The Collective Dimensions of Employment Relations

Tindara Addabbo · Edoardo Ales ·
Ylenia Curzi · Tommaso Fabbri ·
Olga Rymkevich · Iacopo Senatori
Editors

The Collective Dimensions of Employment Relations

Interdisciplinary Perspectives on Workers' Voices and Changing Workplace Patterns

palgrave
macmillan

Editors
Tindara Addabbo
Marco Biagi Department of Economics
University of Modena and Reggio Emilia
Modena, Italy

Edoardo Ales
Department of Law
Parthenope University of Naples
Napoli, Italy

Ylenia Curzi
Marco Biagi Foundation
Modena, Italy

Tommaso Fabbri
University of Modena and Reggio Emilia
Modena, Italy

Olga Rymkevich
Marco Biagi Foundation
University of Modena and Reggio Emilia
Modena, Italy

Iacopo Senatori
Marco Biagi Foundation
University of Modena and Reggio Emilia
Modena, Italy

ISBN 978-3-030-75531-7 ISBN 978-3-030-75532-4 (eBook)
https://doi.org/10.1007/978-3-030-75532-4

This Palgrave Macmillan imprint is published by the registered company Springer Nature Switzerland AG
The registered company address is: Gewerbestrasse 11, 6330 Cham, Switzerland

Contents

Editors and Contributors

About the Editors

Tindara Addabbo is Full Professor in Economic Policy and Coordinator of the Ph.D. Programme in Labour, Development and Innovation at the University of Modena and Reggio Emilia (Italy). Current main research areas: gender economics, employment and wage discrimination by gender, well-being, gender budgeting and policies evaluation, gender gap in education, quality of work, work-related stress, certification of firms in terms of gender equity and work-life balance. Coordinator of the ongoing Project: Leading Towards Sustainable Gender Equality Plans in research institutions—LeTSGEPs (H2020-SwafS-2019-873072) within the Horizon 2020 Research and Innovation Framework.

Website: http://personale.unimore.it/rubrica/curriculum/addabbo.

Edoardo Ales is Full Professor of Labour and Social Security Law at the Department of Law of the University of Naples "Parthenope" (Italy). He also teaches European Labour Law at LUISS—G. Carli in Rome (Italy). He is invited professor of International and European Labour

Law at the Pontifical Lateran University (Vatican State—Rome). He is Member of the Board of Directors of the Giornale del Diritto del Lavoro e delle Relazioni Industriali, Rivista del Diritto della Sicurezza Sociale, *Italian Labour Law Electronic Journal*. He is Member of the Scientific Committee of the Marco Biagi Foundation of the University of Modena and Reggio Emilia (Italy). He is the National Expert for Italy in the ICF-ECE and MoveS Network supporting the EU Commission in the field of Labour Law and Free Movement of Workers.

Ylenia Curzi, Ph.D. in Business Science is Associate Professor of Organization and Human Resource Management at the "Marco Biagi" Department of Economics of the University of Modena and Reggio Emilia (Italy). Teacher responsible of the course on Organization and HRM, master degree course in International Management, and of the course on Organization, bachelor degree in Business Economics and Economy and International Marketing. Member of the Academic Board and coordinator of the course on Organization Theory within the doctoral programme in Labour, Development and Innovation, University of Modena and Reggio Emilia. Member of the Scientific Committee at the Marco Biagi Foundation. She was visiting scholar at Cardiff Business School (Wales, UK). Her research interests include the relationships between organization, digitalization, well-being at work, performance management and innovative behaviour.

Tommaso Fabbri is a Full Professor of Organization and Human Resource Management, Dean of the Department of Economics and vice-director of the interdisciplinary Doctoral School E4E at the University of Modena and Reggio Emilia.

He has written and/or edited 9 books and over 60 articles or chapters on national and international journals and books and his main research interests are organizational learning, well-being at work, performance management work datafication and data-driven human resource management. In his quality of scientific coordinator at Fondazione Marco Biagi, he has been focusing on the interdisciplinary study or work regulation, in the light of the digital transformation of work and organization. He was Visiting Professor at the Pennsylvania State University and he serves as a consultant to several private companies and public institutions.

Olga Rymkevich is a Senior Researcher in Labour Law and Industrial Relations at the Marco Biagi Foundation, University of Modena and Reggio Emilia, Modena (Italy). She graduated from St. Petersburg State University, Russia in foreign languages and international relations and in Economics from the University of Modena, Italy and Reggio Emilia and has a Ph.D. in Labour Law (University of St. Petersburg, Russia). She is a Member of the Academic Advisory Board of the Marco Biagi Foundation, University of Modena and Reggio Emilia. Her research interests include international and comparative labour law, international sports law. She also serves as a managing editor of *The International Journal of Comparative Labour Law and Industrial Relations* (Kluwer Law International) and collaborates with the *Italian Labour Law E-Journal.*

Iacopo Senatori is the Assistant Professor of Labour Law at the University of Modena and Reggio Emilia, Italy. He received a Ph.D. in Labour Law and Industrial Relations at the University of Bologna.

Member of the Academic Advisory Board of the Marco Biagi Foundation, University of Modena and Reggio Emilia; Coordinator of the Labour Law Area in the Ph.D. Programme of Labour, Development and Innovation at the University of Modena and Reggio Emilia; Managing Editor of the *Italian Labour Law E-Journal*. His research interests include EU Labour Law, freedom of association and collective bargaining, workers' well-being, law & tech and the regulation of new forms of work. He is the author of one book and several articles and essays written in Italian and English, published on high-ranking national and international journals.

He has been the principal investigator in several international research projects co-funded by the European Commission.

Contributors

Roberto Albano, Ph.D. in Sociology, is Associate Professor at the Department of Culture, Politics and Society of Turin University, where he teaches Sociology and Methodology of Social Research. His recent research interests include: cultural change in European countries, with a special focus on work values; new forms of work organization, with a special focus on autonomy and control in 4.0, smart working and coworking. His recent publications include: *Work Autonomy, Control and Discretion in Industry 4.0*, in F. Cantoni, G. Mangia (eds.), *Human Resource Management and Digitalization. The Effects of Industry 4.0 on Human Resources*, Routledge/Giappichelli, in press (with Y. Curzi, T. Fabbri); *DigitAgile: The Office in a Mobile Device. Threats and Opportunities for Workers and Companies*, in E. Ales, Y. Curzi, T. Fabbri, O. Rymkevich I. Senatori, G. Solinas, *Working in Digital and Smart Organizations. Legal, Economic and Organizational Perspectives on the Digitalization of Labour Relations*, Palgrave Macmillan, 2018 (with S. Bertolini Y. Curzi, T. Tabbri, T. Parisi); *What's Still Important about Work? A Longitudinal and Cross-country Analysis of Prevalent Attitudes towards Work During the Last 40 Years*, in T. Addabbo, E. Ales, Y. Curzi, I. Senatori (eds.), Well-being at and through Work, Eleven International Publishing/ Giappichelli, 2017 (with T.Parisi).

Ronald C. Brown is a Law Professor at the University of Hawaii Law School teaching labour and Asian international labour law and has served as the University's Director of the Center for Chinese Studies. He has authored numerous articles and has published, East Asian Labor and Employment Law, Understanding Labor & Employment Law in China and Understanding Chinese Courts and Legal Process: Law with Chinese Characteristics

Filip Dorssemont (1970) is Full Professor of Labour Law at the Faculty of Law of the Université catholique de Louvain (in Louvain-La-Neuve). He also is Guest Professor of European Labour Law at the Free University of Brussels (VUB). He is Co-President of the Association Belge de droit du travail et de la sécurité sociale (2020–2022), after serving as President of this association (2014–2016). He is a Member of the Transnational

Trade Union Rights Expert Network (European Trade Union Institute). Dorssemont has lectured law (Antwerp University, master's in law 1993), studied philosophy (bachelor Antwerp University 1990 and a Complementary Studies in Philosophy at the Institute of Philosophy, Leuven University, 1994). Currently he is a Master Student of Art History (Université catholique de Louvain). He has defended a Ph.D. thesis on the legal status of representative trade unions (Antwerp University, 2001).

His main fields of interest are: industrial relations law, fundamental labour rights at work, European Labour Law and labour representation in the history of art.

Anthony Forsyth is Professor of Workplace Law and Leader of the Law Discipline in the Graduate School of Business and Law, RMIT University, Melbourne, Australia. His research focuses on collective bargaining, trade unions, labour hire and the gig economy. He is Vice-President of the Australian Labour Law Association and chaired the Victorian Government Inquiry into the Labour Hire Industry and Insecure Work (2015–2016). He also runs the Labour Law Down Under Blog (https://labourlawdownunder.com.au/) and is the author of the forthcoming book: *The Future of Unions and Worker Representation: The Digital Picket Line* (Hart Publishing).

Federico Fusco is an Assistant Professor of law in the College of law of the Prince Mohammad Bin Fahd University in Al Khobar, Kingdom of Saudi Arabia.

From 2017 to 2019 he has been working as a postdoc in business law at the School of Economics and Management of Lund University in Sweden.

He holds a Ph.D. in Law and Economics from the Scuola Normale Superiore (Pisa-Florence) and a postgraduate specialization course in EU Law from the University Federico II of Naples.

He has constantly attended as a presenter and session organizer the most prominent world labour conferences, and in 2017 he has created an international study group on labour law and industrial relations with participation of scholars from Brazil, Cambodia, Italy, South Africa and Sweden.

He has been lecturing in Italy, Sweden and the Kingdom of Saudi Arabia at bachelor and master level. He has also completed several pedagogical courses focused on best ways to teach and organize courses in higher education.

His main areas of research cover employment contract law, industrial relations, comparative and EU labour law and privacy law. His recent publications include "Betting on the Future: A Comparison Between Trade Unions' Strategy in the Re-structuring of Fiat and Volvo Cars", in *E-Journal of International and Comparative LABOUR STUDIES* (2020), 2; "COVID-19 and Labour Law: Saudi Arabia", in *Italian Labour Law e-Journal* (2020), 1s and "Employee Privacy in the Context of EU Regulation 2016/679: Some Comparative Remarks", in T. Addabbo, E. Ales, Y. Curzi, T. Fabbri, O. Rymkevich, I. Senatori (eds.), *Performance Appraisal in Modern Employment Relations* (2020), Palgrave Macmillan.

Marius Kalanta is a Postdoctoral Research Fellow at the Institute of International Relations and Political Science at Vilnius University. His research focuses on the interaction between political economic institutions, such as industrial relations, corporate governance, the financial system and product market competition, and politics, such as electoral and business groups politics, and on the impact both institutions and politics make on economic performance including comparative institutional advantage, sources of economic growth and trajectories of economic transition. He studies these phenomena by applying theoretical tools developed within the disciplinary field of comparative political economy, notably its branches of varieties of capitalism, growth regimes, and electoral and business groups politics, and focusing geographically on Central and Eastern European political economies.

Tania Parisi is Assistant Professor of Sociology, at the Department of Philosophy and Education Sciences, University of Turin (Italy). Her main research interests include the methodology of social research, social inequality, models of social change and innovation. In the field of work and ICT she recently published "Gli smart workers tra solitudine e collaborazione" in «*Cambio*» (with R. Albano, L. Tirabeni, 2019); "Perceived Autonomy and Discretion of Mobile Workers" in «*Studi Organizzativi*» (with R. Albano, Y. Curzi, L. Tirabeni, 2018); "DigitAgile: The

Office in a Mobile Device. Threats and Opportunities for Workers and Companies", in Ales, E. et al. (ed.), *Working in Digital and Smart Organizations*, Palgrave Macmillan (with Albano R., Bertolini S., Curzi Y., Fabbri T., 2018).

Massimo Resce is an expert in European policies for territorial development and in labour market policies. Former Coordinator of techno-structures of public bodies for the implementation of local development programmes and pilot projects, with particular reference to the areas of the South, he is now a Researcher at INAPP (National Institute for Public Policy Analysis), where he conducts studies aimed at analysing human capital and labour market policies within the National Operational Program "Systems of active employment policies", co-financed by the European Social Fund (ESF). His research has recently focused on the analysis of the wage issue in Italy and on the problems inherent in the low growth of labour productivity. In particular he has studied how the industrial relations system and the collective bargaining model affect these variables.

Enrico Sestili is an expert in the analysis of the labour market and occupations, during the years he has participated in surveys and studies in INAPP (National Institute for Public Policy Analysis) on the subject of skill needs, classification of occupations and industrial relations.

In the fields of Research, University and Higher Education in Art and Music, he operates as a trade union leader at national and regional level and conducts analyses and studies on law, human resources management and training.

Julia Tomassetti is an Assistant Professor of Law at the City University of Hong Kong. She earned a JD from Harvard Law School and doctorate in sociology from UCLA. She has held research fellowships at the Georgetown University Law Center, the Baldy Center for Law & Social Policy at SUNY Buffalo and the Center for Law, Society, & Culture at the Indiana University Maurer School of Law. Dr. Tomassetti's research focuses on work law, contracts, economic sociology and the political economy of contemporary capitalism. Using an interdisciplinary lens, her scholarship has examined technology and work, nonmarket work, service work and the gig economy. Her current projects explore algorithmic management, property rights, neoliberal reasoning and the relationship between employment and the business enterprise. Before entering the academy, Dr. Tomassetti practiced campaign finance and employment law in New York City.

Manfred Weiss (born in 1940). 1974–2008 Full Professor for Labour Law and Civil Law (first at the University of Hamburg and since 1977 at the Goethe University in Frankfurt). Professor emeritus since 2008. Visiting Professor in many universities all over the world. 2000–2003 President of ILERA. 1998–2002 Deputy President of German Lawyers' Association (DJT). For many years Consultant to the ILO 1980 and to the Commission of the EU. Technical Assistance to many countries. Honorary Doctorates: Budapest (2005), Lima (2006), Bordeaux (2011), Northwest University (NWU)/South Africa (2015). Award of the Labour Law Research Network (LLRN) for outstanding contribution to labour law (2015). Fellow of the World Academy of Art and Science (WAAS).

Helena Ysàs Molinero is Lecturer in Labour and Social Security Law at the Universitat Autònoma de Barcelona (Spain) and member of the Institut d'Estudis del Treball (IET), an interdisciplinary research center based in that same academic institution. Her research interests focus on European and national social dialogue, participation of trade unions in public institutions, collective bargaining and employee representation issues, among others. She has frequently adopted a comparative law perspective in her work, especially between Spain and France, where she spent her postdoc period. She has continuously participated in national and international competitive research projects, including a work in progress project on employee representation institutions in a transformative network economy funded by the Spanish Ministry od Science and a project on microtasking work funded by French ANR. She regularly contributes to national and international scholarly events and publishes her work in corresponding reviews and publishers (over 40 contributions to conferences and over 70 published review articles, book chapters and books in the course of 16 years).

List of Figures

List of Tables

1

Introduction

Olga Rymkevich and Iacopo Senatori

This book is the third editorial initiative[1] of an ongoing research project managed by the Marco Biagi Foundation (University of Modena and Reggio Emilia, Italy), seeking to cast light on the new challenges and trends in the world of work accelerated by the advent of digital technologies. The present volume is focused on the implications of the societal and technological changes for the "collective dimensions" of employment, a plural expression that intends to encompass the collective identity of workers, the institutional representation of their interests and the regulatory framework built around it, emphasising the complex characterization of all these factors in the modern society.

O. Rymkevich · I. Senatori (✉)
Marco Biagi Foundation, University of Modena and Reggio Emilia, Modena, Italy
e-mail: iacopo.senatori@unimore.it

O. Rymkevich
e-mail: rymkevich@unimore.it

T. Addabbo et al. (eds.), *The Collective Dimensions of Employment Relations*,
https://doi.org/10.1007/978-3-030-75532-4_1

From a methodological perspective, the combination of an interdisciplinary and multidisciplinary approach represents an original feature of this book, allowing to analyse in a comprehensive way a number of multifaceted and controversial issues linked to the collective dimensions of employment relations and the impact generated by digitalization and workplace "fissurisation". Furthermore, the use of the comparative method offers a wide geographical spread providing an original insight on different national experiences in the countries of Western, Northern, Southern and Eastern Europe, China, Russia and Australia.

The structures of collective representation of workers have always been a crucial tool to advance regulation of employment relations, to grant high levels of protection and to achieve a fair balance between the social and economic needs in society. However, the existence of these structures is now seriously threatened by many factors.

The list of those threatening factors includes: declining union density and collective bargaining coverage, governmental policies, legislative restrictions, austerity measures, uncertain development of transnational union networks in the face of a stronger role played by multinational corporations, enlargement of the sectors of the working population that are not entitled to collective representation, either because of their employment status or due to their contingent position in the company (such as dependent self-employed and workers employed in value chains).

In addition, a disaffection for the collective representation rights is increasingly evident in the institutional framework. At the national level, the action of lawmakers and governments is often accompanied by arguments in favour of "disintermediation", in the sense that the State should deal with employment regulation autonomously, with no need or entitlement for social dialogue to intervene in the drafting or implementation of the legislative process. At the supranational and international levels, the instruments typically envisioned in industrial relations to empower employees and engage them in the drafting and enforcement of employment regulations, i.e. collective bargaining and industrial action, are trumped by the economic rights and freedoms of the enterprise, thus undermining the collective defence of employees' interests. This is clearly the case in the European Union, although arguments aimed at challenging the established status of collective rights have also been put forward within the ILO, with particular reference to the right to strike.

The institutional framework reveals a mismatch between regulatory provisions and the demand for fair working conditions in relation to the emerging economic and social phenomena. The digital revolution gives rise to new organizational arrangements in the workplace, and new ways to perform work that often fail to meet the traditional criteria for the classification of employees. As a result, trade unions and representative bodies face a challenge to their capacity (and legal entitlement) to mobilize collective interests, linked to "virtual" workplaces where in many cases workers are denied minimum employment rights and protection. The digital, "platform" or "gig" economy also calls into question the role of unions in overseeing and influencing employment conditions in relation to key issues such as the measurement, monitoring, assessment and remuneration of the work performance, the protection of work-life balance against the growing intrusiveness of work in private life enabled by mobile devices ("time porosity"), the impact of new technologies on health and safety, the adaptation of occupational skills to new work processes, and the responses to the digital restructuring of undertakings entailing redundancies or the relocation of production.

The "fissured workplace" mentioned above has a negative impact on collective solidarity not only in relation to the classification of individual employment relationships, but also with regard to supply chains, in which large groups of workers are denied the power to influence decisions taken by the lead enterprise, that is the final beneficiary of the production process. In both cases, legal constraints may prevent the collective mediation of interests, given the possible conflict between collective bargaining, competition law and entrepreneurial freedom, as the European experience shows.

Nonetheless, it is possible to detect signs of resilience of the institutions of collective representation, that may result in a renewal, instead of a descent, of the role of those institutions in the regulation and management of the workplace. For instance, in the field of the "gig-economy", in several Western countries and regions an increasing number of initiatives have been undertaken by collective actors, bringing together traditional representation structures and spontaneous grass-roots movements. At times, lawmakers attempt to promote the activation of collective representation and collective bargaining by means of legal and economic incentives, often encouraging social partners to address specific issues linked to productivity and technological development. In the background stands the idea of searching new alliances between traditional and new players, like trade unions and other non-governmental or civil organizations, to pursue combined or joint efforts.

Furthermore, a different characterization of collective employment relations has been attracting increasing attention in recent times: the so-called collective-relational dimension, that identifies the web of relations established among workers belonging to the same workplace, other than the formal representation structures. Such "third" dimension does not constitute a means to achieve countervailing power, but rather a phenomenon inherent in the employment relationship itself. This perspective assumes that conceptualizing the workplace relationship merely in an individual and atomized perspective is likely to be insufficient. On the contrary, it can be argued that, along with situations related to the single binding relationship between employer and employee, different situations will be envisaged, that assume a legal significance only in the perspective of the unitary consideration of the relationships that take place in the organizational community. This emerges clearly from the appreciation of the importance of the organization in the context of the employment relationship, especially in the light of the implementation of new technologies in production processes and in the management of its impact on the workplace patterns. It is evident that the interest of the employer in the organization, as outlined above, cannot be limited to the individual level but necessarily extends to the collective dimension where multiple occupational skills are represented and need to be organized, coordinated and managed.

Against such background, the book aims at putting together under the same conceptual framework the old and new "collective dimensions" of employment, and to offer to the readers a renewed theoretical perspective (and justification) on the role that the dialogue between workers and companies could play in an increasingly complex world of work, where the massive change of well-established interpretative categories is coupled by a substantial continuity of the interests and aspirations expressed by the actors of the employment relationship.

The book is divided into three thematic sections. **The first one** intends to provide a general contextualization of the book by introducing the three "basic" collective dimensions of employment relations: trade unions, workers' representation bodies, the workplace, meant as an organizational community. The aim is to recap the state of the art and provide the analytical elements to stimulate a twofold reflection: on the one hand, how the traditional representational institutions can be revitalized, and on the other hand how they can interact with new concepts and instruments, with a view to reaffirming an updated role of collective relations as a tool to regulate and manage the workplace.

The chapter by **Manfred Weiss** provides a broad overview of the evolution and main challenges for the employee representation and participation structures in the light of the analysis of the relevant European and international legislation. Particular attention is paid to the role of employee in management decision-making through the prism of fundamental human rights and industrial democracy. In the author's view, the idea of employees' participation as a democratic and human rights principle should be promoted everywhere as it represents a powerful tool to counteract to the progressive erosion and fissurization of the workplace and increasing employee disempowerment in the context of the uncertain consequences of digital and technological revolution.

Filip Dorssemont in his contribution proposes a comparative legal and historical analysis of the development of employee and employer organizations at the European and international level and of the role of international legal instruments and essential means in this regard. In particular, he examines certain legal concepts such as the legal definition and status of the main actors involved in representation (trade unions and employers' associations), the notion of representativeness and the complex and controversial nature of their interrelations in the light of fundamental human rights principles. The chapter concludes with a provocative antithesis, *i.e.* how labour law could operate without social partners organizations.

The chapter by **Tommaso Fabbri** and **Ylenia Curzi** presents a conceptual framework, derived from the processual theory of organization, for the analysis of the "third" dimension of work relationships, additional to the individual one, regulated by the contract and to the collective one, regulated by industrial relations settlements. The authors move from the unsolved tension, inside labour law, between contractualist and institutionalist perspectives and claims that the tension is rooted in mainstream, socio-technical theory of organization, where the organizational work system is rationally and thoroughly set before the worker comes into play, either as an executor or a discretionary agent. Conversely, processual theory of organization sheds light on workers autonomous regulatory contribution to the overall work organization, so providing original analytical insights on the dynamics of work relations and, consequently, for their regulation.

In conclusion of this section, the chapter by **Edoardo Ales** aims at demonstrating the existence of several collective dimensions within the employment relationship to be tracked back both to the trade unions' and to the works councils' model. The "agentification" that characterizes each model is likely to jeopardize the enhancement of the interrelational element the most advance organizational theory looks at as main feature of the collective dimension of the employment relationship. The essay tries to make some proposals on which, from a juridical point of view one can reconcile the individual nature of the contractual relationship with the "processual regulation" option inspired by the collective self-coordination of performances within the work community

Considering that digitalization and all the major social and economic transformations that affect the modern world of work have their heart at the workplace, the chapters collected in the **second section** provide a reflection on the role of the company as a specific and autonomous regulatory forum and the responsiveness of the existing employee representation structures to the effects of multiple transformations generated by globalization and digitalization such as workplace fissurization, employees precarization and company disintegration.

In this way, the chapter by **Roberto Albano**, **Ylenia Curzi** and **Tania Parisi** is aimed to identify prevalent trends in control and surveillance in industry since 1990 to present, focusing in particular on the differences between highly digitalized and traditional workers. The authors elaborate three ideal-types of management control, namely controlled autonomy, new-Tayloristic and Panopticon control. Then, they analyse data from the 1991 to 2015 European Working Conditions Survey. Their findings show a growing trend towards forms of control approaching the ideal-type of controlled autonomy, particularly among digital workers. Highly digitalized industrial work practices offer greater opportunities for workers to develop new skills and exercise their autonomy. In contrast to the expectations, however, findings show that this hardly occurs through the involvement in a group or team that has common tasks and can autonomously plan its work. This suggests that the autonomy that workers are allowed to exercise in today's digital work settings has an individual rather than a collective character. In addition, their autonomy does not concern strategic organizational objectives and goes along with work intensification. At least in the countries, sectors and period considered in the analysis, digital workers have no opportunities to participate in decision-making processes regarding the organization's objectives and it seems that they are not able to get out of a growing loneliness, to raise the level of social conflict and to oppose real autonomy to management. These findings contribute to the line of critical research on new post-Fordist work practices, which today gain new momentum thanks to the digital transformation of work.

Julia Tomasetti examines a thought-provoking neoliberal concept which regards an individual as an independent economic agent or neoliberal agent managing his/her human capitalportfolio where working time and other working arrangements become mere human capital assets with certain implications for labour and social security law. She focuses on *SuperShuttle* DFW decision where labour rights were denied to airport shuttle drivers who were considered independent business contractors for themselves. She illustrates the dichotomy between employee rights and property-like entrepreneurial prerogatives reflecting upon liberal conceptualization as opposed to the neoliberal reconceptualization of such notions as firm, entrepreneurialism, productive activity and models of profit generation which as a more extreme implication "transform the living in doing business" and conflates worker discretion with autonomy. The author argues that platforms often adhere to such a neoliberal concept while designing their work modalities. This practice helps them to avoid applying statutory protections to platform workers who are considered neoliberal agents.

Helena Ysàs Molinero highlights significant inconsistencies between the existing employee representation structure and the corresponding company structure in Spain. In her opinion, national regulations often lag behind main economic and social developments related to workplace fissurization, workforce precarization and company disintegration which resulted in progressive weakening of employee representation structures. The author argues that the legislation should provide better opportunities to be fairly represented to all categories of workers, including employees of a "fissured company", small establishments and independent workers.

Finally, the **third section** casts light on various forms and systems of employees' representation and collective action for the defence of workers' interests, in consideration of the increasing number of spontaneous initiatives undertaken by collective players. Moreover, it draws up an original mixture of traditional and innovative practices that involve old and new actors of the collective dimensions. In this perspective the chapters collected in this section are aimed to explore the collective dimensions of labour relations in the context of a range of new business models and examine the ability of the unions and alternative workers representation bodies to represent workers engaged through gig platforms, supply chains, as well as the role and attitude of employers' organizations.

The first chapter of this section by **Federico Fusco** focuses on the compliance with the international provisions (in particular with the ILO and ECHR standards) of the recent changes in the Swedish legislation aimed to restrict the right to strike of those trade unions that are not bound by the collective agreement signed by the employer. The author illustrates controversial global effect of the reform especially if it is placed together with other Swedish legislative provisions. By recognizing the rationale behind the reform, the author however calls for a more weighted case by case approach in order to prevent collateral and potentially dangerous consequences for many conflicting interests at stake. In the author's view, the reform risks to undermine the principle of freedom of association as it limits trade unions regardless of the level of their representativeness to defend working conditions of their members. It may also discourage both the workers to join such unions and the employers to sign the respective collective agreements.

The chapter by **Anthony Forsyth** examines the challenges for collective worker representation posed by new business models in Australia and Italy and assesses the effectiveness of responses from trade unions and emerging worker representative groups in the era of "platform capitalism". By comparing approaches in the two countries and examining the reasons of successful and less successful outcomes of the efforts undertaken by workers representatives (cases of Foodora, Uber, Amazon, Bologna Charter, etc.) the author demonstrates that a new form of solidarity aimed to respond to the new business models challenging the established notions of work is emerging. While providing a critical assessment of the role of collective regulation of platform and other types of fissured work, the author argues that new opportunities for the development of different expressions of collectivism are arising. At the same time, he argues that the involvement of established trade unions using multi-pronged strategy including public campaigning, litigation of individual or group and grass-roots organizing provides better chances for success.

Marius Kalanta in his analysis argues that a lack of the positive impact of European and national policy measures aimed at strengthening social dialogue in CEE countries, particularly, social dialogue institution building via political interventions and the Europeanization through capacity building and dissemination of social standards, can be linked to incomplete assumptions they have been grounded on. These assumptions have overestimated the power of European and national political actors to establish strong and functioning social dialogue and underestimated the role of social partners' motivation to be engaged in it. The chapter focuses on structurally shaped motivation of enterprises to be involved in social dialogue in the Baltic countries. It finds that the Baltic growth regime has recently become strongly export-driven suggesting that coordinated wage-setting could have also become increasingly compatible with the enterprises' interests to improve the competitiveness of exports. However, it is not a component of the current business strategies of Baltic manufacturing enterprises. Instead, enterprises rely on "price taker" strategies that take advantage of favourable market opportunities but not of competitiveness improvements via cooperation and coordination at the intra- or inter-sectorial level. Therefore, in the author's view, these strategies are not complementary with social dialogue institutions.

The chapter by **Olga Rymkevich** and **Ronald Brown** compares the situation of platform workers engaged in ride-hailing and food delivery service in Russia and China. These countries share communist experience, similar trajectory of trade unionism development and have witnessed rapid growth of platform work in the last two decades. The lack of labour rights and benefits for gig workers is a global issue. It is complicated by the diversity of gig workers who generally vary from self-employed, independent contractors, part-timers, irregular workers, etc. However, the facts are becoming clear that platform entrepreneurialism is a business model designed to cut costs by shifting labour costs to the workers. It is particularly true for workers who work for one employer upon whom they are dependent on for their livelihood. Some countries have protected this group of "dependent employees". Stirrings in China and Russia are beginning to call for that recognition. The problem of granting them the status of "employee" thus entitling these workers to an employment contract and eligibility for labour rights and benefits and the right to become members of unions has gained increasing attention both in China and in Russia albeit to a different extent and with different success. In the meantime, the frustrations of these workers sometimes result in public protests. The paper focuses on the experience of Russia and China in relation to ride-hailing and food delivery services. After an overview of the general trends of the development of gig work in these countries the paper analyses the approaches to the problem of legal classification of these workers and trade unions responses.

Massimo Resce and **Enrico Sestili** focus their attention on the policies of supporting collective bargaining in Italy by means of legislative and economic incentives. The chapter provides a quantitative and qualitative assessment of the collective bargaining enacted in response to such legislation. In particular, it investigates upon the main characteristics of the measures adopted for the growth of productivity in decentralized bargaining and their integration at local level and by company size and industry. Moreover, it deals with the problems of measurability of performance increases and the choices made by the companies in terms of objectives and growth indicators. Finally, it provides a summary of the main emerging evidence, also through company profiling, with respect to the choices in adopting the tax incentives.

Note

1. *Working in Digital and Smart Organizations. Legal Economic and Organisational Perspectives on the Digitalisation of Labour Relations*, E. Ales, Y. Curzi, T. Fabbri, O. Rymkevich, I. Senatori, G. Solinas (eds.), Palgrave Macmillan, 2018 and*Performance Appraisal in Modern Employment Relations. An Interdisciplinary Approach*, T. Addabbo E. Ales, Y. Curzi, T. Fabbri, O. Rymkevich, I. Senatori (eds.), Palgrave Macmillan, 2020.

Part I

The Collective Dimensions of Employment: A Taxonomy

2

Challenges for Workers' Participation

Manfred Weiss

Introduction

Employees are not supposed to be mere objects of management's decisions but must participate in management's decision-making in order to live up to human dignity and to establish a democratic workplace. This insight by the founding fathers of labour law (Sinzheimer 1927) is as valid today as it was in the formative era of labour law. Such continuation has recently been confirmed in Europe by Art. 27 of the Charter of Fundamental Rights of the EU (CFREU) and by the 8th Principle of the European Pillar of Social Rights. The question is whether and how labour law has lived up to this goal so far and whether in the future it will be possible to establish a satisfying structure to meet this ambitious goal.

M. Weiss (✉)
Labour Law and Civil Law, Goethe University Frankfurt, Frankfurt, Germany
e-mail: M.Weiss@jur.uni-frankfurt.de

T. Addabbo et al. (eds.), *The Collective Dimensions of Employment Relations*,
https://doi.org/10.1007/978-3-030-75532-4_2

Starting from a sketchy description of the variety of patterns of workers participation within the company and of the advantages of such systems this contribution tries to highlight the approach of the European Union towards workers participation and tries to reflect on the challenges for workers participation in view of modern working patterns, particularly those implied by digitalization.

The Variety of Systems of Workers Participation

Institutionalized patterns of workers' participation exist in many countries. However, there are big differences from country to country. These differences refer to

- the degree of participation, ranging from information and consultation via veto rights up to co-determination where management and workers' representatives are on the same footing in decision-making for a whole range of topics.
- the level of participation, ranging from the shop-floor level up to the headquarters of companies or groups of companies. Some countries even know employee representation in company boards where again the differences are tremendous, in particular as the percentage of seats are concerned.
- the composition of bodies of workers' participation which is different from country to country. In some countries exclusively employees, in others chaired by management side.
- the relationship between bodies of workers' representation and trade unions, thereby, of course also to the relationship between workers' participation and collective bargaining (Biagi and Tiraboschi 2007, p. 503).

There is one common deficiency of the different systems of workers' participation: they only very seldom are implemented in small companies. And often the threshold established by law does not necessarily correspond with implementation—as for example in Germany—where small establishments of at least 5 employees are included in the works council law but by far not implemented in actual practice.

In view of the variety of the systems of workers participation, it is important to stress that they all are embedded in the cultural tradition and overall institutional framework of the respective country in which they are established. Therefore, the institutional arrangements cannot be transferred elsewhere. But, of course, the idea of workers' participation can be spread everywhere.

The Advantages of Workers' Participation

The positive effects of the system of employees' involvement in management's decision-making are well documented by many empirical studies.[1] To just mention the most important of them:

- They lead to a change of focus from shareholder value to stakeholder value and tends to promote sustainability instead of short-term effects at the stock markets.
- They have a big advantage compared to unilateral decision-making by the mere fact that management, who has to justify towards workers' representatives what it wants to do and why it wants to do it, tends to prepare the decisions much more carefully than it would be the case without this obligation. This leads evidently to better decision-making.
- The consciousness that workers' representatives are involved in management's decision-making and that workers' interests are taken into account tends to increase the employees' motivation and thereby the company's productivity.
- Last not least the permanent dialogue between management and workers' representatives leads to mutual trust, changes the attitudes of both sides, employers and workers representatives—and absorbs conflicts.

These findings correspond with Marco Biagi's and Michele Tiraboschi's expectations when they wrote that "employee representation has to fulfil a trust building function" and that "representation must guarantee the legitimacy of management decisions, enhanced by their joint nature, with a favourable impact on their execution" (Biagi and Tiraboschi 2007, p. 554).

The Approach of the European Union

The EU from the very beginning not only was confronted with the diversity of the Member States' systems on workers' participation but particularly with the split between Member States with a tradition of participation and cooperation between business and labour and Member States with a tradition of conflict and antagonism. Instead of leaving this situation as it was the EU opted for participation and cooperation, having in mind the indicated advantages of systems of workers' participation. This approach found its expression in a whole set of Directives, starting in the seventies of last century with Directives referring to specific issues,[2] ending up in the first decade of the new century with a Directive on a general framework on information and consultation.[3] In addition, systems of workers' participation for transnationally operating companies were developed. Most important in this context are the Directive on European Works Councils which after long and controversial debates could be passed in 1994[4] and the Directive on Employee Involvement in the European Company of 2001.[5] The pattern established in the latter Directive has become a model for further Directives as for example the Directive on transnational mergers. Nowadays the set of these Directives can be seen as a success story and as the core of the so-called European Social model.

There is no longer any doubt that the promotion of employees' involvement in company's decision-making has become an essential part of the EU's mainstreaming strategy in its social policy agenda. It has transgressed definitely the "point of no return". This policy is in line with the already mentioned Art. 27 CFREU. This has an important implication: countries with a tradition of exclusively antagonistic structures have no longer a choice but to restructure their systems towards a concept of partnership and cooperation.

Of course, the Directives sketched above have their weaknesses: they are unnecessarily complicated, not always consistent and above all very vague in their terminology. The Directive supplementing the Statute of the European Company as well as the Directive on a national framework for information and consultation has been watered down during the legislative process: the result is a real minimum consent. However, in assessing the importance of these measures for the future of industrial relations in the EU these deficiencies should not be overstated. The decisive element is the fact that these instruments, taken as a whole, force all actors involved—trade unions and workers' representatives, employers' associations, employers and employees—to discuss and reflect on the potential of employees' information and consultation and in the case of the Directive supplementing the Statute on the European Company even on the potential of workers' participation in company boards.

There is another aspect worth to be mentioned. The EU has proved to be a learning system. In the beginning there were illusions of harmonization (Weiss 2019, p. 181), of establishing the same system for all the Member States. Such a strategy would have underestimated the strength of national culture and tradition. Therefore, it is important to stress that the EU's approach no longer is focussing on introducing specific institutional patterns but simply stimulates and initiates procedures for the promotion of the idea of employees' involvement in management's decision-making. This is to be considered as an important step towards the establishment of industrial democracy as a basic feature of the already mentioned European social model. This strategy is based on the assumption that workers' involvement in management's decision-making—as indicated above—is favourable not only for the employees but also for the companies' economic performance.

Even if workers' participation mainly has become a trademark of the EU, it should not be ignored that some Transnational Corporations based in Europe even went further and concluded agreements with Global Union Federations to establish World Works Councils covering all subsidiaries of the globe.

However, so far, the means of these bodies of workers' representation to promote employees' interests worldwide in transnationally operating corporations still remain to be rather modest. Nevertheless, the importance of such strategies barely can be overestimated. Not only the number of transnationally operating companies has increased tremendously. According to the campaign organization "Global Justice Now" in 2016 69 of the 100 largest economies in the world were transnationally operating corporations and not States. Walmart has higher revenues than the government of Spain, Apple has higher revenues than the government of Belgium and the German MNE Daimler has higher revenues than the government of Denmark, to just give you some examples. It is evident that the exercise of such power cannot be left to unilateral decisions by management. Workers' participation in these contexts, reaching the headquarters where ever they are located and covering all subsidiaries all over the world, ideally should be established. This, however, is still a dream due to the lack of transnational rules and also due to the lack of strong international actors on the workers' side.

The Preconditions of Workers' Participation

Instead of further dreaming on more workers' participation within transnational corporations, it might be helpful to have a look on the constitutive elements for efficient functioning of workers participation in management's decision-making. So far, they have been

- an identifiable workplace where employees are working together in the premises of the employer,
- a hierarchical structure between management and employees with more or less homogeneous interests,
- a relatively clear method and easily recognizing criteria on how to identify who is an employee and
- an identifiable employer, namely a company to which the employees belong.

These preconditions have become more and more problematic. And this leads to the question whether and how workers' participation can survive in the future (Klebe and Weiss 2019, p. 263).

The fragmentation, segmentation and dislocation of the workforce are an increasing trend. Not only the diversity of interests of the different groups of employees makes it difficult to articulate a collective voice in participating but perhaps even more the fact that isolation and individualization prevents collective consciousness. The need to be present in the premises of the employer is fading away. Digitalization to a bigger and bigger extent allows that work can be performed from everywhere.

Vertical structures more and more are replaced by so-called flat hierarchies. Instead of subordination autonomy is becoming the new catchword. Thereby the still existing difference of interests between management and employees, of course, is not disappearing. But it is less visible.

Already for quite a long time, it has become evident that the demarcation line between employment and self-employment is very difficult to draw. To an increasing extent there are persons labelled as being self-employed but in reality, being employees. They of course are to be included into the scope of application of labour law, even if it might be difficult to exactly identify their status. But it cannot be ignored that there are to an increasing extent those who undoubtedly are self-employed but economically in a similar or even worse position as employees. This in particular refers to the so-called solo-self-employed who perform the work by themselves in person and who have no employees. The ILO just has created a label for them: "dependent self-employed".

Not only the erosion of the workforce, the disappearance of clear-cut hierarchies and the increase of dependent self-employed are features of the new world of work but also the erosion of the company structures which makes it difficult to define who is the employer. Since quite a while companies have achieved a "new mobility" as regards company patterns and cooperative structures. It makes sense to talk of a "volatility" of legal structures, as virtual corporate networks emerge, areas are outsourced, companies are run without formal group structures and transnational cooperation is becoming more and more a common feature. Dis-locating strategies are on the agenda. The enterprise often is turned into a merely virtual entity. It often has become difficult to identify the employer. The "fissured workplace" has become a sort of catchword of this extremely complex development. Digitalization and globalization are further and mutually pushing this trend.

The Need for Workers' Participation Bigger Than Ever

The transformation of working patterns is so speedy that the legislator evidently is not able to keep up with all these technological changes. Legislation only can provide a relatively flexible framework. Solutions balancing the needs of the companies and the workers are to be developed on a decentralized level, at the workplace and within the companies.

It has to be kept in mind that the consequences of the technological revolution are still quite unclear. For example, the prognoses on job losses due to digitalization are not reliable at all. Some experts expect the job loss to be dramatically, others predict that the volume of new jobs due to digitalization will be bigger than the loss. All this is speculation. On the other hand, it is uncontested that a main effect of digitalization will be that the content of work will be very different compared to today and that other skills will be needed than nowadays. Therefore, one implication of the new scenario is certain: de-skilling and re-skilling will be of utmost importance.

The uncertainty of the quantity of job loss and the certainty of widespread de-skilling and re-skilling imply fears among the workforce which easily might lead to resistance against these new patterns. Unilateral decision-making by management, therefore, might not be able to achieve acceptability in introducing and implementing digital work.

The more workers' involvement already in early stages and throughout the implementation process, the higher will be the legitimacy of decision-making. This is true for all digital types of work ranging from tele-work or smart work to industry 4.0 where robots interact with each other and with human beings up to the platform economy where work is performed on demand via app or online by so-called crowd-workers. Therefore, another catchword is now on the agenda: "cooperative turn".

Employee involvement in management's decision-making in the era of digitalization is particularly important

- in areas of life-long-training where decisions are to be made on measures to maintain and further promote employment,
- in the area of working time in order to shape it in a way which corresponds on the one hand to the employees' autonomous decisions on working time flexibility as well as to the company's needs,
- in the area of risk management in order to prevent the psycho-social diseases which in view of the new technological environment are growing faster and faster
- or in the area of protection of privacy which in the era of digitalization is endangered as never before.

These few examples are by far not comprehensive. But they indicate that employees' involvement in management's decision-making is more urgent than ever. The question, however, is whether and how workers participation meeting all these challenges can be organized in view of all the indicated changes. The old models might not be able to serve the purpose since—as indicated—the constitutive elements on which they are built no longer exist.

Does Workers' Participation Have a Future?

The more urgent the need for workers' participation, the more difficult it might by to maintain or establish such systems in the new world of work. There are quite a few obstacles which have to be overcome in order to maintain or establish functioning workers' representation in modern company structures, including the platform economy.

The first challenge will be to overcome the individualization and isolation of the workers. This applies in particular to tele-workers and to all types of workers in the platform-economy. It is necessary to create a collective consciousness.

There are already many attempts, mainly organized by trade unions, to contact the respective workers by digital tools and bring them together in workshops where useful information is provided. These initiatives particularly try to enable the digital workers—as for example crowd-workers—to communicate with each other, thereby overcoming the isolation. The example of an initiative conducted by the powerful metal-workers-union in Germany shows that the results of such initiatives are quite promising, even if they are still in an experimental stage.

The second and perhaps biggest challenge is how to cope with those who are evidently no employees in the traditional sense. Already for quite a long time, it has become evident that the demarcation line between employment and self-employment is very difficult to draw (Davidov and Langille 2006).

To an increasing extent there are persons labelled as being self-employed but in reality, being employees. The problem on how to draw a demarcation line between employment and self-employed will further increase in the era of digitalization. The degree of autonomy in performing work makes it more and more difficult to categorize the persons involved in such work, even if a closer look reveals that the autonomy is ambiguous because new mechanisms of more efficient control are in place. Many of those who participate in crowd-sourcing certainly are not employees but rather self-employed.

The question is what to do with those who undoubtedly are self-employed and work alone without employees but are economically in a similar position as employees. They are not reached by labour law protection. They are not included in minimum wage schemes, in health and safety arrangements or in guarantees of decent working time, to just give some examples. Theoretically there are different possibilities to provide for them the necessary protection: the broadening of the notion of employee, the creation of a specific intermediate category or the extension of the scope of labour law to economically dependent self-employed (solo-self-employed).

The broadening of the notion of employee is the pattern which can presently be seen in the many lawsuits all over the world determining the question whether Uber drivers are employees or self-employed. In many countries the notion of employee has been extended significantly. However, this strategy has limits. If the notion is extended too far, it is becoming meaningless. And it never will be possible to include all economically dependent employees.

The introduction of an intermediary category between employment and self-employment might be a solution (Waas 2017, pp. 160–162). However, as the examples in quite a few countries show, it only has provoked uncertainties and led to many controversies. It increases the complexity, thereby rather leading to more problems than less.

A more radical possibility would be the inclusion of self-employed up to a certain wage level under the protective roof of labour law and social security law. As far as the inclusion into the social security system is concerned, some countries—as for example Austria—have followed this path already and it seems to work quite well. Whether, however, such a strategy might work also for labour law, may be doubted. It cannot be denied that many protective patterns are linked to the relationship between employer and employee in the employment relationship. The rules on protection against unfair dismissal might be a good example to illustrate what I mean. Therefore, a mere extension of labour law to self-employed might not be the right strategy.

Therefore, a change of paradigm might be more helpful. Instead of putting workers in different categories, we should discuss the floor of rights all working people need, no matter what their status is. This is in line with the universal labour guarantee as suggested by the ILO Commission on the Future of Work (and unfortunately no longer contained in the ILO centenary Declaration of June 2019). It focuses on protection of workers regardless of their contractual arrangement and of their employment status. The focus should be on the shape of the protective umbrella, not on the boxes where workers are put in.

The third challenge will be to define who is the counterpart of worker representatives on the management side. This is getting more and more difficult the more company structures are scattered. And it is particularly difficult in the context of the platform-economy. Who—to just take this example—in case of crowd-work is treated as employer, the platform operator or in case of crowd-work the crowd-sourcer or both of them? The categorization cannot be left to the platforms themselves. Objective criteria and a functional approach—as for example suggested by Jeremy Prassl from the University of Oxford—are necessary to identify the employer. The problem is particularly complex if in a crowd-work structure where not the platform operator but the crowd-sourcer as client of the platform is getting the crowd-workers' achievements. In this tripartite structure, the employer's role might be split between platform and crowd-sourcer or fulfilled by one of the two actors (Prassl and Risak 2016, p. 619; 2017, p. 67).

The problem of tripartite structures is not new. It is well known in the context of temporary agency work. However, it has become much more dramatic in view of the platform economy. Therefore, it is not surprising that efforts are taken to develop appropriate solutions to identify who is in such a constellation the employer and in what way. There is a lively debate on this issue, however, no satisfying solutions are found yet.

The fourth challenge is the fact that the workforce, again particularly in the context of crowd-working is transnational. This leads to the question whether schemes of workers' representation can be established covering all workers, no matter to which country they belong. All those workers might be included to vote for the workers' representatives. And the workers' representatives might possibly speak for all of them. This would need worldwide transnational regulation which—as already indicated above—is not easy to be developed.

Conclusion

Workers' Participation is a necessary precondition for a democratic workplace in which the worker is considered to be a citizen and not a mere object of management's decisions. Mainly in Europe systems of workers' participation are widespread. They differ from country to country. The EU has tried to promote this cooperative pattern to a great extent. However, much remains to be done to end up in a worldwide coverage.

The real question, however, is whether in the new world of work, in particular in view of digitalization, it will be possible at all to maintain or to establish patterns of workers' participation. The sketchy article tried to show that workers' participation is needed more than ever before, and it also tried to indicate the main obstacles which are to be overcome to reach this goal. The efforts to pave the way in this direction are there, but they are still rather modest. Much remains to be done.

Finally, there should be no doubt that the proper functioning of any form of workers' participation depends not only on internal factors within the company but also to a great extent on external factors. It needs a specific climate, an overall pattern of labour relations where the actors on both sides, business as well as trade unions, respectfully recognize each other and have at least a basic willingness to cooperate instead of fighting each other. In this sense it may be reminded what Marco Biagi once wrote: "Participation is a viable option if there is a sufficiently widespread consensus of all stakeholders involved, including social partners, enterprises and employees. ... Only if this condition is met, can employee involvement…be intended as the option to be pursued, to reconcile efficiency values, on the one hand, and social justice and quality of work values, on the other" (Biagi 2002).

Notes

1. See, for example, the comprehensive study on the impact of the German model of workers' participation by Bertelsmann Foundation/Hans-Böckler-Foundation (Eds.), *Mitbestimmung und neue Unternehmenskulturen – Bilanz und Perspektiven*, Gütersloh 1998.
2. See in particular Directive 75/129/EEC of 22 February 1975 OJ 1975, L 48, on protection of workers in case of collective redundancies and Directive 77/187/EEC of 5 March 1977, OJ 1977, L 61, on protection of workers in case of transfer of undertakings.
3. Directive 02/14/EC of 11 March 2002, OJ L 80/29.
4. Directive 94/45/EC of 22 September 1994, OJ L 254/64, amended by Directive 09/38/EC of 6 May 2009, OJ L 122/28.
5. Directive 01/86/EC of 8 October 2001, OJ L 294/22.

References

Biagi, Marco. 2002. "Quality of Work, Industrial Relations and Employee Involvement in Europe: Thinking the Unthinkable?" In *Quality of Work and Employee Involvement in Europe*, edited by M. Biagi. Kluwer Law International 3 (22).

Biagi, Marco, and Michele Tiraboschi. 2007. "Forms of Employee Representational Participation." In *Comparative Labour Law and Industrial Relations in Industrialized Market Economies*, 9th and revised ed., edited by R. Blanpain. Wolters Kluwer.

Davidov, Guy, and Langille Brian, eds. 2006. *Boundaries and Frontiers of Labour Law.* Oxford/Portland.

Klebe, Thomas, and Weiss Manfred. 2019. "Workers' Participation 4.0 – Digital and Global?" *Comparative Labor Law & Policy Journal* 40 (2): 263–285.

Prassl, Jeremias, and Martin Risak. 2016. "Uber, Taskrabbit, and Co.: Platforms as Employers? Rethinking the Legal Analysis of Crowdwork." *Comparative Labor & Policy Journal* 37 (23): 619–651.

Prassl, Jeremias, and Martin Risak. 2017. "Working in the Gig Economy—Flexibility Without Security?" In *European Employment Policies: Current Challenges*, edited by R. Singer and T. Bazzani. Berlin.

Sinzheimer, Hugo. 1927. *Das Wesen des Arbeitsrechts.* Reprinted in Sinzheimer, Hugo. 1976. *Arbeitsrecht und Rechtssoziologie*, Band 1, Frankfurt.

Waas, Bernd. 2017. "Crowdwork in Germany." In *Crowdwork a Comparative Perspective*, edited by B. Waas et al. Frankfurt.

Weiss, Manfred. 2019. "The Development of Employee Involvement in the EU: Lessons to Be Learned." In *Employment Relations in the 21st Century, Bulletin of Comparative Labour Relations*, 107, edited by Valeria Pulignano and Frank Hendrickx.

3

Trade Unions, Employers' Association and the Law

Filip Dorssemont

Introduction

This contribution analyses the legal construction of trade unions and employers' associations. In French one would add: *Bien étonné de se retrouver ensemble* (What an odd couple). Sure, they truly presuppose each other in a sound dialectical manner. They even tend to be qualified as social partners in numerous language versions of Article 155(1) TFEU of which the formulation dates back to the times immemorial of the Single European Act. In the English language version, a more dialectical language has been used: "management and labour". However, social partners would become the winning formula in the end, as is evidenced by the use of these words in the English language version of Article 152 TFEU.

F. Dorssemont (✉)
Université Catholique de Louvain, Ottignies-Louvain-la-Neuve, Belgium
e-mail: filip.dorssemont@uclouvain.be

Vrije Universiteit Brussels, Brussels, Belgium

T. Addabbo et al. (eds.), *The Collective Dimensions of Employment Relations*,
https://doi.org/10.1007/978-3-030-75532-4_3

In *Academia*, labour lawyers tend to have dedicated much more attention to the trade unions than to the employers' associations. This state of affairs is slightly reminiscent of their obsession with the concept of the worker to the detriment of the definition of the concept of the employer. Thus, the thesis of J. Prassl on the concept of the employer already came close to a small Copernican revolution, heralding the promise of a refoundation of labour law in favour of all those economic actors who cannot be considered employers or better as autonomous undertakings (Prassl 2016, p. 288). It is not so difficult to identify a number of causes for this systematic lack of attention. Nomen est omen. Whereas a specific word was invented for associations of workers (trade unions, syndicats, sindacati), the notion "employers' association" sounds like a definition based upon a genus (association) and a differentia specifica of that word, as if a proper word still has to be invented. The invention of a specific word for workers' associations is partially due to the development of specific national legal frameworks for trade unions, which could not be used for employers' associations. At international and European level, the ECHR (1950), the ICCPR (1966) and the CFREU (2000/2007) solely relate to trade unions/syndicats in a specific manner and are mute on employers' associations. In the same vein, the notion of the representativeness of employers' associations is rarely studied, whereas representativeness of trade unions has received ample attention. In the field of collective actions, strike actions have received much more attention than lock-outs.

Both associations play a quintessential role in any system of industrial relations. They will be endowed with prerogatives to represent their constituency. Depending upon their role, the notion of constituency can be interpreted narrowly as referring to their affiliated workers or employers or more broadly as referring to the respective workers and employers affected by the exercise of the prerogatives, irrespective of the fact whether the latter are indeed affiliated or not.

This contribution does not seek to analyse these prerogatives. The focus is on actors and interactions, not on functions. The following interactions come into play:

- Interactions between trade unions and employers' associations;

- Interactions between trade unions and employers;
- Interactions between trade unions and workers' representatives not related to the trade unions.

Thus, this contribution will consist in the best French tradition of two parts. I will focus on the legal construction of trade unions and employers' associations in a static and a conceptual manner. The analysis of the legal principles guiding the interaction will be *in se et* per se more dynamic.

The legal analysis is eclectic and transversal. I will analyse the subject on the basis of elements of international, European and comparative labour law. The choice of the countries involved is restricted to legal orders of Belgium, France, Germany, the Netherlands and the UK, due to the linguistic deficiencies of the author and his intention to study the legal sources in their original language. This contribution will be concluded by a reflection on the added value of trade unions and employers' association based upon the old device of imagining what a world without trade unions and employers' associations looked like and would look like.

Trade Unions and Employers' Associations, What's in a Name?

Trade unions have emerged *avant la lettre*, prior to their legal institutionalization. They have emerged in a context of industrialization and of a progressive depenalization of laws prohibiting combinations, which at a later date were sufficiently lenient to combat collective actions distinct from the former, such as the strike (Jacobs 1986). Contrary to the journeymen associations so typical of the *Ancien Régime*, the collective identity of members of a trade union was not based upon an ethos of craftsmanship jealously transmitted upon a limited number of apprentices, but upon a "professional identity", based upon the involvement of workers in the same branch of industry at the same sectoral level. In other words, the craft ceased to be the defining factor of the collective identity (Lallement 2008, pp. 33–40). Employers' associations have been established mainly as a reaction to the emergence of trade unions *or* they were constituted originally for the purposes of lobbying at the end of nineteenth century (Jacobs 1986, pp. 222–223).

Historically, trade unions need to be distinguished from corporations. To attribute corporatistic attitudes to them is not a textbook example of sound historical knowledge. Corporations of the *Ancien Régime* as well as more contemporary corporations (of doctors, lawyers and architects) are *instituted* by public authorities. They are not associations. They had and have the capacity to enact regulations, not to be confused with products of collective bargaining. They were and are "inclusive" or rather "mixed" bodies of masters and journeymen. Historically, corporations enjoyed privileges, endowing them with a monopoly to produce goods or to provide services at a local or regional level. In absence of schools open to the public, they effectively controlled the access to the profession, limiting competition and ensuring a fair price for their goods or services. In practice, journeymen concentrated on the training of these apprentices. The journeymen association never aimed to open up the training to what might be called outsiders nowadays. Their preferred means of collective action was the recourse to combinations, *id est* the negative freedom of not concluding contracts with masters not willing to pay the price for their services, at the time closer to subcontracting as to genuine employment contracts (Dorssemont 2002, pp. 78–83; Lis and Soly 1997).

Trade unions and employers' associations need to be defined by their "genus". They are associations, *id est* bodies which are not instituted by public authorities but are the result of the exercise of contractual autonomy. From a purely sociological perspective, they could be qualified as associations of workers and employers for the defence, furthering and promotion of interests of workers and employers as workers or employers as such.

The idea that associations in the meaning of Article 11 European Convention on Human Rights have a private law character came to the forefront in the (Belgian) Landmark case *Le Compte, Van Leuven and Demeyere vs Belgium* (1981).[1] In this case, three Belgian doctors contested in vain the obligatory membership of the *Ordre des Médecins* as a prerequisite to practice medicine. The Court made it abundantly clear that such an obligation which obviously affected the livelihood of the persons concerned did not constitute a restriction of the (negative) freedom of association. The Court considered that the *Ordre des Médecins* did not constitute an association. The Court came to this conclusion on the basis of an organic and a functional test. The *Ordre des Médecins* was not created by individuals but instituted by a statutory law. Furthermore, the Ordre essentially exercised a mission in the field of the public interest, rather than just promoting the interests of their members. In the interesting *Asti* judgement, the Court of Justice of the European Union followed a different approach. The Court had to interpret the scope of Article 8 of Regulation 1612/68.[2] This provision which has now been enshrined in Regulation 492/2011 recognizes a principle of "equality of treatment as regards membership of trade unions and the exercise of rights attaching thereto, including the right to vote and to be eligible for the administration or management posts of a trade union". In the present case, migrant workers in Luxembourg were deprived of voting rights in the *Chambre des employés privés*, whereas they were obliged to pay a retribution. Despite the fact that the *Chambre* was instituted by law, the Court of Justice did assimilate this body to a trade union in the meaning of Article 8 Regulation 1612/68. This means that the notion of trade union has a meaning autonomously from Luxembourgish law and from the notion of association/trade union in the meaning of Article 11 ECHR.

Legal definitions of trade unions are enshrined especially in specific national legal frameworks of trade unions as well as in European and international instruments recognizing the freedom of association. As a general rule, these definitions are only relevant for trade unions. The only instrument which defines trade unions as well as employers' associations in an identical way is the ILO Convention nr 87. The use of the word "organization" is a remarkable attempt to construe a word applicable to both types of associations.

Although definitions do not directly attribute rights and impose obligations, they define or delimit the scope of application on an instrument. They do not restrict rights, they delimit a sphere of application of an instrument. An entity is in or outside the sphere of application. Henceforth, these delimitations can affect the scope *ratione personae* of the workers able to invoke the right to organize as trade unions.

As a general rule, the notion of the workers able to invoke the right to organize is seldom made explicit. A judgement of the Grand Chamber of the ECHR seems to us to identify "the worker" in question. In the *Sindicatul Pastoral Cel Bun v. Romania judgment*,[3] the Court had to consider whether members of the clergy of the Romanian Orthodox Church could invoke freedom of association vis-à-vis their bishopric. Romania contested this applicability by denying that the popes (*i.e.* priests) were bound by an employment contract. This exercise presupposed an interpretation of the concept of a worker who could invoke freedom of association. The Grand Chamber seems to insist only on the quid of subordination, work and remuneration. Neither the origin of this relationship (a civil law contract or a vow of a sacral nature) nor the source of financing (the Church or the State) are relevant.

In another earlier judgement on the (negative), freedom of association *Sigurdur Sigurjonsson v. Iceland,* the Court held that the distinction between self-employed and subordinate workers is not relevant in determining whether or not Article 11 ECHR is applicable to the case at hand.[4] The Court held that Article 11 ECHR enshrines both the generic freedom of association and the specific trade union freedom. It seems to us that this position is valid insofar as it concerns the assessment of issues relating to freedom of association or trade union rights at the individual level. However, this distinction seems to be relevant when assessing the question of essential or important means for the defence of the interests of a member of a trade union. This obligation to provide essential means has only been recognized in favour of trade unions, not at all to association in general.

In the case *Liječnički sindikat v. Croatia*, the European Court of Human Rights found a violation of the right of a doctors' and dentists' trade union to strike.[5] There is nothing in this case to suggest that the union was organizing only doctors or dentists with an employment contract. The Government of Croatia did not dispute at all that the union in question could invoke freedom of association and the right to strike. However, it would be presumptuous, in our opinion, to consider that this judgement definitively and explicitly settles the question of the ownership of the right to strike in favour of self-employed workers.

The European Social Charter recognizes freedom of association for workers and employers without specifying these notions. The use of the English word (*workers*) pleads in favour of a broad interpretation of the word "worker". The same is true for the opening up of trade union freedom to retired workers and the unemployed (Jacobs 2017, p. 235).[6] M. Mikkola, a former member of the Committee, also considers that so-called self-employed workers would fall within the scope of Article 5 of the ESC (2010, p. 242)

Convention No. 87, adopted within the International Labour Organization, takes a stronger stance. Its Article 2 states that "Workers and employers, without distinction whatsoever, shall have the right to establish and, subject only to the rules of the organisation concerned, to join organisations of their own choosing without previous authorization" (Hodges-Aeberhard 1989).

The phrase "without distinction of any kind" seems to argue, in our view, also for the broadest possible understanding of the word "worker". This is what the latest version of the Compilation of Decisions of the Committee on Freedom of Association, renamed Compilation (2018), states:

> By virtue of the principles of freedom of association, all workers – with the sole exception of members of the armed forces and the police – should have the right to establish and join organizations of their own choosing. The criterion for determining the persons covered by that right, therefore, is not based on the existence of an employment relationship, which is often non-existent, for example in the case of agricultural workers, self-employed workers in general or those who practice liberal professions, who should nevertheless enjoy the right to organize.[7]

It should also be noted that this maxim of jurisprudence, which was listed in the previous case law of 2006, has been confirmed in posterior case law by the Committee on Freedom of Association.[8]

The reference to agricultural workers is not purely coincidental. Convention No. 141 (ILO) defines its scope of application very broadly. Article 2 states that:

> For the purposes of this Convention, the term ***rural workers*** means any person engaged in agriculture, handicrafts or a related occupation in a rural area, whether as a wage earner or, subject to the provisions of paragraph 2 of this Article, as a self-employed person such as a tenant, sharecropper or small owner-occupier.

Convention No. 141 tries to delimit its scope according to the concept of employer. It thus reverses the classic semantic approach of defining that concept according to the worker. In the spirit of the Convention, there is a watertight division between the worker and the employer. The Convention applies to "all categories of rural workers, whether they are wage earners or self-employed" (Article 3). Article 2 (2) states:

> This Convention applies only to those tenants, sharecroppers or small owner-occupiers who derive their main income from agriculture, who work the land themselves, with the help only of their family or with the help of occasional outside labour and who do not—
>
> (a) permanently employ workers; or
> (b) employ a substantial number of seasonal workers; or
> (c) have any land cultivated by sharecroppers or tenants.

Instead of examining the question of whether a worker is in a state of subordination to an employer, a revolution of a Copernican nature is needed. The question should be asked whether a worker can be qualified as an employer. If not, he or she could invoke freedom of association. In other words, although employers are disqualified in a second stage, self-employment does not exclude falling within the scope of the Convention. In short, the first real question is whether a farmer is an employer who employs workers. If he is not, he falls within the scope of Convention No. 141. It is interesting to note that the Convention does not settle the question of whether an agricultural worker managing an undertaking has economic "autonomy".

The right of farmers to form or join a "trade union" is to be assessed on an autonomous basis. It is sufficient in my view that farmers have the right to set up a professional organization which is endowed with the essential prerogatives for the collective defence of the interests of its members. In fact, this idea was put forward in a judgement of the European Court of Human Rights, stating that the mere fact that domestic law prevents farmers from joining a trade union within the meaning of domestic law is irrelevant, provided that the constitution of such a professional organization is indeed possible according to another statute.[9]

The statutory legal frameworks for trade unions also set teleological limits to the objectives an association is allowed to pursue in order to benefit from the recognition and the protection of the freedom of association under the statute concerned. It is important to underpin whether the nature of these interests to be defended is being restricted as well as. The most favourable definitions might be those where interests are not being made subject to a *differentia specifica*. Thus, the Organic Law on the institution of the Belgian Conseil National du Travail defines trade unions as structures having a statutory objective to defend workers' interests («avoir pour l'objet statutaire la défense des intérêts des travailleurs»). The definition of organizations of workers or employers enshrined in Article 10 ILO Convention nr 87 defines them as any "organization of workers or of employers for furthering and defending the interests of workers or of employers". The French definition of a "syndicat" stemming from the Loi Waldeck Rousseau adopts a seemingly more restrictive stance defining the "syndicat professionnel" as structures exclusively dealing with the study, and the defence of rights as well of the material and moral interests, both collectively as well as individually of the persons envisaged by the statutes («Les syndicats professionnels ont exclusivement pour objet l'étude et la défense des droits ainsi que des intérêts matériels et moraux, tant collectifs qu'individuels, des personnes visées par leurs statuts»). Given the large scope of this *differentia specifica*, this provides leeway for a broad interpretation of the interests at stake and is effectively interpreted in that manner, despite the fact that the notion of "professionnel" was intended historically to restrict the interests at stake. Thus, in the field of collective action, strikes will need to serve a rather immediate "professional" aim, jeopardizing the legitimacy of sympathy strikes.

This restriction of the interests is made more explicit in the definition of what constitutes a "union professionelle" in the Belgian law on professional unions, defining the "*union professionelle* as an association constituted exclusively for the study, the protection and the development of professional interests of their members" («L'union professionnelle est une association formée *exclusivement* pour l'étude, la protection et le développement des intérêts *professionnels* de ses membres»). The law provided an optional framework for trade unions which they never embraced. The Law was recently abolished. Also the German constitutional provision (Article 9 GG) enshrining the right to organize adopts a *differentia specifica* of the interests to be protected and promoted which cover both working conditions as well as economic conditions ("das Recht zur Wahrung und Förderung der Arbeits- und Wirtschaftsbedingungen Vereinigungen zu bilden").

Another issue is whether the ambit of antagonists against whom these interests need to be defended is being restricted. Thus Article 1 of the British TURCLA defines trade unions as "an organisation (whether temporary or permanent) –

(A) which consists wholly or mainly of workers of one or more descriptions and whose principal purposes include the regulation of relations between workers of that description or those descriptions and employers or employers' associations".

Thus, it neglects that trade unions need to defend and promote interests in their relation to the State as the architect of legislation and policies which directly affect the interests of workers.

Although the issue is more semantic than legalistic, some definitions present trade unions as being solely in the defensive rather than in the offensive as well. Thus, the telos of trade unions enshrined in Article 11 ECHR and in the French Waldeck Rousseau Law strikes as being too defensive (protection of interests/étude et defense). The posterior formula of the right to organize enshrined in Article 8 ICESCR (promotion and protection of his economic and social interests) is more offensive and in line with the seminal formula of Article 10 ILO Convention nr 87 (furthering and defending the interests).

Some delimitations impose limits to the governance and the autonomy of the structure invoking the right to organize, such as the necessity to function in a democratic way. Thus, Article 39 Italian Constitution provides that the registration of trade unions has to be made subject to the condition that the statutes of the trade unions provide sufficient guarantees of a democratic functioning ("*É condizione per la registrazione che gli statuti dei sindacati sanciscano un ordinamento interno a base democratica*"). Since no statutory framework has been established for the registration of trade unions entailing the acquisition of corporate personality, this provision is not of immediate practical relevance. Despite the absence of any reference to the democratic constitution of trade unions, Gamillscheg also insists on the democratic character of associations of employees for the sake of their constitutional recognition as so-called *Koalitionen* (Gamillscheg 1997, pp. 401–403). In France, the application of the Loi Waldeck Rousseau which is a mandatory legal framework does not ensure as such that *syndicats* function in a democratic manner. There are no rules about the governance structure, providing, e.g. the democratic election of trade union leaders. The same observation is valid for the Belgian Law on Professional Unions.

Other delimitations seek to avoid that structures which are not sufficiently independent from the antagonists they seek to combat can profit from the recognition. The condition of independency is a condition formulated by F. Gamillscheg in respect of *Koalitionen* (1997, pp. 415–425). The French Law Waldeck Rousseau is mute on this issue, whereas the criteria for representativeness established under French Law (Article L2121-1) do insist on independence. In my view, this is not a condition of representativeness, it needs to be rephrased as an essential characteristic of all trade unions.

The Acquisition of Legal Personality

It is important to stress in my view, that trade unions or employers' associations are not per se legal persons. Thus, Article 7 of the ILO Convention just states that:

> The acquisition of legal personality by workers' and employers' organisations, federations and confederations shall not be made subject to conditions of such a character as to restrict the application of the provisions of Articles 2, 3 and 4 thereof.

Articles 2, 3 and 4 ILO Convention nr 87 deal with a number of specific issues. It is relevant that statutory frameworks do not restrict the identity of the workers or employers eligible for membership (article 2). The statutory framework should provide sufficient autonomy for the organizations "right to draw up their constitutions and rules, to elect their representatives in full freedom, to organise their administration and activities and to formulate their programmes" (article 3) Last but not least, the statutory framework should not allow for the dissolution or suspension by administrative authority (Article 4).

Belgian trade unions have historically refused to embrace legal frameworks entailing legal personality for different reasons which are not referred to in the ILO Convention nr 87. They are suspicious about the rise that strategic information would be made public as a result of the acquisition of the legal personality. In their view, any kind of publicity or a risk of publicity of the identity of the members or of financial situation of the trade unions is to be avoided. Thus, the trade unions do not want antagonists to be able to know the amount of their "caisse de résistance" (the fund to support workers on strike). Furthermore, they fear the consequences of a regime of liability which could force them to pay damages resulting out of collective actions deemed illicit. Since at present the trade unions cannot be held liable, it is extremely blurry for them what the consequences of the acquisition of legal personality might entail. This would require less insecurity with regard to the question what illicit strikes are, a clear cut answer to the question to what extent trade unions are required to act as an actor preventing damages and for which actors the trade unions can be held liable (Dorssemont 2006).

The baseline of this provision is sound. There is no obligation to impose legal personality to trade unions and employers' associations. There is no incompatibility between the acquisition of legal personality and the full enjoyment of the freedom of association. Historically, the Belgian Socialist Party, known as the *Parti Ouvrier Belge*, which was founded by trade unions demanded the adoption of a legal framework allowing the trade unions to acquire legal personality. The aforementioned cases *Sindicatul* and *Manole* concern trade unions eager to acquire legal personality and challenging a refusal to be registered. The Italian Constitution does contain a provision regarding the acquisition of legal personality as a mere consequence of registration, obliging the legislator just to impose a democratic structure as a condition. This could be seen as a good practice in the light of the admonishment of the ILO Convention nr 87 not to impose conditions restricting the freedom of association. As already mentioned in the above, such a statutory instrument was never adopted. Few countries have actually adopted specific legal frameworks, *solely* dealing with the legal status of trade unions.[10] Many statutory legal frameworks rather deal with the very issue of the freedom of association of workers.[11] It is more common for trade unions to adapt to more generic frameworks applicable to associations in general. These frameworks might or might not leave a choice between a corporate status and a purely contractual status. The absence of corporate personality is not as uncommon as one might assume Thus, the Belgian, the German and the Italian trade unions lack legal personality. The Belgian associations are called factual associations (*associations de fait).* The qualification is problematic, since there is nothing factual about a phenomenon which is purely contractual in nature. The German trade unions constitute *nicht eingetragen Vereine* and the Italian trade union are *associazioni non riconosciute.*

In my view, the lack of corporate personality cannot be used as a pretext to deny a *locus standi* to a trade union, since this is an essential means to defend workers' interests. Thus, in *Adefdromil v. France* the European Court on Human Rights ruled that such a *locus standi* affects the core of the freedom of association. The denial of a trade union deprived of legal personality of such a *locus standi* was considered to be a violation of Article 11 ECHRM. The absence of this legal personality was linked to the prohibition for the military to create a trade union. As a consequence, their trade union could not be considered as a "syndicat" which is endowed with legal personality *iuris et de iure.*[12]

The Issue of Representativeness

The notion of a trade union or an employers' organizations needs to be distinguished from that of a representative organization of workers or employees. It is well known that the notion of representativity originated from the Constitution of the ILO and was subsequently embraced by national legislators.

Indeed, Article 3 of the ILO Constitution fleshes out the tripartite nature of the General Conference, forcing Member States to designate delegates representing the employers and the workpeople of their State. The latter have to be nominated "*in agreement with the industrial organizations, if such organizations exist, which are most representative of employers or workpeople, as the case may be, in their respective countries*".

The ILO does not give a satisfactory definition of what constitutes representativity. As was highlighted by Lucien François in his seminal Treaties, a proper understanding of representativeness depends upon the perspective adopted (François 1980, pp. 212–214).[13] For a sociologist, representativeness refers to a relation of adequacy between a constituency and a representative. A trade union could be described as a representative actor, if its position reflects what the constituency thinks. François pointed out that the notion of representativeness functions rather differently from a legal perspective. A trade union or employers' association is representative, since it has been empowered to exercise prerogatives which go beyond the defence of the interests of the members and extend to non-affiliated workers or employers. In fact, every trade union is representative, *id est* empowered to represent its members. If in the case of collective agreements, these agreements are applicable beyond the sphere of the members affiliated to the signatory parties, there is a need to construe a notion of representativeness which can trigger something the *figura* of agency (mandate) cannot generate. Based upon a standing case law of the freedom of association committee, the General Conference has adopted the Collective Bargaining Recommendation nr 163 (1981) which provides the following principle:

> (b) in countries in which the competent authorities apply procedures for recognition with a view to determining the organisations to be

> granted the right to bargain collectively, such determination is based on pre-established and objective criteria with regard to the organisations' representative character, established in consultation with representative employers' and workers' organisations.

The ILO Constitution does not provide criteria which should guide the determination of the most representative trade unions and employers' associations with which the States should reach an agreement in order to nominate the respective delegates. Formally, this is not contrary to the Recommendation, which deals with collective bargaining at national level.

Both the French and the Belgian legislator have established criteria of representativity for trade unions which match the Collective Bargaining Recommendation.[14] A recent French reform has also introduced exhaustive criteria for employers' associations which seem ILO proof.[15]

Interactions with and Between Trade Unions and Employers' Associations

Article 2 ILO Convention nr 98 states that:

> Workers' and employers' organisations shall enjoy adequate protection against any acts of interference by each other or each other's agents or members in their establishment, functioning or administration.

This principle is illustrated by a more specific rule, prohibiting behaviour stemming from the managerial side against trade unions. It states in the subsequent paragraph:

> 2. In particular, acts which are designed to promote the establishment of workers' organisations under the domination of employers or employers' organisations, or to support workers' organisations by financial or other means, with the object of placing such organisations under the control of employers or employers' organisations, shall be deemed to constitute acts of interference within the meaning of this Article.

A nice example of "implementation" of this principle is provided by the Italian *Statuto dei lavoratori* (Act nr 300 of 1970). It has implemented this principle in a generic way to the sole benefit of the workers' organizations and in a more specific way by prohibiting *sindacati di commodo.* In the same vein Article 13 of the Spanish Organic law on the freedom of association (*Ley Organica de Libertad Syndacal*: Act n. 11 of 1985) qualifies acts of interference as violations of the freedom of organization, thus opening up all the remedies prescribed in the law. It also defines acts of interference as acts aimed at encouraging the formation of unions dominated or controlled by an employer or business association, or at supporting, financially or otherwise, unions for the same purpose of control.

Interactions Between Trade Unions and Employers

Employers have developed a very efficient strategy in order to neutralize the impact of trade unions striving for the defence and the protection of their workers' interests, *i.e.* discriminating employees applying for a job or effectively working in their enterprise.

This practice is explicitly prohibited by Article 1 of the ILO Convention 98 which also enumerates two textbook examples of anti-union discrimination:

a. to make the employment of a worker subject to the condition that he shall not join a union or shall relinquish trade union membership; and
b. to cause the dismissal of or otherwise prejudice a worker by reason of union membership or because of participation in union activities outside working hours or, with the consent of the employer, within working hours.

In the same vein, the European Court on Human rights introduced the notion of discrimination in the landmark case *Danilenkov v Russia*,[16] by warning that the presence of criminal law provisions must not lead to a situation where discrimination in the area of freedom of association can no longer be combatted through the measure of the lighter civil burden of proof. Without explicitly stating that this civil law evidence should be facilitated by a reversal of the burden of proof, the Court did, however, state in § 130 that:

> It therefore agrees that the clear negative effects of DUR membership on the applicants were sufficient to constitute a prima facie case of discrimination in the enjoyment of the rights guaranteed by Article 11 of the Convention.[17]

The expression of the words "prima facie" gives the impression that the Court believes that evidence based on indications could suffice.

> In the subsequent *Tek Gıda İş Sendikası v. Turkey* case, the Court had to dwell on a dismissal of employee as a retaliation of their membership of a trade union involved in collective actions. The European Court on Human Rights has in *Tek Gıda* ruled that the subjective choice incumbent upon an employer between reinstatement and a compensation of one year constituted a disproportionate restriction of the freedom of association.[18]

Whereas the impetus in the ILO Convention nr 98 is on the discriminatory use of the stick, the *Statuto dei lavortori* innovates by prohibiting a more insidious discriminatory use of the carrot to undermine trade union affiliation and activity. Article 16 prohibits the "concessione di trattamenti economici di maggior favore" which could be used to seduce workers not to affiliate to a trade union or not to engage in trade union activity. The *Statuto dei lavoratori* highlights the discriminatory character of such a form of management by seduction. The stance adopted against these practices prefigurates the landmark judgement in *Wilson and Palmer vs the UK* of the European Court on Human rights, condemned the UK for "permitting employers to use financial incentives to induce employees to surrender important union rights", *in casu*, the fact of giving trade union a mandate for the sake of collective bargaining.[19]

Interactions Between Trade Unions and Workers' Representatives not Related to the Trade Unions

An interaction which does not directly concerns the relationship between trade unions and employers' associations, but which might undermine the position of trade unions at the level of the undertaking concerns the potential competition between trade unions and workers' representatives which are not directly related to trade unions. An issue to be addressed is the notion of workers' representatives. The notion of a workers' representative has been defined in Article 3 of ILO Convention No. 135.[20] In combination with Article 1, this definition refers to workers' representatives who function within an undertaking (*dans l'entreprise*) and covers both:

> (a) the trade union representatives, namely, representatives designated or elected by trade unions or by members of such unions;
> (b) elected representatives, namely, representatives who are freely elected by the workers of the undertaking in accordance with provisions of national laws or regulations or of collective agreements and whose functions do not include activities which are recognised as the exclusive prerogative of trade unions in the country concerned.

Various ILO standards allow for a role for such workers' representatives on the condition that they do *not* undermine the position of trade unions within the undertaking. The workers representatives concerned are not "trade union representatives, namely representatives designated or elected by trade unions" or by the members of such unions, but "elected representatives, namely representatives who are freely elected by the workers of the undertaking".[21]

Conclusion

Labour law is older than the invention of the employment contract. In France and Belgium statutory frameworks for trade unions predate the invention of the employment contract. In the era of the *Ancien Régime*, journeymen associations managed to increase wages through boycotts and through reducing the number of apprentices being trained, but they need to be distinguished from modern trade unions. The collective identity of trade union affiliates is based on a different bound and they have recourse to a modern type of collective action, the strike. Just as the boycotts allowed them to receive an adequate remuneration, the involvement of trade unions has amounted to reach the same objective, through the exercise of collective autonomy, not just at a local level, but at a sectoral and intersectoral level. The absence of bargaining agents will deprive labour law regulations of their autonomous character. It will force individual employers to engage in a form of individual bargaining which will result in higher transaction costs. The representation of workers would be left to elected workers representatives who will never be able to represent a constituency in an efficient and adequate way without being backed up by an organization.

A recent proposal for an EU directive focused on adequate minimum wages highlight the essential role of social partners in setting adequate minimum wages.[22] This avenue is fleshed out prior to a statutory intervention. It stresses the role of the State in promoting collective bargaining and in ensuring a proper enforcement of these agreements as well as the involvement of social partners in case a statutory setting of minimum wages might be privileged.

Notes

1. ECHR, 23 June 1981, 7238/75, 6878/75 (*Le Compte, Van Leuven and Demeyere vs Belgium).*
2. CJEU, 4 July 1991, C-213/90 (Asti).
3. ECHR, 9 July 2013, 2330/09 (*Sindicatul Pastoral Cel Bun c Romania*).
4. ECHR, 30 June 1993, 16130/90 *(Sigurdur Sigurjonsson v Iceland).*
5. ECHR, 27 November 2014, 36701/09 (*Hrvatski liječnički sindikat v. Croatia*).
6. See in this regard: Jacobs, Antoine. 2017. "Article 5. The Right to Organise." In *The European Social Charter and the Employment Relation*, edited by Niklas Bruun, Klaus Lörcher, Isabelle Schömann, Stefan

Clauwaert, 235. Oxford: Hart Publishing, where the author refers to a 2010 Statement of Interpretation of the European Committee of Social Rights.

7. ILO. 2018. *Freedom of Association—Compilation of Decisions of the Committee on Freedom of Association.* 6th ed. Geneva: International Labour Office, para. 387.
8. See in this respect the cases listed in Borelli, Silvia and Juana María Serrano García. 2019. "Il Necessario Riconoscimento Dei Diritti Sindacali Ai Lavoratori Dell'economia Digitale." In *Impresa, lavoro e non lavoro nell'economia digitale*, edited by Cristina Alessi, Marzia Barbera, and Luciana Guanaglione, 537–556. Bari: Cacucci, and cases n. 2686 (Dominican Republic); n. 2868 (Panama); n. 2888 (Poland).
9. ECHR, 16 June 2015, 46551/06 (*Manole and the Direct Farmers of Romania v. Romania*).
10. Examples concern France (The Loi Waldeck Rousseau), Belgium (the recently abolished Loi sur les Unions Professionnelles).
11. Spain (*Ley organica de libertad sindical* (1985) and Greece (Act No. 1264/82, on the democratisation of the trade union movement and the protection of workers' trade unions) and UK (TULRCA 1992).
12. ECHR, 2 October 2014, 32191/09 (*Adefdromil versus France*): §§ 60: «La Cour considère qu'en lui interdisant par principe d'agir en justice en raison de la nature syndicale de son objet social, sans déterminer concrètement les seules restrictions qu'imposaient les missions spécifiques de l'institution militaire, les autorités internes ont porté atteinte à l'essence même de la liberté d'association».
13. On the issue of representativeness, see Dorssemont, Filip. 2020. "La représentativité revisitée." In *Organes et instruments de la Concertation sociale: Enjeux contemporains. Actes du colloque organisé sous la direction scientifique de F.Dorssemont, P.-P. Van Gehuchten, L. Dear et J.-P. Cordier à l'UCLouvain par le CRIDES et l'AJPDS le 30 novembre 2018*, edited by Filip Dorssemont, Pierre-Paul Van Gehuchten, Laurent Dear, and Jean-Philippe Cordier, 61–82. Liège: Wolters Kluwer.
14. See for the criteria of representativeness of trade unions under French Law, Article L. 2121-1 and Article L. 2122 of the French Code du Travail:

    Article L. 2121-1

    La représentativité des organisations syndicales est déterminée d'après les critères cumulatifs suivants:

    1. *Le respect des valeurs républicaines;*

2. *L'indépendance;*
3. *La transparence financière;*
4. *Une ancienneté minimale de deux ans dans le champ professionnel et géographique couvrant le niveau de négociation. Cette ancienneté s'apprécie à compter de la date de dépôt légal des statuts;*
5. *L'audience établie selon les niveaux de négociation conformément aux articles L. 2122-1, L. 2122-5, L. 2122-6 et L. 2122-9;*
6. *L'influence, prioritairement caractérisée par l'activité et l'expérience;*
7. *Les effectifs d'adhérents et les cotisations.*

Article L. 2122-1

Dans l'entreprise ou l'établissement, sont représentatives les organisations syndicales qui satisfont aux critères de l'article L. 2121-1 et qui ont recueilli au moins 10% des suffrages exprimés au premier tour des dernières élections des titulaires au comité d'entreprise ou de la délégation unique du personnel ou, à défaut, des délégués du personnel, quel que soit le nombre de votants.

For Belgium, see Article 2 § 4 of the Loi sur le Conseil national du Travail:

§ 4. *Les membres représentant les organisations les plus représentatives des travailleurs sont choisis parmi les candidats sur base d'une liste double de candidats présentée par ces organisations.*

Sont considérées comme organisations les plus représentatives des travailleurs les organisations qui répondent à tous les critères suivants:

1. *être constituées sur le plan national et avoir un fonctionnement interprofessionnel;*
2. *représenter la majorité absolue des secteurs et des catégories de personnel dans le secteur privé et le secteur public, pour autant que la majorité des travailleurs soit également représentée;*
3. *au cours de la période de quatre ans précédant les nominations prévues à l'article 5, compter en moyenne au moins 125.000 membres cotisants, y compris les membres des organisations affiliées ou associées;*
4. *avoir pour objet statutaire la défense des intérêts des travailleurs.*

15. See Articles L. 2152-1 to L. 2152-7 of the French Code du Travail.
16. ECHR, 30 July 2009, *67336/01 (Danilenkov and others v Russia).*
17. ECHR, 30 July 2009, *67336/01 (Danilenkov and others v Russia)*, § 130.
18. ECHR, 4 April 2017, 35009/05 (*Tek Gıda İş Sendikası v. Turkey*).
19. ECHR, 2 July 2002, 30668/96, 30671/96 and 30678/96 (*Wilson, National Union of Journalists and others vs UK*).
20. Article 3, ILO Convention No. 135:

For the purpose of this Convention the term ***workers' representatives*** *means persons who are recognised as such under national law or practice, whether they are—*

a. *trade union representatives, namely, representatives designated or elected by trade unions or by members of such unions; or*
b. *elected representatives, namely, representatives who are freely elected by the workers of the undertaking in accordance with provisions of national laws or regulations or of collective agreements and whose functions do not include activities which are recognised as the exclusive prerogative of trade unions in the country concerned.*

21. See Article 5, ILO Convention No. 135: "*Where there exist in the same undertaking both trade union representatives and elected representatives, appropriate measures shall be taken, wherever necessary, to ensure that the existence of elected representatives is not used to undermine the position of the trade unions concerned or their representatives and to encourage co-operation on all relevant matters between the elected representatives and the trade unions concerned and their representatives*". See also Recommendation, 1952 No. 94 concerning Consultation and Co-operation between Employers and Workers at the Level of the Undertaking: "*consultation on matters of mutual concern not within the scope of collective bargaining*"; and Recommendation 1960 No. 113 concerning Consultation and Co-operation between Public Authorities and Employers' and Workers's Organisations at the Industrial and National Levels: "*Such consultation and co-operation should not derogate from freedom of association or from the rights of employers' and workers' organisations, including their right of collective bargaining*".
22. COM (2020) 682 final.

References

Borelli, Silvia, and Juana María Serrano García. 2019. "Il Necessario Riconoscimento Dei Diritti Sindacali Ai Lavoratori Dell'economia Digitale." In *Impresa, lavoro e non lavoro nell'economia digitale*, edited by Cristina Alessi, Marzia Barbera, and Luciana Guanaglione, 537–556. Bari: Cacucci.

Dorssemont, Filip. 2002. *Rechtspositie en Syndicale actievrijheid van representatieve werknemersorganisaties*. Brugge: Die Keure.
Dorssemont, Filip. 2006. "La loi belge sur les Unions professionnelles de 1898: avatar de la loi Waldeck-Rousseau de 1884?" *Annales de la Faculté de droit de Strasbourg* 8: 169–191. Strasbourg: Presses universitaires de Strasbourg.
Dorssemont, Filip. 2020. "La représentativité revisitée." In *Organes et instruments de la Concertation sociale: Enjeux contemporains. Actes du colloque organisé sous la direction scientifique de F.Dorssemont, P.-P. Van Gehuchten, L. Dear et J.-P. Cordier à l'UCLouvain par le CRIDES et l'AJPDS le 30 novembre 2018*, edited by Filip Dorssemont, Pierre-Paul Van Gehuchten, Laurent Dear, and Jean-Philippe Cordier, 61–82. Liège: Wolters Kluwer.
François, Lucien. 1980. *Théorie des relations collectives du travail en droit belge*. Bruxelles: Bruylant.
Gamillscheg, Franz. 1997. *Kollektives Arbeitsrecht: ein Lehrbuch. Grundlagen, Koalitionsfreiheit, Tarifvertrag, Arbeitskampf und Schlichtung*. Band 1. Munich: Beck.
Hodges-Aeberhard, Jane. 1989. "The Right to Organise in Article 2 of Convention No. 87: What Is Meant by Works 'without Distinction Whatsoever'?" *International Labour Review* 128 (2): 177–194.
ILO. 2018. *Freedom of Association—Compilation of Decisions of the Committee on Freedom of Association*. 6th ed. Geneva: International Labour Office.
Jacobs, Antoine. 1986. "Collective Self-Regulation." In *The Making of Labour Law in Europe*, edited by Bob Hepple, 193–241. London: Mansell Publishing Limited.
Jacobs, Antoine. 2017. "Article 5. The Right to Organise." In *The European Social Charter and the Employment Relation*, edited by Niklas Bruun, Klaus Lörcher, Isabelle Schömann, and Stefan Clauwaert, 220–248. Oxford: Hart Publishing.
Lallement, Michel. 2008. *Sociologie des relations professionnelles*. Paris: La Découverte.
Lis, Catharina, and Hugo Soly. 1997. "Ambachtsgilden in vergelijkend perspectief: de Noordelijke en de Zuidelijke Nederlanden 15de -18de eeuw." In *Werelden van verschil: ambachtsgilden in de Lage Landen*, edited by Catharina Lis and Hugo Soly, 11–42. Brussels: VUB Press.
Matti, Mikkola. 2010. *Social Human Rights of Europe*. Porvoo: Legisactio Ltd.
Prassl, Jeremias. 2016. *The Concept of the Employer*. Oxford: Oxford University Press.

4

Organization as Collective Rule-Making

Tommaso Fabbri and Ylenia Curzi

Introduction

According to a number of prominent Italian labor law scholars, the collective dimension of the work relationship features an inherent and unescapable component which is *additional* to the collective-*trade union* dimension and to the *individual* dimension regulated by the employment contract and is also sometimes associated with the idea of "community"; some scholars refer to this as the "collective-relational" dimension, others as the "third" dimension.

The work at the Fondazione Marco Biagi and the interdisciplinary approach that prevails there offer an excellent vantage point for observing

T. Fabbri · Y. Curzi (✉)
Marco Biagi Department of Economics and Marco Biagi Foundation,
University of Modena and Reggio Emilia, Modena, Italy
e-mail: ylenia.curzi@unimore.it

T. Fabbri
e-mail: tommaso.fabbri@unimore.it

T. Addabbo et al. (eds.), *The Collective Dimensions of Employment Relations*,
https://doi.org/10.1007/978-3-030-75532-4_4

the intimate connections between the arguments of labor law and the economic/managerial perspective of analysis, connections that lately have taken concrete shape in the so-called "principle of adjustment," whereby framing the dynamics of labor and the firm in organizational terms precedes (*prius*) the jurist's regulatory decisions. The aim of this chapter, therefore, is to shed light on the organizational roots of the *collective-relational* or *third* dimension of the work relationship.

Interdependence

The rejection of an institutionalist view of the work relationship, in Italy, goes far back in time—to Lodovico Barassi's foundational work of 1901—and is acknowledged in the Constitution, where the principle of collaboration is relegated to Article 46, the poorly practiced article on workers' participation in the management of enterprises. However, the idea that the opposing, and prevalent, individualistic-contractualistic view of the work relationship has insufficient regulatory power is attracting renewed attention from jurists. As it is beyond the scope of the present chapter to discuss this at length, we will limit ourselves to offering two recent, and illuminating, quotations.

The first is from Riccio (2018): "*The effort to link all of the various aspects of the employment relationship to contract law, making the contract impenetrable to the firm where the job is performed, eventually led to underestimate one interest of the employer that would not possibly have entered into such contractual arrangement. We refer to the employers' interest in the organization, as the integration/coordination of each task with the other tasks and with the firm's production factors. In satisfying this interest, the employer can rely on a general power of organization […]*" (pp. 25–26). To catch this "*interest in the organization,*" Riccio specifies (idem, p. 28–29) that it is necessary to "*focus on the question of the interrelationships between the subjective positions of the workers in a given organization*" (p. 29), interpreting the latter, as Art. 3 of Law 604/1966 does, "*as the key to bring to unity the unavoidable fact of the division of labor*" (p. 28): "*Considering corporate activity as production activity that is organized, even as regards individual tasks, clearly points to an unavoidable interrelationship between workers' jobs*" (p. 23).

The second is taken from two papers by the same author, Luca Nogler, published in 2014 and 2015: "*Those who think in pro-labor terms, however, should admit that there is a third dimension, separate and distinct from the individual and trade union dimensions, which has to do with the fact that subordinate work is carried out* "à cote de"*. The worker cannot claim to be sealed off on his own like an isolated monad, as if he did not work alongside others (and as if this were not contemplated by the contract). In reality, the contract requires him to make himself "organizable" or, to put it another way, to cooperate in the problem of the organizational "bringing together" of workers*" (Nogler 2015, p. 15). "[…] *The third dimension is situated, as it were, between the individual and collective dimensions, and concerns the relationship that is established (through social contact) between the workers in the work organization: it is sometimes spoken of as a horizontal interconnection of work relationships*" (Nogler 2014, p. 902).

This third dimension, then, is collective but not via the trade unions, inherent in the work relationship, and relational, i.e., it consists in the social relationship that arises between workers as they each strive to connect their working activities into a coordinated unit, an organization, with a view to achieving a common—though not necessarily shared—outcome. It is the interdependence between the workers and between the jobs in the organization: This, in the reconstructions we have just quoted, is what appears to exceed the traditional bounds of the bilateral contract and thus calls for a "third," dedicated thematization. And it is something on which organizational theory can shed light.

Let us see how.

Coordination

The "collective" character of the organization lies in its being a "social relationship" in the Weberian sense, viz., "*the behavior of a plurality of actors insofar as, in its meaningful content, the action of each takes account of that of the others and is oriented in these terms*" (Weber 1922a,

p. 26), and in its being "*a system of consciously coordinated activities*" rationally oriented toward the pursuit of a common outcome (Barnard 1938; Simon 1947; March and Simon 1958). Social relationships, inasmuch as they are purposeful collective actions, and inasmuch as they are cooperative actions oriented toward a common—even if not shared—outcome, entail some sort of logical and technical mechanism whereby individual rationalities can converge on a collective, organizational goal; in the lexicon of organizational theory, this mechanism is called coordination: "*The term coordination denotes the process that enables each participant to know and/or predict the others' behavior, and thus to ground his decisions and actions in that knowledge. In other words, it designates the set of rules that make it possible to integrate an individual's behavior with that of the other participants in the organization*" (Albano 2013, p. 42). This is "organizational rule-making." This is the phenomenology for/to which legal rules are formulated and applied. And what does organizational theory tell us about this phenomenology? How does it enable us to frame it in terms of rationality, thus providing the groundwork (*prius*) for "legal rule-making"?

Interpreting Coordination: Alternative Options

Essentially, organizational theory gives us two alternative options for interpreting organizational rule-making.

The first, the mainstream alternative, and as such the only one familiar to the overwhelming majority of jurists, and consequently the only one that figures in their arguments, is the *predetermination* option: Organizational rule-making equates to the set of *prior heteronomous* rules by which coordination of collective action is achieved. There are two variants of predetermination: "*Imposition*" and "*discretion.*" In the "*imposition*" or Fordist variant, the decision-maker/rule-maker has access to full information and can thus set out the details of jobs and requires that they be carried out in sequence and/or in parallel as part of meticulous production programs. In the "*discretion*" or post-Fordist variant, the decision-maker/rule-maker's controlling omniscience is undermined by the environmental uncertainty and the workers, the executors, are consequently required to make a "greater effort," as Burns and Stalker (1961) point out: They must not only *execute* the detailed instructions given to them, but they must also *adjust the instructions* to contingent needs, or in other words interpret their job correctly in accordance with their superiors' expectations; likewise, they must direct their skills flexibly and adaptively toward achieving the outcome set beforehand by the decision-maker/rule-maker.

In the "*imposition*" variant, the interrelations or interdependencies between workers, or in other words, between the individual "*tasks*," are known and worked out exhaustively *beforehand* and ordered sequentially and/or in parallel in a production program. In the "*discretion*" variant, by contrast, each individual "*role*" has the additional responsibility of determining how to coordinate with the other roles with which it is interdependent: The worker must proactively seek results, strive to integrate his work in the organization, and feel a duty, to use a term with legal overtones, to *become an organic part of the firm*, to make himself *organizable*, over and above "executive" obedience to the employer's orders.

Today, many jurists believe the difference between the Fordist *task* and the post-Fordist *role* to be the most significant break in the organizational phenomenology of the last decades, which is precisely why they see such urgency in acknowledging the *third, collective-relational dimension*. In truth, however, the difference between Fordism and post-Fordism is one of degree and not of kind, as transpires from the words of Taylor himself, father of Fordism and predeterminist utopian-in-chief. Taylor writes (1903): "*The two qualities that count most for success in this kind of executive work are grit and what may be called 'constructive imagination'—the faculty which enables a man to use the few facts that are stored in his mind in getting around the obstacles that oppose him, and in building up something useful in spite of them. [...].*" In Taylor's perspective, thus, management is all about prompting and obtaining workers' initiative. And similarly, Fayol (1916), in many ways Taylor's European equivalent at the turn of the last century, uses the term "*initiative*" to express the quality that, together with responsibility, a supervisor must do his utmost to "*encourage and develop*" in his subordinates. Not surprisingly, "initiative" is also the term that Mattia Persiani (1966) was to use a few decades later to explain the *duty of loyalty* that, along with subordination to the employer's managerial authority, is the *only* way of ensuring that the employer's interests are satisfied. Thus, the empirical impossibility of resolving a priori all of the interdependencies between jobs by means of a well-thought-out production program peeps out from beneath the veil of the two *ethea*—that of Taylor and Fayol's determinism, and that of Persiani's contractualism.

This impossibility is brought front and center by the second alternative for interpreting organizational phenomenology, which we suggest should be called the *processual regulation* option.

The Nobel laureate Herbert A. Simon (Simon 1947; March and Simon 1958) made a distinction between two modes of coordination: *Prior coordination*, which is planned in advance and precedes execution, and *self-coordination*, or *autonomous* coordination, which is expressed *in the course of action* by the workers and/or work groups. Prior heteronomous coordination and self-coordination at the time of the action, Simon tells us, are both necessary for cooperative effort.

This brings us to another distinction, between working autonomy, or in other words the workers' *organizational autonomy*, as opposed to *discretion*, with which it is invariably confused in the mainstream perspectives (Maggi 2016). "Autonomy" is the ability to produce one's own rules for taking action and making decisions for the self-governance of the processes in which one is involved and is expressed "*both in the choice of appropriate means for pursuing the desired ends, and in changing the goals and sub-goals, i.e., in reframing the problem to reflect the lessons learned with the means chosen earlier*" (Albano et al. 2020, p. 17). "Discretion", by contrast, is a mode of heteronomy, distinct from thorough rules imposed from above, in that it involves the "*scope for action and decision-making envisaged by a heteronomous rule that obliges the subject to choose between multiple alternatives*" (idem, p. 17).

Simon then makes a further point about the two modes of coordination: Prior heteronomous coordination and autonomous coordination in the course of action are not only both necessary for collaborative effort, but they are also always present (March and Simon 1958, p. 69). This means that, outside of the Taylorist utopia, decision and execution can only be distinguished and separated *analytically*, not empirically: Each action is regulated *simultaneously* by prior rules, which can be either autonomous or heteronomous, and by rules that are produced at the same time as the action and are intrinsic to it, and for that reason are necessarily autonomous (Maggi 2016). It is only in this light, writes Albano, that we can address the question of workers' autonomy in the production process "*without preconceptions*" (Albano 2013, p. 53): Coordinating and regulating the *interrelation between jobs* is not the exclusive prerogative of the employer, nor could it be linked to the latter through the employer's imposition of discretion (what is usually, and often improperly, called workers' "empowerment"). In fact, workers yield autonomous regulatory contribution, both as regards the content of the job and how it is coordinated with other jobs, which does not erode the employer's authority but adds to and supplements it. What we have here is "*travail d'organisation*" ("work of organization"), as Terssac calls it (Terssac 2002), carried out by the workers in the interests of the work process and hence in the interests of the employer, supplementing the latter's managerial and organizational authority which, being guided by *bounded* rationality (Simon 1947), cannot predetermine everything.

This essential regulatory contribution takes the shape of an autonomous, non-discretionary collaboration *on the part of* interdependent workers, and *distributed among* interdependent workers in the interest of the work process, because the regulation is "*more precise and more rational as it is participatory*," as Angelo Salento writes in Barbera, Dagnes, Salento, Spina (eds.), 2016. This gives rise to a notion of *worker participation* which is neither granted (from above) nor claimed (from below), but is an *inescapable* ingredient of the regulation of collective action. It is a notion of participation rooted in a view of the organization as a process of actions and decisions, "*which on the one hand is not free from preordination,* [but] *on the other hand can never be thought of as "done and delivered", as an organized setting, as an institution, as dominium*" (Salento and Masino 2013, p. 194). It is thus a notion of participation, and this is crucial as regards the long-standing and still unresolved opposition between contract and organization in labor law doctrine, which does not rely, because it does not need to rely, on a concept of the organization-firm as an *institution*.

Beyond the Fiction

The two options presented here, predetermination and processual regulation, are two alternatives for interpreting coordination that reflect two different ideas of the organization: the mainstream view of the organization as an entity, a socio-technical system, and the other view of organization (itself no less a part of the dictionary definition of organization) as the act of organizing, as a process of actions and decisions.[1] This latter view of the organization as process springs from a third epistemological posture (Weber 1922b; Abbagnano 1959; Maggi 2016; Fabbri 2010; Albano et al. 2020) which stands apart from both the institutionalists' objectivism and the contractualists' subjectivism.

It is only by means of this third, processualist epistemological posture that we can go beyond the opposition between contract and organization, because it is only from this perspective that we can see the analytic, rather than empirical, nature of the distinction. Without this epistemological turn, and without the theory of regulation that stems from it, any attempt to resolve the opposition between contract and organization will in fact end by reasserting it, either by bringing the institutional back into the contractual (as in the case of the proposed *third dimension* mentioned earlier), or, conversely, by seeking the contractual in the institutional (as developments in the sphere of industrial democracy have once again attempted to do[2]).

"*It is nothing but fiction,*" as a prominent jurist wrote nearly thirty years ago, "*to suppose that the individual contract can be considered* per se *capable of guaranteeing truly and precisely how much subordination, and conversely, the content (and limits) of the employer's managerial authority, that will be required in the concrete implementation of the contractual programme*" (Perulli 1992, p. 139). This brief introduction to an alternative, processual perspective on organization, which differs epistemologically and substantively from the socio-technical mainstream that informs the post-Fordist narrative, is thus an invitation to Labor Law to look beyond the fiction.

Notes

1. "*The organization is processual in nature, not only for the trivial reason that the end products are the sum of multiple activities taking place at different times. It is a process because the structuration of activities is itself an action oriented in time, based on trial, error and correction, and can only in part be ordered beforehand* [...]" (Albano, 2013, p. 52).
2. For instance, cf. Pedrazzoli (1985).

References

Abbagnano, Nicola. 1959. *Problemi di sociologia.* Torino: Taylor, excerpt reprinted in P. Rossi, M. Mori, M. Trinchero, 1975, *Il problema della spiegazione sociologica,* Loescher, Torino.

Albano, Roberto. 2013. "Razionalità e regolazione organizzativa." In *Organizzare il servizio sociale,* edited by R. Albano, M. Dellavalle, 19–56. Milano: Franco Angeli.

Albano, Roberto, Ylenia Curzi, and Tommaso Fabbri. 2020. *System, Actor, and Process: Keywords in Organization Studies.* London and New York: Routledge / Turin: Giappichelli.

Barassi, Lodovico. 1901. *Il Contratto di lavoro nel diritto positivo italiano,* Società editrice libraria, Milano.

Barbera, Filippo, Joselle Dagnes, Angelo Salento, and Ferdinando Spina, eds. 2016. *Il capitale quotidiano. Un manifesto per l'economia fondamentale.* Roma: Donzelli editore.

Barnard, Chester I. 1938. *The Functions of the Executive.* Cambridge, MA: Harvard University Press.

Burns, Tom, and G. M. Stalker. 1961. *The Management of Innovation.* London: Tavistock Publication Ltd.

Fabbri, Tommaso. 2010. "L'organizzazione: sistema predeterminato, entità emergente, processo di azioni e decisioni." In *L'organizzazione: concetti e metodi,* edited by T. Fabbri, 15–35. Roma: Carocci.

Fayol, Henri. 1916. *Administration industrielle et générale.* Paris: Dunod (English ed., *General and Industrial Management*, Pitman, London, 1988).

Maggi, Bruno. 2016. *De l'agir organisationnel. Un point de vue sur le travail, le bien-être, l'apprentissage*. Tao Digital Library, Bologna (1st ed. Octarès Editions, Toulouse 2003).
March, James G., and Herbert A. Simon. 1958. *Organizations*. New York: Wiley.
Nogler, Luca. 2014. "Contratto di lavoro e organizzazione al tempo del post-fordismo." *Argomenti di diritto del lavoro* 19 (4/5): 884–902.
Nogler, Luca. 2015. *La subordinazione nel d.lgs. n. 81 del 2015: alla ricerca dell' «autorità del punto di vista giuridico"*, Working Paper Centre for the Study of European Labour Law "Massimo D'Antona", n. 267: 1–31.
Pedrazzoli, Marcello. 1985. *Democrazia industriale e subordinazione. Poteri e fattispecie nel sistema giuridico del lavoro*. Milano: Giuffrè.
Persiani, Mattia. 1966. *Contratto di lavoro e organizzazione*. Roma: CEDAM.
Perulli, Adalberto. 1992. *Il potere direttivo dell'imprenditore*. Milano: Giuffrè.
Riccio, Antonio. 2018. *Il potere di scelta del datore di lavoro. La dimensione collettivo-relazionale del lavoro subordinato*. Roma: Aracne Editrice.
Salento, Angelo, and Giovanni Masino. 2013. *La fabbrica della crisi. Finanziarizzazione delle imprese e declino del lavoro*. Roma: Carocci Editore.
Simon, Herbert A. 1947. *Administrative Behavior*. New York: Free Press.
Taylor, Frederick W. 1903. *Shop Management*. Saratoga: American Society of Mechanical Engineers.
Terssac, Gilbert de. 2002. *Le travail: une aventure collective*. Toulouse: Octarès Editions.
Weber, Max. 1922a. *Wirtschaft und Gesellschaft*. Tübingen: Mohr. English edition: Weber, M. 1978. *Economy and Society: An Outline of Interpretive Sociology*, vol. 1. Edited by G. Roth and C. Wittich. Berkeley, Los Angeles, London: University of California Press.
Weber, Max. 1922b. *Gesammelte Aufsätze zur Wissenschaftslehre*. Tübingen: Mohr. English edition: Weber, M. 1949. *On the Methodology of Social Sciences* (Translated by: E. A. Shils and H. A. Finch). Glencoe, IL: Free Press (2nd ed. 2011 with a new introduction by R. J. Antonio and A. Sica).

5

The Collective Dimensions of the Employment Relationship: Ways Beyond Traditional Views

Edoardo Ales

Dimensions Is Not a Typo

Labour Lawyers usually understand the work relationship as structured into two dimensions—the individual and the collective. The individual is the cornerstone of juridical relationship of any kind, in the sense that therein the parties express their willingness of establishing reciprocal rights and duties. The individual dimension may be also relevant when it comes to the regulation of the working conditions in case an

E. Ales (✉)
Department of Law, Labour Law and Industrial Relations, University of Naples "Parthenope", Naples, Italy
e-mail: edoardo.ales@uniparthenope.it; eales@luiss.it; ales@pul.it

Department of Political Sciences, Social and Labour Market Regulation, LUISS University Rome, Rome, Italy

Comparative and International Labour Law, Pontificial Lateran University, Rome, Italy

T. Addabbo et al. (eds.), *The Collective Dimensions of Employment Relations*,
https://doi.org/10.1007/978-3-030-75532-4_5

employee possesses individual capacities that enable him or her to negotiate arrangements different from the standard ones as regulated in the collective dimension. Despite its repeatedly forecasted end, the latter is still, by far, the most common and effective 'place' of working conditions regulation, at least in continental Europe (Ales 2020a).

However, in some legal orders, the collective dimension is not unitary. As highlighted by Dorssemont (in this book), the same ILO *Workers' Representatives Convention* 1971 (n. 135) revels that there are at least two actors who operate in the collective realm of the employment relationship, i.e., "(a) trade union representatives, namely, representatives designated or elected by trade unions or by members of such unions; or (b) elected representatives, namely, representatives who are freely elected by the workers of the undertaking in accordance with provisions of national laws or regulations or of collective agreements and whose functions do not include activities which are recognised as the exclusive prerogative of trade unions in the country concerned" (Article 3).

This not a merely theoretical distinction: It entails some relevant practical consequences. As a matter of fact, according to the ILO *Collective Bargaining Convention*, 1981 (n. 154), "where national law or practice recognises the existence of workers' representatives as defined in Article 3, subparagraph (b), of the Workers' Representatives Convention, 1971, national law or practice may determine the extent to which the term ***collective bargaining*** shall also extend, for the purpose of this Convention, to negotiations with these representatives." Furthermore, "where, in pursuance of paragraph 1 of this Article, the term ***collective bargaining*** also includes negotiations with the workers' representatives referred to in that paragraph, appropriate measures shall be taken, wherever necessary, to ensure that the existence of these representatives is not used to undermine the position of the workers' organisations concerned" (Article 3).

A very sensitive issue, since, again according to the *Collective Bargaining Convention*, "the term ***collective bargaining*** extends to all negotiations which take place between an employer, a group of employers or one or more employers' organisations, on the one hand, and one or more workers' organisations, on the other, for– (a) determining working conditions and terms of employment; and/or (b) regulating relations between employers and workers; and/or (c) regulating relations between employers or their organisations and a workers' organisation or workers' organisations" (Article 2).

The point is that, under the *Collective Bargaining Convention*, negotiations with the workers' representatives referred to in Article 3, subparagraph (b), of the Workers' Representatives Convention not necessarily falls with the very notion of collective bargaining, thus lacking the status granted by Convention n. 154. On the consequences of such exclusion, we will come back later. Nevertheless, right now, it is worth mentioning that the Court of Justice of the EU has adopted a radically different position affirming that "the works council's right of co-decision (...) and the right of opposition (...) constitute two expressions of the fundamental right of collective bargaining."[1]

However, at least according to the just mentioned ILO conventions and to some national legislations, one could argue that the collective dimension is split into two areas as far as workers' representation is concerned. The first area is based on freedom of association, as recognized, among the others, by the ILO *Freedom of Association and Protection of the Right to Organise Convention*, 1948 (No. 87), according to which "workers and employers, without distinction whatsoever, shall have the right to establish and, subject only to the rules of the organisation concerned, to join organisations of their own choosing without previous authorisation" (Article 2). The second, in which "representatives who are freely elected by the workers of the undertaking," in most of the cases works councils, are active, is based on a decision of the national legislator, specifically addressed to establish a representation system within the undertaking, supported and framed by the law, according to a 'recognition of rights approach.' As a matter of fact, it is usually up to the workers to decide whether such a representation will exist in practice.

If the national legislator decides that the term collective bargaining does not include negotiations with the works councils, therefore excluding agreements signed between the latter and the relevant employer from determining "working conditions and terms of employment" and/or regulate "relations between employers and workers" (argument *ex* Article 2 Convention n. 154), one has to reflect on what remains to be negotiated and agreed upon. I will come back on this topic in the following (par. 2), together with some remarks on the denial of the right to collective action, typical of legislations introducing the works councils' model.

Nevertheless, such a reflection stimulates further considerations on certain aspects of the collective dimension that shall not necessarily be connected to the regulation of working conditions. They belong rather to the working modalities in the employment relationship, which consists of the subordination of the employee to the employer. As highlighted by Fabbri and Curzi (in this Book), quite recently some scholars have declared themselves unsatisfied with the dichotomic alternative individual (contractual)—collective (trade union) in Labour Law, thus developing the idea of a further relational collective dimension, immanent in the interaction between the employer and the employees as well as among employees within the organization, understood as work community. Those scholars criticize the individualistic/monadic approach that characterizes the traditional view of the employment relationship, at turn based on the assumption that the organization—seen as a precondition of the modalities in which employees perform their tasks, can be and actually is predetermined by the employer. Fabbri & Curzi respond that organizational theory has moved forward from the old deterministic paradigm—based on predetermination in its two variants of imposition and discretion, to a newly conceived 'processual regulation' option that entails an "inescapable workers' participation." Such a (inter)relational collective dimension has nothing to do either with the trade union or (perhaps) with the works councils' one.

In the paragraphs that follow, I will discuss (a) the relationship between the trade union (freedom-of-association-based) and the works councils (legislatively-supported) collective dimensions (par. 2) as well as (b) the interrelational collective dimension linked to the modalities in which the tasks are performed within an employment relationship (par. 3), wondering how from the juridical point of view the individualistic/contractualistic/predeterministic approach can be substituted by the processual regulation approach (par. 4).

2. Beyond Freedom of Association: The Legislatively-Supported Collective Dimension in the Regulatory Perspective

As pointed out above, freedom of association plays a crucial role in the regulation of working conditions. In many Industrial Relations Systems, it even overlaps with the collective dimension, which is dominated by trade unions and employers' organizations. In some legal orders, only trade unions are entitled to the right to collective bargaining, i.e., the main regulatory working conditions regulatory instrument. To the exclusive entitlement to collective bargaining corresponds an equally exclusive entitlement to collective action, which can be lawfully exercised by employees only if called by a trade union (so defined by case law). Such a rigid scheme—materialized in a few legal orders (the German and the Austrian, for example)—is likely to attach to the collective (trade union) dimension a (negative) conflictual character, with the consequence that freedom of association tends to be kept away from the workplace and to be confined to the branch/sectoral level where employers may be supported by their organizations. In these cases, the collective (trade union) dimension would remain outside the undertaking, at least as far as the regulation of working conditions is concerned.

However, one shall note that legislators try to strike a balance between employees' and employers' conflicting interests to have or not voice mechanisms within the undertaking. Solutions range from the provision of a right to establish workers' representation bodies at plant level within the framework of most representative trade union for the mere purposes of unionization and employees' rights enforcement (Italy), to the introduction of a works councils' system, by definition deprived of collective bargaining and collective action rights, as exclusive employees' agent at plant level (Germany). In the middle, one finds a variety of recognition procedures, based either on employees' balloting in order to appoint an exclusive representative (USA) or on an employees' request voluntarily accepted by the employer or imposed by an independent committee (the CAC in the UK). In both cases, the aim is to be entitled to conduct collective bargaining on behalf of a group or groups of workers.

One may wonder whether these are all 'filter mechanisms' aiming at avoiding that "The denial by some employers of the right of employees to organize and the refusal by some employers to accept the procedure of collective bargaining lead to strikes and other forms of industrial strife or unrest, which have the intent or the necessary effect of burdening or obstructing commerce (…)" (US National Labor Relations Act—NLRA 1935, Section 1).

Even in the Italian case, the entitlement to collective bargaining and action rights, as recognized to trade union representations at plant level (*Rappresentanze Sindacali Unitarie*—RSU) in the early Nineties, has been made conditional, by the same Social Partners, upon the introduction of a double-level collective bargaining system in which the branch collective agreement determines the room for maneuver of negotiation within the undertaking, thus restraining and embedding the exercise of those rights. *Mutatis mutandis*, a similar approach has been adopted by the German legislator in the *Betriebsverfassungsgesetz* (BetrVG), when it provides that the right to codetermination of the works councils can be exercised only if matters that fall within their scope of action have not been already regulated by the legislator or by collective agreements (BetrVG § 87, 1). In case of disagreement between the employer and the works council, a plant-level arbitration committee (*Einigungsstelle*) will decide, without collective action coming into question.

The Italian situation is rather different, since RSU are entitled to the right to call a strike. However, if they do it for contractual purposes, its scope will be limited to the already bargained matters and to their implementation conditions as decided at the branch level.

If the German and Italian approach is based on a (more or less strong) limitation of trade union/works councils' objective scope of action at the undertaking level, the Anglo-American solution is grounded on a selection of the bargaining agent according to the 'single representation principle,' which is aimed at establishing a privileged relationship between the person or the organization representing the employees and the employer.

In the NLRA (Section 7), the 'single representation principle' is extremized into a 'union shop mechanism' that can derogate to the negative freedom of association principle to the extent that the latter "may be affected by an agreement requiring membership in a labor organization as a condition of employment (…) if such labor organization is the representative of the employees as provided in section 9(a), in the appropriate collective-bargaining unit covered by such agreement when made." However, "no employer shall justify any discrimination against an employee for non-membership in a labor organization (A) if he has reasonable grounds for believing that such membership was not available to the employee on the same terms and conditions generally applicable to other members, or (B) if he has reasonable grounds for believing that membership was denied or terminated for reasons other than the failure of the employee to tender the periodic dues and the initiation fees uniformly required as a condition of acquiring or retaining membership."

From these brief reflections one can derive that, in a regulatory perspective, the collective dimension of the employment relationship cannot be seen as one. To the already mentioned distinction between freedom-of-association-based and legislatively-supported representation, a further and consequent one has to be added between the branch/sectoral and the company level. The access to the latter, in fact, is 'filtered' most of the times by legislators in order to avoid that the undertaking becomes a battlefield where "all's fair." Controlled decentralization of collective bargaining, regulated competition among organizations, recognized agents, arbitration procedures: Although to different extends, depending on the approach adopted by each legal order, everything seems to strive for a peaceful and orderly working conditions setting, at least at company level.

This is particularly true when it comes to legislatively supported representation embodied by works councils, based on the principle of cooperation (*Zusammenarbeit*) with the employer and the exclusion of conflict. If legislator and collective bargaining leave enough room for works councils' agreements (*Betriebsvereinbarungen*), they may represent an alternative or complementary way forward for a collective dimension that entails codetermination rights to be exercised on organizational and managerial issues otherwise unilaterally decided by the entrepreneur. This could be seen as a 'protected collective dimension of dialogue' between the employer and the employees, in which the interest of the business (*Betrieb*), as something beneficial to both sides, is at stake.

Despite their differences, one common feature of the trade unions' and the works councils' collective dimensions has to be found in the 'agentification' of the relationship between the employer(s) and the employee(s). By 'agentification' I mean that employers (at least at branch level) and employees (both at branch and at company level) interact via agents who synthetize and represent a collective interest that, by definition, standardizes the individual ones. Consequently, in the regulatory perspective, employees are seen as a collective entity, in which individual behaviors and attitudes toward the performance matter, mainly if not exclusively, in the view of the pathology of the employment relationship. This is the case of collective agreements regulating the exercise of the disciplinary power in case of misconducts.

Trade unions' diffidence to get involved into the qualitative appraisal of the contribution each employee may bring to the outcome of the business—that they often prefer to be ascertained in mere quantitative terms (e.g., the respect of working time)—is revealing of their difficulty to grasp the interrelational element inherent to the very notion of 'collective' they should embody. One could even argue that the same qualification as collective of the trade unions' dimension, at least internally, might be questioned to the extent that they neglect such an interrelational element. This can be seen as a paradox of 'agentification' in relation to which the individual dimension is not only 'cleansed' of its egoistic component but also deprived of its interrelational one.

On the other hand, the same works councils' codetermination rights, despite their explicit reference to the organization of the business (*Ordnung des Betriebs*) and to the behavior of the employee (*Verhalten des Arbeitsnehmer*) (§87 par. 1 n. 1 *BetrVG*), do not apply to the way in which work duties are discharged. However, in the realm of wage setting, in case the undertaking has adopted achievement-related pay-systems, works councils are entitled to codetermination rights as far as their fair application is concerned (§87 par. 1 n. 11 *BetrVG*). This is an important role works councils may play in the view of enhancing the interrelational element of their collective dimension, since, according to case law,[2] the very functioning of such systems shall be based on the previous setting of a reference performance (*Bezugsleistung*) and the amount of the wage shall be assessed according to the relationship between the output of the employee with that reference.

A further important role works councils may play in the view of enhancing the interrelational element of their collective dimension refers to the exercise of codetermination rights in relation to the implementation of group work (*Gruppenarbeit*). This is defined by §87 par. 1

n. 13 *BetrVG* as the case in which a group of employees performs an overall task (*Gesamtarbeit*) assigned by the employer essentially under its own responsibility. As far as the interrelational element of the collective dimension is concerned, codetermination rights can be exercised by the works council—but also by the group itself in case they have been transferred, on the cooperation among employees in the group or with other groups as well as in order to cope with internal conflicts. A works council agreement has to be sign for this purpose. In case of disagreement, the arbitration committee (*Einigungsstelle*) will decide.

In light of this, one may argue that within the works councils' collective dimension the interrelational element is taken into greater consideration than in the trade unions' one, mainly because of the existence of codetermination rights recognized by the law. Something that is difficult to achieve though freedom of association and its conflictual method.

Beyond the "Fiction": The 'Inescapable Workers' Participation' in the Relational Perspective

'Agentification' as a common feature of the collective dimensions of the employment relationship shows all its weakness when it comes to the enhancement of the interrelational element as the one allowing the functioning of the undertaking understood as work community. This is quite apparent for the trade unions/freedom-of-association-based dimension, which looks at employees as a group rather than as individuals reciprocally interacting with their own different behaviors and attitudes toward the way in which tasks are performed. Uniformity of treatment with the professional group is, in most of the cases, the main precept of collective bargaining. Diversification is not at the top of trade unions' concerns and skills. On the other hand, one cannot take for granted that the employer would like trade unions to be involved into Performance Appraisal Systems (PAS: see Curzi et al. 2020) that seem to fall, mainly if not exclusively, within the managerial prerogatives, from which trade unions are quite systematically excluded.

Accepting diversities connected to individual attitudes and capabilities is the first step toward acknowledging the interrelational element that characterizes the collective dimension. Its denial in the view of guaranteeing uniform working conditions is likely to produce dysfunctional consequences on the appraisal of the individual performance (that may become indistinguishable) as well as on the organization of working modalities. The latter, more than working conditions, seem to be at the center stage of the interrelational element and therefore of any genuine collective dimension. One could argue that predetermined *basic* working conditions frame working modalities that, on the other hand, are associated with the idea of organization as a coordinated process (Fabbri and Curzi in this Book).

Coordination of individual performances seems to be the binding force of the interrelational element that makes the collective dimension operational. Such an approach does not necessarily question the employment relationship as based on individual subordination to the extent that it relies on the organizational power of the employer, which can be exercised heteronomously in the form of coordination of subordinated performances. From such a perspective, one could even accept the individual performance to be regulated by the employment contract, if one recognizes that *interrelational* managerial prerogatives necessarily place themselves outside it, based as they are on the freedom to conduct a business. The latter, at turn, is limited by legislation and collective or individual bargaining to the extent that legislators and the parties so decide.

In this case, the 'agentification' may be neither needed nor requested, since it refers to working modalities that are (individually) subordinated to and (collectively) coordinated by the employer. Unless, as already mentioned, it takes the form of codetermination, in the sense that the legislator imposes a duty of cooperation between the employer and the works council in the view of a negotiated exercise of managerial prerogatives, coordination included, as happens in the German system with group work.

In my view, the real issue the 'processual regulation' option encounters with the traditional vision of the employment relationship is that of "*self-* or *autonomous* coordination, which is expressed *in the course of action* by the workers and/or work groups" (Fabbri and Curzi, in this Book). Under traditional vision I understand the idea that the contractual qualification of the relationship as subordinated does automatically excludes any degree of autonomy of the employees. Such an exclusion is not necessarily linked to the duties deriving for the employee from the employment contract. In fact, if employers so decides, they can exercise their managerial prerogatives in the strictest and most pedant way. The point is whether one admits that the employer may also leave employees free to coordinate their performances without producing an unsustainable legal uncertainty in relation to the applicable legislation.

The application to hetero-organized collaborations, i.e., collaborations organized by the employer, of the 'subordinate protection package' is the solution adopted by the Italian legislator to tackle such a risk (art. 2 Legislative Decree n. 81 of 2015). On the other hand, the same Italian legislator has admitted and regulated the existence of negotiated coordination between a contractor and a self-employed service provider (coordinated continuous collaborations *ex* art. 409 civil procedure code). Last but not least, once again the Italian legislator has provided some employee-like protection to autonomous riders, operating also through digital platforms (art. 47-*bis* ff. Legislative Decree n. 81 of 2015). A highly complicated situation, which cannot be investigated here.

Nevertheless, also from a juridical perspective, one could assume the viability of an individual 'autonomized subordination' within the employment relationship, above all in undertakings in which PAS are in place (Ales 2019, 2020b). On the contrary, more difficult to conceive is the existence of an 'autonomized coordination,' since (self)coordination, by conforming individual performances, is able and likely to create collective subdimensions within the undertaking that are neither organized nor governed by the employer. Not by chance, codetermination rights are limited to the implementation of group work, falling its establishment or withdrawal within the managerial prerogatives to be unilaterally exercised by the employer.

Concluding on this point, one can argue that if one remains within the legal framework of the employment relationship, it will be up to the employer to decide whether and to which extent autonomy will be allowed as for individual subordination as well as collective coordination. However, in relation to the latter, one may wonder whether the collective dimension typical of the subgroup will be compatible with that legal framework without overflowing into a subcontracted provision of services.

Therefore, the question could be who (but the employer) and in which quality coordinates the self-coordination among the employees or within the group, exercising organizational prerogatives that, in light of the 'processual regulation' option cannot be entirely predetermined, not only through the individual employment contract but also according to the freedom to conduct a business, which should be referred to the employer. From a juridical perspective, the same 'inescapable workers' participation' (so Fabbri & Curzi in this Book) that characterizes the 'processual regulation' option is confronted with the issue of managerial prerogatives either in the sense of investigating to which extent and how employees are involved in hetero-organization or in order to understand what exactly self-coordination means in terms of responsibilities, above all as far as individual outcomes are concerned. One may wonder whether, at least from a juridical point of view, the 'inescapable workers' participation,' inherent to self-coordination, does need a kind of 'agentification,' which allows to lead it back to the equally inescapable individual nature of any obligation, toward both the employer and the group-leader.

The Prescriptive Perspective, Its Demands, and Some Solutions

The inescapable individual nature of any obligation is at the very basis of the idea of retributive and remunerative justice, at turn strictly linked to the punishment/reward approach, in which any negative and positive contributions to the common endeavor of the parties shall matter. Even if, as suggested (Ales 2019), subordination does not necessarily rely on a strict command-and-control mechanism, thus allowing to look at the performance as a flow of hetero- and self-decision, the deep sense of the individual effort, albeit understood in its relational collective dimension, cannot be forgotten or neglected. At the end of the day, the boundaries of the individual obligation have to be clearly drawn in the interest of both parties, although most notably in that of the weaker one.

The prescriptive perspective, which activates whenever mismatches arise regarding stances and conducts seen as dysfunctional by one of the parties, does require effective accountability/liability mechanisms to be available in the view of guaranteeing the restoration of a positive relational climate within both the individual and the collective dimension(s). One may wonder whether the latter may help in such a restoration and, even more, in the anticipation or prevention of dysfunctionalities. This largely depends upon the nature of the dysfunctionality.

Mismatches or different expectations and claims on working conditions can be easily traced back to the disputes on interest that, also according to art. 28 CFREU, do belong to the realm of collective bargaining, now including also works councils' agreements, and collective action, on the contrary exclusive feature of the freedom-of-association-based collective dimension. Negotiation, conflict, and arbitration (in case of works councils) are collective tools which are likely to produce a satisfactory settlement of individual expectations, avoiding, though, the individualization of the claim. Due to their inherent transactional nature, the trade unions' and works councils' collective dimensions are the most effective environment in which the prescriptive perspective may operate on working conditions without paying any duties to the individual dimension. Furthermore, one has to highlight the monitoring function trade unions and works councils may exercise on the agreements they have signed and on their proper application to individuals, which is typical of the rights and duties provided by those agreements in relation to working conditions.

One may wonder whether the language of rights and duties fits to the discourse on work modalities, which are the core of the interrelational collective dimension, above all within the 'processual regulation' option perspective. This does not seem to be the case. The same presence of the interrelational element brings us back to the fluid and uncertain interests' realm, the ordering factor of which is the continuing negotiation of participative and/or egoistic demands among the parties involved. One might argue that negotiation will end up into agreements providing rights and duties. However, the same ongoing nature of negotiation is likely to determine a structural dynamism typical of the processual approach, which does not tune with the rights and duties discourse, at least in its traditional, static posture. In such a context, the same manager has to be reconsidered as a facilitator instead of a leading person, as it was and still is within the command-and-control approach.

In the self-coordination perspective, one may advocate that each of the parties involved within the organization has to play the facilitator in order to avoid the process to stop and the flow to clot. In fact, any clots easily correspond to an individual issue that brings the right and duties dimension back in the game. Participative regulation seems to be the most viable solution even if activated outside any 'agentification' perspectives, as substituted by a personal and direct involvement in which the employer and the employees are placed at the same level. This falls, evidently, outside the traditional notion of subordination and necessitates the process to progress smoothly, without any needs of exercising managerial prerogative in a constricting way.

The idea of 'flat hierarchy' seems to be the most suitable in displaying the full potential of the interrelational collective dimension. At turn, 'autonomized subordination' may be looked at as an adequate juridical shell in which the interrelational collective dimension may work swiftly, without loosing the full integration within a work community essential for its very existence.

Notes

1. CJEU, 4 April 2019, C-699/17, *Allianz Vorsorgekasse*, par. 55.
2. BAG, 25.05.1982, 1 ABR 19/80; BAG, 13.09.1983, 1 ABR 32/81.

References

Ales, Edoardo. 2019. "Subordination at Risk (of "Autonomisation"): Evidences and Solutions from Three European Countries". *Italian Labour Law e-Journal* 1: 1.

Ales, Edoardo. 2020a. "The Regulatory Function of Collective Agreements in the Light of Its Relationship with Statutory Instruments and Individual Rights: A Multilevel Approach." In *The Sources of Labour Law*, edited by T. Gyulavári, M. Menegatti, 37. Alphen aan den Rijn: Kluwer Law International B.V.

Ales, Edoardo. 2020b. "Is Performance Appraisal Compatible with the Employment Relationship? A Conclusive Plea in Favour of an Achievement-Oriented Approach to Work Organisation." In *Performance Appraisal in Modern Employment Relations: An Interdisciplinary Approach*, edited by T. Addabbo, E. Ales, Y. Curzi, T. Fabbri, O. Rymkevich, and I. Senatori, 255. London, New York, and Shanghai: Palgrave Macmillan.

Curzi, Ylenia, Fabbri Tommaso, and Barbara Pistoresi. 2020. "Performance Appraisal Criteria and Innovative Work Behaviour: The Mediating Role of Employees' Appraisal Satisfaction." In *Performance Appraisal in Modern Employment Relations: An Interdisciplinary Approach*, edited by T. Addabbo, E. Ales, Y. Curzi, T. Fabbri, O. Rymkevich, and I. Senatori, 11. London, New York, and Shanghai: Palgrave Macmillan.

Dorssemont, Filip. *Trade Unions, Employers' Associations and the Law*, in this Book.

Fabbri, Tommaso, and Ylenia Curzi. *Organization as Collective Rule-Making*, in this Book.

Part II

The Collective Dimensions and Workplace Organisation

6

Does Control Change Nature in Industrial Digital Work? A Secondary Analysis of the 1991–2015 European Working Conditions Surveys

Roberto Albano, Ylenia Curzi, and Tania Parisi

The present chapter is the result of the joint work of the authors. However, sections were authored as follows: "Introduction" and "Discussion and Conclusions" by Roberto Albano; "Theoretical Framework" and related sub-sections ("Control Based on Actual Direct Surveillance", "Control Based on the Possibility of Direct Surveillance", and "Controlled Autonomy (and Internalized Control)") by Ylenia Curzi; "Research Methodology" and related sub-sections ("Data Sources", "Cases and Variables Selection", and "Data Analysis") by Tania Parisi.

R. Albano
Department of Cultures, Politics and Society, University of Turin, Turin, Italy
e-mail: roberto.albano@unito.it

Y. Curzi (✉)
Marco Biagi Department of Economics and Marco Biagi Foundation, University of Modena and Reggio Emilia, Modena, Italy
e-mail: ylenia.curzi@unimore.it

T. Parisi
Department of Philosophy and Education Sciences, University of Turin, Turin, Italy
e-mail: tania.parisi@unito.it

T. Addabbo et al. (eds.), *The Collective Dimensions of Employment Relations*,
https://doi.org/10.1007/978-3-030-75532-4_6

Introduction

The nature of work practices has already been heavily transformed by new digital technology, and this trend is likely to continue to grow in the future. The intensive use of last-generation *Information and Communication Technologies* (hereinafter, ICTs) is associated with the emergence of new work practices in different kinds of organizations. Work activities are increasingly being performed within workflows hosted in organizations' digital platforms; the growing use of digital instruments, among which are mobile devices, allows workers to access and process flows of digital information and communication—in real-time or later—and to connect to the organization's databases and data analysis software from anywhere (Fabbri 2018).

The digital transformation of organized work alters the modes of producing the information and communication used to perform work, which increasingly become formalized, codified, and explicit. Consequently, digitalization opens up the opportunity to make work more and more standardized. In addition, new digital technologies have an unprecedented capacity to gather, store, record, analyze, and assess data, thereby offering new opportunities to expand the scope and reach of workers' surveillance. Namely, they open up new opportunities for management to classify, evaluate, and compare organizational members' behaviors, and to compare actual workers' behaviors with abstract models, with the purpose of rationalizing and imposing order to increase efficiency. Consistently, some research studies indicate the emergence of a renewed, even more radical taylorism in new digital organizations (Cattero and D'Onofrio 2018; Rosenblat and Stark 2016; Staab and Nachtwey 2016; Schörpf et al. 2017). Other scholars underline the primacy of forms of control that emulate and increase the pervasiveness of the Panopticon (Fernie and Metcalf 1998; Fuchs 2011, 2015; Menzies 1996; Sia and Neo 2008; Rosanvallon 2011; Sewell and Wilkinson 1992).

Although these interpretations seem to be reaching increasing consensus among scholars, they are contrasted by other studies focusing on the opposite trend. More specifically, the latter emphasize the emergence, in highly digitalized workplaces, of forms of work organization that have clear similarities with post-fordist organizational solutions such as *Business Process Reengineering*, *Total Quality Management*, *Lean Production*, and *Socio Technical System* approach to work organization (Hirsch-Kreinsen 2016; Johansson et al. 2017; Kagermann et al. 2013; Wilson 1999). These forms of work organization rely on a different and more complex way of controlling work.

In light of these heterogeneous interpretations, it is still unclear what forms of control and work organization are indeed emerging in digitally transformed organizations and what consequences they have on workers' behaviors and sense making. This is especially true in industry. Here, the application of new digital technologies is in the early stage, and there have been only a few attempts to examine the phenomenon empirically (Johansson et al. 2017; Pfeiffer 2017; Pfeiffer and Suphan 2015; Salento 2016, 2017). Existing studies mainly tend to formulate scenarios of the likely future implications of the digitalization of work for industrial employees, which, however, lack strong empirical foundations.

Moreover, the digital transformation of work practices has further stimulated the taylorism/fordism vs. post-fordism debate, originally developed in the 1980s and 1990s. A central issue of this debate was and continues to be whether one should consider so-called post-fordist organizational solutions as radical alternatives to those based on the *Scientific Management* principles, which can overcome the limits of the latter, or contrarily whether they stand in strict continuity with tayloristic solutions.

Since its initial development in industry, the tayloristic/fordist organizational system has been widely criticized by different scientific communities. Bio-medical disciplines have highlighted the inconsistencies between the "organizational" machine and the "human" one. The psychology of work has pointed out the harmful effects of monotonous work. Sociologists and anthropologists have denounced the social isolation of workers in time and space within tayloristic production systems and the denial of the autonomy that human beings need and aspire to exercise, at least to some extent, in the transformative action of their surrounding environment. Taken together, these features shape a totalitarian and alienating system, especially if one claims to consider it as the basis for the organization of society as a whole, as Taylor himself and his followers wished for (on the modernity of Taylor's dystopia, see Solé and Maggi 2007).

In the late 1970s, so-called "new" post-fordist organizational forms (i.e., the previously cited ones) became established in industry. The prefix *post-* suggests that they break with fordism. However, an extensive body of critical literature, most of which is known as *Critical Management Studies*, has shown that behind formal changes there is continuity between the underlying principles of fordist solutions (which are not as homogeneous as they are often depicted today) and those of so-called post-fordist ones.

Giovanni Masino has proposed a careful historical analysis of fordism, a systematic review of *Critical Management Studies*, and a theoretically informed interpretation of the substantial continuity between fordist and post-fordist organizational solutions, which goes beyond the mainstream managerial rhetoric (Masino 2005). According to his interpretation,[1] post-fordist organizational solutions do not differ from the tayloristic/fordist ones because managerial control diminishes. Quite the opposite, they differ because managerial control changes form so as to expand its scope and reach complex activities where it is impossible to apply the tayloristic principle of clear-cut separation between decision and execution, and thus, it is necessary to maintain a much stricter control over the worker's value-laden, cognitive, and decision premises.

In this chapter, we seek to contribute to this stream of research that aims at unveiling the main "illusions of postfordism" (Masino 2005). Namely, the illusion that workers have greater opportunities to participate in setting the decision premises that shape organizational processes. The illusion that the introduction of new technologies automatically results in workers' upskilling. The illusion that a highly centralized administration of organizations can be replaced by a democratic and polycentric governance of intra- and inter-organizational relationships that would bring about more consensus and simultaneously greater quality and efficiency of organizational processes.

In particular, we will deal with the aspects of control and surveillance in new work practices, with a particular focus on highly digitalized ones.

Our general research question is: What are the prevalent trends characterizing the formal organization and control of work in the current transformation phase? In particular, we are concerned with the following more specific research questions: Is there a growing trend toward forms of external control among industrial organizations in the current phase of work transformation? Or, in contrast, can we observe a stronger tendency toward internalized control?

To address these issues, we have identified three different modes for management to intensify control over workers (and work practices), drawing on theoretical literature and qualitative research. They are three ideal-types in the Weberian sense (Weber 1904, Eng. transl. 1949/2011).[2] The key features of each ideal-type may occur simultaneously—in different degree, and in an articulated and fuzzy way—in any real organization.

The first ideal-type of control is based on visible, actually exercised direct surveillance. The second one consists of less visible, potential direct surveillance. Both the abovementioned ideal-types assume that workers will behave opportunistically if they do not perceive that they are subject to external control. On the contrary, the third ideal-type is based on tight workers' self-control, which is demanded by a communitarian view of the organization that requires workers' loyalty and monitors only performance outcomes.

We begin by illustrating in greater depth the main features of the three ideal-types.

These abstract conceptualizations of management control are then used as a basis for exploring the major trends characterizing work organization in industry from 1990 to present. We especially focus on industrial work carried out within the employment relationship. Moreover, we analyze a considerable number of variables drawn from the 1991–2015 *European Working Conditions Surveys* (European Foundation for the Improvement of Living and Working Conditions 2017), using the three ideal-types as a theoretical foundation for organizing our data analysis as well as for interpreting and understanding the findings.

In the last section, we set out the prevalent trends characterizing the forms of control and surveillance of work performed within the employment relationship in industry, particularly focusing on the main differences between employees who intensively use new digital technologies (i.e., highly digitalized workers, here referred to as "digital" workers) and those who do not (i.e., low digitalized workers also referred to as "traditional" workers).

Theoretical Framework

For the purpose of the present study, we choose a very broad and general definition of organizational control in terms of the capacity to influence individuals and groups, managers and employees so that they take actions and make decisions which are consistent with organizational goals (Flamholtz et al. 1985). Moreover, we distinguish organizational control from surveillance, the latter indicating any process of gathering, recording, storing, processing, sorting, assessing, and using data and information useful for exercising control on individuals and groups (Ball 2010; Fuchs 2011, 2013; Lyon 2001; Walker 2017). In addition to surveillance, control may be based on other mechanisms, such as socialization and indoctrination (Ouchi 1979, 1980; Simon 1947/1976). The greater the effectiveness of socialization and indoctrination, the lesser the need for surveillance.

In order to understand how control operates in new digitalized work practices, we distinguish three ideal-types of control. They are based on the theoretical literature on organizational control and surveillance, especially in post-fordist work practices (Ball 2010; Callaghan and Thompson 2001; Carugati et al. 2018; Child 1972, 1973; Edwards 1979; Masino 2005; Ouchi 1977, 1979, 1980; Ouchi and Maguire 1975; Orlikowski 1991; Perrow 1972; Sewell 2012; Wilson 1995, 1999). The three ideal-types of management control are respectively: (1) control based on visible, actually exercised constant surveillance of organizational members' behavior; (2) control based on less visible, potential constant direct surveillance; (3) self-control of workers derived from the internalization of values and norms which are part of the organizational culture, and strengthened by horizontal control exercised by peers. The first two types strongly rely on the use of surveillance. Instead, the last ideal-type assumes that surveillance plays a secondary and exceptional role in workers' control. In the following, we deeply describe the three types of control and we briefly present the results from some qualitative empirical studies on the forms of control emerging in new digital work settings, which in many respects seem to approach the ideal-types under analysis.

Control Based on Actual Direct Surveillance

The first ideal-type, i.e., New Tayloristic Control, is primarily based on top-down and visible surveillance. Organizational members are subject to continuous and pervasive surveillance exercised by a hierarchical superior who checks whether they conform to pre-set rules and standard operating procedures while they are performing their jobs. Direct control is either exercised through face-to-face hierarchical supervision or mediated by technical artifacts (Cavazotte et al. 2014; Halford 2005; Sewell and Taskin 2015).

In its current materialization, surveillance through technology consists in the use of intelligent algorithms and/or wearable devices, which automatically guide workers step by step through their working activities or the stages of decision-making processes, and automatically identify any deviations in execution from the prescribed procedures (Gorecky et al. 2014). This type of control is one of the essential features of the organizations based on the *Scientific Management* principles (Taylor 1911).

It goes along with the stable assignment of completely predetermined tasks to the worker. Task rotation is not admitted, nor do workers have the opportunity to interact with one another while they are performing their tasks. They are also given complete instructions describing their methods, means, exact time, and place of work in detail. Coordination of individuals takes place through standardization. The assigned tasks, in turn, are part of a process of transforming inputs into outputs whose whole structure is completely and rigidly predetermined by industrial engineers in the planning department (nowadays, ICTs specialists). Since there is no room for workers to deviate from the prescribed procedures, they have no opportunity to learn new things while they are performing their jobs. Employees are required to develop a totally other-directed organization personality. In this regard, a key role is played by the scientific selection and training of workers in the exact methods that must be used to perform the job in the *best way*. Training is mostly done on the job by a functional supervisor, once and for all until the procedures change. To induce workers to accept formal authority and discipline, management offers economic and material inducements, whose entities must be correlated with productivity.

A number of qualitative empirical studies, conducted in different work settings and times, document the use of new digital technologies as a means to intensify actual direct surveillance. For example, Halford's (2005) study of the multiply located ICT-supported work practices introduced in a large UK-based financial service company and Cavazotte et al.'s (2014) study on the use of smartphones by professionals in a Brazilian law firm. The latter shows that superiors have intensified their communication and exercised closer monitoring of their subordinates' day-to-day work activities after the introduction of the new digital work practices. Sewell and Taskin (2015), in their study of teleworking in a Belgian biopharmaceutical company, also observe higher predetermination and closer control of teleworkers' tasks, of the time allowed for tasks completion, as well as of working time arrangements. Similarly, Davenport (2013) suggests that the use of decision support systems based on big data and data visualization technologies at Procter & Gamble has led to the tighter predetermination of the key steps of managers' decision-making processes.

Probably, the most striking examples of digital new taylorism are provided by the empirical studies on the digitalization of Amazon's 'fulfilment centres' (Cattero and D'Onofrio 2018; Staab and Nachtwey 2016) and on the use of digital platforms by global enterprises (e.g., Amazon and Uber) to mediate the provision of both physical and digital services and tasks (Bergvall-Kåreborn and Howcroft 2014; Rosenblat and Stark 2016). Schörpf et al. (2017) observe that also platforms designed for creative work tend to establish a tayloristic logic of work organization. This finds expression in the allocation of standardized and fragmented work tasks to isolated workers; experience and skill requirements largely predetermined by the platform providers through pre-set rules inscribed in the design of the platform; clear tasks specifications; request that workers provide high output within small time frames and close monitoring of their activities through performance reviews conducted by the clients following the criteria laid down by the platform providers.

Control Based on the Possibility of Direct Surveillance

Like the previous one, also the ideal-type of Panopticon Control is based on top-down pervasive surveillance of organizational members' execution of tasks.

However, it operates through less visible, Panopticon surveillance based on three key mechanisms (Foucault 1977; Sewell 1998; Sewell and Wilkinson 1992; Simon 2005; Wilson 1995, 1999). First, a system of permanent, exhaustive, omnipresent one-way visibility, which ensures that any deviation from pre-set rules can be immediately detected. Second, the dissociation between the seeing/being seen dyad so that the surveilled workers never know whether they are actively being watched at any one moment, but they can be sure that they may always be so. Third, a system of threats and sanctions. Under these conditions, individuals must be sure that it is impossible to hide unacceptable behaviors and avoid the related sanctions. In this way, the disciplinary effect is constant even if surveillance is not.

This kind of control primarily rests on the constant *possibility* of direct and invisible surveillance of workers' behaviors. In this case too, control is external as it achieves individuals' compliance leveraging their fear of being seen while they are behaving in unacceptable ways. Compared to the *Scientific Management* method, however, Panopticon surveillance makes it possible to continuously monitor the activities of a larger number of employees with fewer supervisors. At the extreme level, a totalitarian system would make "disobedience" almost unthinkable, reducing the necessity of applying the sanctions.

This ideal-type of control goes along with a formal organization of work which entails the almost comprehensive predetermination of the key structural aspects of the transformation process (i.e., the standard time for the completion of the work process, the single stages, activities and tasks of it, the methods of work, the allocation of tasks to workers, and the practical abilities that workers should possess to perform their tasks). From this point of view, this ideal-type seems to be similar to the one based on *Scientific Management* principles. However, they differ in the form of coordination of interdependences (Thompson 1967/2003): Coordination is by standardization in the former, whereas it is by planning in the latter.[3] Coordination by planning goes along with the request that workers adhere to a partially self-directed organization personality and thus exercise a certain degree of discretion in the execution of their tasks to obtain the prescribed outcomes. For example, discretion can regard changes in the work pace or in the order of execution of the tasks. Workers may be required to make such discretionary decisions to cope with variations occurring at one stage of the process and threatening the possibility of completing work tasks within the pre-set standard time in that stage and next ones.

Despite these differences with respect to *Scientific Management*, the consequence of the formal organization for workers is the same: They have no opportunity to exercise their autonomy over task design and execution and other key aspects regarding the organization of their work. Nor do they have possibility to develop new competences.

New technological developments (such as enterprise resource planning, customer relationship management, supply chain management software applications, cloud computing, artificial intelligence-based expert systems) promise to open up new opportunities for Panopticon surveillance. They enable a completely new level of work visibility (e.g., never ending, far reaching, and relentless); they make it possible to streamline human supervisors' work of comparing, classifying, and evaluating behaviors, and to free the "reach of the gaze" from spatial and temporal constraints, thereby making the watcher *potentially* omnipresent not only in space but also in time (Galič et al. 2017; Simon 2005).

Many empirical studies on the use of ICTs document the emergence of forms of organizational control that approach this ideal-type (Fernie and Metcalf 1998; Fuchs 2011, 2015; Menzies 1996; Rosanvallon 2011;

Sia and Neo 2008). In particular, Delbridge et al. (1992), Sewell (1998), and Sewell and Wilkinson (1992) show that the use of ICT-supported management information systems with a Panopticon effect is an essential component of the implementation of JIT/TQM production systems and a means to speed up and intensify work in a number of different work settings. Panopticon surveillance ensures that workers make discretionary decisions to cope with unexpected problems during the execution of their tasks. At the same time, it enables management to detect any positive discretionary work practices immediately and to transform them into new standard procedures.

Similarly, Elmes et al. (2005) document the Panopticon effect of the use of an enterprise resource planning system in an American-owned global manufacturing organization. In this case, workers perform their jobs in line with management expectations—that is, they conform to the rules and procedures for tasks completion embedded into the system, but also exercise discretion to deal with exceptions so as to avoid ripple effects. Finally, Leclercq-Vandelannoitte (2011) argues that the adoption of mobile technologies in a French large building company is part of a wider management control strategy consisting in the implementation of invisible and pervasive surveillance of site foremen's activities as well as in the imposition of new constraining obligations on them (i.e., the obligation to make greater discretionary efforts in order to manage the building site expenses).

Controlled Autonomy (and Internalized Control)

The third ideal-type of managerial control rests on organizational members' tight self- (i.e., internalized) control. It is related to a communitarian view of the organization in which management trusts workers, requires their loyalty, and asks them to adhere and identify with a unitary set of organization's values and goals.

Individuals are responsible for the achievement of specific results but they can decide by themselves the ways to reach them. Consistently, they can take initiative to prevent and solve unexpected problems that could have negative consequences for the effectiveness of the transformation process. They can also assess the quality of their own work. They can even participate in making decisions affecting their work. In other words, management admits that workers make autonomous decisions. However, workers' autonomy displays a peculiar character. Using an oxymoron, it can be called "controlled autonomy'" (Appay 2007). It rests on the workers' capability to find the most appropriate ways to achieve specific pre-set goals and performance targets, which are defined in accordance with overall organizational goals established by top managers. The above-mentioned organizational requirements entail the need to expand the capabilities of each individual worker so that he/she can appropriately respond to any situation that may confront him/her.

One way to achieve this is training, both initial intensive skill training (Ouchi 1979; Simon 1947/1976) and permanent training. The latter includes on-the-job training (e.g., in the form of job rotation), formalized training programs, even organized by institutions outside the organization, and more generally any other training opportunities that workers undertake autonomously in order to strengthen and enhance their skills and knowledge.

Training also aims at promoting the individuals' identification with the organization, mostly intended as a community. For this purpose, management organizes meetings, lectures, and speeches with external consultants, training workshops on the organization's culture and values, as well as parties and other moments of conviviality. Teamwork is another way to expand workers' capabilities to cope with unexpected events and problems. Within a team, knowledge, skills, and ability of different workers are combined in a highly flexible manner, according to the nature of the problem to be solved.

When the level of uncertainty of organizational process increases, the need to leverage complex competences at several stages of the process increases as well. Under these conditions, the complete alignment between individual and organizational goals is paramount. For this purpose, however, management cannot effectively rely on forms of external control. Therefore, in addition to material inducements, management turns to other techniques such as persuasion, workers' involvement, and the internalization of values and norms, which are part of the organizational culture. These mechanisms are more powerful and even manipulative as they aim at inducing organizational members not only to do what management wants but also to perceive this as the result of their own free choice (Wilson 1999).

The individual's ability to effectively mobilize and contribute with his/her knowledge and skills to the achievement of the organizational goals and to become socialized into the values and norms of the organizational culture is a source of reputation. It is also under the constant scrutiny of his/her peers. Thus, a system of horizontal (many-to-many) surveillance among organizational members, which is functional to the culture of the organization (i.e., the culture of those who control the organization), also contributes to strengthen individuals' self-control (Barker 1993).

Finally, there is another key feature that characterizes the ideal-type of Controlled Autonomy. That is, management only temporarily accepts that operators exercise their autonomy when doing their job in order to ensure the smooth operation of the process. Indeed, management continuously attempts to transform such an autonomy into discretion, which, to the extreme, can be embedded into intelligent machines in highly digitalized work processes. Similarly, management admits and even requires that workers learn new things while they are performing their work, but continuously seeks to appropriate and codify their knowledge and skills.

According to some scholars (Hirsch-Kreinsen 2016; Johansson et al. 2017; Kagermann et al. 2013; Taskin 2010; Wilson 1999), digitally transformed organizations (e.g., virtual organizations and smart factories) and new highly digitalized work practices (e.g., virtual teams, distance and mobile work, smart or agile working) would be increasingly supported by management control strategies and forms of work organization that approach this ideal-type. In his study of sales teleworkers in an electronics company, Dambrin (2004) indeed observes that teleworkers exercise autonomy over the means used to complete their work and in order to solve unexpected problems, as well as greater discretion over their working schedules. At the same time, they are responsible for achieving specific pre-set measurable targets. Similar findings emerge from a research on smart working carried out among a large number of Italian organizations of different size and economic sectors (Smart Working Observatory 2016). Valsecchi's (2006) study of teleworkers in an Italian telecommunication company also shows that the main mechanisms used by management to control teleworkers are internal training to socialize teleworkers into the organization values and a greater emphasis on trust. Finally, some empirical studies carried out in Germany point out that the extensive use of new digital technologies in industry would be accompanied by the following major changes in work organization (Bonekamp and Sure 2015; Pfeiffer et al. 2016): management's expectation that workers autonomously undertake the necessary training to improve their skills; greater importance of work teams; greater demand for workers' flexibility, capacities in troubleshooting, and improvisation in the execution of their work; workers' ability to innovate. At the same time, however, workers would have a diminished ability to shape the wider contours of the system, as this one would be increasingly predetermined by ICTs (Edwards and Ramirez 2016).

In light of the discussion carried on so far, we can summarize and compare the essential features of the three ideal-types of modes for intensifying management control over workers and work practices in Table 6.1.[4]

Research Methodology

Data Sources

Alongside the theoretical elaborations and the analysis of the available literature on the topic, we made a secondary analysis of the data from the European Working Condition Surveys (hereinafter, EWCS; European Foundation for the Improvement of Living and Working Conditions 2017), as some of the collected variables are useful proxies of the concepts proposed in the chapter. The EWCS is a repeated cross-national sample survey that has been conducted every five years since 1991 (first wave) to 2015 (sixth wave).[5] The number of countries involved in the survey has gradually increased over the years, from 12 European countries of the first edition to the current 35, which also include non-European countries. The survey comprises a body of questions that have remained

Table 6.1 Ideal-types of management control

New Tayloristic Control	Panopticon Control	Controlled Autonomy
Comprehensively and tightly pre-set program of activities	Almost comprehensive and tightly pre-set program of activities	Tightly pre-set objectives and admitted variations in the regulation of the ways to get the work done during work performance
Rigid and stable tasks, lack of discretion	Rigid and flexible tasks; highly circumscribed degree of discretion to govern highly circumscribed stages of the work process	Organizational roles requiring complex tasks and a high degree of discretion
Visible, pervasive, actually exercised surveillance of tasks' execution based on (one-to-a few) hierarchical supervision or on intelligent algorithms and wearable devices	Pervasive, invisible, potential (one-to-many) surveillance of tasks' execution	Outcome control; peer (many-to-many) control; trusty relationships based on reputation
Other-directed organization personality. Management disallows any possibility of workers' autonomy	Partially self-directed organization personality. Management disallows any possibility of workers' autonomy	Completely self-directed organization personality. Management temporarily accepts workers' autonomy but continuously attempts to transform it into discretion

(continued)

unchanged over the years and therefore in many cases allow us to observe trends over a period of more than twenty years.

Table 6.1 (continued)

New Tayloristic Control	Panopticon Control	Controlled Autonomy
No opportunity for workers to learn new things when they perform their work	No opportunity for workers to learn new things when they perform their work	Opportunity for workers to learn new things when they perform their work. Management continuing attempt to codify and appropriate new knowledge and skills developed by workers
Workers' training in the methods and procedures for tasks completion in accordance with pre-set training contents and techniques	Workers' training in the methods and procedures for tasks completion in accordance with pre-set training content and techniques	Initial intensive skill training for filling complex roles. Permanent training, through external training activities or on-the-job training. Demand for workers' personal responsibility for their continuing professional development
Coordination by standardization	*Coordination by planning*	*Coordination by planning*
Productivity-based material and economic inducements as key mechanisms for management to induce workers to accept formal authority and discipline	Material inducements and individuals' fear of being seen as key mechanisms for management to induce workers to accept formal authority and discipline	Material and immaterial inducements, persuasion, strengthening of the organizational culture until the manipulation of individual identities as key means for management to ensure individual and organizational goals congruence

Source Authors' own elaboration

Cases and Variables Selection

Since our focus is on the effects of the digitalization of work, we conducted all the analyses separately for workers who use ICTs intensively[6] and those who do not. We called the first "digital workers" and the others "traditional workers."

Given the scope of this study, we also decided to limit the analysis to the group of workers employed in the industrial sector.[7] To have a sufficient number of cases, we considered 12 countries: Austria, Belgium, Denmark, Finland, Germany, Ireland, Italy, Netherlands, Portugal, Spain, United Kingdom, and Sweden.[8] Table 6.2 shows the absolute frequencies of the cases considered for each wave and the percentages of prevalence of digital and traditional workers on the total cases.

We also estimated the number of *mobile digital workers*. As it is known, there are many definitions of mobile workers, depending on how the intensity of use of ICTs and the frequency of work outside the office are defined.[9] Therefore, their impact on total workers is not easy to calculate. Despite the ever-increasing use of mobile technologies at work—such as laptops, mobile phones, and tablets—the majority of employees is still working within the company's premises. In our samples, for instance, the amount of industrial digital workers performing their activities for several times a week in different locations—such as customer sites, in the car, in open spaces, at a coffee shop, or at the airport—varies from 2% in Italy to 14% in Sweden.

Then, from the EWCS dataset, we selected the variables on which it was possible to formulate hypotheses regarding the three ideal-types proposed in the chapter: New Tayloristic Control (T1); Panopticon

Table 6.2 Cases considered for each wave and prevalence of digital and traditional workers

	1991	1995	2000/01	2005	2010	2015
Traditional workers (%)	84	79	75	66	61	60
Digital workers (%)	16	21	25	34	39	40
Total cases	10,122	13,424	18,136	12,211	17,309	18,224

Source: Authors' own elaboration based on 1991–2015 EWCS data

Control (T2); and Controlled Autonomy (T3). In general, we favored long-trend variables (indicatively starting from the second wave), but we made some exceptions due to the relevance of some variables with respect to the ideal-types.

Data Analysis

For each ideal-type, we formulated specific assumptions concerning the level or trend of each variable, on the basis of the theoretical framework illustrated in the previous pages.

These assumptions are summarized in Table 6.3. The table is organized as follows:

- Column 1: synthetic variable label;
- Columns 2 to 4: expected situation in accordance with the theoretical framework related to each ideal-type, which is the same for traditional and digital workers. "Pos" means that, according to the theory, we should expect a percentage higher than 70% (on average) over the period and/or an increase higher than 3 percentage points between the first and the last wave. "Neg" means that, according to the theory, we should expect a percentage lower than 30% (on average) over the period and/or a decrease of more than 3 percentage points;
- Columns 5 to 7: observed situation for each ideal-type, split by "traditional workers" (T) and "digital workers" (D). Three asterisks (***) indicate the cases in which data meet our expectations, both for average period level and for trend (positive or negative). Two asterisks (**) indicate the cases in which data meet our expectations just for average period level, lower than 30% in case of expected negative trend and higher than 70% in case of expected positive trend. One asterisk (*) indicates the cases in which data meet our expectations just for trend. Lastly, empty cells () indicate the cases in which no expectations are confirmed.

Table 6.3 Variables included in the analysis: Expected and observed trend/period average

	Expected level or trend			(Dis)confirmation		
	T1	T2	T3	T1	T2	T3
Period: 1991–2015 (6 waves)						
Working at very high speed	Pos	Pos	Pos	(D/T)*	(D/T)*	(D/T)*
Working to tight deadlines	Pos	Pos	Pos	(T)*	(T)*	(T)*
Being able to choose or change your speed or rate of work	Neg	Pos	Pos		(D)***; (T)*	(D)***; (T)*
Earnings from your main job include piece rate or productivity payments	Pos	Pos	Neg			(D/T)**
Period: 1995–2015 (5 waves)						
Pace of work dependent on numerical production targets or performance targets	Neg	Pos	Pos		(D)*	(D)*
Pace of work dependent on automatic speed of a machine	Pos	Neg	Neg	(T)*	(D)***	(D)***

(continued)

We summarize what emerged from the exploration of levels and trends in Table 6.4 and refer to the next paragraph for the discussion of the results.

Table 6.3 (continued)

	Expected level or trend			(Dis)confirmation		
	T1	T2	T3	T1	T2	T3
Pace of work dependent on the direct control of your boss	Pos	Neg	Neg			
Job involves assessing yourself the quality of your own work	Neg	Neg	Pos			(D/T)**
Job involves solving unforeseen problems on your own	Neg	Pos	Pos		(D/T)**	(D/T)**
Job involves learning new things	Neg	Neg	Pos	(T)*	(T)*	(D)**
Being able to choose or change order of tasks	Neg	Pos	Pos		(D)**	(D)**
Being able to choose or change methods of work	Neg	Neg	Pos	(T)*	(T)*	(D)**
Rotating tasks between yourself and colleagues	Neg	Neg	Pos	(D/T)*	(D/T)*	

(continued)

Discussion and Conclusions

Since the mid-1970s, the combination of large international changes of a technological, economic, and cultural nature has defined a new social organization of the countries that from 1945 until then had

Table 6.3 (continued)

	Expected level or trend			(Dis)confirmation		
	T1	T2	T3	T1	T2	T3
Earnings include extra payments for additional hours of work/overtime	Pos	Pos	Neg	(D/T)*	(D/T)*	
Fixed starting and finishing times	Pos	Pos	Neg			(D/T)*
Period: 2000/2001–2015 (4 waves)						
Working in a group or team that has common tasks and can plan its work	Neg	Neg	Pos	(D/T)*	(D/T)*	
Period: 2005–2015 (3 waves)						
Being able to take a break when you wish	Neg	Neg	Pos			
Job gives you the feeling of work well done	Neg	Neg	Pos			(D)**; (T)***
Being able to apply your own ideas in your work	Neg	Neg	Pos	(D/T)*	(D/T)*	
Having the feeling of doing useful work	Neg	Neg	Pos			(D)**; (T)***
Training paid by yourself	Neg	Neg	Pos	(D/T)**	(D/T)**	

(continued)

adopted a fordist social model. Despite important aspects of discontinuity, "the underlying logic of capitalist accumulation and its crisis tendencies remain the same" (Harvey 1989, p. 189).

Table 6.3 (continued)

	Expected level or trend			(Dis)confirmation		
	T1	T2	T3	T1	T2	T3
On-the-job training (co-workers, supervisors)	Neg	Neg	Pos	(T)**	(T)**	(D)*
Working hours fit in with family or social commitments outside work (% Very well)	Pos	Pos	Neg			(D/T)*
Period: 2010–2015 (2 waves)						
Being consulted before objectives are set for your work	Neg	Neg	Pos	(D)*	(D)*	
Being involved in improving the work organisation or work processes	Neg	Neg	Pos			(T)*
Being able to influence decisions that are important for your work	Neg	Neg	Pos			(D/T)*

(continued)

Focusing solely on the organizational structures of the company, new organizational forms have grown up impetuously firstly in the industrial sector and then in the service sector. Compared to the fordist ones, they are based on lower levels of standardization and predetermination of work as well as on less direct hierarchical control over daily work activities. On the other hand, however, they require greater flexibility, responsibility, and self-regulation skills from workers.

Table 6.3 (continued)

	Expected level or trend			(Dis)confirmation		
	T1	T2	T3	T1	T2	T3
Period: 2015 (1 wave)						
Your immediate boss gives you praise and recognition when you do a good job	Neg	Neg	Pos			(D)**
Employees are appreciated when they have done a good job (% Agree)	Neg	Neg	Pos			(D/T)**
The management trusts the employees to do their work well (% Agree)	Neg	Neg	Pos			(D/T)**

Note (D) = Digital workers; (T) = Traditional workers; (*) Expected Trend = Observed Trend; (**) period average over 70% (if positive trend expected) or under 30% (if negative trend expected); (***) Expected Trend = Observed Trend and period average over/under threshold; ( ) empty cells mean disconfirmation of expected level or trend. Dummies (%Yes) unless otherwise specified
Source Authors' elaborations based on 1991–2015 EWCS data

Much of the managerial and sociological literature calls these forms post-fordist, thereby suggesting a caesura with the logic that inspired the taylor-fordist organization of work.

An optimistic interpretation of post-fordist models considers the (true or presumed) novelties as sources of improvement in several organizational dimensions, such as effectiveness and efficiency, autonomy of the workers and innovation capacity, quality of products and services, workers' well-being and work-life balance, and customers' satisfaction.

On the other side, an equally extensive body of literature offers critical interpretations of these models. According to it, expressions such

Table 6.4 Number of variables consistent to expectations (AV and relative frequencies on 29 examined variables)

	New Tayloristic Control (T1)		Panopticon Control (T2)		Controlled Autonomy (T3)	
Traditional workers	9* 2** 0***	0.38	9* 3** 0***	0.41	7* 5** 2***	0.48
Digital workers	6* 1** 0***	0.24	7* 3** 2***	0.41	6* 11** 2***	0.66

Note (*) Expected Trend = Observed Trend; (**) period average over 70% (if positive trend expected) or under 30% (if negative trend expected); (***) Expected Trend = Observed Trend and period average over/under threshold
Source Authors' own elaborations based on 1991–2015 EWCS data

as "enhancement of workers' skills," "decision-making decentralization," "continuous learning," and "participation in the construction of corporate values" are typical of rhetorical discourses, and they hide the real aims pursued through the new organizational forms, namely: predetermination of work outcomes, objectification and codification of workers' expertise, engineering of the corporate culture aimed at indoctrination, and even at the colonization of the employees' self. Briefly, the real aim would be decision-making centralization and increasing control over the several regulations present in every complex organizational process.

Extant empirical research shows that the new organizational forms have often proved to be methods of pervasive control, capable of succeeding where taylorism failed because they are better suited to less standardized work processes, which require more abstract knowledge and skills. An extensive and intensive radicalization of control of work practices is made possible also by new digital technologies and their high level of integration, both on a virtual and on a material level.[10]

Several case studies document that other forms of management control have become established, alongside the more traditional form of direct and personal supervision of work practices, already implemented in fordism-taylorism solutions, and today appropriately renewed thanks to ICT innovation. Therefore, it could be interesting to try to understand whether and how much these forms are frequent, particularly in the industrial sector. Here, the application of new digital technologies is in the early stage. Although optimistic predictions have been made about the consequences for workers of organizational changes associated with the intensive use of ICTs in industry,[11] there is still little empirical evidence on what forms of work organization and managerial control are indeed emerging (Johansson et al. 2017; Pfeiffer 2017; Pfeiffer and Suphan 2015; Salento 2016, 2017).

On the basis of the analysis of EWCS data, we have an opportunity to give a first, although rough answer to this question. The variables that we selected from the EWCS dataset for our empirical analysis allow us to say to what extent in the industrial sector real work practices approach each of the three ideal-types illustrated previously. Our data also permit us to distinguish between "digital" and "traditional" workers in order to see if the three ideal-types have a different weight in the interpretation of current trends in control. The number of digital workers is increasing constantly and sharply, even if traditional ones still represent most of workers (see Table 6.2).

Our findings confirm the existence of growing processes of intensification of work pace, individualization of activities, and salary flexibility (based on the flexibility of hours worked); these processes are taken for granted to some extent, once companies have accepted the rules of hyper-competition in the globalized economy (Goeltz 2014).

Both the digital and the traditional workers are subject to them, the latter in a more marked way.

Among the traditional workers, the intensification of work pace seems to be more linked to the speed of the machines; this is probably due to the fact that in this category many workers still perform mainly manual and motor activities. As for the digital ones, among whom the number of those who perform intellectual work is presumably greater, the intensification appears more linked to production or performance objectives.

Over the considered period, we can also observe an increasing number of both digital and traditional industrial workers that experience problems in finding a satisfactory fit between their working hours and their family and social commitments outside work, even though they have the opportunity to work according to flexible working schedules. In this regard, and with particular reference to digital workers, our empirical analysis seems to challenge the optimistic prediction that an increasing number of employees in digitally transformed industrial organizations would be able to better combine work and private life (Kagermann et al. 2013).

The analysis of the average period levels and trends of the selected variables clearly shows the prevalence and growth of forms of control approaching the ideal-type of Controlled Autonomy, for both digital and traditional workers (see Table 6.4). In particular, an increasing number of industrial workers report that they are able to assess themselves the quality of their own work and to affect decisions that are important for their work[12]; they also stress the importance of such immaterial inducements as the feeling of doing useful or well-done work, and the development of trusting relationships between management and workers, based on recognition and reputation.

We observe a greater prevalence of signals indicating external control (New Tayloristic Control and Panopticon Control) among traditional workers. Indeed, an increasing number of traditional workers perceive a reduced ability to change or choose the methods of work, to learn new things while they are performing their job as well as fewer on-the-job training opportunities. In contrast, digital workers appear to be scarcely subject to direct and explicit surveillance, and slightly more subject to the Panopticon one (see Table 6.4).

Instead, digital workers appear to be much more clearly subject to forms of management control approaching the Controlled Autonomy. In particular, over the considered period, an increasing number of digital industrial workers report that they have to cope with a demand for flexibility and adaptability in the execution of their tasks. Such flexibility refers to the possibility of solving unforeseen problems on their own, changing or choosing the pace of work, the methods, and order of execution of their tasks. This, in turn, appears to go along with the opportunities for them to learn new things while they are performing their work.

For a significant number of digital workers, flexibility is also spatial. A signal of that is the proliferation of terms such as remote workers, mobile workers, agile workers, e-workers, and e-nomads to indicate workers who spend a significant part of their time working outside the company boundaries and communicating with colleagues and superiors through digital technologies. According to the report of two specialists in the field of smart working implementation, Andy Lake and Tim Dwelly, issued in 2014 and sponsored by three influential international companies in the field of mobile work: "Mobile working, supported by new technologies, is developing fast. Some 25% of EU workers are classed as 'e-nomads', and globally more than a third of the workforce is expected to be mobile by 2015" (Lake and Dwelly 2014, p. 4). However, the large majority of workers is still working at company's premises for the main part of the week, especially in the industrial sector as confirmed by EWCS data (cf. the Research Methodology section above).

In brief, as compared to traditional workers, digital employees seem to have greater scope to exercise their autonomy over the way to get their work done, being responsible only for achieving pre-set performance targets.

However, the autonomy of digital workers seems to be even more restricted than expected. In particular, we expected to find an increasing number of digital workers who "are consulted [by management] before objectives are set for their work" and who "are able to apply their own ideas in their work" over the considered period. Instead, the two above-mentioned variables do not show positive trends.

In this regard, our empirical investigation provides further evidence in support of the few empirical studies showing that in highly digitalized industrial work settings workers can exercise their autonomy at the level of their specific tasks but cannot shape the wider contours of the work processes in which they participate (Bonekamp and Sure 2015; Edwards and Ramirez 2016).

To summarize, we can conclude that the new work practices, that are currently emerging in the industrial sector, certainly open up new opportunities for workers to use their knowledge and develop new skills; this is especially true for digital workers, a category that, as we have said, is rapidly growing in the countries of the sample. From this point of view, we agree with what some scholars have pointed out about the application of digital technologies in industry (a phenomenon also called Innovation 4.0), in light of qualitative and quantitative research carried out in some companies in Germany (homeland of Innovation 4.0): The expertise of workers, their ability to perform "living labor," still plays a key role even in highly routinized and standardized production processes (Pfeiffer 2014; Pfeiffer and Suphan 2015). On the other hand, however, the available, albeit still limited, empirical evidence casts doubt on the fact that this living work manifests itself in full autonomy. Full autonomy, in fact, entails the opportunity for workers to influence the objectives of the organization. Instead, today we see—at least in the countries, sector, and period considered in our analysis—that a managerial elite group does not grant margins of effective workers' participation in the decision-making processes regarding strategic decisions. On the other hand, in the current phase of hyper-competitive capitalism, it does not seem that workers are really able to get out of a growing loneliness, to raise the level of social conflict, and to oppose real autonomy to management.

Consistently, our findings provide further evidence in support of the stream of critical thinking aiming at unveiling the many illusions of post-fordist organizational solutions that today seem to gain new momentum thanks to ICTs innovation. In particular, the illusion that the emergence of new work practices involves a shift toward a democratic and polycentric governance of organizations, or even toward "heterarchies" (Stark 2011), which provide greater opportunities for workers to participate in setting the decision premises that shape organizational processes. In contributing to this line of critical thinking, we have also proposed the ideal-type of Controlled Autonomy as a theoretical foundation for appreciating the complexity of the forms of control of new work practices in highly digitalized work settings.

Notes

1. Even though we believe that Masino's comparative analysis of fordist and post-fordist organizational forms shows a more systematic character, similar interpretations can be found in other fields of the international scholarly literature. See, for example, Barker (1993), Delbridge et al. (1992), Sewell (1998), Sewell and Wilkinson (1992), and Wilson (1995, 1999).

2. They have been formed by abstracting and accentuating certain conceptually essential elements (traits, features, or tendencies) from a great deal of diffuse, discrete, more or less present and occasionally absent concrete individual phenomena, and arranging them into a unified, internally consistent construct which enlightens the essential features of an empirical phenomenon from a particular analytical point of view (Weber 1904, Eng. transl. 1949/2011, p. 100).
3. Coordination by planning involves the establishment of schedules for governing the action of sequentially interdependent organizational units or members and it "does not require the same high degree of stability and routinization that are required for coordination by standardization" (Thompson 1967/2003, p. 56).
4. Of course, in any real organization, there can be hybrid solutions which can also include features not considered here.
5. EWCS Integrated data file 1991–2015. The EWCS dataset is accessible via the UK Data Archive (UKDA) of the University of Essex at www.esds.ac.uk. To access data files, users are required to register to the UKDA. Information on the registration procedure is available at www.esds.ac.uk/aandp/access/login.asp. The archive also provides access to survey documentation and guidance for data users.
6. That is, they work with digital technologies (e.g., computers, laptops, and smartphones) three-quarters of the time.
7. NACE sectors: Industry, Transportation, Storage, and Communications.
8. We didn't consider Luxembourg because of its small sample size, and France and Greece because of their low value in the index of digitalization of industrial work (da Empoli 2017).
9. For a review of the main definitions, see Eurofound and the International Labour Office (2017).
10. The scope of our reasoning is limited to control in the individual organizations, but a similar argument can be extended to the whole social organization.
11. See, for example, Kagermann et al. (2013, p. 5) who argue that in the smart factories, flexible work arrangements will allow workers "to combine their work, private lives and continuing professional development more effectively, promoting a better work-life balance".
12. An increasing number of traditional workers also report that they are involved in improving the work organization and work processes.

References

Appay, Béatrice. 2007. "Dualismes et paradoxes au travail. L'autonomie contrôlée." *Sociologia del lavoro* 105: 19–34.

Ball, K. 2010. "Workplace Surveillance: An Overview." *Labor History* 51 (1): 87–106. https://doi.org/10.1080/00236561003654776.

Barker, J. R. 1993. "Tightening the Iron Cage: Concertive control in Self-Managing Teams." *Administrative Science Quarterly* 38(3): 408–437. https://doi.org/10.2307/2393374.

Bergvall-Kåreborn, B., and D. Howcroft. 2014. "Amazon Mechanical Turk and the Commodification of Labour." *New Technology, Work and Employment* 29(3): 213–223. https://doi.org/10.1111/ntwe.12038.

Bonekamp, Linda, and Matthias Sure. 2015. "Consequences of Industry 4.0 on Human Labour and Work Organisation." *Journal of Business and Media Psychology* 6 (1): 33–40.

Callaghan, G., and P. Thompson. 2001. "Edwards revisited: Technical Control and Call Centres." *Economic and Industrial Democracy* 22 (1): 13–37. https://doi.org/10.1177/0143831x01221002.

Carugati, Andrea, Aurélie Leclercq-Vandelannoitte, and JoaoVieira da Cunha. 2018. "Work Control and Surveillance in the Age of Digital." In *Human Resource Management and Digitalization*, edited by Franca Cantoni and Gianluigi Mangia, 115–140. London: Routledge.

Cattero, Bruno, and Marta D'Onofrio. 2018. "Organizing and Collective Bargaining in the Digitized 'Tertiary Factories' of Amazon: A Comparison Between Germany and Italy." In *Working in Digital and Smart Organizations. Legal, Economic and Organizational Perspectives on the Digitalization of Labour Relations*, edited by Edoardo Ales, Ylenia Curzi, Tommaso Fabbri, Olga Rymkevich, Iacopo Senatori, and Giovanni Solinas, 141–164. Cham: Palgrave Macmillan.

Cavazotte F., A. H. Lemos, and K. Villadsen. 2014. "Corporate Smart Phones: Professionals' Conscious Engagement in Escalating Work Connectivity." *New Technology, Work and Employment* 29 (1): 72–87. https://doi.org/10.1111/ntwe.12022.

Child, J. 1972. "Organization Structure and Strategies of Control: A Replication of the Aston Study." *Administrative Science Quarterly* 17 (2): 163–177. https://doi.org/10.2307/2393951.

Child, J. 1973. "Predicting and Understanding Organizational Structure." *Administrative Science Quarterly* 18 (2): 168–185. https://doi.org/10.2307/2392061.

da Empoli, Stefano, ed. 2017. "Thinking the Future of European Industry. Digitalization, Industry 4.0 and the role of EU and national policies." ICom Report. https://www.i-com.it/. Accessed 30 November 2020.

Dambrin, Claire. 2004. "How Does Telework Influence the Manager-Employee Relationship?" *International Journal of Human Resources Development and Management* 4 (4): 358–374.

Davenport, Thomas H. 2013. "How P&G Presents Data to Decision-Makers." *Harvard Business Review*, April, 4. https://hbr.org/2013/04/how-p-and-g-presents-data. Accessed 30 November 2020.

Delbridge, R., P. Turnbull, and B. Wilkinson. 1992. "Pushing Back the Frontiers: Management Control and Work Intensification Under JIT/TQM Factory Regimes." *New Technology, Work and Employment* 7 (2): 97–106. https://doi.org/10.1111/j.1468-005x.1992.tb00024.x.

Edwards, Richard C. 1979. *Contested Terrain: The Transformation of the Workplace in the Twentieth Century*. New York and London: Basic Books and Heinemann.

Edwards, P., and P. Ramirez. 2016. "When Should Workers Embrace or Resist New Technology?" *New Technology, Work and Employment* 31 (2): 99–113. https://doi.org/10.1111/ntwe.12067.

Elmes, M. B., D. M. Strong, and O. Volkoff. 2005. "Panoptic Empowerment and Reflective Conformity in Enterprise Systems-Enabled Organizations." *Information and Organization* 15 (1): 1–37. https://doi.org/10.1016/j.infoandorg.2004.12.001.

Eurofound and the International Labour Office. 2017. *Working Anytime, Anywhere: The Effects on the World of Work*. Luxembourg: Publications Office of the European Union, and Geneva: the International Labour Office. https://www.eurofound.europa.eu/publications/report/2017/working-anytime-anywhere-the-effects-on-the-world-of-work. Accessed 30 November 2020.

European Foundation for the Improvement of Living and Working Conditions. 2017. *European Working Conditions Survey Integrated Data File, 1991–2015* [data collection], 4th Edition. UK Data Service, SN: 7363.

Fabbri, Tommaso. 2018. "Digital Work: An Organizational Perspective." In *Working in Digital and Smart Organizations. Legal, Economic and Organizational Perspectives on the Digitalization of Labour Relations*, edited by

Edoardo Ales, Ylenia Curzi, Tommaso Fabbri, Olga Rymkevich, Iacopo Senatori, and Giovanni Solinas, 29–38. Cham: Palgrave Macmillan.

Fernie, Sue, and David Metcalf. 1998. *(Not) Hanging on the Telephone: Payment Systems in the New Sweatshops*. London: Centre for Economic Performance, London School of Economics and Political Science. https://cep.lse.ac.uk/_new/publications/abstract.asp?index=390. Accessed 30 November 2020.

Flamholtz, E. G., T. K. Das, and A. S. Tsui. 1985. "Toward an Integrative Framework of Organizational Control." *Accounting, Organizations and Society* 10 (1): 35–50. https://doi.org/10.1016/0361-3682(85)90030-3.

Foucault, Michel. 1977. *Discipline and Punish: The Birth of the Prison*. London: Penguin Books.

Fuchs, Christian. 2011. "How to Define Surveillance?" *MATRIZes* 5 (1): 109–133.

Fuchs, C. 2013. "Political Economy and Surveillance Theory." *Critical Sociology* 39 (5): 671–687. https://doi.org/10.1177/0896920511435710.

Fuchs, Christian. 2015. "Surveillance and Critical Theory." *Media and Communication* 3 (2): 6–9.

Galič, M., T. Timan, and B.-J. Koops. 2017. "Bentham, Deleuze and Beyond: An Overview of Surveillance Theories from the Panopticon to Participation." *Philosophy & Technology* 30: 9–37. https://doi.org/10.1007/s13347-016-0219-1.

Goeltz, Donald R. 2014. "Globalization and Hypercompetition: Drivers, Linkages, and Industry Differences." *Journal of International Business and Cultural Studies* 8: 1–15.

Gorecky, Dominic, Mathias Schmitt, Matthias Loskyll, and Detlef Zühlke. 2014. "Human-Machine-Interaction in the Industry 4.0 Era." 12th IEEE International Conference on Industrial Informatics (INDIN), 289–294.

Halford, S. 2005. "Hybrid Workspace: Re-spatialisations of Work, Organisation and Management." *New Technology, Work and Employment* 20 (1): 19–33. https://doi.org/10.1111/j.1468-005x.2005.00141.x.

Harvey, David. 1989. *The Condition of Postmodernity: An Enquiry into the Origins of Cultural Change*. Oxford: Blackwell.

Hirsch-Kreinsen, H. 2016. "Digitization of Industrial Work: Development Paths and Prospects." *Journal for Labour Market Research* 49: 1–14. https://doi.org/10.1007/s12651-016-0200-6.

Johansson, J., L. Abrahamsson, B. Bergvall Kåreborn, Y. Fältholm, C. Grane, and A. Wykowska. 2017. "Work and Organization in a Digital Industrial Context." *Management Revue* 28 (3): 281–297. https://doi.org/10.5771/0935-9915-2017-3-281.

Kagermann, Henning, Wolfgang Wahlster, and Johannes Helbig. 2013. *Recommendations for Implementing the Strategic Initiative Industrie 4.0*. München: National Academy of Science and Engineering. https://en.acatech.de/publication/recommendations-for-implementing-the-strategic-initiative-industrie-4-0-final-report-of-the-industrie-4-0-working-group/. Accessed 1 December 2020.

Lake, Andy, and Tim Dwelly. 2014. "It's Work But Not as We Know It. An Exploration of What the Future of Work Means for Business, Society and Public Policy." http://flexibility.co.uk/ItsWorkBut/index.asp. Accessed 1 December 2020.

Leclercq-Vandelannoitte, A. 2011. "Organizations as Discursive Constructions: A Foucauldian Approach." *Organization Studies* 32 (9): 1247–1271. https://doi.org/10.1177/0170840611411395.

Lyon, David. 2001. *Surveillance Society: Monitoring Everyday Life*. Milton Keynes, UK: Open University Press.

Masino, Giovanni. 2005. *Le imprese oltre il fordismo. Retorica, illusioni, realtà*. Roma: Carocci.

Menzies, Heather. 1996. *Whose Brave New World? The Information Highway and the New Economy*. Toronto, Canada: Between the Lines.

Orlikowski, W. J. 1991. "Integrated Information Environment or Matrix of Control? The Contradictory Implications of Information Technology." *Accounting, Management and Information Technology* 1 (1): 9–42. https://doi.org/10.1016/0959-8022(91)90011-3.

Ouchi, W. G. 1977. "The Relationship Between Organizational Structure and Organizational Control." *Administrative Science Quarterly* 22 (1): 95–113. https://doi.org/10.2307/2391748.

Ouchi, W. G. 1979. "A Conceptual Framework for the Design of Organizational Control Mechanisms." *Management Science* 25 (9): 833–848. https://doi.org/10.1287/mnsc.25.9.833.

Ouchi, W. G. 1980. "Markets, Bureaucracies and Clans." *Administrative Science Quarterly* 25 (1): 129–141. https://doi.org/10.2307/2392231.

Ouchi, W. G., and M. A. Maguire. 1975. "Organizational Control: Two Functions." *Administrative Science Quarterly* 20 (4): 559–569. https://doi.org/10.2307/2392023.

Perrow, Charles. 1972. *Complex Organizations*. Glenview, IL: Scott Foresman.

Pfeiffer, Sabine. 2014. "Digital Labour and the Use-Value of Human Work. On the Importance of Labouring Capacity for Understanding Digital Capitalism." *tripleC: Communication, Capitalism & Critique. Open Access Journal for a Global Sustainable Information Society* 12 (2): 599–619.

Pfeiffer, Sabine. 2017. "The Vision of 'Industrie 4.0' in the Making—A Case of Future Told, Tamed, and Traded." *Nanoethics* 11: 107–121.

Pfeiffer, Sabine, Horan Lee, Christopher Zirnig, and Anne Suphan. 2016. *Industrie 4.0—Qualifizierung 2025*. Frankfurt/M.: VDMA. https://www.fachportal-paedagogik.de/en/literatur/vollanzeige.html?FId=1095421#vollanzeige. Accessed 1 December 2020.

Pfeiffer, Sabine, and Anne Suphan. 2015. "The Labouring Capacity Index: Living Labouring Capacity and Experience as Resources on the Road to Industry 4.0." Working Paper 2015 No. 2. Stuttgart: University of Hohenheim, Chair for Sociology. www.sabine-pfeiffer.de/files/downloads/2015-Pfeiffer-Suphan-EN.pdf Accessed 1 December 2020.

Rosanvallon, Jérémie. 2011. "Le contrôle du travail, entre réalités et perceptions: le cas de la messagerie électronique." *Sociologies pratiques* 1 (22): 19–33.

Rosenblat, Alex, and Luke Stark. 2016. "Algorithmic Labor and Information Asymmetries: A Case Study of Uber's Drivers." *International Journal of Communication* 10: 3758–3784.

Salento, Angelo. 2016. "Note sui problemi di ricerca su Industria 4.0 e sulle conseguenze per i lavoratori e le lavoratrici." *Inchiesta* 191 (gennaio-marzo): 44–49.

Salento, Angelo. 2017. "Industria 4.0, imprese, lavoro. Problemi interpretativi e prospettive." *Rivista Giuridica del Lavoro e della Previdenza Sociale* ANNO LXVIII (No. 2): 175–194.

Schörpf, P., J. Flecker, A. Schönauer, and H. Eichmann. 2017. "Triangular Love–Hate: Management and Control in Creative Crowdworking." *New Technology, Work and Employment* 32 (1): 43–58. https://doi.org/10.1111/ntwe.12080.

Sewell, G. 1998. "The Discipline of Teams: The Control of Team-Based Industrial Work Through Electronic and Peer Surveillance." *Administrative Science Quarterly* 43 (2): 397–428. https://doi.org/10.2307/2393857.

Sewell, Graham 2012. "Organization, Employees, and Surveillance." In *Routledge Handbook of Surveillance Studies*, edited by Kirstie Ball, Kevin Haggerty, and David Lyon, 303–312. New York: Routledge.

Sewell, G., and L. Taskin. 2015. "Out of Sight, Out of Mind in a New World of Work? Autonomy, Control, and Spatiotemporal Scaling in Telework." *Organization Studies* 36 (11): 1507–1529. https://doi.org/10.1177/0170840615593587.

Sewell, G., and B. Wilkinson. 1992. "'Someone to Watch over Me': Surveillance, Discipline and the Just-in-Time Labour Process." *Sociology* 26 (2): 271–289. https://doi.org/10.1177/0038038592026002009.

Sia, S. K., and B. S. Neo. 2008. "Business Process Reengineering, Empowerment and Work Monitoring: An Empirical Analysis Through the Panopticon." *Business Process Management Journal* 14 (5): 609–628. https://doi.org/10.1108/14637150810903020.

Simon, B. 2005. "The Return of Panopticism: Supervision, Subjection and the New Surveillance." *Surveillance & Society* 3 (1): 1–20. https://doi.org/10.24908/ss.v3i1.3317.

Simon, Herbert A. 1947. *Administrative Behavior*. New York: Free Press (1976 3rd ed.).

Smart Working Observatory. 2016. *(Smart) work in Progress!* Milan: Politecnico of Milan, Department of Management Engineering.

Solé, Andreu, and Bruno Maggi. 2007. "Société, entreprise, individu: la surprenante actualité de la 'vision du monde' de Taylor." *Cahier de recherche du Groupe HEC* Paris, n° 869. https://hal-hec.archives-ouvertes.fr/hal-00580144. Accessed 1 December 2020.

Staab, P., and O. Nachtwey. 2016. "Market and Labour Control in Digital Capitalism." *tripleC: Communication, Capitalism & Critique. Open Access Journal for a Global Sustainable Information Society* 14 (2): 457–474. https://doi.org/10.31269/triplec.v14i2.755.

Stark, David. 2011. *The Sense of Dissonance. Accounts of Worth in Economic Life*. New York: Princeton University Press.

Taskin, Laurent. 2010. "La déspatialisation. Enjeu de gestion." *Revue française de gestion* 3 (202): 61–76.

Taylor, Frederick W. 1911. *The Principles of Scientific Management*. New York/London: Harper & Brothers Publishers.

Thompson, James D. 1967. *Organizations in Action*. New York: McGraw-Hill (2003. New Brunswick (USA)/London: Transaction Publishers).

Valsecchi, R. 2006. "Visible Moves and Invisible Bodies: The Case of Teleworking in an Italian Call Centre." *New Technology, Work and Employment* 21 (2): 123–138. https://doi.org/10.1111/j.1468-005x.2006.00168.x.

Walker, Kasey L. 2017. "Surveillance." In *The International Encyclopedia of Organizational Communication*, edited by Craig R. Scott and Laurie Lewis, 1–7. New York: Wiley.

Weber, M. 1904. "Die Objektivität sozialwissenschaftlicher und sozialpolitischer Erkenntnis." In *Gesammelte Aufsätze zur Wissenschaftslehre*. Mohr: Tübingen. English edition: Weber, M. 1949. *On the Methodology of the*

Social Sciences (Translated by E. A. Shils and H. A. Finch). Glencoe, IL: Free Press (2nd ed. 2011 with a new introduction by R. J. Antonio and A. Sica).

Wilson, F. 1995. "Managerial Control Strategies Within the Networked Organization." *Information Technology & People* 8 (3): 57–72. https://doi.org/10.1108/09593849510098271.

Wilson, F. 1999. "Cultural Control Within the Virtual Organization." *The Sociological Review* 47 (4): 672–694. https://doi.org/10.1111/1467-954x.00191.

7

Neoliberal Conceptions of the Individual in Labour Law

Julia Tomassetti

Introduction

This chapter explores neoliberal conceptions of the individual as an economic agent in legal disputes over companies' obligations towards their workers. I focus on companies that use digital platforms to coordinate the production of goods and services ('platform companies'). The main legal issue in these disputes is whether the workers are entitled to rights and protections under labour law as statutory 'employees' or 'workers', or excluded from labour law as 'independent contractors'. The companies contend that they bear no responsibility to the workers as their employers, because the workers are in business for themselves and even 'entrepreneurs'. The chapter shows how platform companies can depict their workers as neoliberal subjects through practices and discourse, and how these techniques can shape legal evaluations of

J. Tomassetti (✉)
City University of Hong Kong, Hong Kong, China
e-mail: jtomasse@cityu.edu.hk

T. Addabbo et al. (eds.), *The Collective Dimensions of Employment Relations*,
https://doi.org/10.1007/978-3-030-75532-4_7

the work relationships. I conclude that the neoliberal subject in legal reasoning stands in a relation of 'elective affinity' (Weber 1946, p. 42) with the practices and rhetoric of platform companies.

To demonstrate my argument, I analyse *SuperShuttle DFW, Inc. and Amalgamated Transit Union Local 1338* (2019) (hereafter '*SuperShuttle DFW*'), a recent decision by the US National Labor Relations Board (NLRB). In *SuperShuttle DFW*, an NLRB majority ruled that airport shuttle drivers for the platform company SuperShuttle DFW (hereafter 'SuperShuttle') were independent contractors rather than employees of the company. Therefore, the drivers had no statutory rights to unionize and bargain collectively with the company.

SuperShuttle arranged its work relationship with drivers in ways that cued neoliberal conceptions of the individual and of what it means for an individual to be in business for herself. To account for these practices, SuperShuttle invited the Board to re-imagine its workers as neoliberal agents, and the Board did so. This shaped the Board's assessment of the drivers' legal status, convincing it that the workers were independent contractors. By construing the drivers as neoliberal agents, the company persuaded the NLRB that shuttle drivers engaged in repetitive and unskilled work organized by, controlled by, and for the benefit of the company were entrepreneurs in business for themselves.

What are these neoliberal conceptions? And what company practices and rhetoric facilitate their reception by legal decision-makers?

The neoliberal individual is modelled on the neoliberal firm (Gershon 2011), and to understand the neoliberal firm, we should begin by distinguishing it from its liberal form.

Liberal theory rendered the firm as a productive enterprise, an organization that coordinated the financing, development, production, and sale of goods and services (Chandler 1977; Hart 1995). The liberal firm sought profit mainly through successful competition in product markets. Its corporate form facilitated this goal (Kraakman 2001).

Neoliberal theory displaces the liberal concept of the firm as a productive enterprise almost entirely with that of its legal form, the corporation. It also reconceives the main purpose of the corporate form. Instead of serving the productive enterprise, its primary purpose is to manage contractual nexuses among stakeholders and serve as an investment portfolio, a 'portfolio of assets' (Davis 2009). Its primary goal is not necessarily to maximize profit through product market competition, but rather to appreciate the value of its portfolio (Fligstein 1990; Dore 2008). To do so, it may prioritize financial activity (Davis 2009). It may engage in financial speculation, regulatory arbitrage, regulatory entrepreneurship (Pollman and Barry 2017), and rentier capitalism.

Neoliberal theory telescopes the corporation to the individual subject through the concept of 'human capital'. What is human capital? Simulating the emic perspective of the neoliberal subject, Feher (2009, p. 26) provides: 'my human capital is me, as a set of skills and capabilities that is modified by all that affects me and all that I effect'. Whereas liberal agency is grounded in possessive individualism (Gershon 2011), neoliberal agency is based on human capital (Feher 2009; Brown 2015). Neoliberalism transmutes the firm from a coordinator of labour to the manager of an asset portfolio, and the worker from an owner of labour to the manager of a human capital portfolio.

The shift from labour to human capital reflects 'neoliberal rationality', which views neoliberalism as an 'order of normative reason' (Brown 2015; Foucault 2008). From an analysis of policies, economic arrangements, and other contemporary institutions, Brown (2015) distils neoliberal rationality as a complex of categories, practices, logics, and principles that differ from their liberal counterparts. Scholars have been addressing how platform companies, as part of the 'gig economy', enact, benefit from, and propel neoliberal policies and work arrangements (Zwick 2018). We see less work examining neoliberalism as a form of rationality. Yet, scholars are beginning to explore how neoliberal rationality and its construction of the individual manifest in and shape different social relations, including work. Moisander, Groß, and Eräranta (2018), for example, explore how a digital platform company, in order to manage precarious labour, sought to shape its workers' subjectivity so that workers thought of themselves as little enterprises, or neoliberal agents.

This chapter argues that we can also see neoliberal rationality at work in legal reasoning, when companies, and sometimes legal decision-makers, construe workers as neoliberal agents.

Using the *SuperShuttle DFW* dispute as my primary example, I show how a company can index the worker and 'entrepreneur' in neoliberal terms through practical and discursive techniques. The worker becomes an 'entrepreneur', but with a meaning far removed from a liberal understanding of the term. For example, on the practical side, the company designs the labour process to permit/require workers to determine their own working times by logging in and out of the platform. The platform then argues that, since workers can earn more money the more hours they log in, they are deploying a managerial strategy in deciding when and how long to work. For the liberal subject, choosing to work longer hours under the command of another for mostly fixed returns is not entrepreneurial. However, for the neoliberal subject, a decision to work longer hours reflects her discretionary commitment of human capital—her time.[1] Human capital is like any other capital. It is 'invested' like other capital and earns 'profit' like any other capital. Therefore, working longer hours is the equivalent of risking any other capital for the sake of gain, like investing additional money in a business to expand production or enter a new market.

This is how the practice of permitting—requiring—workers to determine their own schedules facilitates a neoliberal legerdemain: the company provides the individual, as holder of human capital, the opportunity to make decisions about the use of this capital. In fact, it *requires* the worker to make these decisions. As a consequence, no matter how unskilled the work, and even where the costs and returns vary little or not at all with the duration of the work, time management becomes an entrepreneurial venture.

The analysis of *SuperShuttle DFW* shows how neoliberal rationality can transform discretion in carrying out work tasks into economic autonomy. Conceptualizing the worker as a manager of human capital makes it possible to interpret almost all worker discretion as entrepreneurial opportunity. As illustrated by the working hours example, within neoliberal rationality, the discretion need not be exercised in the context of product market competition to be entrepreneurial or involve activities characteristic of product market competition, like investing in advertising or making production more efficient. Nor does the desired end need to be monetary, because neoliberal rationality does not distinguish between the domains of production and reproduction (Feher 2009). Thus, taking time off from work can be an entrepreneurial opportunity. Further, the discretion need not be exercised in as methodological a fashion as expected under a liberal notion of entrepreneurialism. It can be more speculative and sporadic.

By showing how neoliberal rationality can shape legal evaluations of platform work, including what it means to be an entrepreneur, my analysis carries some implications for our understanding of digitally coordinated work. Advancements in information and communications technology have facilitated changes in how companies organize production and exchange. Yet, these changes do not always involve major shifts in the organization of authority relations, sites of entrepreneurial ferment, or loci of power. The analysis of *SuperShuttle DFW* suggests that some of these apparent transformations in the organization of work are artefacts of changes in our conception of individuals as economic agents.

The chapter unfolds as follows: the section "The Neoliberal Subject" introduces neoliberal conceptions of the firm and the individual. The section "The Neoliberal Subject in Labour Law" shows how companies arrange work relationships in ways that invoke these conceptions, using *SuperShuttle DFW* as its main example. It also illustrates how these conceptions shape evaluations of the legal status of workers. The final section critiques the neoliberal rendering of the individual in labour law and concludes.

The Neoliberal Subject

The neoliberal subject is modelled on the neoliberal firm (Brown 2015). Therefore, to illuminate the nature of this subject, the section begins by comparing liberal and neoliberal conceptions of the firm.

The Liberal Firm

The liberal firm was an organization engaged in the financing, production, and sale of goods and services for profit (Chandler 1977; Hart 1995). Liberal economic theory even defined the boundaries between the 'firm' and the 'market' according to how productive activity was organized—whether by centralized coordination or by the price mechanism (Coase 1937). The purpose of the corporation in liberal economic theory was to serve the firm in its pursuit of profit in product markets. The corporate form gave the firm a coherent legal subjectivity, provided a means for raising capital, and helped govern relationships among different stakeholders (Kraakman 2001).[2]

The Neoliberal Firm

Neoliberal theory dispenses with the notion of the firm as a productive enterprise and relaxes the tenet that the purpose of incorporation is to facilitate successful product market competition. In an influential article entitled 'Theory of the Firm', Jensen and Meckling (1976) argued that the firm was a 'nexus of contracts' among stakeholders, a 'legal fiction' to accommodate contracts with workers, shareholders, suppliers, investors, and other stakeholders. As such, the firm was no longer a productive enterprise or even an organization. It was a convenient legal shorthand for a network of contractual relationships, a conventional device for contracting parties to pursue gain. Since the neoliberal firm is not an organization but a 'nexus', the 'boundary' metaphor is less apt. However, to define the limits of its business identity and legal responsibility, it looks to its formal legal relations, such as property rights, contracts, and equity (Davis 2009; Jensen and Meckling 1976).[3]

This notion of the firm better accommodates new conceptions of corporate interests and valuation that do not give precedence to profit-seeking through product market competition. Davis (2016) noted that a reductionist conception of the firm as a 'legal fiction' was ideologically suited for the era of mergers and acquisitions. It likewise provides a better justification than liberal theory for contemporary pursuits like financial speculation, asset manipulation, regulatory arbitrage (Tomassetti 2016), regulatory entrepreneurship (Pollman and Barry 2017), and rentier capitalism. Davis (2009) theorized that, in an era of financialization, the corporation often serves as a 'portfolio of assets', a sort of malignant outgrowth of what Fligstein (1990) called the 'financial conception' of corporate control. Evidence suggests that companies have been orienting their competitive activities towards financial markets and away from product markets (Davis 2009; Dore 2008). For example, corporations have increasingly earned income from portfolio activity (Krippner 2005). The goals of the neoliberal firm are to increase its stock value and speculate successfully in financial markets.

The Neoliberal Subject and Neoliberal Rationality

The depiction of the neoliberal individual in this section draws from the neoliberal firm limned above and from recent literature on neoliberal rationality (Brown 2015) and subjecthood (Feher 2009; Gershon 2011, 2014, 2018), where neoliberal rationality comprises practices, principles, and logics that differ from their liberal counterparts (Brown 2015).

The neoliberal individual is modelled on the neoliberal firm. As noted above, under neoliberalism, the firm is no longer a productive enterprise, an organization that coordinates production and facilitates cooperation among stakeholders for purposes of product market competition. The individual as corporation need not embody this purpose either to be a legitimate economic agent. The purpose of the neoliberal individual as a corporation is to manage a portfolio of assets (Brown 2015; Gershon 2014). She is the 'CEO of me' (Gershon 2018).

The concept of 'human capital' is central to telegraphing the corporation as an asset portfolio to the human being. The neoliberal subject is a bundle of usable human capital assets, including knowledge, skills, experiences, alliances, and capacities (Feher 2009). The individual manages this portfolio through continuous, reflexive, means-ends calculations (Gershon 2011). Each exchange she chooses reflects a strategy for managing configurations of risk, responsibility, and reward (Gershon 2018). Embodied by and embodying human capital, the individual is 'for himself his own capital, his own producer, the source of his earnings' (Foucault 2008, p. 226).

Neoliberal rationality implies a different theory of the worker and of the employment relationship. Human capital, rather than possessive individualism, is the basis of economic subjecthood (Feher 2009). In a liberal imagining of the individual, a worker 'owns' her capacity to labour. She lends this property to an employer for a certain time. In the neoliberal reimagining of the individual, the worker manages a collection of assets, of human capital (Brown 2015). Instead of lending her labour to an employer, the individual invests human capital.

The goal of the neoliberal subject is appreciating her human capital. To do so, she prioritizes investing in human capital, attracting other investors, and taking risks in a context of 'macroeconomic vicissitudes' (Brown 2015, p. 84). Not only might these pursuits take place outside of product markets, but they may also take place outside of what liberal theory conceptualizes as the domain of production. Neoliberal rationality makes no distinction between the domains of production and reproduction (Feher 2009). As such, the neoliberal subject may value her returns by means that are illegible in the liberal domain of production because they elude quantification. For the neoliberal subject, 'everything I earn — be it salary, returns on investments, booty, or favors I may have incurred — can be understood as the return on the human capital that constitutes me' (Feher 2009, p. 26).

The Neoliberal Subject in Labour Law

This section illustrates how companies and legal decision-makers construe workers as neoliberal agents in legal disputes over whether workers are independent contractors. In particular, I show how some platform companies draw on particular work practices to invite legal decision-makers to interpret their work arrangements in neoliberal terms. The companies invoke and describe these practices to cue neoliberal conceptions of what it means to be an independent contractor and 'entrepreneur'. They thereby seek to demonstrate that their workers are not employees of the company. In comparison with liberal conceptions of the independent contractor and entrepreneur, neoliberal conceptions presuppose a subject with different goals, engaged in different economic activities, and using a different means-end rationality to pursue these activities. The neoliberal subject is a very different kind of economic agent than her liberal counterpart.

The legal standards for distinguishing independent contractors from workers who are entitled to rights and protections under statutory labour law vary. However, a common consideration is whether the worker is in business for herself. This suggests that the worker is an independent contractor. In some jurisdictions, decision-makers have focused on the concept of 'entrepreneurial opportunity' as a significant, if not decisive, factor in determining whether an individual is an independent contractor. For example, in *SuperShuttle DFW*, the tribunal asks whether the workers' positions afford opportunities for 'entrepreneurial' gain and loss, and it promotes this inquiry above all other considerations in the legal standard.

The argument uses examples from a few cases but focuses on *SuperShuttle DFW*, a recent NLRB decision evaluating the employment status of airport shuttle drivers for SuperShuttle. The NLRB is the agency responsible for enforcing US collective bargaining law, the National Labor Relations Act (NLRA). It sits as an appellate tribunal in NLRA disputes. SuperShuttle is part of a nationwide organization that provides ground transportation to and from airports through a central reservation and payment system.

SuperShuttle serviced the main airports in the Dallas-Fort Worth region of Texas through a fleet of drivers. Until 2005, the company recognized its drivers as employees. In 2005, it changed to a putative franchise model and began categorizing the drivers as independent contractors. Drivers were required to enter one-year franchise agreements. SuperShuttle charged drivers in the form of an initial fee and flat weekly fees. According to the company, the weekly fees covered use of the company's brand, equipment, access to transportation requests ('bids'), and payment processing. The company also charged drivers a flat weekly fee for insurance.

Drivers were required to purchase or lease a van meeting the company's specifications, and to cover various costs associated with the van's upkeep and operation, like maintenance, gas, and tolls. SuperShuttle assisted some drivers in acquiring van leases through its affiliated leasing company. Most drivers leased their vans instead of purchasing them.

SuperShuttle paid a driver the difference between the fares SuperShuttle charged passengers transported by the driver and the fees it charged the driver, minus other payments the driver owed to the company (e.g. insurance, van payment (if applicable), etc.). SuperShuttle established the fees and fares unilaterally.

The franchise agreement with drivers did not limit SuperShuttle's right to control the drivers' work. It obliged drivers to 'follow standards, specifications and operating procedures as specified in this Agreement… in order to ensure uniformity and quality of services offered to the public' (p. 26). The company required drivers to follow detailed rules regarding uniforms, van appearance, eating and drinking, and other aspects of customer service.[4] The agreement permits SuperShuttle to unilaterally alter its terms, including vehicle specifications.

The company took several measures to ensure that drivers produced a particular branded service. It trained drivers to meet its 'brand standards' (p. 26); supervised drivers through its communications system, GPS tracker, and paperwork requirements; and inspected the vans periodically.

Drivers could receive transportation requests ('bids') through SuperShuttle's Nextel hand-held device issued to drivers; by waiting in queue at a hotel, airport, or other designated location; or by driving a regularly scheduled hotel-airport circuit (for which a driver had to pay an additional weekly fee). Regardless of the kind of 'bid', all passenger transportation had to be processed through the Nextel device, which was connected to the company's reservation and dispatch system. Drivers could not use any other means or system. The case record suggested that drivers could generally select the 'bids' that they wanted and turn down others without penalty; however, drivers testified that SuperShuttle had penalized them for not accepting requests.

The franchise agreement imposed additional requirements on drivers not directly related to customer service. It prohibited drivers from working for SuperShuttle competitors or being involved in any other transportation work, whether as an employee or as a business principal. Drivers could not solicit passengers, advertise, or otherwise seek passengers. Each driver could operate only one vehicle, must be the principal driver, and must directly supervise the vehicle's operation. A driver could not use the vehicle for any purpose outside of her work for SuperShuttle.

The *SuperShuttle DFW* dispute issued from the efforts of SuperShuttle's Dallas-Fort Worth drivers to unionize. After drivers voted to unionize, SuperShuttle refused to bargain with them. The company alleged that it had no statutory obligation to bargain with the drivers, because they were independent contractors rather than employees. A majority of the NLRB agreed with the company.[5]

Using the SuperShuttle example, the next subsections explore how companies can promote neoliberal conceptions of the individual as an economic agent in ways that suggest the individual is in business for herself.

Modelling the Individual on the Corporation

One method of arranging relationships to suggest neoliberal conceptions of the individual is to have workers become a corporation quite literally. Some companies require or encourage workers to register themselves as business entities and then delineate workers as business enterprises in their contracts. As an example of the latter, building service companies have designated individual janitors as 'franchisees' (*Awuah v Coverall North America* 2010; *De Giovanni v Jani-King Int'l* 2013). SuperShuttle calls its drivers 'franchisees'.

Some companies impose a formal 'individual-as-business' requirement on workers as a condition of holding the job. For instance, the package delivery company FedEx began requiring individual drivers to incorporate themselves in the midst of growing legal scrutiny of its treatment of drivers as independent contractors (Litvak 2010).

Platform companies have also done this. The on-demand ride company Uber's agreement with UK drivers depicts each driver position as being held by two distinct entities—a 'Partner' and a 'Driver'. A court observed that, in the 'vast majority' of cases, the 'partner' and 'driver' were the same individual (*Aslam & Farrar v Uber* 2017, p. 13). Uber in the United States also contracts only with an 'independent company in the business of providing transportation services'. According to its agreement with Uber, this 'independent company' is responsible for entering a similar agreement with a driver and ensuring that the driver complies with the agreement (*Razak v Uber Technologies* 2018, p. 6). The company construes the individual as a neoliberal agent almost literally: the individual is both a business entity and a human capital asset in a portfolio that must be wisely managed (Becker 1962).

Moisander et al. (2018) argue that construing the worker as a business entity is a technique of 'neoliberal governmentality', a means of managing precarious workers by mobilizing them as neoliberal agents.

This technique also shapes legal evaluations of the worker's status. Whether the worker is incorporated or formally established as an enterprise is not normally an express factor in the legal tests for determining worker status. Further, under these tests, the label the parties place on their relationship is not supposed to be determinative (*Lawson v Grubhub* 2018). Nonetheless, decision-makers sometimes find incorporation or a contractual depiction of the alleged independent contractor as a business entity to be evidence that the individual is an independent contractor (*FedEx Home Delivery v NLRB* 2009). In *SuperShuttle DFW*, the majority remarked: 'five franchisees entered into the franchise agreement as corporations. Such a relationship is rare in employer-employee relationships and is associated with independent-contractor status' (p. 14).

As illustrated above, one means of cueing neoliberal conceptions of the individual worker in labour law disputes is to ask the worker to embody the corporate form expressly.

Replacing Labour with Human Capital: Choosing Working Times

Companies can also prompt neoliberal conceptions of workers in legal disputes by permitting—requiring—workers to determine their own schedules, and then arguing that this practice proves the worker has entrepreneurial opportunities.

A common feature of platform production is for the company *not* to require that individuals commit to work *ex ante* at any particular time or for any particular length of time as a condition of the position. Platform workers generally choose when to log into the system and how long to stay logged in. Logging in indicates that the worker is available to receive assignments/requests from the platform.[6] So long as the worker does not log out before completing an assigned or accepted task, the worker can generally choose when to log out. Some platforms require a worker to log in occasionally to maintain her position, but others do not.

As typical of platform companies then, SuperShuttle did not schedule its drivers. A driver chose when to log into its system. This indicated that she was available to receive transportation requests from the dispatch system or to receive passengers while waiting in line at a hotel or airport. Drivers also chose when to log out of the system.

The NLRB majority repeatedly argued that drivers' discretion to choose when and how long to work was evidence of their entrepreneurial opportunity.[7] For instance, the majority argued, '[S]o the more they work, the more money they make', demonstrating that 'franchisees have significant opportunity for economic gain and significant risk of loss' (p. 12). It also contended that 'franchisees' freedom to keep all fares they collect, coupled with their unfettered freedom to work whenever they want, provides them with significant entrepreneurial opportunity' (p. 13).

Grubhub, a food delivery platform, made a similar argument in litigation over the employment status of its delivery workers. To demonstrate that the workers were 'entrepreneurial' and had 'an opportunity for profit or loss', Grubhub pointed to their 'discretion over where and for how long to perform deliveries… and the opportunity to participate in bonus promotions and earn the minimum hourly guarantee' (*Lawson v Grubhub* 2017, Defendant's Reply Brief, p. 16).[8]

Time as Capital

In contending that being resourceful with one's time or working longer hours is an entrepreneurial strategy, these arguments conjure the worker as a neoliberal agent. They displace the concept of labour with that of human capital, so that 'labor disappears as a category' (Brown 2015, p. 38). The worker becomes a holder of human capital rather than the owner of labour. Her time and flexibility in using her time are marketable assets in her portfolio of capital.

Time becomes capital like any other form of capital. Like other capital, when deployed it is an 'investment'. When its deployment leads to gain, this gain is 'returns' or 'profit', not 'wages'. If labour persists at all in this neoliberal rendering, it does so in a decomposed form (perhaps as 'energy'), as one element in a bundle of assets that includes time and flexibility.

When labour 'disappears as a category' (Brown 2015, p. 38), so must the liberal distinction between labour and capital. Human 'capital', as capital, is like any other resource one might venture for gain (Brown 2015). We see this lack of differentiation in the *SuperShuttle DFW* majority's attempt to reconcile drivers' 'entrepreneurial opportunities' with the business restrictions the company imposed on them:

> We acknowledge that the [contract's] prohibition on franchisees entering into business relationships with SuperShuttle's competitors limits to some extent the potential for entrepreneurial opportunity that would otherwise come with ownership of their vans. However, that limitation is mitigated by the fact that SuperShuttle does not limit its hours of service and that the franchisees can drive for SuperShuttle whenever and for as long as they choose. Thus, the franchisees do not need the option to work for SuperShuttle's competitors to maximize their entrepreneurial opportunity to the same extent that they would need that option if SuperShuttle's hours of service were limited or if SuperShuttle limited the number of hours that they could drive. (n. 29)

Here, the majority depicts working additional hours as equivalent to expanding one's business or investing in other undertakings. The drivers' time is human capital, and as such, it is no different than other forms of capital, like money or real or intellectual property. Working longer hours is just as entrepreneurial as using one's vehicle to start a new company or work for a competitor.

What invites or facilitates this semiotic (and ideological) election of human capital over labour in the legal evaluation of the SuperShuttle drivers' work?

At first glance, this seems rather implausible. Where individuals are providing hourly work that requires little skill or expertise, it seems difficult to dismiss the prominence of labour in the arrangement. In *SuperShuttle DFW*, the drivers are performing the same work, subject to about the same costs. Certainly, the longer drivers work the greater the chance they receive trip requests. Yet, working long hours does not provide a means of manipulating the cost/revenue ratio to their advantage. SuperShuttle controls trip requests and establishes fares. Nor does the decision to work longer hours change drivers' weekly payments to SuperShuttle or the company's pricing structure for fares. It also seems difficult *not* to 'see' labour here where the core of the arrangement is an individual's agreement to apply her faculties in accordance with the direction of another. Recall that, the *SuperShuttle DFW* franchise agreement placed no limits on what the company could require drivers to do while working.

In fact, the *SuperShuttle DFW* decision and Grubhub's arguments are illegible within liberal discourse. Working a requisite number of hours to earn a bonus is not a 'managerial tactic' within a liberal system of meaning. Working longer hours to earn more in hourly compensation or to increase the probability of receiving passengers is not 'entrepreneurial'. These arguments conflate the liberal distinction, often recited by courts, between 'working smarter, not just harder' (*Corporate Express Delivery Systems v NLRB*, p. 780). Working longer hours is a quintessential case of 'working harder'.

However, *requiring* that workers choose their work times facilitates labour's disappearance and human capital's incarnation: by requiring the individual to make decisions about when and how long to work (and thus when and for how long to potentially earn income), the company makes time management look like a business strategy. We presume that the worker calculated the expected risk-cost-reward of investing her human capital. She is expected to manage and invest her time prudently (even in deciding when and for how long to activate her obligations under an agreement to follow instructions). Therefore, by choosing one's hours to earn hourly wages and bonuses, a worker 'did, in fact, exercise skill and managerial tactics in an effort to increase profitability' (*Lawson v Grubhub* 2017, Defendant's Reply Brief, p. 13). Decisions about working times are 'managerial' since they require managing one's human capital. And workers who are making managerial decisions look less like employees and more like persons in business for themselves.

Skill

Another legal consequence of construing the individual as a neoliberal agent is to diminish the importance of 'skill' as a factor in the tests for determining employment status.

Whether the work is skilled or unskilled is often a relevant inquiry in determining whether someone is an independent contractor or not. If the work is unskilled, the individual is more likely to be an employee/worker and less likely to be an independent contractor. In the industrial era, 'skill' generally referred to a proficiency in a productive task or set of productive tasks associated with an occupation or industry. Skill was a specialized ability garnered through experience, training, education, and/or professional qualification. Applying this understanding of skill helped to differentiate agreements in which an individual subjected her capacity for purposive action to the commands of another (employment), from agreements in which an individual sold services encapsulating expertise that the hirer did not cultivate in-house, and that the hirer could not meaningfully direct and monitor. If the work was unskilled, it was likely that the workers were in the former kind of arrangement—employment. Those hired to perform unskilled work were also less likely to be in business for themselves.[9]

Under a neoliberal rendering of the individual, the weight of skill in legal evaluations of employment tends to decrease, and, in some manner, the meaning of the term itself shifts. In neoliberal rationality, 'entrepreneurialism' includes nearly any exercise of discretion involving 'human capital'. Decision-makers who adopt this understanding of entrepreneurialism tend to see skill as a relatively insignificant factor: a neoliberal construction of the individual as the manager of a bundle of assets can transform even unskilled work into an 'entrepreneurial strategy'. Being 'entrepreneurial' in the neoliberal sense *is* a skill. Recall Grubhub's argument that choosing to work when the platform was offering hourly wages and bonuses demonstrated 'skill and managerial tactics' (*Lawson v Grubhub* 2017, Defendant's Reply Brief, p. 13).

Many platforms design their work arrangements so that the worker must always make decisions about when and how long to work for it, thereby always exercising entrepreneurial 'skill'. The *SuperShuttle DFW* majority, for instance, recognizes that the drivers' work does not require specialized abilities. However, it devotes the least space to this discussion out of all the factors in the test. It concludes, without analysis, that other factors—particularly drivers' entrepreneurial opportunity—outweigh the skill factor and other factors probative of an employment relationship.[10]

The dissent's critique of the majority highlights the contrast between liberal and neoliberal evaluations of the weight and meaning of skill. The dissent argued that the majority did not give due significance to the fact that the work was unskilled. It also attributed more weight to other factors the majority thought were overshadowed by the drivers' 'entrepreneurial opportunity'. These factors were that SuperShuttle trained the drivers, and that the drivers were performing services constituting the core of SuperShuttle's business (not their own businesses).

Discretion as Autonomy

Within a neoliberal rendering of the individual in legal reasoning, discretion at work often masquerades as autonomy. Simply by permitting the worker to decide when and how long to make herself available for assignments, platform companies seem to transform hourly labour into a strategic investment by someone in business for herself. Fabbri (2018) shows that, while digitalized work processes may incorporate worker discretion, this does not necessarily provide workers autonomy in decision-making.

This observation applies to many platform workers, including the drivers in *SuperShuttle DFW*. According to the majority, the drivers had 'total autonomy to set their own work schedule' (p. 12). In one sense, this was true. Drivers could make themselves available for work when they pleased and generally for how long they pleased, without risking termination. And yet, the company organized the work relationship so that the drivers were, as a practical matter, required to work some quantum for SuperShuttle. SuperShuttle only entered one-year agreements with drivers and charged them weekly fees to keep their positions. Drivers also had vehicle payments. The company also prohibited drivers from otherwise working in the transportation industry. Drivers were required to use, and depended upon, SuperShuttle's information and communications technology—its dispatch system and equipment—to receive paid work. In the light of these economic, contractual, and technological constraints imposed by the company, the majority's conclusion that the company afforded drivers considerable 'independence to pursue economic gain' (p. 9) conflates discretion and autonomy.

This conflation of discretion and autonomy is also apparent in the majority's claim that 'control and entrepreneurial opportunity are opposite sides of the same coin' (p. 9). The majority contended that the less that the hirer controlled the individual in the performance of her work, the more entrepreneurial opportunity she had. This inverse relationship sometimes obtains within a liberal rationality, but not always. The dissent provides one example where it does not: an employer that hires a chef does not exercise much control over how the chef goes about cooking, but this does not in itself present an entrepreneurial opportunity to the chef in the liberal sense. Under neoliberal rationality, however, many kinds of discretion can present entrepreneurial opportunity since many kinds of choices require the management of one's human capital.

Blurring Production and Reproduction

Brown (2015) argues that neoliberal rationality, by applying a particular kind of economistic reasoning to all domains of activity, eliminates liberalism's distinction between the productive and reproductive. We see this elimination where platform companies permit/require workers to determine their own schedules and then construe these choices as entrepreneurial decisions, since 'the more they work, the more money they make' (*SuperShuttle DFW* 2019, p. 12). This mode of reasoning transforms not just making a living, but living itself, into running a business. Decisions about when to eat or sleep are entrepreneurial, because they are simultaneously decisions about when to make oneself available to work. Physiological discipline is a business strategy. Metabolic rationalization is a profit opportunity. Neoliberal individuals are 'the managers of a portfolio of conducts pertaining to all the aspects of their lives' (Feher 2009, p. 30).

Consider the argument in *SuperShuttle DFW* that permitting drivers to hire a 'relief driver' presented an entrepreneurial opportunity. This is one of the few instances where SuperShuttle's terminology was not entirely obfuscatory: providing 'relief' from work suggests making time for non-work undertakings, like a vacation day. As noted, drivers' agreement with SuperShuttle and the company's compensation-cum-indenture system all but required drivers to make themselves available to work with some regularity to make their required payments. Drivers might indeed want some 'relief' from work.[11] However, both the lower tribunal and NLRB majority interpreted the right to hire a relief driver as a profit opportunity. Neoliberal rationality reflects a 'desire to overcome the divide between the intimate man and the entrepreneur' (Feher 2009, p. 33).

Reimagining Business Activity and Entrepreneurialism

The arguments regarding the 'entrepreneurial opportunities' that additional hours of work provide presuppose a neoliberal understanding of business activity by an individual. Different categories, practices, logics, and principles shape the individual subject under neoliberal rationality than under liberal rationality. The subject is a neoliberal agent, again modelled on the neoliberal corporation. We see a normative shift away from the practices that liberal rationality valorizes as business activity. We see a different understanding of commercial risk-taking and of means-ends rationality. Overall, we see a general indifference to the institutional context in which the individual agent pursues her interests.

Liberal Rationality and Business Activity

Liberal rationality—its categories, principles, logics, and practices—focuses on production and product markets. Socially valuable business activity is oriented towards product markets. They deal with productive efficiency (e.g. input/output ratios and scale economies), marketing and finding new customers, expanding production, and innovating in product markets. A liberal means-ends logic aims at maximizing profit through successful product market competition. This product market context distinguishes liberal business activity and entrepreneurialism from other activities, like performing well at a job to receive a promotion or raise, hustling, or speculation.

Within liberal rationality, it would have been difficult to find that the SuperShuttle drivers were in business for themselves. SuperShuttle transferred some 'opportunity for loss' to drivers in requiring drivers to assume the cost of SuperShuttle vans and pay the company for their jobs. However, SuperShuttle did not provide drivers a meaningful opportunity for commercial gain. It prohibited drivers from engaging in product market competition. Drivers could not compete for passengers on the basis of price, quality, or service differentiation. The company established fares and required that drivers follow strict customer service standards. Drivers had some discretion to choose which trip requests to accept, but there is no evidence that this gave them the ability to alter cost-return ratios (i.e. to make their operations more efficient): SuperShuttle controlled the revenue side by establishing fares, and there is no indication in the record that drivers could do much to shape their costs. The company set drivers' weekly fees. A driver could try to find a cheaper van, but this was presumably difficult given that the vehicles needed to meet particular specifications, such as age and model.[12] They could decline transportation requests that required the driver to travel a long distance to the pickup point. As one driver noted, however, this was a matter of 'common sense', not business strategy.

The company foreclosed the major activities that characterize liberal entrepreneurship. It prohibited drivers from expanding their 'business[es]' (p. 6) by acquiring additional vans or routes. It prohibited drivers from soliciting passengers or otherwise marketing themselves. Nor could drivers work for competitors or in any other kind of transportation business. Drivers could not use work tools in which they had a putative 'proprietary interest', including the vans[13] and communications equipment, for any commercial purpose except driving for SuperShuttle. Thus, SuperShuttle constrained drivers' opportunity for profit via entrepreneurial activity, understood in liberal terms.

Neoliberal Business Activity and Indifference to Institutional Context

Within neoliberal rationality, these constraints become largely irrelevant. Working longer hours is the equivalent of scaling up a business or going into business for oneself. As noted, the majority argued that drivers' ability to drive for SuperShuttle for additional hours 'demonstrated that the franchisees have significant opportunity for economic gain and significant risk of loss' (p. 12), even though drivers had *no* control over how many requests they received, and even though they could do little to alter cost/return ratios. Likewise, the majority claimed that the prohibition against drivers using their vans for other transportation work did not matter, because drivers could still 'maximize their entrepreneurial opportunity' by driving additional hours.[14]

The terminology that the company and NLRB majority used reflects this neoliberal re-imagining of business activity. Accepting transportation requests, including when arriving at the front of the line at the airport, was 'bidding'. As noted, however, drivers could not, in fact, compete ('bid') for passengers based on price, quality, or service differentiation. Nor could they negotiate with SuperShuttle to increase its fare or lower its fees in exchange for accepting a trip request. They 'bid' by being first in line or the first to accept a request. To provide another example, according to the majority, when SuperShuttle sent a transportation request and the driver accepted it, the driver 'obtain[ed] business' (p. 5). Again, drivers had no control over, or means of controlling, trip requests. Yet, the more requests that SuperShuttle sent and that drivers accepted, the greater 'amount of business' the driver 'generat[ed]' (p. 4). The majority also suggested that, whenever SuperShuttle transferred its business costs to drivers, including the costs of vans, fuel, and tolls, it created a potential 'profit margin' for drivers (p. 7).

Just as the neoliberal corporation is less concerned about profiting from returns in product markets, so is the neoliberal individual as an economic agent. She is less focused on maximizing gains from market exchange. Thus, she is less engaged with the activities necessary to maximizing these gains, like producing efficiently, innovating in product markets, and marketing.

We also see a devaluation of product market competition and indifference to institutional context in the majority's argument over the meaning and role of 'entrepreneurial opportunity' in the legal test for employment status. The *SuperShuttle DFW* majority expressly and strongly disagreed with the contention of the dissent and the majority of a previous NLRB decision. The latter insisted that 'entrepreneurial' activity was an aspect to be considered in assessing whether an individual was 'providing services as an independent business'. One moulded in a liberal milieu might query: what is being an 'independent contractor' if not running an independent business? The *SuperShuttle DFW* majority preferred the term 'independence to pursue economic gain' (p. 9). This pursuit was no less entrepreneurial when it took place outside a market, for instance, in a social network or among co-workers (as in hiring a relief driver). Under neoliberal rationality, a corporation—and the individual as a corporate homunculus—pursue economic gain in many venues.

A Contrast for Emphasis

The stark contrast between liberal and neoliberal conceptions of entrepreneurialism is evident in the majority and dissenting opinions in *SuperShuttle DFW*. The *SuperShuttle DFW* dissent distinguished the drivers from independent business operators by drawing upon activities characteristic of operating a business under liberalism. She noted that drivers could not solicit customers, offer discounts, advertise, or do anything else to generate business—evidence that would indicate drivers 'operate in a marketplace' rather than in an employment relationship (p. 28) (dissenting opinion).

The dissenting NLRB member insisted on a notion of entrepreneurialism grounded in the liberal notion of operating an independent business. The dissent critiqued the majority's adoption of the company's argument and terminology that drivers 'bid' on transportation requests:

> SuperShuttle drivers 'bid' on trips, but unlike in conventional bidding (in which contractors contend for work), drivers here lack the ability to compete on price, quality of service, or any other distinguishing variable. Instead, drivers compete primarily to be the first to register interest in a job via the mandated Nextel device—hardly the type of competition that favors entrepreneurial skill. (p. 28) (dissenting opinion)

Another example, from the UK, illustrates the contrast between liberal and neoliberal notions of business activity. In *Aslam & Farrar v Uber* (2018),[15] the Court of Appeal upheld a lower tribunal's finding that Uber drivers were 'workers' under UK law and thus entitled to certain statutory rights. The Court looked for liberal indicia that the alleged independent contractors were in business for themselves. Quoting a previous decision, the Court argued as follows:

> 'a focus upon whether the purported worker actively markets his services as an independent person to the world in general (a person who will thus have a client or customer) on the one hand, or whether he is recruited by the principal to work for that principal as an integral part of the principal's operations, will in most cases demonstrate on which side of the line a given person falls'. (para. 38)

The lower tribunal had rejected Uber's understanding of being in business:

> The notion that Uber in London is a mosaic of 30,000 small businesses linked by a common 'platform' is to our minds faintly ridiculous. In each case, the 'business' consists of a man with a car seeking to make a living by driving it. Ms Bertram spoke of Uber assisting the drivers to 'grow' their businesses, but no driver is in a position to do anything of the kind, unless growing his business simply means spending more hours at the wheel. (As*lam & Farrar v Uber* 2016, para. 90)

In the above quote, we see that the tribunal rejects the suggestion that working longer hours is the equivalent of a scaling up a business. Likewise, the tribunal does not transmute labour into human capital so that labour disappears. It recognizes that Uber drivers are 'seeking to make a living by driving' (As*lam & Farrar v Uber* 2016, para. 90).

Neoliberal Rationality and Means-Ends Logic

We also see a neoliberal understanding of entrepreneurship in the speculative and amorphous means-ends logic the majority depicts as rational calculation. The majority argued that 'the absence of control over franchisees' routes affords franchisees considerable opportunity and independence during those times they choose to work' (p.12). Yet, it did not explain how drivers could strategically use this 'geographic freedom' to increase their income (p. 12). The majority also appeared to endorse the lower tribunal's argument that drivers made 'calculated choices between which trips to choose', arguing that drivers could 'weigh the cost of a particular trip (in terms of time spent, gas, and tolls) against the fare received' (p. 12). These are hardly the kind of 'calculated choices' envisioned within liberal rationality for improving the efficiency of one's operations in a methodological and predictable manner.[16] The dissent notes that, according to a driver who testified in the proceeding, 'deciding whether to accept or decline a bid was "commonsense stuff," based on the time and distance involved in picking up a passenger' (p. 24) (dissenting opinion). What under liberal rationality appears as 'common sense' is a 'calculated choice[]' under neoliberal rationality.

Even the argument that drivers could increase their 'profit' by working longer hours reveals the majority's more speculative notion of entrepreneurship. The majority seems to endorse the lower tribunal's suggestion that deciding when and how long to work was a form of entrepreneurial risk-taking: 'a driver's determination of when and how much he will work impacts his profit margin. All drivers take similar risks, but by their decisions and efforts, they do not all achieve the same profits' (p. 7) (quoting SuperShuttle DFW 2010, p. 21). Working as long as possible increased the *chance* of receiving more trip requests, but, again, drivers could not strategically leverage the latter through longer hours.

Just as risk-taking by the neoliberal firm in financial markets and regulatory venues entails a different means-end logic than risk-taking oriented towards product markets, so does the risk-taking of the neoliberal individual. She is less concerned with the means-ends calculations that go into input/output ratios, advertising, and responsiveness to product demand. She is less methodological and more prone to speculation.

The majority's lack of concern with identifying the commercial gain that drivers might generate through the exercise of their discretion, as well as its depiction of speculation and adventitious possibility as proper entrepreneurial risk-taking, suggests another feature of neoliberal rationality. As others have argued, neoliberal rationality merges the realms of production and reproduction (Feher 2009; Brown 2015). In doing so, however, it does not simply extend economistic reasoning to reproductive domains of activity. It seems also to extend the logic and principles of the reproductive realm to productive domains of activity. We see use-value, the incommensurable, and the unquantifiable attenuating the rational means-ends calculations of the market.

The NLRB majority's notion of entrepreneurialism in *SuperShuttle DFW* is far removed from the liberal notion of entrepreneurialism, which bears some relation to running an independent business and successfully competing by developing, producing, and selling goods or services at a profit. The majority's notion of entrepreneurialism dispenses with the traditional indicia of running a business, like seeking goodwill, marketing oneself, generating new business, creating new products, or producing more efficiently. Liberal calculability associated with these activities is likewise less relevant: sporadic, speculative means-ends determinations replace the methodological logic of liberalism. Neoliberal gain is not about maximizing profit through product market exchange or rational cost–benefit analysis (Brown 2015). Returns from productivity are less important than those from speculating and hedging (Brown 2015). Further, the *SuperShuttle DFW* majority construes every chance a driver has to earn (or lose) money, no matter how detached from the context of product market competition, as an entrepreneurial opportunity.

Over-Contractualization

Over-contractualization is another company practice that tends to cue neoliberal depictions of the worker in legal reasoning. Companies seeking to avoid the statutory obligations of employers often impose or encourage seemingly superfluous contracts between workers.

Some companies include 'substitution rights' in their independent contractor agreements, which permit a worker to contract with a co-worker to perform her work. SuperShuttle's agreement with drivers provided for such an arrangement. Some SuperShuttle drivers provided service to hotels on a regular schedule. If a driver could not work her regular shift, she needed to find a replacement. The contract between a driver and SuperShuttle permitted the driver to use a substitute driver who was the driver's 'employee, agent, shareholder or partner' (p. 6). The majority mostly accepted the company's argument that a driver was 'responsible for finding a replacement, with no involvement from SuperShuttle' (p. 5). However, a driver had to provide written notice to SuperShuttle to use a replacement. And a replacement driver looked much like another SuperShuttle driver, albeit one without a vehicle. The replacement driver needed to undergo SuperShuttle's training and meet SuperShuttle's eligibility requirements for drivers.

FedEx, which characterized its drivers as independent contractors, also engaged in over-contractualization by requiring contractual relationships among co-workers and between superiors and subordinates. For instance, according to FedEx, when a FedEx driver needed someone to cover her shift, or if the workload assigned by FedEx required two persons instead of one, the driver 'hired' another FedEx driver. Superiors (workers who oversaw more than one delivery route) 'hired' their subordinates (FedEx drivers who drove the routes). Some courts interpreted these agreements as evidence that FedEx provided entrepreneurial opportunities to drivers and that drivers were engaged in business on their own accord (*FedEx Home Delivery v NLRB* 2009; *In re FedEx Ground Package System* 2010).

Where a company, as in the case of FedEx and SuperShuttle, places many constraints on the worker's right to 'hire' another, it is often unrealistic for a worker to increase her income in any systematic or substantial fashion by taking advantage of these contracting rights. In *SuperShuttle DFW*, only one or two drivers had used a relief driver. And, while a franchisee driver could hire a relief driver, the former was still obligated to be the principal driver and to supervise directly the vehicle's operation (p. 6).

Contrast these arrangements to how some other service positions work. Employers often simply allow employees to exchange shifts with one another, or they coordinate replacements, without requiring a formal 'contract' between co-workers. Restaurant workers sometimes arrange their own shift exchanges and replacements without using co-worker contracts, for example. Interchanging fungible personnel across positions within a centrally managed process of production would appear to be something employers and co-workers do all of the time without such contracts.

In one sense, these redundant, or pseudo, contracts merely create an illusion that workers are engaged in activities consistent with liberal conceptions of running an independent business, such as hiring employees and managing an efficient productive process.[17]

Yet, neoliberal conceptions of the individual also seem to be at work here in convincing legal decision-makers that these contracts reflect entrepreneurial opportunity. Under a neoliberal conception of entrepreneurial activity, the fact that these contracts are not market exchanges or likely to provide a realistic opportunity for commercial gain is, in part, irrelevant. The contract reflects the worker's reflexive management of her human capital assets—a calculated allocation of risk, obligation, and reward. It entails the prudent management of time.

Further, this exercise of discretion and exchange qualifies as entrepreneurial within neoliberal rationality even where its object is something that liberalism would relegate to the domain of reproduction rather than production. Even finding a replacement to relieve oneself of a day of work is entrepreneurial. We see this notion in the lower tribunal's decision from *SuperShuttle DFW*, which the NLRB majority referenced with approval. The lower tribunal stated that drivers had the 'potential to generate more gross revenue while spending less time driving when a relief driver is hired' (p. 7) (quoting *SuperShuttle DFW* 2010, p. 21). In this statement, the tribunal seems to represent the returns in the cost/return ratio that the driver seeks to minimize *not* in monetary units or quantifiable terms at all. Rather, the returns are the *absence* from work ('spending less time driving').[18] And still, the tribunal finds that the right to hire a relief driver presents an entrepreneurial opportunity.

Conclusion

A neoliberal rendering of the worker tends to conflate discretion with autonomy, and this conflation can become a justification for denying statutory protections to workers. Within neoliberal rationality, where 'control and entrepreneurial opportunity are opposite sides of the same coin' (*SuperShuttle DFW* 2019, p. 9), a worker's exercise of discretion will often appear entrepreneurial. And legal decision-makers can find entrepreneurialism—even of the neoliberal variety—compelling evidence that an individual is an independent contractor excluded from labour law.

A consequence of displacing labour with human 'capital' and erasing the differentiation among kinds of capital is also to erase power differences between workers and capital: whenever the company provides the worker with some discretion, the worker appears to possess *additional* resources apart from her capacity to work (labour power) to bring to the market to earn a living. In other words, 'As capitals, every subject is rendered as entrepreneurial, no matter how small, impoverished, or without resources, and every aspect of human existence is produced as an entrepreneurial one' (Brown 2015, p. 65). This semblance of autonomy contributes to the challenge of establishing that workers who are provided with some discretion in carrying out their work are not independent contractors.

Platform workers certainly take risks, but these are often risks associated with being precarious workers (Weil 2014; Doorn 2017), not independent business owners. In becoming a SuperShuttle franchisee, the driver takes a risk that she will not receive enough trip requests to cover her weekly payments to the company and van lease. And, given the company's control over costs, passenger requests, and fares, she cannot much mitigate this risk or leverage it to her benefit through entrepreneurial acumen. Whenever a driver decides not to work some hours, she likewise takes this risk. The driver also takes the risk that the company will unilaterally change the terms of the franchise agreement to her detriment. Again, this is a risk she cannot mitigate or leverage through entrepreneurial savvy.

Platform companies in particular have been adept at designing work practices that facilitate the neoliberal conflation of discretion and autonomy, and thus at avoiding statutory obligations under labour law. Digital technologies provide many opportunities for a company to programme/design a labour process that permits or requires a worker to undertake discrete exercises of discretion without diminishing the calculability of production for the company. For instance, a platform can permit workers to select their own working times, but the platform can at the same time ensure that it has enough workers available at any particular time to satisfy service requests by hiring workers in excess numbers. It can also transfer business costs to workers, but set pay rates so low that workers can only realize income if they make themselves available at times when the company is offering higher rates of pay.

The use of platform technology in the coordination of production has not provided such a degree of economic autonomy so as to transform all platform workers into independent businesses. Rather, it has facilitated a neoliberal interpretation of the individual worker as a corporate homunculus—a tiny but accurate replica of the neoliberal firm. There is an elective affinity (Weber 1946) between the practices and rhetoric of platform companies and the neoliberal subject. As the platform companies displace—practically and rhetorically—liberal economic norms, practices, and logics with their neoliberal counterparts, the individual worker appears as a new kind of 'entrepreneur', a neoliberal agent.

The liberal ideology of possessive individualism resolved one political obstacle to capitalism. There were no more serfs or slaves, but only a republic of proprietors: one possessed labour as one's property and had a right to make decisions with respect to the disposal of this property. Thus, the class of persons who had nothing to bring to the market to earn a living except their labour was no less autonomous than those with other forms of property. On the doctrinal side, transforming a master-servant relationship into an employment 'contract' was one of liberalism's great legal feats. By partially erasing the distinction between servitude and contract, it lent the legitimacy of law to help obscure the worker's class condition of subordination. Anointing the master-servant relationship with 'freedom of contract' made it easier to reconcile relationships of servitude with liberal ideals of self-governance.

Still, liberal ideology struggled with its own contradictions and legal paradox. Labour is a false commodity, and trying to subject it to the laws of supply and demand creates painful social dislocations (Polanyi 1957). Further, as the economist Oliver Hart (1995) recognized, rights in other kinds of property confer control over human assets (aka workers). Labour is 'complementary' to other property rather than 'autonomous' (Hart 1995). The worker cannot produce marketable goods or services without combining her labour with the property of others. So, the class of persons with other property rights generally dictates the terms of this combination. They much prefer an agreement whereby the worker places her *ability* to labour within their disposal over agreements for the exchange of labour itself. In other words, they often agree only to an employment arrangement, not an independent contracting one. But, by calling employment a 'contract', the law posited that one *can* in fact exchange—*alienate*—one's ability to work, or one's very faculty to take purposive action. Yet, this faculty made one a citizen subject capable of contracting in the first instance.

Liberal ideology and legal reasoning never successfully overcame this contradiction. Instead, there was struggle, compromises, and workarounds. Workers organized to gain greater autonomy and legislatures passed statutory protections. And employers found various ways around statutory protections, for instance, by deeming employees to be independent contractors.

Neoliberal ideology seeks to surpass the accomplishments of liberalism and neuter its contradictions. The liberal ideology of 'freedom of contract' and the employment contract suppressed the distinction between servitude and autonomous exchange. As noted, however, this entailed a legally and politically difficult proposition: that one could buy a person's faculty to take purposive action without actually buying the person. Neoliberalism aspires to moot this problem by erasing the remaining distinction between the employment 'contract' and other contracts. The neoliberal individual is the manager of human capital, capital like any other capital. This individual does not sell her person to an employer but rather invests this human capital, like time and energy, in a temporary alliance. The consequence of introducing this neoliberal subject in legal reasoning is to make statutory protections for workers appear obsolete and further obscure class subordination.

Notes

1. In a previous paper, I explore how platform companies obscure their role as employers by promoting neoliberal conceptions of the firm to account for their labour practices (Tomassetti 2016).
2. In practice, the corporate form often served other purposes, for instance, as a holding company for combinations, a portfolio for income streams, and a speculative vehicle (Fligstein 1990; Roy 1999). As discussed *infra*, a neoliberal theory of the firm better accommodated this reality.
3. For example, only by defining the boundaries of its enterprise according to its contractual and property relations can the on-demand ride company Uber plausibly state that its drivers are engaged in a separate business than Uber. This is because Uber rides are produced via Uber's centralized direction, not the price system: Uber sets passenger fares, assigns drivers and cars to passengers, and strategically suppresses market signals by programming its algorithm to conceal market information from drivers and passengers (Tomassetti 2016). Instead of defining its enterprise according

to the firm/market boundaries of liberal theory however, Uber contends that its enterprise boundaries are located where its formal legal relations with drivers begin (a putatively arms-length technology 'license'), and where its formal property relations end (between ownership of its information technology and lack of ownership of drivers' vehicles). Under a liberal understanding of the firm, such as the definition of economist Ronald Coase (1937), the drivers would be located within Uber as a firm. However, this would make it quite difficult to claim that the drivers were independent contractors (Tomassetti 2016).

4. Some regulations were intended to ensure passengers received a standardized experience reflecting the 'unique' SuperShuttle brand, and others were intended to meet its clients' specifications (*SuperShuttle DFW* 2019, p. 26). The regulations could be quite specific. For example, van seats could have 'no more than two small holes' (p. 4).
5. Although *SuperShuttle DFW* is an agency decision rather than a court decision, its legal consequence extends beyond the underlying dispute. Subsequent decisions have since adopted its reasoning. Further, the NLRB's General Counsel relied on the reasoning from *SuperShuttle DFW* in an advice memorandum (2019). The memorandum finds that drivers for the on-demand platform Uber are independent contractors. Since the General Counsel is responsible for representing workers before the NLRB, the memorandum in effect deprives these drivers of the statutory rights to organize and collectively bargain, and signals that the NLRB is likely to deprive other platform workers of their rights as well (Mishel and McNicholas 2019).
6. The worker generally must begin committing her effort and attention to the platform as soon as she logs in. Upon her logging in, the platform treats her as part of its active workforce. It may provide only a matter of seconds to accept an assignment/request (*Aslam & Farrar v Uber* 2017, p. 5). However, platforms often pay the worker only for the time she is directly servicing customers, for instance, when transporting a passenger or delivering a meal (*Aslam & Farrar v Uber* 2017; *R (on the application of Independent Workers Union of Great Britain) v Central Arbitration Committee* 2018).
7. A driver could transfer her franchise to another driver if she met SuperShuttle's requirements and received its consent. The chapter does not discuss this right, because the decision does not argue that this right reflects entrepreneurial opportunity and does not focus on it in its analysis.

8. The court ruled against Grubhub on the summary motion in which it made these arguments (*Lawson v Grubhub* 2017). The court later ruled that the delivery worker was an independent contractor (*Lawson v Grubhub* 2018). The decision was not based on the argument that the plaintiff had any entrepreneurial opportunity, however. In fact, the court found that the delivery worker was not 'engaged in a distinct occupation or business' (p. 1089). Rather, the court ruled on behalf of Grubhub because it found that Grubhub did not exercise sufficient control over the manner and means of the plaintiff's work for the plaintiff to qualify as its employee. The decision illustrates that not all legal tests and courts consider entrepreneurial opportunity to be the determinative factor in disputes over employment status. It also illustrates that not all courts interpret employer-designed discretion, including a worker's discretion to establish her own hours, as entrepreneurial opportunity. The case is now on appeal.
9. The obverse is not necessarily true. The author is unaware of any jurisdiction where the law precludes professionals from being employees.
10. The majority recognized, for example, that SuperShuttle was 'clearly involved in the business of transporting customers' and that this factor weighed in favour of finding employment status (*SuperShuttle DFW* 2019, p. 14).
11. Only one out of eighty-eight drivers had hired a relief driver. Neither the lower tribunal's decision nor the NLRB decision indicates why drivers did not seek to make greater use of relief drivers. The dissent suggested it might be due to SuperShuttle's strict requirements for working as a relief driver. SuperShuttle also imposed restrictions on a driver's ability to use a relief driver. Drivers had to be trained by SuperShuttle and meet the company's other eligibility requirements for drivers. The company had to approve of the relief driver and receive advance written notice of a driver's decision to use one.
12. The decision does not mention this possibility or whether this was a realistic option. Perhaps drivers could also look to purchasing cheaper gas and hiring cheaper mechanics. Again, the decision does not address these questions or how they would present a realistic means for drivers to better their livelihoods. However, in a dispute over the employment status of FedEx delivery drivers, who were also required to pay for delivery vehicles, FedEx argued that the potential to find cheaper mechanics was evidence of drivers' entrepreneurial opportunity (*FedEx Home Delivery v NLRB* 2009, Brief of Petitioner/Cross-Respondent).

13. The franchise agreement apparently did not prohibit expressly drivers from using the vans for other purposes; however, it severely restricted their ability to use the vehicles for any commercial purposes by prohibiting their involvement in any other kind of transportation business. That the vans had to be outfitted for passengers and display SuperShuttle's colours and insignia also limited their usefulness in other undertakings.
14. The majority argued that, because the market for airport transport was 'competitive', drivers could probably earn just as much by working longer than by doing other work (*SuperShuttle DFW* 2019, n. 29). The dissenting NLRB member observed that this reckoning was speculative. The dissent also noted it was suspect to conclude that the market was 'competitive' when SuperShuttle restricted drivers from doing any other transportation work.
15. The UK Supreme Court recently upheld this decision in a unanimous ruling (*Uber BV v Aslam*).
16. Further, from SuperShuttle's website, it appears that one element of 'time spent'—the time required to drive the passenger to her destination—was likely already incorporated in the fare (SuperShuttle Express blog, March 17, 2019). If so, this was not a variable by which drivers could substantially shape their income.
17. Over-contractualization also helps a company depict multilateral relationships of production among co-workers, which the company centrally coordinates, as dyadic market exchanges (Tomassetti 2015). Positing contracts between co-workers likewise helps conceal the hub-and-spoke authority relations between the company and its workers. The company's role in directing production is thereby less visible, also making its role as an employer less visible.
18. The statement is somewhat ambiguous. Perhaps the tribunal presumed that the franchisee driver would hire a relief driver in order to spend time at a commercial pursuit.

References

Aslam & Farrar v Uber, [2015] Nos. 2202550/2015 (London Employment Tribunal, Oct. 28, 2016).

Aslam & Farrar v Uber, [2017] No. UKEAT/0056/17/DA (London Employment Appeal Tribunal, Nov. 10, 2017).

Aslam & Farrar v Uber, [2018] EWCA Civ 2748, 2018 WL 06625651 (Court of Appeal, Dec. 19, 2018).

Awuah v Coverall North America, Inc., 707 F.Supp.2d 80 (US District Court, District of Massachusetts, March 23, 2010).

Becker, Gary S. 1962. "Investment in Human Capital: A Theoretical Analysis." *Journal of Political Economy* 70 (5): 9–49.

Brown, Wendy. 2015. *Undoing the Demos—Neoliberalism's Stealth Revolution.* New York: Zone Books.

Chandler, Alfred D. 1977. *The Visible Hand: The Managerial Revolution in American Business.* Cambridge, MA: Belknap Press of Harvard University Press.

Coase, Ronald H. 1937. "The Nature of the Firm." *Economica* 4 (16): 386–405.

Corporate Express Delivery Systems v NLRB, 292 F.3d 777 (US Court of Appeals, D.C. Circuit, June 11, 2002).

Davis, Gerald F. 2009. *Managed by the Markets: How Finance Reshaped America.* Oxford: Oxford University Press.

Davis, Gerald F. 2016. "What Might Replace the Modern Corporation: Uberization and the Web Page Enterprise." *Seattle University Law Review* 39 (2): 501–516.

De Giovanni v Jani-King Int'l, Inc., 968 F. Supp. 2d 447 (US District Court, District of Massachusetts, Sept. 12, 2013).

Doorn, Niels van. 2017. "Platform Labor: On the Gendered and Racialized Exploitation of Low-Income Service Work in the 'On-Demand' Economy." *Information, Communication & Society* 20 (6): 898–914.

Dore, Ronald. 2008. "Financialization of the Global Economy." *Industrial and Corporate Change* 17 (6): 1097–1112.

Fabbri, Tommaso. 2018. "Digital Work: An Organizational Perspective." In Working in Digital and Smart Organizations: Legal, Economic and Organizational Perspectives on the Digitalization of Labour Relations, edited by Edoardo Ales, Ylenia Curzi, Tommaso Fabbri, Olga Rymkevich, Iacopo Senatori, and Giovanni Solinas, 29–38. Cham: Palgrave Macmillan.

FedEx Home Delivery v NLRB, 563 F.3d 492 (US Court of Appeals, D.C. Circuit, April 21, 2009).

Feher, Michel. 2009. "Self-Appreciation; or, The Aspirations of Human Capital." *Public Culture* 21 (1): 21–41.

Fligstein, Neil. 1990. *The Transformation of Corporate Control*. Cambridge: Harvard University Press.

Foucault, Michel. 2008. *The Birth of Biopolitics: Lectures at the Collège de France, 1978–1979*. New York, NY: Palgrave Macmillan.

Gershon, Ilana. 2011. "Neoliberal Agency." *Current Anthropology* 52 (4): 537–555.

Gershon, Ilana. 2014. "Selling Your Self in the United States." *PoLAR: Political and Legal Anthropology Review* 37 (2): 281–295.

Gershon, Ilana. 2018. "Employing the CEO of Me, Inc.: US Corporate Hiring in a Neoliberal Age." *American Ethnologist* 45 (2): 173–185.

Gerth, Hans, and Charles Wright Mills. 1946. *From Max Weber: Essays in Sociology*. New York: Oxford University Press.

Hart, Oliver. 1995. *Firms, Contracts, and Financial Structure*. Oxford: Oxford University Press.

In re FedEx Ground Package System, Inc., 734 F.Supp.2d 557 (US District Court, Northern District of Indiana, Aug. 11, 2010) *reversed*, *in re* FedEx Ground Package Sys., Inc. Emp't Practices Litig., 792 F.3d 818 (US Court of Appeals, 7th Circuit, July 8, 2015).

Jensen, Michael C., and William H. Meckling. 1976. "Theory of the Firm: Managerial Behavior, Agency Costs and Ownership Structure." *Journal of Financial Economics* 3 (4): 305–360.

Kraakman, Reinier. 2001. "The Durability of the Corporate Form." In *The Twenty-First-Century Firm: Changing Economic Organization in International Perspective*, edited by Paul DiMaggio, 147–60. Princeton, NJ: Princeton University Press.

Krippner, Greta R. 2005. "The Financialization of the American Economy." *Socio-Economic Review* 3 (2): 173–208.

Lawson v Grubhub, Inc., No. 15-CV-05128-JSC, 2017 WL 2951608 (US District Court, Northern District of California, July 10, 2017).

Lawson v Grubhub, Inc., 302 F. Supp. 3d 1071, 1073 (US District Court, Northern District of California, Feb. 8, 2018).

Litvak, Anya. 2010. "FedEx Ground Makes Change to Independent Contractor Model." *Pittsburgh Business Times*. http://www.bizjournals.com/pittsburgh/stories/2010/06/14/story4.html?page=all. Accessed on Jan. 18, 2021.

Mishel, Lawrence, and Celine McNicholas. 2019. *Uber Drivers Are Not Entrepreneurs: NLRB General Counsel Ignores the Realities of Driving for Uber*. Washington, DC: Economic Policy Institute. https://www.epi.org/

publication/uber-drivers-are-not-entrepreneurs-nlrb-general-counsel-ignores-the-realities-of-driving-for-uber/. Accessed on Jan. 15, 2021.

Moisander, Johanna, Claudia Groß, and Kirsi Eräranta. 2018. "Mechanisms of Biopower and Neoliberal Governmentality in Precarious Work: Mobilizing the Dependent Self-Employed as Independent Business Owners." *Human Relations* 71 (3): 375–398.

National Labor Relations Board Office of the General Counsel. April 16, 2019. Advice Memorandum. *Uber Technologies, Inc.*

Polanyi, Karl. 1957. *The Great Transformation.* Boston, MA: Beacon Press.

Pollman, Elizabeth, and Jordan M. Barry. 2017. "Regulatory Entrepreneurship." *Southern California Law Review* 90 (3): 383–448.

R (on the application of Independent Workers Union of Great Britain) v Central Arbitration Committee, [2018] EWHC 3342, 2018 WL 06330550 (High Court of Justice Queen's Bench Division Administrative Court, Dec. 5, 2018).

Razak v Uber Technologies, Inc., No. 16-573, 2018 WL 1744467 (US District Court, Eastern District of Pennsylvania, April 11, 2018) *Vacated and Remanded*, 951 F.3d 137 (US Court of Appeals, 3rd Circuit, March 3, 2020).

Roy, William G. 1999. *Socializing Capital*. Princeton, NJ: Princeton University Press.

SuperShuttle DFW, Inc. and Amalgamated Transit Union Local 1338, Case 16–RC–010963. (National Labor Relations Board Region 6, Aug. 16, 2010).

SuperShuttle DFW, Inc. and Amalgamated Transit Union Local 1338, 367 N.L.R.B. No. 75, 2019 BL 24595 (National Labor Relations Board, Jan. 25, 2019).

SuperShuttle Express, "How to Find Pricing Ahead of Time." March 27, 2019, https://www.supershuttle.com/blog/find-advance-pricing-supershuttle/. Accessed on Jan. 16, 2021.

Tomassetti, Julia. 2015. "From Hierarchies to Markets: FedEx Drivers and the Work Contract as Institutional Marker." *Lewis & Clark Law Review* 19 (4): 1083–1152.

Tomassetti, Julia. 2016. "Does Uber Redefine the Firm: The Postindustrial Corporation and Advanced Information Technology." *Hofstra Labor & Employment Law Journal* 34 (1): 1–78.

Uber BV v Aslam, [2021] UKSC 5 (Supreme Court, Feb. 19, 2021).

Weil, David. 2014. *The Fissured Workplace: Why Work Became So Bad for So Many and What Can Be Done to Improve It*. Harvard: Harvard University Press.

Zwick, Austin. 2018. "Welcome to the Gig Economy: Neoliberal Industrial Relations and the Case of Uber." *GeoJournal* 83 (4): 679–691.

8

Is the Structure of Employee Representation Institutions in Europe Adapted to the Economic Transformations? Analysis and Proposals from the Spanish Case

Helena Ysàs Molinero

Background: New Production Structures, Same Worker Representation Bodies?

Workplaces and work centres have been affected in recent years by multiple and deep transformations that have altered the company and its production structures. Transformations have been driven by a number of factors, among which globalization, increased competence between companies, the emergence of new economic power in the global world scenario, industrial offshoring processes, technological innovation, and new forms of production organizing (flexible production, just-in-time, lean production): all of them, and some others, have contributed to a profound redefinition of companies and of the space they occupy in

H. Ysàs Molinero (✉)
Labour and Social Security Law, Universitat Autònoma de Barcelona, Barcelona, Spain
e-mail: Helena.Ysas@uab.cat

T. Addabbo et al. (eds.), *The Collective Dimensions of Employment Relations*, https://doi.org/10.1007/978-3-030-75532-4_8

the wealth creation processes (Riesco-Sanz 2012). Outsourcing, digitalization and changes in the share of employment corresponding to industrial and service sectors, among other factors, have determined the downsizing of companies' individual workforce in many pre-existing establishments (Fita Ortega 2017) and completely different structures in newly created companies. Establishments are now frequently much smaller or composed by employees pertaining to different companies. This phenomenon has been accompanied by a blurring of the work centre as a permanent standpoint, consequently to the increasing of jobs implying daily mobility and distance work. Platform economy business models are probably the main exponent of maximizing a profit by minimizing (employee status-recognized) workforce and pose extremely serious problems to the building of employee representation structures, to the point of making them unviable in the terms of current legislations, with very scarce room also to trade union representations where a double channel exists (Esteban 2018; Gutiérrez 2019; Guerrero 2019). Finally, in some countries it is not unusual that employees who lose their jobs start activities as independent workers as the only way out of unemployment. This happened very clearly, i.e. in Spain, in the employment crisis that followed the 2008 financial crackdown. In fact, public powers have encouraged such an individual response to massive unemployment, by trying to build a discourse—or a tall tale—on entrepreneurship. Reality is that these independent workers often perform tasks previously developed by employees under similar subordination conditions but they are not recognized as employees. All in all, companies have considerably enlarged forms of obtaining economic activity from a large number of producers without the need of hiring them as employees, thus, they provide services under real but no legal subordination: "companies without workers and workers without companies" (Riesco-Sanz 2012).

All these phenomena have a strong impact on employee representation, most especially in small- and medium-sized companies (SMEs), whose employees risk losing access to representation as consequence of downsizing. At the same time, many of these SMEs act as subcontractors for other firms—as much as half of them, according to Bouquin et al.'s estimations (2007)—and consequently their staff will probably be spread across a number of contractors' establishments, making it very difficult to build representation structures for these employees.

In fact, counteracting the effects of contracting out on employee representation bodies is one of the major challenge representation institutions need to face across Europe. It is not only a technical matter of reaching thresholds, that can be solved by legislative changes, it is also a more profound issue as outsourcing of activities might imply both a physical dispersion of workers and a dispersion of their interests leading to a weakening of trade unions' capability to represent workers' interests with exceptions in branches where trade union presence is strong and consolidated (Fita Ortega 2017). That weakening will make it more difficult to create representation structures even where this would hypothetically be possible.

Notwithstanding, a previous problem needs to be solved. It is related to the nowadays existing employee representation structure, which is often inconsistent with the corresponding company structure.

European Legislative Shortcomings: The Spanish Case as Example

National regulations on employee representation in the workplace have not always accompanied all these transformations. On the contrary, they have frequently remained petrified, so that the disparity between company structures and workplace reality and legal provisions intended at guaranteeing employees a representation to supervise regulatory accomplishment on the part of the company and to defend their rights and interests, including collective bargaining, has strongly increased. The fact that many EU countries exclude workers in small- and medium-sized companies from employee representation by fixing high thresholds in countries where precisely SMEs are majority "seriously reduce the potential for collective representation and the exercise of union rights at the workplace level" (Bouquin et al. 2007, p. 18). However, as Supiot (2007) reminds, worker representation has not ceased to be, together with negotiation and collective action, one of the pillars of social dialogue, which cannot develop if there are no actors to represent the interests in place.

This is the reason why employee representation structures should be revised.

To illustrate this assertion with cyphers, the following can be mentioned: for EU countries with employee representatives (work councils or equivalent institutions), the thresholds are changing in a wide range of 5 to 50 employees. Industrial relations systems have of course different characteristics and direct comparisons do not always reflect comparable situations. Also many other items can nuance the effect of a particular regulation, starting with the fact that the employee representation body is based, and so the threshold calculated, at company or establishment level, a decisive issue that will be further developed in this paper. The existence of trade union representations and how they relate to employee-elected representations is relevant. Just as an overview, examples of countries with low thresholds (5–6) are Austria, Czech Republic, Germany, Latvia, Slovakia or Spain. Other countries such as Portugal, Estonia or Lithuania do not fix a threshold at all. At the same time, other countries such as the UK, Poland, Norway or the Netherlands establish thresholds as high as 50 employees, even though in some cases minor representative bodies can exist in smaller production units (Eurofound 2014).

Despite the fact that by only mentioning these numbers the picture is for sure incomplete or even inaccurate, they transmit quite clearly the idea that an extremely high number of establishments and employees in the EU lack collective representation at the workplace.

Therefore, strong shortcomings can be identified in many countries' current legislations regarding worker representation structures and thresholds, as these often fail to guarantee that large numbers of workers effectively do have voice in their companies as contemplated in these same regulations. This aggravates severely the deficiencies made evident in the last decades in the field of industrial democracy and stirs very interesting debates on how industrial democracy could be deepened. Lately some proposals have been formulated in this context, such as that of Ferreras (2017), who advocates for a democratization of companies by granting employees at least the same political rights in the governance of the company as the capital owners have, through a mechanism she names "economic bicameralism", where capital and labour investors would be represented equally. Certainly, the debate on how the dissociation of democracy and the institutional structure of companies should be addressed but as interesting as it might be, it is not the focus of this paper. However, bringing on the table Ferreras' reflections on the lack of voice citizens experiment when they become employees is pertinent to the main point of this paper. She argues that people raised as citizens in a democracy aspire to have a say in their lives, but that ambition is in total contradiction with the functioning of companies, and so experience in the world of work can be very frustrating in this respect and does not respond to the aspiration of large segments of the population. This makes the case for defending at very least the need of strong representation structures.

However, the lack of voice within the company is glaring if we consider the large amounts of workers who do not even have a representative to stand for their rights and interests. Consequently, legal changes to grant that every employee does have a voice within the firm through a representative are urgent. This argument is in line with more general statements proposed by prestigious labour law scholars such as Alain Supiot (2007), who holds that representation of workers is one dimension of collective relations affected by the changes in the organization of labour occurred during the last years, while the field of small companies remains free from collective representation. He concludes that an adaptation of collective labour law to the new forms of organizing developed by companies is needed.

From this standpoint a discussion on how the problem regarding unadapted workplace representation structures could be solved, or, at least, mitigated, will follow. First, some specific maladjustments that are key to producing the mentioned results need to be identified.

I intend to do that by using one blatant example: one of the countries where the imbalance is particularly serious is Spain, as its legislation on employee representation structures has never undergone a reform since it was approved in 1980—a legislation that had some serious shortcomings already at the time. That categorical statement can be sustained even though at first glance—see figures published by Eurofound and mentioned above—Spain could be classified among the countries with a lower threshold and, consequently, among those who guarantee to a greater extent representation rights. It is true that the law fixes a threshold of 6 employees. However, the Spanish regulations base employee representation on the establishment level, banning the use of the undertaking level to elect representatives. That point, together with some other issues that will be mentioned next, is key to understand why so many Spanish employees lack workplace representation. At the same time, the notion of establishment defined by the law and the interpretation given by the courts result in considering every single production unit, the small and simple it might be, as an establishment. The courts also restrict the possibility of modifying employee representation structures through collective agreements. The only provision existing in order to facilitate the grouping of two or more establishments to obtain employee representation is limited to those with 10 or more employees each and settled in the same province (Spain has 57 of them), thus a possibility extremely limited. In the following lines these issues will be developed.

As mentioned, the consideration of the establishment as constituency, that is, that employee representatives are not elected at company level but at establishment level is highly relevant. In fact, the law is not completely clear on that point. On the contrary, its wording is quite confusing: Article 62.1 and 63.1 of the Statute of Workers[1] say that "representation of employees in the company or working centre (…) corresponds to worker delegates" and that "The works council is the representative body for all workers in the company or in the work centre (…)". This led a number of academics in the 80s and 90s to maintain that there was no obstacle to interpret the legal provision so as a choice between the company as a whole or its establishments was possible (scholar positions compiled by Rojo (1999), who shared the view that a flexible understanding of articles 62 and 63 was possible). However, it is also true that it is not unreasonable to interpret that the employee representatives need to be elected at establishment level or at company level only when the company does have one only establishment. That interpretation can be upheld by the same Article 63.1 "(…) by creating [a works council] in every establishment employing 50 or more people", as well as by Article 63.2, mentioning the precise cases in which establishments can elect a joint works council. By using these arguments the Supreme Court declared in two 2001 judgements—and has maintained ever since—that no choice is possible and that the constituency is the work centre.[2] Excluding the possibility of constituting the workers' representation bodies at company level entails of course very serious consequences, especially in a context where, as described above, companies and work centres are downsizing.

That key element to the exclusion of many employees from being entitled to elect representatives is accompanied by a number of other factors, all of them leading to the same direction. These are mainly related to the huge restrictions to joint representation structures in the Spanish legislation and judicial interpretation.

As for the legal regulation of joint representation structures, Article 63.2 of the Statute of Workers sets a limited geographical criterion: work centres can only elect joint representation bodies if they are situated in the same province (administrative geographical division) or in the rare case of being situated in a town pertaining to another province but bordering the first. If the geographical criterion in these terms could have some sense in 1980, this is certainly unjustified in 2020. Communication technologies make it perfectly possible that groups of employees geographically far one from the other but sharing working conditions and interests keep in touch and are represented together in front of the company.[3]

A further restriction derives from the fact that the law contemplates that in case some establishment reaches the number of 50 employees within the eligible geographical framework that establishment will not participate in the joint representation, that is, if for example one establishment has 51 employees and the other establishments together 48, the first will have its own works council but the others will enjoy no worker representation at all, as, once excluded the first one, the others do not reach the number of 50 employees. In that case, the law leaves little room to interpretation, as it is quite clear in this point.

Additionally, and very importantly, the severe deficiencies of the legal regulation are shown by the fact that the law does not mention the possibility of adding work centres to elect not a joint works council but a joint personnel delegate or delegates. Note that in Spain personnel delegates and works councils are attributed exactly the same functions; the constitution of one or the other depends on the number of employees an establishment has (up to 49 employees personnel delegates and 50 employees or more works councils). Having both figures exactly the same functions and being the only difference between them the number of employees they represent and the number of representatives (1–3 in the case of personnel delegates and 5–75 in the case of works councils) a justification to admit joint works councils but no joint personnel delegates is hard to find: if joint works councils are used to enable employee representation in case of a plurality of work centres that don't reach the threshold required to elect works councils separately, the same rule should be applied for those establishments that do not reach the threshold to have personnel delegates separately but they would reach the threshold together. The legal gap could have given place to an interpretation of the Supreme Court by resorting to analogy or even by using purpose interpretation instead of limiting to a word-by-word interpretation of the law (both interpretation means are considered in the Spanish Civil Code). In fact, admitting the possibility of choosing joint delegates would by itself expand to a large extent employee representation in small- and medium-sized companies with more than one work centre in the same geographical area.

Still, limitations to joint works councils do not finish here. Works centres with less than 6 employees are excluded form electing representatives; this is the threshold applicable in Spain, as in other countries other thresholds apply. But the law does not say whether these employees will be counted to determine whether the threshold is reached to constitute a joint works council. Despite the law being silent on that point, the Supreme Court has determined that these employees are not to be counted. The argument used is debatable, because not having enough dimension to elect their own representatives does not necessarily lead to the conclusion that they cannot be considered to elect a joint body representing a plurality of establishments. The logic of the threshold is of course that in small works centres employees do not need representatives as they are capable to represent themselves because they are few and close to the employer. But in the case maybe not of small-sized companies but of medium-sized or even of large companies with many small works centres, can employees really represent themselves in front of the employer? Is really the employer so close to them that negotiations can take place directly without the need of intermediaries? The answer is probably not, so thresholds should maybe not be the same for single work centre small-sized companies than for plural work-centre larger companies, or at least in that case small work centres should be able to join in order to obtain common representatives. As it is the case with the current jurisprudence, employees in a company with many small works centres cannot elect representatives, no matter how many workers the company employs in a specific geographical area and no matter how many works centres it has. Therefore, large companies with large workforce can avoid employee representation if they are organized in small works centres.

Here the legal definition of a work centre and its interpretation appears again as decisive. The work centre is defined in Article 1.5 of the Statute of Workers as "a production unit with specific organization and registered with the Public Administration". The last requirement is purely formal, as its absence does not determine that the unit is not considered a work centre. In fact, the most relevant element is the "specific organisation", which is in general understood in quite flexible terms, so that the fact that a middle-level manager is based at the work centre and that he or she is able to take some decisions regarding day-to-day organization, such as hiring or distribution of working time is enough to consider that a separate work centre exists. Consequently, as Pastor Martínez (2018, p. 224) puts it, the application of that regulation "is not neutral and it does not necessarily respond to objective realities", uninfluenced by the interests of the parties. On the contrary, the employer has room to determine the boundaries of his or her work centres by taking some organization decisions and so he or she can manoeuvre to obtain wished results in terms of division of the company in work centres and to minimize the presence of employee representatives.

Further limitations to joint representation bodies need to be related. Not only employees working in work centres under 6 employees are not counted, but employees in work centres with 6 to 10 employees are only counted if such employees previously organize a vote and decide for that participation. This statement set by the Supreme Court in judgement of 20th February 2008 and others has been severely criticized by scholars (for instance, Cabeza Pereiro 2009), especially since the Constitutional Court had previously established in the case of a work centre by work centre election that a vote to decide whether a vote to choose a representative is organized is not needed. On the contrary, the vote to choose a representative can be organized and if employees participate by majority to it, it will be considered that they consent the vote. The Constitutional Court privileges that interpretation (judgement of 8th March 2004), by arguing that it is the interpretation needed to sufficiently safeguard the fundamental right to trade union freedom of association. Therefore, it can be interpreted that the restriction set by the Supreme Court, as far as it is not a direct requirement of the law, is contrary to the fundamental right of union freedom of association.

Finally, one last mention to the—again—very limited possibility that the Spanish legislation offers to create a joint committee at company level ("inter work centre committee" in a direct linguistic translation) that groups the different works councils or personnel delegates already existing in the respective work centres. That is, the so-called joint committee is a second-degree representative body that is created so that companies with multiple workplaces can count with a space where issues common to the different workplaces can be discussed. However, it must be underlined that the joint committee presupposes the existence of a plurality of work centre representative bodies. That is, it does not solve the problem of employees who do not have representatives in their work centres. Even in the cases of companies including work centres with representatives and other work centres without them, the joint committee will be composed by the previously elected representatives, so none of them will come from the establishments that could not elect representatives. Consequently, a distance between members of the joint committee and employees in work centres without representation is inevitable. Furthermore, the creation of the joint committee is not automatic once more than one work centre elect representatives. It will only be possible if the applicable collective agreement includes and regulates that institution. Also, the joint committee will have the competences that the collective agreement includes. Its functioning is also determined by the agreement.

As a result of all the above described regulatory limitations and Court interpretations, the number of employees who are not covered by employee representation in Spain is extremely high. The following data illustrate the preceding affirmation: 78.7% of companies have no establishment with employee representatives, as none of them has 6 employees or more. As for the resting 21.3% of companies, they might not have worker representation in some of their work centres. Moreover, less than half of the Spanish employees (47.4%) do have employee representatives, and the percentage is especially low in the case of precarious workers (37%), women (44.2%) and young employees under 25 (34%) (Alós et al. 2015).

The previous data also bring about the need of a reflection on abidance by Directive 2002/14/EC establishing a general framework for informing and consulting employees in the European Union. First, it is true that the Directive is lax in its definitions, leaving room to Member States to maintain very dissimilar definitions of undertaking and, especially, establishment, resulting in extremely different demands in terms of where employees will have to be consulted. The States can choose to apply the Directive whether to undertakings with at least 50 employees or to establishments with at least 20 employees. In countries where employee representation bodies are based on establishment level the second option will be chosen, as the first one would imply having to inform and consult at a level where no representatives are often found (e.g. in Spain many companies with more than 50 employees but divided in small establishments under 6 employees have no representatives at all). In that case, the obligation or non-obligation to inform and consult employees will depend on the national definition of the concept "establishment". The definition provided by the Directive considers that it means "a unit of business defined in accordance with national law and practice, and located within the territory of a Member State, where an economic activity is carried out on an ongoing basis with human and material resources". From a formal point of view, the Spanish definition of establishment is probably consistent with the Directive, as it is defined as a production unit with "a specific organization". However, interpretation of that last requirement by Courts is so broad that, as mentioned above, almost every production unit will be defined as an establishment. This results in a multiplication of establishments that makes it very often difficult to reach the threshold of 20 employees, and so it reduces to a great extent the scope of the Directive. That practical result can bring into question whether Spain—and probably many other States—is really providing the legal framework necessary to accomplish with the Directive's material provisions, consisting in consulting "at the relevant level of management and representation" (Article 4.4 (b)) on the recent and probable development of the undertaking's or establishment's activities and economic situation; on the situation, structure and probable development of employment within the undertaking or establishment and on any anticipatory measures envisaged; and on decisions likely to lead to substantial changes in work organization or in contractual relations (Article 4.2). If a State uses a very restrictive definition of establishment that even allows employers to artificially split companies, isn't it failing to fulfil with the obligations fixed by the Directive?

The Court of Justice of the European Union (CJEU) has never pronounced on that specific matter. However, other cases might bring light to that point. In Judgement AMS v. CGT (C-176-12, 14 January 2014) the Court stated that the examined national legislation (in that case it was a French provision excluding a category of employees from being counted to determine if thresholds were reached) "has the consequence of exempting certain employers from the obligations laid down in Directive 2002/14 and of depriving their employees of the rights granted under that directive. Consequently, it is liable to render those rights meaningless and thus make that directive ineffective" (paragraph 25). In following paragraph 27, the Court affirms that "the margin of discretion that the Member States in matters of social policy cannot have the effect of frustrating the implementation of a fundamental principle of European Union law or of a provision of that law". The Court also reminds (paragraph 28) that Article 11 of the Directive requires Member States to take all necessary steps enabling them to guarantee the results imposed by Directive 2002/14 and declares that a provision of the Directive cannot be interpreted so that it allows Member States to evade the obligation to reach a clear and precise result imposed by European Union law. This issue would certainly deserve a deeper analysis and it is a path that to my mind is worth going through, but the limited extension of this work makes it necessary to leave it for future developments.

Alternatives to Be Found in the European Context: In Particular, the French Model

This work aims to explore regulatory alternatives that other countries have adopted to ensure a wider coverage of employee representation institutions, with a particular attention to the recent reforms that France has implemented in that field.

As a matter of fact, France's worker representation structure is worth taking into consideration. Even though quite a complex institution, regulations on the new social and economic committee (CSE) (works council) guarantee to a much wider extent than that of other European countries that a larger number of employees are represented. In fact, the old institutions, personnel delegates, works councils and hygiene and security committees also did that (Giraudet 2018). Starting from the company level, where a works council is compulsory if the company as a whole has at least 11 employees, a range of possibilities are deployed, from establishment works councils plus a centralized works council to an "economic and social unit" works council, which might regroup different companies with close economic linkages, to "inter-companies" works councils joining employees and employers of different companies sharing the workplace. Collective agreements are called to specify the possibilities offered by the law. Collective bargaining can also define the boundaries of the concept "establishment" to these effects in every single case.

In essence, the main difference between the Spanish and the French model is the space where employee representation is based: whereas in Spain employee representation is based on the workplace and the possibilities of pushing representation to a larger level, whereas company or even multi-work centre level are extremely limited, in France the representation is based *at least* in the company level and maximum flexibility is then used to create representative bodies in lower or higher-level spaces depending on the interests at stake and with the participation of the parties implied.

The main possibilities offered by the French legislation have been mentioned, but it is interesting to observe some more details of the French legal framework as it is an example of how worker representation can be regulated so that a much larger number of employees obtain representation in the workplace, compared to Spain.

To be more precise, the perimeter of the representation bodies is to be negotiated by the social partners, that is, trade union representatives, or by the company works council itself, together with the employer. They can determine the boundaries of a "distinct establishment", that can correspond to one single or multiple workplaces. Only if the agreement could not be reached (lack of agreement with the trade unions or lack of legitimated trade unions and impossibility to reach an agreement with the works council), can the employer determine unilaterally a distinct establishment. In any case, the fixation of distinct establishments can never be used as a tool to avoid the constitution of employee representation bodies,[4] as a company works council will always exist (whereas a company CSE if no distinct establishments are fixed or a central CSE otherwise). Additionally, the employer's decision can be contested in front of the administrative authority, which will decide whether justification enough to the fixation of a distinct establishment following the legal criteria is proved. These legal criteria can be reduced to the fact that the distinct establishment is an appropriate context to carry out the functions corresponding to personnel representatives, where significant management autonomy concerning the staff decisions is exercised by a head of establishment; the distinct establishment is then a legal concept not necessarily corresponding to a physical establishment.

The company collective agreement can also include the creation of another figure: the proximity delegate. That delegate, who can be a member of the CSE or simply designed by it, will be designed in a more reduced field compared to the company CSE or even the distinct establishment CSE and its functions, quantity and functioning will be determined by the collective agreement itself. The idea is that they stay close to the employees to defend their rights by, for instance, presenting claims to the employer.

A group works council can also be established so that employees can be consulted at group level about strategic business orientations. At the same time, a collective agreement signed by two or more companies can establish an intercompany CSE whenever the nature and importance of the problems common to these companies, settled in the same site or even in a shared geographical zone, justify the need of a common body. Here again, the regulation of all the details is left to the social partners, who will establish the number of representatives, the functions associated to that body, etc. In any case, an intercompany CSE will not substitute each participating company's CSE.

Another possibility offered by the French legislation is the constitution of a so-called economic and social unity (UES) works council. The economic and social unity is defined as an ensemble of separated companies closely bonded one to the other. A UES is not a group of companies, which is defined as an ensemble of companies where one company is the parent company and the others are subsidiary or controlled companies. In the UES ties can be conformed in many ways, but there must be a common interest for employees of the different companies that justifies the convenience of establishing a joint representation body. UES's are established by collective agreement or by court decision in case no agreement has been reached upon that point. It can be divided in distinct establishments as if it were one only company.

As we can see, French regulations on employee representation leave a considerably wide margin to the social partners, so that they can agree upon a broad range of possibilities to determine the structure of employee representation in companies or even within wider frames, based on common interest criteria that will be determined by the social partners themselves. In fact, the social partners can decide the structure of a company or an ensemble of companies to the effects of employee representation with multiple possibilities to choose from and to divide or assemble employees. However, the freedom left to the social partners in order to decide such compositions will never be detrimental to the representation of one single employee, as a company representation body will be in any case guaranteed, no matter if distinct establishments, economic and social unities or intercompany bodies are agreed upon.

Underlying the regulation of the CSE (but also the previous and equivalent works council and personnel delegates) is the idea that the company is not only an economic entity but also a social entity and that it is not only defined under economic parameters but also by its social composition. This explains the fundamental idea that the determination of the "space" where a CSE needs to be constituted has to be guided by the effectiveness in the defence of the workers' rights and interests. A clear contrast between the French and the Spanish system can be verified in that point.

Despite the logical and reasonable that the French approach to employee representation might look like, in fact many other European countries apart from Spain base worker representation structures not in the company but in the workplace/establishment. This is the case of Germany or Austria, where the threshold is however lower, of 5 employees, or the Netherlands, with a minimum threshold of 10 employees. As consequence, problems faced in Spain in the field of workplace representation might be common, at least partially, to other European countries.

This work has as one of its main goals to formulate proposals in order to rebuild the structures of employee representation institutions that could not only contribute to solve Spanish deficiencies in this respect but also provide ideas to face adaptations that other countries might need.

Proposals to Increase Employee-Elected Representation Coverage and to Improve Its Effectiveness

Some proposals are therefore here discussed.

The starting point in the reshaping of personnel representation institutions should be a shift in the centre of gravity of employee representation: it should move from the establishments to the company. As we have seen, many countries have chosen the establishment as the space where representatives are to be elected. Even though different both regulatory and structural conditions influence the dimension establishments tend to have in each country, giving as a result disparate representation coverage rates, it can be maintained that global transformations in company structure generally produce a reduction in large production units and a widespread of small or very small production units. This also happens as consequence of outsourcing and the growing use of independent contractors. Consequently, whenever employee representation is based on establishments, and as long as thresholds regarding the minimum number of employees an establishment needs to have—fixed by almost all national regulations—are maintained, it will be inevitable that large numbers of employees do not have access to representation in the workplace. Therefore, a shift from the establishment to the company as representation field as general rule would open access to representation to a larger percentage of employees. A further argument to the defended position is that in doing so employee representation bodies would come closer to the spaces where the main decisions affecting staff are taken. That is, the centralization of corporate power also demands a centralization of worker representation for the latter to be effective.

All in all, it is quite a simple move: by transferring employee representation bodies to the company level, the impossibility to choose them in so many establishments in so many companies disappears, and so the lack of representation for so many employees is solved.

Increasing the effectiveness of employee representation is of course not as simple as that. Despite the proposed correction, strict centralization of employee representative bodies might still not be operational in companies with a wide geographical extension, especially in the bigger countries. This would be the case of Spain as of many other countries. In that case some adjustments can be recommended. First level works councils—establishment level—could be settled on a geographical basis that should be specified according to the national context. In the case of Spain the existing administrative divisions under the name of provinces could be suitable in some cases. However, the geographical criterion is not necessarily the only one that can be proposed today. Communication technologies make it possible to keep permanent contact between employees based in different production units, as well as between employees and employers. The geographical distance is then a side item if a common interest exists. In this sense, the French idea of the establishment not as a physical reality, but as a community of interest regarding contractual and working conditions is very interesting, as it brings about the idea of dividing the company so that all employees are represented and so that they are represented at the most suitable level. In fact, academics acknowledge elsewhere that the "working community" is defined by the sharing of interests and worries (Fita Ortega 2017), but the French legal framework has the particularity of effectively basing employee representation structures on that notion. It is true that, as Fita Ortega (2017) points out, fragmentation of production processes and precariousness are powerful vectors of common interest disintegration. We could nevertheless regard that common interest from a different point of view and understand that sometimes traditional spaces of common interests might dissolve but other spaces of common interest might appear, such as the common interest of employees geographically disperse in very small production units but working for the same company under the same working conditions. Such common interest could not be united in the past and it can be today by using technologies, as above-mentioned.

In such a case a second level works council formed by members of all the first level works councils should be set. In fact, whenever a division of the company is implemented to the effects of establishing employee representation, a second or third level body grouping should be set to guarantee that representatives exist at each level where the company may take decisions affecting the personnel and its working conditions. It should not be a possibility only applicable under agreement but contemplated by the law.

The latter correction might not necessarily offer a satisfactory response to the objection that can be opposed to centralizing employee representation at company level, because in day-to-day activity the distancing of representatives to the daily contact with represented employees and their needs might persist with territory works councils. Even though technologies can help, they do not solve the problem, as it is more a matter of permanent and informal contact, also building trust. That is why creating the figure of a "unit delegate" could be interesting. It should preferably be a member of the company works council based in the affected production unit. However, in very fragmented companies or in those with production units of diverse size, it can be the case that not all production units are represented in the works council. In such cases, the works council could designate an employee so that he or she exercises that task. In both cases, and especially if the unit delegate is a member of the works council, a direct connection between employees and the works council is secured. In fact, as already mentioned, this figure is contemplated by the French Code du Travail. It is called "proximity representative" and it will only be activated if the social partners agree upon it in a company agreement. Following the line of wide competences left to the social partners in determining the structure of collective representation, the law establishes that the proximity representative's functions will be determined by the collective agreement. In my opinion, the possibility to appoint a proximity or a unit delegate should not be left as an option to the social partners. It should be part of the representation structure designed by the law, that is, it should be obligatory when a company with multiple production units has one only company works council or territory works councils grouping several establishments in a more or less broad territorial level. A further possibility to rationalize the system—also contemplated by the French legislator—and that appears to be reasonable enough is that a proximity delegate is designed for more than one production unit. It would to my view be an appropriate response in the case of very small but geographically close production units, for example those in the same town. Proximity representatives should be equipped with prerogatives to exercise control of compliance of labour regulations in the workplace and to interact with the establishment management in parallel to their functions as works council's members when they are or in permanent contact with a correspondent works council member.

Even though the law should contemplate complete representation structures, collective bargaining is a very adequate instrument to adapt the structure of worker representation bodies to the particularities of every sector and every company. This is the reason why sectoral agreements and even in more precise terms company agreements should be able to determine that structure. However, in doing so, negotiators should take care not to produce a structure that provide workers with narrower possibilities of making worker representation bodies real. That is, representative coverage deriving from legislative provisions should be granted and changes in the structure of worker representation by collective agreements should only be accepted if they result in an equivalent or larger coverage. This is in fact what the French legislation stipulates, by establishing a company works council when no distinct establishment CSEs are created.

Finally, when discussing the personnel representation in the company, a special mention to representation issues in outsourcing contexts is relevant. Outsourcing generates two types of problems related to employee representation. First, it eminently contributes to the fragmentation of workplaces and to the reduction in dimension of productive units. If the definition of establishment to the effect of employee representation remains linked to the separate production unit, as occurs in Spain, and if grouping establishments is severely limited by the existing legal frameworks, the result will inevitably be—again—that many employees remain unrepresented. This is clearly the case of Spain, where the unchanged definition of establishment combined with decentralization of production result in large numbers of micro-establishments where the number of workers does not reach the thresholds fixed by this same non-updated regulation to elect representatives. A solution to that issue could be provided by the aforementioned proposals in themselves, insofar employees pertaining to the principal company as well as those pertaining to contractors and subcontractors would be represented at least in their respective company works council, while works council members would at the same time act as delegates in the workplace. However, further provisions could be necessary to ensure that the contractors' and subcontractors' staff is represented in front of the principal company, which is the one that will be taking many decisions affecting them. For that purpose a workplace council, formed by works council members elected in the workplace for every intervening company, might be suggested.

Even if legislations were reformed to establish representation bodies (at least) at company level and so representation coverage in multiple work centre companies was extended, still many employees working in small companies with one only work centre would be excluded from representation. In fact, it is reasonable to maintain that in these cases employees can directly interact with their employer and therefore they do not need representation. Still, they might share interests with other employees in the same sector or geographical surrounding; the above-mentioned inter-company works council can be an alternative when a limited number of companies easily identifiable are affected. However, sectoral territorial-level representation bodies could also be envisaged, especially to deal with health and security matters.[5] Experiences of inter-enterprise representatives or district delegates created by collective agreement or even simply the reduction of thresholds through collective bargaining can also be found across Europe (Bouquin et al. 2007); the severe exclusion of collective bargaining from changing representation structures or reducing thresholds dictated in Spain by the Supreme Court results the more incomprehensible if we adopt a comparative perspective.

Employees undoubtedly need legislations that are not an obstacle but facilitate the constitution of representation bodies to represent those who cannot interact directly with a decision-making employer and to do that in the most appropriate level. However, as Gumbrell-McCormick and Hyman (2006) show, it has to be considered that institutional representation structures do not always predict the reality of industrial relations. First, because legal provisions deploying an accurate employee representation system do not always guarantee that these institutions are effectively created everywhere they should. To picture that statement almost any European country can be taken as example concerning employee representation structures in small and medium companies. It is the case for Germany, for France and for Spain, among others. In the German case, Schlömer et al. (2008) qualify the existence of works' councils (Betriebsräte) as exceptional in small- and medium-sized work centres (specifically, a study by IAB (Institute for Employment Research)-Betreibspanels conducted in 2004 gave as result that only about 10% of small- and medium-sized work centres who could have a works' council did have such an institution, compared to 93% of big-sized work centres).[6] Additionally, many other contextual factors determine the development of collective relations in companies. The case of France is paradigmatic: it is described as the European country where managerial practices are probably more paternalistic, authoritarian and resembling to those common in the USA (Gumbrell-McCormick and Hyman 2006) despite having one of the most complete and elaborate worker representation system. At the same time, the lack of an institutionalized representation body does not always mean that employees do not have opportunities to collectively defend their rights and interests, as alternative mechanisms might exist. Schlömer et al. (2008) found that in Germany in medium-sized establishments forms of collective representation other than works councils were more frequent than these (works councils existed in 17.1% of work centres employing 20–49 employees, whereas other forms of collective representation such as round tables, employee committees, employee designed as intermediary or spokesman or spokeswoman, existed in 18.2% of work centres the same size). Eurofound (2014) coincides in sustaining that "the ability to establish institutionalized structures/bodies of employee interest representation seems to be more heavily influenced by the relevant industrial relations framework and in particular the organizational strength of trade unions and their presence at company level than by legal regulation", and cite as example the Nordic countries or Belgium, where thresholds are high but the real presence of representation structures in small- and medium-sized companies is quite extended. This publication provides very interesting data demonstrating that in small- and medium-sized companies, even if representation bodies can be set up, reality is quite different and such companies mostly do not have employee representatives.[7] However, Schlömer et al. (2008) also found that whenever a conflict arises the need of a works council is frequently verified.

A further and very interesting debate refers to representation of workers who do not have employee status, and that have been mentioned in this work's background section. Surprisingly, the ILO takes sides in a very clear manner: in the World Report on the Future of Work (2019), it openly advocates for including independent workers in collective representation bodies, even though it does not specify how. It should be noted that the Report does not refer to the creation of specific representation bodies for independent workers, but apparently proposes the inclusion of that category in existent employee representation institutions. This is an idea that can be explored, especially for independent workers who permanently work a considerable number of hours as subcontractors for one same company and who share some interests with employees. Nevertheless, it would be very difficult to realize from the practical point of view: How can we determine which independent workers should be included in the list of voters? Should they be represented by employees or should a share of representation positions be attributed to independent workers? How can both employees' and independent workers' conditions be included in one single negotiation when the legal framework applicable to them is totally different? All these questions should not lead to discarding such proposal; on the contrary, they should invite to further reflection on that matter. For example, it is arguable that the inclusion of independent workers can be easier in sectoral or territorial-level representation bodies than in a particular company, as issues discussed are more general compared to the ones dealt with at a company level. In any case, the ILO's assertion contributes to laying the discussion on the table.

Finally, it must be underlined that the idea that legislation guaranteeing that employees do have voice in the company by updating representation structures, so that they cover in the future a much larger portion of employees than they do today, is in line with the concept of industrial citizenship, which has been discussed by scholars throughout the years, and its updating in a fast evolving world of work (Fudge 2005). It is a thoroughly insufficient yet indispensable basis of industrial democracy.

In line with that, the ILO states in the recent World Report on the Future of Work (ILO 2019, p. 41), that "collective representation of workers and employers through social dialogue is a public good that lies at the heart of democracy". The ILO refers of course to social dialogue to a much larger extent than the company level, but also to the company level. Furthermore, representativeness to participate at sectoral, interprofessional and even international level is gained in many countries at company level. This would be the case of Spain, where trade unions are representative at national level when they obtain at least 10% of the total number of representatives elected in all companies. This is the reason why the unjustified exclusion of employees from choosing representatives does not only have effects on industrial democracy, but also on democracy to a much wider extent.

Notes

1. Royal legislative decree 1/2015, of October 23rd (new version of Law 8/1980, including no changes in these articles).
2. Judgements of 31st January and 19th March 2001.
3. In fact, the ILO encourage trade unions to adopt innovative organizing techniques, including the use of digital technology, to organize labour. It insists that digital technology provides workers' organizations with the potential to connect with workers outside traditional workplaces. Therefore, if technology should be used for the mentioned purposes, the use of it to facilitate employee representation should also be accepted and these technological possibilities should give place to the revision of legislation created when they did not exist.
4. It might though be used to undermine the representation capacity by reducing the number of representatives and representation hours compared to the previous situation, as now one single establishment can be fixed where in the past multiple establishments each one of them with their own representation could exist.
5. Eurofound (2014) cites as an example Sweden's Regional Safety Representatives, established as far back as 1949 in the construction and forestry industries, but later extended to all sectors in 1974. Also in Italy territorial representation bodies were established in 1989 in the craft sector. In Spain, collective agreements can create representation bodies with competences exclusively in health and safety issues for all work centres under that collective agreement.
6. Note that these data do not coincide by those provided by Eurofound (see following note).
7. For instance (percentage of companies or establishments with representation bodies where they could be elected): Austria: companies with 5–10 employees: 3%; Estonia: 5–9 employees: 2.3%; Germany: 5–50 employees: 6%; the Netherlands: 10–49 employees: 16% works council and 12% mini works council. However, Denmark: 5–9 employees: 67%. It is interesting to see the results for France as this work has put its model as an example of a better regulation of employee representatives: 11–19 employees: 37%, which is more than other countries but less than could be expected considering the broadness of its legislation. In the case of Spain, the data offered by Eurofound do not refer to employee representatives in small- or medium-sized establishments. However, doubts on these data should be expressed, as

they are quite different from those offered by Eurofound itself in a 2011 publication: coverage of employees by employee representation bodies in establishments between 10 and 19 employees: Austria 10%; Denmark 57%, Germany 39%; France 29%; the Netherlands 26%. The difference could be partly explained by the fact that in the 2014 report only legal structures were considered, whereas in the 2011 report also bodies derived from collective bargaining were contemplated. Still, the differences can hardly be explained by that single factor or by the 3 years passed between the publication of both reports. Also, Eurofounds' 2011 report finds that 46% of Spanish establishments between 10 and 19 employees do have representation bodies.

References

Alós, Ramon, Beneyto Pere J., Jódar Pere, Molina Oscar, and Sergi Vidal. 2015. *La representación sindical en España*. Madrid: Fundación 1º de Mayo.

Bouquin, Stephen, Leonardi Salvo, and Sian Moore. 2007. "Introduction: Employee Representation and Voice in Small and Medium-Sized Enterprises—The SMALL Project." *Transfer: European Review of Labour and Research* 13 (1).

Cabeza Pereiro, Jaime. 2009. *Las elecciones sindicales*. Albacete: Bomarzo.

Esteban Legarreta, Ricardo. 2018. "Cuestiones sobre la articulación de la representación del personal al servicio de plataformas colaborativas." *Descentralización productiva: nuevas formas de trabajo y organización empresarial: XXVIII Congreso Nacional de Derecho del Trabajo y de la Seguridad Social* 2 (57).

Eurofound. 2011. *Employee Representation at Establishment Level in Europe. European Company Survey 2009*. Dublin. http://www.eurofound.europa.eu/pubdocs/2011/43/en/1/EF1143EN.pdf. Accessed on February 2, 2019.

Eurofound. 2014. *Social Dialogue in Micro and Small Companies*. Dublin. https://www.eurofound.europa.eu/publications/report/2014/industrial-relations-business/social-dialogue-in-micro-and-small-companies. Accessed on February 15, 2019.

Ferreras, Isabelle. 2017. *Firms as Political Entities. Saving Democracy through Economic Bicameralism*. Cambridge: Cambridge University Press.

Fita Ortega, Fernando. 2017. "El impacto del actual contexto productivo en los derechos de participación y representación de los trabajadores en Europa." *Revista General de Derecho del Trabajo y de la Seguridad Social* 46.

Fudge, Judy. 2005. "After Industrial Citizenship. Market Citizenship or Citizenship at Work?" *Relations Industrielles/Industrial Relations* 60 (4): 631–656.

Giraudet, Carole. 2018. "Nécrologie juridique du comité d'entreprise: transformation et succession d'une institution juridique." *La Revue de l'IRES* 94–95 (1–2): 29–56.

Guerrero Vizuete, Esther. 2019. "La digitalización del trabajo y su incidencia en los derechos colectivos de los trabajadores". *IUSLabor* 1: 267–285.

Gumbrell-McCormick, Rebecca, and Richard Hyman. 2006. "Embedded Collectivism? Workplace Representation in France and Germany." *Industrial Relations Journal* 37 (5): 473–491.

Gutiérrez Colominas, David. 2019. "¿Es eficaz la configuración actual de constitución de la representación sindical de trabajadores en las empresas dispersas?" *IUSLabor* 1: 297–306.

ILO—Global Commission on the Future of Work. 2019. *Work for a Brighter Future.* Geneva: International Labour Office. https://www.ilo.org/wcmsp5/groups/public/---dgreports/---cabinet/documents/publication/wcms_662410.pdf. Accessed on February 20, 2019.

Pastor Martínez, Alberto. 2018. "Una aproximación a la problemática de la representación colectiva de los trabajadores de las plataformas "colaborativas" y en entornos digitales." *Iuslabor* 2: 214–233.

Riesco-Sanz, Alberto. 2012. "Empresas sin asalariados y asalariados sin empresas: apuntes sobre la crisis y transformación del empleo." *Lan Harremanak - Revista de Relaciones Laborales* 27.

Rojo Torrecilla, Eduardo. 1999. "Elecciones provinciales de delegados de personal." *Aranzadi Social* 5: 873–878.

Schlömer, Nadine, Kay Rosemarie, Rudolph Wolfgang, and Wolfram Wassermann. 2008. "Arbeitnehmerbeteiligung in mittelständlichen Unternahmen." *WSI Mitteiligungen* 5: 254–260.

Supiot, Alain. 2007. *Critique du droit du travail.* Paris: PUF—Presses Universitaires de France.

Part III

Challenges and Perspectives for the Collective Dimensions of Employment: National Focuses

9

The Right to Strike: The ILO and ECHR Legal Frameworks and the Potential Non-compliance with Those Standards of the New Swedish Legislation

Federico Fusco

Introduction

The present paper focuses on the compliance with the ILO and ECHR standards of the recent changes in the Swedish legislation. The reform aims to restrict the right to strike of the trade unions that are not bound by the collective agreement signed by the employer.

The study will be divided in three parts: (1) part one will offer a brief description of the relevant features of the Swedish industrial relations system, of the socio-economic factors that triggered the reform and of its content; (2) part two will study the notion and extension of the right to strike in accordance with the ILO system and the European Convention of Human Rights (hereafter ECHR); (3) part three will focus on the

F. Fusco (✉)
College of Law, Prince Mohammad Bin Fahd University, Khobar, Saudi Arabia
e-mail: ffusco@pmu.edu.sa

T. Addabbo et al. (eds.), *The Collective Dimensions of Employment Relations*,
https://doi.org/10.1007/978-3-030-75532-4_9

compliance of the resulting Swedish legal framework with the ILO and ECHR standards.

Background

The Swedish Trade Union Movement Between Pluralism and Lack of Competition Among Different Unions

In Sweden, there are over a hundred national contracting parties for over 650 agreements at the national level (Swedish Trade Union Confederation 2011, p. 2; Eriksson 2010, p. 3). Those numbers suggest the idea of a high competition between different trade unions and of overlapping agreements. However, thanks to the structure of the industrial relations it results in a much more ordered model than the one that could appear at first glance. In fact, the trade unions are organized not only on the basis of the economic activity performed by the employer, but also on the basis of the workers' category. Thus, in the same economic sector, there are different unions for blue-collars, white-collars, and graduated employees. This scheme is reproduced also at the confederal level, where the three main confederations (LO, TCO and SACO) are formed by unions representing, respectively, blue-collars, white-collars, and graduated employees.[1] In addition, each confederation has its own internal rules in order to decide which of its federations is entitled to bargain with a certain employer's organization. The outcome of this structure is that "every company in a sector has one collective agreement for each group (blue-collars, white-collars, and graduated employees)" (Westregård and Milton 2016, p. 2). On the other hand, for each group within a sector only one trade union exists (generally speaking) that represents the majority of the workers.

In other words, it is possible to stress that in the Swedish system a high pluralism exists, combined with very low competition among different trade unions. In fact, each of them has its own sphere of action.

For this reason, in each contractual area there is a single trade union interested in bargaining. This element is crucial because the collective agreement represents the centre of the entire system. In fact, Swedish trade unions set as their primary scope to secure good working conditions for their members thanks to this type of agreement. In this process, if it is necessary to put additional pressure on the counterpart, the union can resort to the industrial action. Thus, the right to strike stems from the right to bargain collectively and, therefore, it cannot be used once the latter has been exercised. For those reasons, the conclusion of a collective agreement entails a duty of peace for the trade unions that have signed it (and for their members) (Bruun and Johansson 2014, pp. 259–260).

The combination of the explained factors (duty of peace for the union signing the agreement and existence of a single—relevant—trade union for each contractual area) leads to a situation in which, once the agreement has been signed, a condition of peace is ensured.

Moving from this frame, it is possible to understand the peculiarity of the Göteborg harbour where 85% of the workers are organized by an independent union. This union does not belong to the federation that has signed the (national) collective agreement applied by the employer, nor was, until a few months ago, linked to him by any agreement at all. Thus, it was free to resort to the industrial action and this had a strong impact on the entire Swedish system.

The Industrial Conflict in the Göteborg Harbour

Between 2016 and 2019, in the Göteborg harbour an industrial conflict was fought, whose consequences were so severe to push the government to draft a bill restricting the right to strike.

The conflict opposed APM Terminals (the company who on 2012 won the public procurement to run the harbour) and "Svenska Hamnarbetarförbundet avdelning 4" (hereafter Hamnfyran), the local branch of the Swedish Dockworkers Union (SHF).

This union was born in 1972 as a spin-off of Transport, the major national union of transportation workers and it constitutes a peculiar case in the Swedish industrial relation scenario. The separation was due to the different ideology that still marks this dockworkers union. The outcome is that, as an independent association, it is not linked to any of the major confederations and to their set of statutory rules. In addition, it is keener to the industrial conflict.

Under a national perspective, the low share of workers joining this union renders it devoid of any relevant power. However, the situation is the opposite in the Göteborg harbour where Hamnfyran represents 85% of the blue-collar, while Transport is just a minority.

In spite of the greater representativeness of Hamnfyran, the companies running the harbour traditionally sign the collective agreement with Transport, which on the national level is more important. This happened also with APM Terminals which, running also other harbours in Sweden where Transport is the prevailing union, claims that it needs to apply a unique contract. However, the consequences for Hamnfyran of not being part of a collective agreement have traditionally been almost nil. In fact, its members used to benefit from the collective agreement signed by Transport,[2] while the management was unilaterally bestowing to the union similar rights to the ones reserved by the law to the trade unions that were part of an agreement.

The outcome of this situation was very convenient for Hamnfyran because it could enjoy the benefits stemming from the collective agreement, without having to bear its costs (*in primis* the duty of peace).

The equilibrium was broken in fall 2015 when the new APM Terminals management started to exclude Hamnfyran from every kind of industrial relation. The trade union responded calling some strikes (even if limited in both number and duration) between spring 2016 and January 2017. Later on, it started to put blockades against overtime and contract workers from other agencies. In November 2016, the National Mediation Office stepped in, but even after several months of mediation, it was not possible to find a solution. In particular, SHF suggested to join Transport and Sveriges Hamnar (the employers' union to whom APM Terminals belongs) in the renewal of the collective agreement, which was expiring in 2017. In this way, SHF would have become part of the contract and, thus, it would have been bound by the duty of peace. This solution would have led to the termination of the conflict, but Transport refused it.

On the other side, APM Terminals reacted to the Hamnfyran actions with 371 hours of lockout (the container terminal was totally closed all the weekdays between 4 p.m. and 7 a.m. from May 19 to June 30).[3]

The outcome of this situation was that in 2017, while the sector was globally growing and the Stockholm terminal performed a +11%, the container trade in Göteborg shrunk by 19%, causing major economic losses to the national economy. In fact, the harbour is the biggest in Sweden and until 2015, it was handling 60% of the national import–export. As the export industry is one of the major pillars of the domestic economy, the malfunctioning of the harbour hindered several industries' shipping, increasing the difficulty and expense of shipping products.

For those reasons, the conflict arose as national debate and the Minister of Labour Ms. Ylva Johansson endorsed the idea to restrict the right to strike.

It should be mentioned that, after some other harsh moments,[4] the conflict was eventually solved on March 5th 2019, when SHF and Sveriges Hamnar signed a so-called second agreement (*andraavtal*).[5] This expression indicates a collective agreement signed when the employer is already bound by an agreement with a different trade union and whose content can be equivalent or different from the first one. In SHF's case, the content of the two agreements is identical and this should prevent future clashes.

The Law on the Limitation of the Right to Strike

Even though the Göteborg conflict has been solved, the debate concerning the need to restrict the right to strike had been pushed beyond the breaking point and, thus, remained actual.

Specifically, in June 2017 the government appointed a special investigator. His mission was to suggest how to extend the peace obligation linked to the conclusion of a collective agreement, by limiting the possibility to strike for trade unions that were not part of the agreement.

However, a few days before the presentation of the results of the investigation, LO, TCO and SACO, together with the Confederation of Swedish Enterprises (*Svenskt Näringsliv*), submitted an autonomous proposal.

The government decided to prioritize the vision of the social partners and started to implement this latter suggestion. The reform amended the so-called Co-determination Act (1976:580) prohibiting an employee from taking part in a collective action against an employer who is already bound by a collective agreement. However, this ban should not be applied if all the following conditions are met:

1. the action is legally organized by the trade union;
2. the action aims to sign a collective agreement (which entails a duty of peace);
3. there has been a previous negotiation between the trade union and the employer on the demands of the trade union;
4. the trade union does not require the employer to apply the new agreement in a way which would constitute a violation of the agreement that the employer has already signed with another union.[6]

In addition, the ban of collective actions is extended to all the disputes of rights, whereas before it was limited only to the rights stemming from the collective agreement.

This new law entered into force on August 1st 2019.[7]

The described legislation limits the right to strike and poses important issues concerning its compliance with the international standards. However, before proceeding to their analysis, it seems desirable to frame which is the exact dimension of the right to strike within the ILO and ECHR legal systems.

The Right to Strike in the Context of the ILO Clash of 2012 Between the Employers and Workers' Groups

The right to strike is not expressly mentioned in the Treaty of Versailles, that, while establishing the ILO (part XIII), refers in art. 427 to the "right of association". Similarly, the core conventions nn. 87 and 98 make an explicit reference only to the freedom of association and the right to organize and collective bargaining. In 1952, the right to strike made its first appearance in the ILO legal framework, being clearly recognized in a decision of the Committee of Freedom of Association[8] and since that moment it has been reasserted and specified in an increasing number of occasions (Bellace 2014, pp. 47 ff.).

This trend was abruptly interrupted during the meeting of the Committee of Application of Standards (CAS) in 2012, when the Employers' group expressed its disagreement about parts of the General Survey of the Committee of Experts on the Application of Conventions and Recommendations (CEACR). In its view, this body was guilty of laying down a detailed regulation of the right to strike without having any power to do so (Bellace 2014, p. 57). The reproach moved from the remark that the Convention n. 87 is silent concerning this right. Therefore, there would be no ground for the CEACR to specify how the countries should behave while dealing with the right to strike. In other words, the position of the Employers' group was that, even if the right to strike exists in many national legal systems (International Labour Conference 2012, p. 27/4), the ILO Conference is the appropriate body to set its regulation and not the CEACR (International Labour Conference 2012, 27/4 and part. I/22 para. 82; Novitz 2014, p. 374). In fact, its mandate would be limited to provide technical evaluation on the compliance with international labour standards and not to "interpret" the conventions.[9] In addition, the fact that it is not a tripartite body could have contributed to the development of an unbalanced set of rules.[10]

For those reasons, the Employers' group refused to examine the cases in which the CEACR was addressing the right to strike. This refusal led to a clash with the Workers' group that resulted in a lack of agreement concerning the list of cases to examine, thus paralysing the regular supervisory system. After two years of uncertainty,[11] the deadlock seemed to have been solved in 2015 thanks to a Joint Statement of Workers' and Employers' Groups. This statement acknowledges that "the right to take industrial action by workers and employers in support of their legitimate industrial interests is recognized by the constituents of the ILO". Moreover, it recognizes that it is part of the mandate of the CEACR to "determine the legal scope, content and meaning of the provisions of the Conventions", but it specifies that "its opinions and recommendations are non-binding" (International Labour Organization 2015, Appendix I, 2). This compromise appears to have smouldered the debate, but not to have ended it. In fact, in a communication to its members, the International Organization of Employers has clarified that: "the statement recognized the right to industrial action in general – which it claims the Employers never denied – but did not recognize that there was a right to strike within the scope of Conv. n.87, and certainly did not accept the extensive guidance provided by the CEACR" (Hovary 2016, p. 403).

The position of the Employers' group has been strongly criticized because it was based on a lack of understanding concerning both the functioning of the regular supervisory system and the process that led to the statement of the freedom of association. Moving from the former, the CEACR would not be able to provide an evaluation of the state of application of the international labour standards without clarifying the content and the extent of the rights settled by the conventions. When negating this power, the Employers' group clearly endorses the old conception proposed by Montesquieu. For the French philosopher, the judge (here conceived as the one that must apply the law) must be an inanimate being, confined to represent the mouth that pronounces the words of the law.[12] However, in the eighteenth century this conception was justified by the need to separate those powers that—during the *ancien régime*—were concentrated in the hands of the king. Instead, in the contemporary reality, a similar claim displays a lack of understanding of the commonly accepted theories of interpretation of legal texts (Guastini 2011, p. 39; Bellace 2018, p. 501).

Concerning the latter—i.e. the misconception of the process that led to the statement of the freedom of association—it has been observed already that art. 427 of the Treaty of Versailles was also meant to protect the industrial action. This statement derives from the assumption that, while recognizing "the right of association for all lawful purposes by the employed as well as by the employers", the parties were referring to the right of the workers to join a trade union and to undertake its typical activities. Among those should be encompassed the collective bargaining and the industrial action. In fact, the strike is a normal and foreseeable consequence of the fact of forming a union (Novitz 2009, p. 126). Moreover, in the British legal framework (whose characteristics played an important role in drafting part XIII of the Treaty) it constituted a tort. However, no action was admitted against a trade union if the said union had respected due procedures while organizing the strike. For those reasons, the "freedom of association" must be read as synonymous of "trade union rights", thus encompassing also the right to strike (Bellace 2014, pp. 34–35; 2018, p. 509).

Moving from those remarks, it is possible to affirm that the right to strike exists in the ILO legal framework (Borzaga and Salomone 2015, p. 6) and its features should be the ones specified in the reports of the CEACR. This statement is backed up by the fact that in 2012, during some informal consultations aimed to solve the deadlock, it became evident that the real concern was the extent of the CEACR's mandate, which for the Employers' group "was not tasked with interpreting the conventions" (Hofmann and Schuster 2016, p. 1). In this light, the thesis of those Authors that interpreted the 2012 clash as a way to contest the ILO's monitoring system in order to rebalance the powers within the organization can be endorsed.[13]

Moreover, it should be observed that, even if not binding, the CEACR's "jurisprudence" is increasingly playing a role in defining the content of the labour standards across the world. In fact, resorting to what has been called an "integrated approach" (Mantouvalou 2013, pp. 529 ff.), several bodies which are able to produce hard law have started to refer to the principles enucleated by this Committee while adopting their provisions or judicial decisions. Thus, such phenomenon is transforming non-binding opinions, which derive their persuasiveness from the moral authority of the Committee of Experts, in a set of rules that can be coactively enforced (Borzaga and Salomone 2015, p. 13). The integration of the ILO core labour standards not only in private initiatives (i.e. codes of conducts or international framework agreements), but also in economic partnerships between countries (such as the EU generalized system of preferences) represents a clear example of this trend (Borzaga and Salomone 2015, p. 11; Novitz 2014, p. 362). On top of that, it is significant that several national and transnational courts resort to the ILO decisions as a guideline for the determination of the cases, as it happens with the European Court of Human Rights (Dorssemont 2016, p. 69).

Under this perspective, it is understandable the concern of the Employers' group and, in this light, the decision to question the ILO regular supervisory system can be seen as an effort to contain the consequences of the described "integrated approach".

The Links Between Right to Strike and Freedom of Association in the ECtHR Case Law

As known, the European Convention of Human Rights does not mention the right to strike. Nevertheless, art. 11 protects the freedom of association, including the freedom to form and join trade unions. In this context, the right to strike has been outlined by the Court as one of the means making that freedom effective.[14] If on the one hand, this reasoning permits to protect the right to strike under the European Convention, on the other hand it leaves open the issue concerning its essentiality. In other words, the right to strike does not enjoy an autonomous protection, but it must be granted only as a means to safeguard the freedom of association. Thus, it is important to understand if the right to strike is an essential aspect of the freedom of association or not. In the former case, its restrictions would automatically entail a violation of the Convention, while in the latter it would be necessary to take also into account the eventual restriction of the other means that the trade unions have in order to pursue their activity.

As it has been pointed out, the Court has sometimes been hesitant concerning the essentiality of the right to strike.[15] However, from an analysis of its newest case law, it is possible to conclude that it conceives the strike as an "important means" to secure trade unions' freedom, but not an essential one. Such classification emerges very clearly from the recent decision *Association of Academics* where the Court highlights the hard boarder between "essential" and "non-essential" elements of the trade union freedom. The former cannot be restricted and, even if their number is not fixed, depending on the evolution of the labour relations, insofar it includes: (1) the right to form and join a trade union; (2) the prohibition of closed-shop agreements; (3) the right for a trade union to seek to persuade the employer to hear what it has to say on behalf of its members; (4) the right to bargain collectively with an employer. The right to strike, instead, is not included in this list.[16]

This approach has been confirmed in the case *Ognevenko v. Russia*[17] with the result that it is possible to affirm that the right to strike "is not absolute and may be subject under national law to regulation of a kind that limits or conditions its exercise in certain instances" (ECtHR 1976, para 36; 2009, para 32; 2018b, para 58).

It is interesting to notice that, as already mentioned, the Court reinforces its reasoning also referring to principles and provisions stemming from legal sources other than the Convention. Those sources include the European Social Charter and resolution n. 2033/2015 of the Parliamentary Assembly of the Council of Europe (titled "Protection of the right to bargain collectively, including the right to strike"), but most of all the ILO jurisprudence (ECtHR, 2018b, para 70).[18] As previously noted, this reasoning of the Court has not been affected by the abovementioned clash within the ILO concerning the existence of the right to strike. On the contrary, when the issue has been raised, the Court dismissed it arguing that it was an internally confined ILO contrast and restricted solely to the Employers' group. For this reason, it was not able to affect the vision of the entire organization, especially considering that the governments' group was firmly supporting the CEACR's decisions (ECtHR 2014, para 97; for a deeper analysis Novitz 2014, p. 376; Vogt 2018, pp. 541–542).[19]

Moving from all the elements explained above, it is possible to affirm that in both the ILO and ECHR legal frameworks the right to strike is recognized and protected. However, its regulation is deeply linked to the necessity to safeguard the freedom of association. In other words, limitations of the right to strike are more likely to conflict with the mentioned international standards when they result in a violation of the stated freedom.

The next section analyses the Swedish legal framework on the basis of this principle. Thus, it will be important to scrutinize if, taking into account the other means available for the trade unions to pursue their goals, the limitation of the right to strike does or does not affect the freedom of association itself.

The Swedish Reform in the Light of the Legal Constraints Stemming from the ILO and the European Convention of Human Rights

As mentioned in the introduction, the core of the Swedish industrial relation system is represented by the collective agreement: the industrial action is conceived as a leverage to convince the counterpart to sign it and, once that is in place, it automatically implies a duty of peace for the signing trade union and its members (Bruun and Johansson 2014, pp. 260–261). Eventual conflicts among different trade unions concerning the right to bargain are usually solved in advance resorting to the internal rules of their confederation (Regeringskansliet Arbetsmarknadsdepartementet 2018, p. 10). The outcome is a situation in which, generally speaking, once the collective agreement has been signed with a trade union (or a group of trade unions in the sectors where they bargain together),[20] no other union has anything to demand and, thus, the collective peace is ensured. Moreover, in application of the so-called Britannia principle (Arbetsdomstolen—Swedish Labour Court, 1989), it is not legal for another trade union to take an industrial action to try to replace an existing agreement (Bruun and Johansson 2014, p. 269).

In this context, eventual remaining strikes not aimed to reach an agreement, even if eventually legal, are perceived as a misuse of the right that contrasts with the basic principles of the Swedish model and, thus, should not be protected.[21]

Finally, the Labour Court's case law regulates the hypothesis in which the employer is bound by a second agreement (*andraavtal*) and the two agreements are not mutually coordinated. In this case, the working conditions (included salary) are regulated exclusively in accordance with the older agreement, disregarding the trade union affiliation of the workers (Arbetsdomstolen 1937, 1939, 1974, 1977). Thus, the second agreement would mainly serve the union in order to obtain the set of rights laid down in the contract or reserved by the law to the collective agreement-based organizations. However, under certain conditions, the employer can be liable for damages if he signs a second agreement that cannot fully produce its effects (Arbetsdomstolen 1977).

Those observations are essential in order to understand the impact of the Swedish reform and its controversial aspects. In fact, while in most of the cases, it would not produce a significant change in the flow of the industrial relations, it will instead deeply affect the position of trade unions such as Hamnfyran, risking to hinder the freedom of association of those organizations.

As an initial remark, it is observed that, as shown by the duty of preliminary negotiations, the proposed legislation fosters the idea of the strike as the last resort. Under this aspect the European Committee of Social Rights has previously expressed some concerns regarding the lawfulness of such an approach, particularly when it gives the judge the power to state if the action can take place or not.[22] This is relevant because before the start of an industrial action the Labour Court can be asked to issue an interim injunction concerning its lawfulness. While doing that the judges will now have to assess if the trade union's purpose is to reach an agreement entailing a duty of peace. However, this assessment will be based on unsatisfactory criteria. In fact, according to the explanatory memorandum of the new legislation, the judge should also take into account if the trade union has been previously bound by a collective agreement with the employer and even the economic content of the requests. In particular, the circumstance that the trade union's claims would deviate from what normally applies in the labour market can contribute in deeming the action specious. This reasoning is in principle acceptable because it prevents claims so unreasonable to conceal a *fraus legis*. However, some doubts arise from the fact that the benchmark to judge the reasonableness of the claim will be the main agreement between the blue-collar confederation (LO, to whom Transport belongs) and the Confederation of Swedish Enterprise (Regeringskansliet Arbetsmarknadsdepartementet 2018, p. 21).

Summing together the two requirements (to be usually part of collective agreements and to raise claims in line with the policy of the major trade unions) results in a situation that imposes some further elaboration. In fact, there is the risk for a trade union with a different vision to fail the judicial control respective to the duty of preliminary negotiation just because it fosters different claims from those of the major organizations. This would create an inadmissible control on the content of the union's claims, whose effect would be the denial of the right to strike for some unions.

This scenario would particularly affect the trade unions not belonging to the major confederations, without any regard to their representativeness in the specific workplace. In addition, this unfair balance would be aggravated by the fact that the majority of the members of the Swedish Labour Court are appointed by the major confederations of employers and employees, which are the subjects that have the greater interest in getting rid of the autonomous unions. For those reasons, there is the risk that in its practical implementation the new legislation could force all the trade unions to align their claims to the requests of the bigger ones. This effect would constitute a clear violation of their freedom of association as defined in the above-mentioned international norms.

Other doubts concerning the presented legislation arise from the global effect that it is going to create when combined with the other features of the Swedish system. In particular, major issues result from the combination with the case-law rule that impedes two collective agreements to be contemporarily applicable in the same area (even if addressed to workers affiliated to different organizations).

As already mentioned, in this hypothesis the older agreement would be applied towards all the workers, even if affiliated to the trade union that has signed the second agreement.

Combining this case law with the new legislation on the strike would result in a situation in which the trade unions without an agreement would see their freedom of association hindered. In fact, they would be able to initiate an industrial action only in order to conclude a collective agreement. However, this agreement will not produce any effect on the working conditions of their members, that would be still regulated by the older agreement signed by a different union.[23] On top of this, the employer would be refrained from signing the second agreement because to not apply it would still constitute a tort and, thus, he would be exposed to liability for damage (Arbetsdomstolen 1974).

In this scenario from one hand, the employer would be highly discouraged from signing a second agreement, while from the other, the trade union would still not be able to obtain the application of the working conditions corresponding to its vision.[24] As a practical outcome, it would be impossible for all the trade unions other than the one signing the first agreement to have any impact on the balance of power between employers and employees. In fact, in the impossibility of obtaining the application of the standards laid down in their agreement, their sole weapon consisted in the strike. However, such behaviour is no longer an option. As observed, this situation could hinder the survival of the trade unions themselves, whose members gather together with the expectation of having some impact. If this does not happen, they can deem their efforts futile and, thus, leave the organization.[25]

It is important to highlight that this result would depend exclusively upon the chronological criteria based on being or not being the first trade union signing the agreement. Instead, the representativeness of the trade union would have no relevance. In the majority of the cases, this will not be an issue because the major trade union and the one signing the contract usually correspond. However, in cases such as the one of the Göteborg harbour, a union would be set aside in spite of its greater representativeness.[26] Considering that the new legislation has been specifically studied in order to produce such effect, some doubts can arise concerning its compliance to the freedom of association as recognized by the ILO and ECHR.

Conclusion

The Swedish system of industrial relations is very rational and well-functioning and the proposed legislation aims to foster those characteristics. This objective is pursued thanks to the contrast of the phenomenon of free riding that can arise when a union signs a collective agreement and others do not. In fact, because of the recalled "*normerande verkan*", all the workers would enjoy the agreement's conditions, but the duty of peace would bind only the signing unions. In this scenario, the unions devoid of the agreement could abuse their possibility to strike, starting action only meant to disrupt the production. In other words, the main concern for the legislator and the social partners is to avoid some individuals or organizations enjoying the positive outcome of the existence of the collective agreement, without bearing its burdens. In this light, the link between the right to strike and the conclusion of a contract entailing the duty of peace appears a good solution.[27]

On the other hand, the rationalization of the system should not jeopardize the freedom of association of any union, who should be let free to pursue its programmes even if not in line with the ones of the major organizations. Under this aspect, there is the need to assess case by case if the new legislation, combined with the other features of the Swedish system, limits the freedom of association to the point to devoid this freedom of its substance. In this light, situations such as the one of the Göteborg harbour seems to stand on the borderline,[28] because broadly representative unions would not be able to influence in any way the working conditions. In fact, the strike would be admitted only in order to sign an agreement, but this agreement would not affect the working conditions of the union's members.

In such a situation, the great majority of the workers would be ruled by another organization, which in the specific workplace could represent only a minority of them. Thus, the right of the union to strike and to collective bargain would be merely on paper and its possibility to seek its goals would be severely hindered. Finally, this lack of impact could discourage the union's members, pushing them to leave it.

For all of those reasons, we believe that in some cases the described limits to the union's activity can hinder the substance itself of the freedom of association and, thus, contrast with the recalled ILO and ECHR legal frameworks.

Notes

1. LO is formed by 14 blue-collar unions, TCO by 14 white-collar ones, and SACO by 23 unions of graduated employees. There is some overlapping between TCO and SACO in some sectors, but the issue is often solved by negotiating together.
2. For the Swedish labour law an employer bound by a collective agreement must apply it, unless otherwise stated, to all the employees, irrespective of their affiliation (so-called *normerande verkan*). This obligation eliminates any stimulus to hire (cheaper) non-unionized employees. On this point, see Bergström (2014, p. 11) and Malmberg (2002, pp. 203 ff.). For the case law, see Arbetsdomstolen—Swedish Labour Court (1977) which states that the collective agreement can contain the obligation for the employer to apply it also to workers not belonging to the signing union. While interpreting a collective agreement, such obligation should be deemed to exist unless specific circumstances would suggest otherwise.
3. For a full description of the conflict see Bergsten and (Makboul 2018) and SHF (2018).
4. The (long) list of strikes and lockouts during the first two months of 2019 can be found here: http://hamn.nu/article/2690/Samlad-lista-over-strejker-och-lockouter.html.
5. This is the first SHF's collective agreement since the union's formation in 1972. The text of the contract is available here: http://hamn.nu/assets/files/Avtalet.pdf (accessed on November 1, 2019).
6. It should be noted that this ban does not affect the possibility to take part in secondary actions, whose lawfulness continues to be linked to the main action's one.
7. SFS 2019:503, published on 2 July 2019.
8. Committee on Freedom of Association (1952, point 68): "The right to strike and that of organizing union meetings are essential elements of trade union rights (...)".
9. See International Labour Conference (2012, 27/4), where the Employers' group clearly contests that the "experts' interpretations of the right to strike are legal jurisprudence or even soft law". Concerning the interpretation of the ILO Conventions the task should lie, in accordance with art. 37 of the ILO Constitution on the International Court of Justice, but the lack of judicial power of the CEACR would prevent to refer to the Court a case based on its interpretation.

10. See the proceedings of the CAS Conference during the 104th session of the International Labour Conference (2015, par. 39).
11. In 2013, the agreement on the list of countries to analyse was found on the precondition that the right to strike should have not been addressed because "the employers do not agree that there is a right to strike recognized in Convention No. 87" (International Labour Conference 2013, par. 232). In 2014, such statement was not repeated because of the opposition of the Workers' group, but the supervisory system continued to suffer for the ongoing conflict (Hofmann and Schuster 2016, p. 2).
12. "Mais les juges de la nation ne sont, comme nous avons dit, que la bouche qui prononce les paroles de la loi; des êtres inanimés, qui n'en peuvent modérer ni la force ni la rigueur" (Montesquieu 1777, Liv. XI, Chap. VI, p. 327).
13. See Borzaga and Salomone (2015, pp. 7–8) where the Authors observe that in the last years the lack of the majority required to adopt new labour convention pushed the ILO to shift its focus on the better implementation of the already existing standards. In this new scenario, the leading role is played by the CEACR, while the constituents "have experienced a decline in their importance".
14. For an analysis of the relevant case law of the ECtHR, see Dorssemont (2016).
15. See Dorssemont (2016, pp. 68–70), where the Author offers a detailed analysis of the evolution of the ECtHR's case law.
16. See ECtHR (2018a, para 23–24). For the exclusion of the industrial action from the essential elements of the freedom of association, see also ECtHR (2014, para 84). On the contrary, in the ILO framework the CFA conceives the right to strike as an "essential means" (see ILO 2018, p. 753).
17. See also ECtHR (2018b, para 55): "Article 11 of the Convention does not secure any particular treatment of trade unions or their members and leaves each country a free choice of the means to be used. (…) The granting of a right to strike constitutes without any doubt one of the most important of such means".
18. On the contrary, the Court does not recall the ILO legal framework in the *Association of Academics* case (ECtHR 2018a). For an analysis of the differences between those cases, see Novitz (2019).
19. Within the ILO, the clear endorsement of the CEACR's jurisprudence has been reaffirmed by the government group during the session of June 2015 of the Committee of Application of Standards. See Bellace (2018, p. 500).
20. See above, note 1.

21. See Regeringskansliet Arbetsmarknadsdepartementet (2018, p. 18) where it summarizes the vision of the major Swedish social partners. An exception is represented by short-term protests for economic-political reasons, which are protected as long as they do not significantly affect the employer (Arbetsdomstolen 1982, 1984).
22. See Novitz (2014, p. 365), where the Author recalls (European Committee of Social Rights 2010). On the contrary, no concerns regarding the *ultima ratio* principle in Germany are expressed by Bruun & Johansson. However, they underline that in that country this rule is alleviated by "a margin of appreciation" of the trade union (Bruun and Johansson 2014, p. 263).
23. Concerning the extended effect of the collective agreement (*normerande verkan*) see note 2.
24. Thus, the positive outcome of the signature of the agreement would solely consist of providing the union with some additional rights of consultation, information, and codetermination.
25. See Bellace (2018, p. 528). Concerning the importance of the right to strike as one of the means to realize the workers' interests protected by the freedom of associations see Novitz (2003, p. 197). In this regard, it is possible to observe that the effective implementation of the freedom of association is affected by the new Swedish legal framework almost as much as it would be in case of negation of the right itself. In fact, to be able to strike in order to obtain a collective agreement that cannot be applied results in a clear limitation of the freedom of association.
26. The need to solve the conflict between several applicable collective agreements has recently been at the center of the discussion also in Germany. However, it is important to note that in this country, the agreement signed by the union that organizes the majority of the workers in the company prevails (see *Tarifvertragsgesetz* §4a par. 2). Moreover, the Constitutional Court has clarified that the substitution process cannot lead the interests of a specific professional group to be neglected (Bundesverfassungsgericht 2017, which led, with effect from January 1st 2019, to the amendment of the §4a par. 2 of TVG).
27. On the necessity of do not abuse the right of strike in the Nordic countries see Bruun and Johansson (2014, pp. 270–271).
28. Even if the conflict in the harbour has now been solved due to the signature of the collective agreement, it cannot be excluded that other problems may arise in the future in both the harbour and different companies.

References

Arbetsdomstolen. 1937. *n.149.*
Arbetsdomstolen. 1939. *n. 24.*
Arbetsdomstolen. 1974. *n. 14.*
Arbetsdomstolen. 1977. *n. 14.*
Arbetsdomstolen. 1982. *n. 311.*
Arbetsdomstolen. 1984. *n.91.*
Arbetsdomstolen—Swedish Labour Court. 1977. *n. 49.*
Arbetsdomstolen—Swedish Labour Court. 1989. *n. 120.*
Bellace, Janice R. 2014. "The ILO and the Right to Strike." *International Labour Review* 153 (1): 29–70.
Bellace, Janice R. 2018. "ILO Convention No. 87 and the Right to Strike in an Era of Global Trade." *Comparative Labour Law & Policy Journal* 39 (3): 495–530.
Bergsten, Henrik, and Lina Makboul. 2018. "How the Labour Conflict in the Port of Gothenburg Became of Critical Importance for the Entire Swedish Labour Market." SVT, January 17.
Bergström, Ola. 2014. "Managing Restructuring in Sweden–Innovation and Learning After the Financial Crisis." IRENE Policy Paper (12).
Borzaga, Matteo, and Riccardo Salomone. 2015. "Challenging the Right to Strike or Attacking the ILO's Monitoring System? The Possible Consequences of Recent Employers Claims on the Enforcement Perspectives of International Labour Standards." SIS Working paper n. 4/2015.
Bruun, Niklas, and Caroline Johansson. 2014. "Sanctions for Unlawful Collective Action in the Nordic Countries and Germany." *International Journal of Comparative Labour Law and Industrial Relations* 30 (3): 253–271.
Bundesverfassungsgericht. 2017. *Urteil des Ersten Senats vom 11. Juli 2017*. July 11. http://www.bverfg.de/e/rs20170711_1bvr157115.html
Committee on Freedom of Association. 1952. *Case n.28, The World Federation of Trade Unions vs UK (Jamaica), Report n. 2.*
Dorssemont, Filip. 2016. "The Right to Take Collective Action in the Council of Europe: A Tale of One City, Two Instruments and Two Bodies." *King's Law Journal* 27 (1): 67–88.
ECtHR. 1976. *Schmidt and Dahlström vs. Sweden.* 6 February.
ECtHR. 2009. *Enerji Yapi-Yol Sen vs. Turkey.* 21 April.
ECtHR. 2014. *RMT vs. UK*. 8 April.
ECtHR. 2018a. *Association of Academics vs Iceland*. 7 June.

ECtHR. 2018b. *Ognevenko v. Russia*. 20 November.

Eriksson, K. 2010. *The Swedish Rules on Negotiation and Mediation: A Brief Summary*.

European Committee of Social Rights. 2010. *Conclusion Concerning the Fulfillment of Art. 6.4 of the European Social Charter by The Netherlands*. December 14. http://hudoc.esc.coe.int/eng/?i=2010/def/NLD/6/4/EN.

Guastini, Riccardo. 2011. *Interpretare e argomentare*. Milan: Giuffrè Editore.

Hofmann, Claudia, and Norbert Schuster. 2016. "It Ain't Over'til It's Over: The Right to Strike and the Mandate of the ILO Committee of Experts revisited." Global Labour University Working Paper No. 40. International Labour Office, Geneva.

Hovary, Claire L. 2016. "The ILO's Employers' Group and the Right to Strike." *Transfer: European Review of Labour and Research* 22 (3): 401–404.

International Labour Conference. 2012. *Conference Committee on the Application of Standards: Extracts from the Record of Proceedings. 101st Session*. Geneva: International Labour Office.

International Labour Conference. 2013. *Conference Committee on the Application of Standards: Extracts from the Record of Proceedings. 102nd Session*. Geneva: International Labour Office.

International Labour Conference. 2015. *Conference Committee on the Application of Standards: Extracts from the Record of Proceedings. 104th Session*. Geneva: International Labour Office.

International Labour Organization. 2015. *Tripartite Meeting on the Freedom of Association and Protection of the Right to Organize Convention, 1948 (No. 87), in Relation to the Right to Strike and the Modalities and Practices of Strike Action at National Level*.

ILO. 2018. *Freedom of Association—Compilation of Decisions of the Committee on Freedom of Association*. 6th ed. Geneva: International Labour Office.

Malmberg, Jonas. 2002. "The Collective Agreement as an Instrument for Regulation of Wages and Employment Conditions." *Scandinavian Studies in Law*: 189–213

Mantouvalou, Virginia. 2013. "Labour Rights in the European Convention on Human Rights: An Intellectual Justification for an Integrated Approach to Interpretation." *Human Rights Law Review* 13 (3): 529–556.

Montesquieu, Charles L. de Secondat. 2011. *L'esprit des lois. 1777*. Paris: Classiques Garnier.

Novitz, Tonia. 2003. *International and European Protection of the Right to Strike: A Comparative Study of Standards Set by the International Labour Organization, the Council of Europe and the European Union.* Oxford: Oxford University Press.

Novitz, Tonia. 2009. "Workers' Freedom of Association." In *Human Rights in Labor and Employment Relations: International and Domestic Perspectives*, edited by James A. Gross and Lance Compa, 123–154. Ithaca, NY: Cornell University Press.

Novitz, Tonia. 2014. "The Internationally Recognized Right to Strike: A Past, Present and Future Basis upon Which to Evaluate Remedies for Unlawful Collective Action?" *International Journal of Comparative Labour Law and Industrial Relations* 30 (3): 357–380.

Novitz, Tonia. 2019. "To Protect the Right to Strike or Not? The Question Before the European Court of Human Rights in app no 2451/16 Association of Academics v Iceland and app no 44873/09 Ognevenko v Russia." *Comparative Labor Law & Policy Journal*. Dispatch No. 15.

Regeringskansliet Arbetsmarknadsdepartementet. 2018. *Ds 2018:40, Fredsplikt på arbetsplatser där det finns kollektivavtal och vid rättstvister*.

SHF. 2018. "Frågor & svar om situationen på APM Terminals." Accessed on February 20, 2018. www.hamn.nu.

Swedish Trade Union Confederation. 2011. *The Swedish Model—The Importance of Collective Agreements in Sweden.* www.lo.se

Vogt, Jeffrey. 2018. "Comments for 'On the Justification of the Right to Strike in the ILO System of Standards', Friedrich Ebert Stiftung (FES), Berlin, 2–3 April 2016." *Comparative Labor Law & Policy Journal* 39 (3): 537–542.

Westregård, Aannamaria, and Jonas Milton. 2016. "Recent Trends in Collective Bargaining Structures in the SWEDISH Model." 11th ILERA European Regional Congress, Milan.

10

'Prova di Solidarietà': How Effectively are Unions and Emerging Collective Worker Representatives Responding to New Business Models in Australia and Italy?

Anthony Forsyth

Introduction

This chapter examines the challenges for collective worker representation posed by new business models in Australia and Italy, and assesses the effectiveness of responses from trade unions and emerging worker representative groups. The relentless process of change in the nature of work and business enterprises over the last 25 years has contributed to the steady decline of trade union membership in many countries. Through franchising, labour hire, independent contracting, complex supply chains and the gig economy, labour costs have been driven down and work has become 'fissured' for many (Weil 2014).

In this era of 'platform capitalism' (Srnicek 2017), collective representation of workers' interests is under significant threat (a 'test of

A. Forsyth (✉)
Graduate School of Business and Law, RMIT University, Melbourne, VIC, Australia
e-mail: anthony.forsyth@rmit.edu.au

T. Addabbo et al. (eds.), *The Collective Dimensions of Employment Relations*,
https://doi.org/10.1007/978-3-030-75532-4_10

solidarity'). The gig economy is highly individualised, operating on the assumption of the worker as an independent contractor rather than an employee (Prassl 2018). Employment-based rights, such as minimum wages and leave entitlements, are dealt out of the equation—along with the right to engage in collective bargaining through unions.[1] Much of the emerging research on legal responses to the gig economy focuses on its *individual* employment law aspects: the categorisation of platform workers and whether existing categories of 'employment' need to be broadened (Menegatti 2018; Stewart and McCrystal 2019).

This chapter draws upon literature relating to various forms of worker representation, to explore the *collective* dimensions of labour relations in the context of a range of new business models in Australia and Italy. It examines how unions have sought to represent workers in these fissured work contexts, and the emergence of other forums for collective representation. The main objective is to evaluate the effectiveness of worker representation in the two countries.

The discussion is organised as follows. Part 2 sketches the comparative landscape of Australia and Italy. Part 3 examines literature on different approaches to representation of workers' interests, including freedom of association, trade union functions and employee 'voice'. This provides a framework for the assessment, in Part 4, of the effectiveness of responses by unions and other forms of collective representation to the deployment of various business models in Australia and Italy. The analysis covers four different (although sometimes overlapping) strategies to advance workers' interests: collective bargaining; lobbying to obtain improvements in the regulatory framework; litigation to challenge particular business models; and self-organisation or spontaneous worker protests. Part 5 sets out the chapter's conclusions.

Comparing the Landscape: Trade Unions, Labour Law and New Business Models in Australia and Italy

Trade Union Organisation and the Legal Framework for Worker Representation

Italy

Italy is generally situated within the southern European model of trade unionism and labour relations, characterised historically by: 'relatively late industrialisation, a large agricultural sector, and a high proportion of self-employment ... Trade unions have been ideologically divided ... and there is a tradition of extensive state regulation of employment conditions' (Gumbrell-McCormick and Hyman 2013, p. 20) The post-war period in Italy saw the emergence of three main 'rival trade union confederations': the Communist/socialist-oriented Confederazione Generale Italiana del Lavoro, the Christian Democrat-led Confederazione Italiana Sindacati Lavoratori and the smaller Unione Italiana del Lavoro 'formed by right-wing Socialists and republicans'. Italian union membership grew considerably following the wave of industrial militancy in the 'hot autumn' of 1969 (Gumbrell-McCormick and Hyman 2013, p. 23). The 1970 Workers' Statute provided a strong legal basis for representation at the workplace through trade unions, revised under a tripartite agreement in 1993 establishing the 'RSU' structure for workplace representative rights ('rappresentanza sindicale unitaria') (Regalia and Regini 2018, p. 65).

Italian unions have always had a role in the implementation of government programmes (e.g. social security, welfare) and engagement with public authorities. However, they faced 'a more hostile environment' under a centre-right government from the early 2000s (Regalia and Regini 2018, p. 65). Union density in Italy fell from 48% in 1980 to 33% in 2010, but experienced a rebound to 37.3% by 2013 (Gumbrell-McCormick and Hyman 2013, p. 5; Regalia and Regini 2018, p. 68). Collective bargaining coverage reduced marginally, from 85% in

1980 to 80% in 2010, but remained at that fairly high level in 2013 (Gumbrell-McCormick and Hyman 2013, p. 5; Regalia and Regini 2018, p. 69). Italy was (apart from Norway and the Ghent-system countries: Denmark, Finland, Iceland, Sweden) 'the only advanced economy' which experienced an increase in its union density rate during the Global Financial Crisis, and the only southern European nation where bargaining coverage remained stable through this period (Regalia and Regini 2018, p. 69).

The legal framework for union organisation in Italy begins with the right to trade union freedom in Article 39, paragraph 1 of the Italian Constitution. Trade union freedom, for these purposes, has both a positive connotation (e.g. to join a union, collect dues, hold meetings, take part in union campaigns) and a negative one (refraining from engagement in these types of activities) (Carinci 2015, pp. 279–280). Trade union freedom is legislated in Articles 14–15 of the 1970 Workers' Statute, including protection of workers from discrimination in hiring on the basis of trade union membership or non-membership, and in dismissal, transfer or disciplinary measures on the grounds of union membership or engaging in union activity (Carinci 2015, p. 283). Article 19 of that legislation provides for the formation of company-based trade unions ('rappresentanza sindicali aziendali' or 'RSAs') by unions affiliated with the main confederations, in businesses employing over 15 workers (Pallini 2016, p. 7; Ales and Senatori 2015, p. 2). As noted above, since the 1993 social pact, another type of union-based workplace representative body—RSUs—can be formed, resulting in overlap between the representative and bargaining functions of RSUs and RSAs (Carinci 2015, pp. 288–289). Collective bargaining rights are also founded in the Constitution (article 39, paragraph 1; and article 40 establishing the right to strike). Bargaining occurs at the national level through collective agreements negotiated by the major union confederations to apply across industries. The system allows limited derogations from the national agreements through firm-level bargaining (Regalia and Regini 2018, pp. 65–66; Pallini 2016).

Australia

Australia sits alongside the USA, UK and other '"firm-level bargaining" countries' (OECD 2017, p. 134), sharing a 'single channel' approach to worker representation dominated by trade unions.[2] Strong legal support for the role of unions formed a cornerstone of the conciliation and arbitration system adopted in 1904, contributing to the considerable growth of the Australian union movement (Rimmer 2004). Australia has one major union confederation, the Australian Council of Trade Unions (ACTU), with a transition in the last 30 years from a large number of craft-based unions to a group of around 20 industry-based organisations. This amalgamation process was one response to the significant decline in union membership levels from around the mid-1980s,[3] when pressure built for reform of centralised wage determination by industrial tribunals.

This led to successive waves of deregulatory legislation, commencing with the shift to enterprise-based bargaining in the early 1990s (Ronfeldt and McCallum 1995), followed by laws facilitating individualised bargaining and prohibiting the 'closed shop' and other forms of support for union activity (Cooper et al. 2009). Union density plummeted, from 50.6% in 1985 to 34.7% in 1996, then continuing to fall to 20% in 2009, 17% in 2013 and 14.7% in 2018 (ABS 2010, 2013, 2018). Collective bargaining coverage has also declined, although not as precipitously: from 83.4% in 1980 to 58% in 2010 (OECD 2017, p. 138), then holding steady at around that level (58.9% in 2018) (ABS 2019). In the last five years, however, collective agreement coverage in the private sector has shrunk (Pennington 2018). Despite falling membership, unions remain influential due to close ties with the Australian Labor Party (ALP).

The *Fair Work Act 2009* (Cth) provides a moderately favourable framework for collective bargaining at the enterprise level, situated above a 'safety net' of industry-level employment conditions ('modern awards'). Unions are the default bargaining representative of any members they have in the workplace. They may obtain recognition from employers for bargaining through a simple petition-based process. They can also access assistance from the Fair Work Commission (FWC) to progress collective negotiations (e.g. good faith bargaining orders). However, unions are not the *exclusive* bargaining representatives of employees (e.g. individual employees may represent themselves). Experience over the eleven years of operation of the *Fair Work Act* has exposed the effectiveness of employer strategies to undermine the statutory supports for union organisation and bargaining (McCrystal et al. 2018).

Adoption of New Business Models

Analyses of Australia (Hardy 2017) and Italy (Menegatti 2018) reveal that the forms and consequences of fissured work are quite similar in these two countries.

Italy

Italian firms began to utilise complex contracting chains from the mid-1970s, segmenting manufacturing processes in order to address skills gaps ('subcontracting of "capacity"') but later engaging more in 'subcontracting aimed merely at cost reduction'; and outsourcing of production to EU countries with lower labour costs became increasingly common (Menegatti 2015, pp. 91–92). Among other developments, the loosening of restrictions on indirect employment from the late 1990s and allowing a role for temporary work agencies meant that:

> Italian law at the beginning of the new millennium [had] therefore definitely opened up the door to business models very similar to those described by David Weil, having the effect of decreasing working conditions for those who work to supply goods or services to or on behalf of the lead company. (Menegatti 2015, p. 100)

Independent contractor arrangements (including misclassification of employees) are widespread in Italy; franchising is also common, although it has received less attention from labour lawyers (Menegatti 2015, pp. 112–113, 115–116). Recently, the 'work-related platform economy' has grown to engage between 700,000 and 1 million workers (concentrated in northern Italian cities with high population density)—a new form of fissuring involving exclusion of workers from social and labour protections (De Stefano and Aloisi 2018, pp. 3, 5).

Australia

Similar developments have occurred in Australia, beginning with various forms of outsourcing, followed by the growth of the labour hire industry, franchising, supply chains and the gig economy (Hardy 2017). I have noted previously that: 'These various [business] models have been used increasingly to distance employers from legal responsibility for workers' minimum employment standards, shifting that burden to smaller business units operating in highly competitive markets' (Forsyth 2017, p. 3). Significant attention has focused recently on the employment practices of labour hire firms and franchise networks amid evidence of widespread breaches of workplace laws (Forsyth 2017; Hardy 2019). Simultaneously, there has been rising concern about the contracting model utilised by gig platforms (i.e. the assumption of independent contractor status for workers who are really employees) (Minter 2017, pp. 441–442; Stewart and McCrystal 2019).

Assessing the Effectiveness of Collectivist Responses to New Business Models

In evaluating responses to the proliferation of business models which have produced fissured work in Australia and Italy, what measures of effectiveness might be utilised?[4] Traditionally, workers' interests are best advanced through freedom of association and collective bargaining, as reflected in standard-setting instruments of the International Labour Organization (ILO). As Hayter (2011, p. 7) states, these are fundamental rights: 'an essential means through which workers are able to ... negotiate improvements in their working conditions'. Intrinsic to freedom of association is the right of workers to form and join organisations for the furthering of their interests (trade unions).

Unions act as the main representative of employees in collective bargaining, offering a countervailing force to employer power (Hayter 2011, pp. 4–5). As well as determining wages and employment conditions, collective bargaining ensures workers' demands on job security, working time regulation and training are heard by management (OECD 2017, p. 129). For Ewing, collective bargaining forms part of the workplace representation function of unions. Collective representation may have a regulatory impact, in that 'its outcomes will typically apply to all the workers in the bargaining unit represented by the union' (Ewing 2005, pp. 3–4; Ford and Novitz 2020). In contrast, individual workplace representation may involve a union acting on behalf of an employee in a grievance or other kind of employment dispute (Ewing 2005, p. 3).

Ewing delineates several other functions performed by trade unions,[5] including a service function: the provision to members of professional services (e.g. legal advice) and 'friendly society'—like benefits (e.g. car insurance). Ewing also points to the regulatory function of unions: 'a process of rule-making that extends beyond their members'. This regulatory role may be direct, through multi-employer collective bargaining; or indirect, through 'legislation which trade unions play a part in securing'. Linked to this, Ewing highlights the governmental and public administration functions of unions: engaging with government to obtain laws that help unions fulfil their other purposes, through 'organised political representation' and involvement in developing and implementing government policy. He views this regulatory function as 'perhaps the most important … this being the most visible manifestation of the trade union role in promoting fairness and social justice not only at work but within the economy as a whole' (Ewing 2005, p. 13; 2014).

Hyman (2001, pp. 1–2) has expounded upon the market, societal and class orientations of unions, explaining his 'three ideal types of European trade unionism' as follows:

> In the first, unions are interest organizations with predominantly labour market functions; in the second, vehicles for raising workers' status in

> society more generally and hence advancing social justice; in the third, 'schools of war' in a struggle between labour and capital ...

In relation to the first of these models, unions traditionally acted to secure economic benefits for their members, primarily through collective bargaining (Hyman 2001, p. 6). As to the second, 'unions emerged as social movements challenging key principles of the social and economic order' (Hyman 2001, p. 60). And on the third, 'class struggle' of the kind envisaged by Marx and Engels has seen 'trade unionism [establish] an alternative set of principles to the logic of capitalism' (Hyman 2001, p. 17).

Freeman and Medoff (1984, p. 8) conceived of collective bargaining as a necessary expression of employee 'voice' in the workplace, a mechanism: 'for providing workers as a group with a means of communicating with management'. They considered this 'collective voice' could 'fundamentally alter the social relations of the workplace'; reduce wage inequalities; and 'alter nearly every other measurable aspect of the operation of workplaces' (Freeman and Medoff 1984, pp. 10, 16–17, 19). Less potent manifestations of worker voice are found in human resource management theory, including 'voice as a means to keep workers from quitting' and 'voice as a means to perfect the employer's organization [through] useful feedback' (Bogg and Novitz 2014, p. 12; Hirschman 1970). These expressions of voice, embodied in quality circles, team-building and reward systems, are usually management-initiated alternatives to trade unions (Bogg and Novitz 2014, p. 13). Somewhere in the middle, measured by influence on managerial decision-making, are information and consultation mechanisms underpinned by a regulatory framework (e.g. the German works council system) (Rogers and Streeck 1995).

Union and Emerging Collectivist Responses in Australia and Italy: A New Model of Solidarity for the Changing World of Work?

The examination in Part 3 of the functions traditionally performed by unions, and other manifestations of worker voice, provides a useful basis for measuring the effectiveness of collectivist responses to new business models in Australia and Italy. In this section, the strategies adopted by unions and emerging forms of collective representation in the two countries are discussed and evaluated, focusing on the four different types of representation mentioned in Part 1 above.

Overview

In Italy, unions have used their historic collaboration with non-standard workers as a basis for engagement with gig workers (Johnston and Land-Kazlauskas 2018, pp. 7–8). According to De Stefano and Aloisi (2018, p. 20): 'Almost every national trade union confederation has set up a working group on "digital transformation of work" with a specific focus on platform work'. Regalia and Regini (2018, p. 71) note that the Italian union movement has intensified 'strategies to contact and protect temporary and freelance workers'. Platforms are not only attracting increasing interest from Italian trade unions; in addition, 'new organisations have been launched in an attempt to "proto-unionise" platform workers' (De Stefano and Aloisi 2018, pp. 5–6). However, Italian unions face challenges in constructing effective forms of collectivism for gig workers, including their geographic isolation and innate resistance to being organised (e.g. due to concerns about management reprisals) (De Stefano and Aloisi 2018, p. 20). These problems are also encountered in Australia, where concerns have been raised 'about the capacity of on-demand workers to negotiate better wages and conditions' (Industrial Relations Victoria 2018, p. 12). Despite this, Australian unions are making headway in organising precarious workers. The ACTU made the proliferation of business structures which threaten secure work a focus of its recent campaign to 'change the rules' governing labour relations (McManus 2018). However, the unexpected re-election of the Coalition Government in the May 2019 federal election means these reform proposals (including sectoral and supply chain bargaining) will not be implemented.

Collective Bargaining/Attempts to Negotiate Collective Agreements

Italy

Amazon

The poor treatment of workers in Amazon 'fulfilment centres' is widely known (see, e.g., Bloodworth 2019): 'logistics work processes are characterized, on the one hand, by an extensive digitization and, on the other hand, by minimal automation, which makes human labour still required' (Cattero and D'Onofrio 2018, p. 143). Amazon engages minimally with trade unions, relies heavily on labour hire agencies to supply a mostly temporary workforce and closely monitors work performance with constant pressure to meet demanding targets. Amazon commenced operations in Italy in 2010 and uses temporary labour as a supplement to its permanent workforce in peak sales periods. Amazon workers have been prevented from joining unions or subjected to 'hostile attitudes' from management, and their temporary status has further deterred union involvement (Cattero and D'Onofrio 2018, pp. 143–146, 156–158).

However, the Filcams CGIL Nazionale union secured a collective agreement with Amazon in May 2018, following strike action during the 'Black Friday' sales period in late 2017 (Walker 2018; Casilli 2017). The agreement (for the company's regional hub in Piacenza) addressed worker concerns around fairness of scheduling and the allocation of weekend/night shifts; and provided for 25% higher pay rates at night (Walker 2018; UNI Global Union 2018). Taking effect on 17 June 2018, this was hailed as: 'the first-ever direct agreement between unions and the company anywhere in the world' (UNI Global Union 2018; Cattero and D'Onofrio 2018, p. 157).[6] Amazon stated, though, that this would not set any precedent for its approach to work organisation elsewhere (Sciotto 2018).

Australia

Airtasker

Airtasker is similar to platforms like TaskRabbit, matching tasks which consumers want performed with people to do the work.[7] Through their Airtasker accounts, 'job-posters' create tasks by providing details and indicating the rate to be paid (payment is per task, and the advertised rate must include Airtasker's 15% fee). Workers interested in completing the task can pitch for it at the advertised rate or seek to 'bid down' the rate of pay which has been offered (Unions NSW 2016, p. 3; Minter 2017, pp. 443–445). In 2016, the peak union body in the state of New South Wales, Unions NSW, argued in a public report that Airtasker 'has used a cloak of innovation and progress to re-introduce archaic and outdated labour practices' (Unions NSW 2016, p. 1). Further, Airtasker relies on its *User Agreement* description of a worker being selected by a job-poster as 'winning', to establish a 'task contract' between job-poster and worker, despite Airtasker's *Marketplace Rules* specifying various forms of control (e.g. deactivation of an account if the rules or agreement are violated) (Unions NSW 2016, pp. 3–4). Unions NSW's report led to the negotiation of an agreement with Airtasker, finalised in April 2017 and described by the union body as a 'world first' for the gig economy (Minter 2017, p. 449; Taylor 2017; Patty 2017). The key features of this agreement are as follows (Minter 2017, pp. 446–449):

- Airtasker now posts recommended pay rates on its website based on the minimum wage rates in modern awards.
- The parties would work together with insurance companies 'to develop an optional insurance policy which provides workers with coverage for personal injury'; and work on 'task-specific safety guidelines for both workers and job-posters, identifying potential workplace hazards and necessary safety precautions'.
- Unions NSW and Airtasker also sought the assistance of the FWC to develop a dispute resolution process for workers and job-posters in which the Commission would act as final arbitrator.

Under the Airtasker agreement, Unions NSW aims 'to address the lack of regulatory protection for workers using digital platforms' (Minter 2017, p. 442), although it acknowledges the limitations of the deal. The recommended pay rates are not mandatory, and the agreement 'cannot single-handedly eliminate the risks of exploitation and the downward bidding of labour standards in platform businesses' (Minter 2017, p. 450). After 12 months' experience under the agreement, Unions NSW Secretary Mark Morey argued that 'workers on the site have enjoyed better income and also have injury protection insurance available to them' (Workplace Express 2018a). Badges and licensing for trades-qualified work have also been integrated into the platform (Gregory 2018).

Transport Workers Union/Coles Accords

In May 2018, the Transport Workers Union (TWU) and the Coles supermarket chain entered into two memoranda of understanding (MOUs) relating to the fair treatment of workers in the company's supply chain and in its engagement of on-demand workers (Workplace Express 2018b). In the first MOU, the parties committed to developing a Charter 'to ensure that the transportation of Coles' freight by road is conducted in a manner that best secures safety and fairness for transport workers', guided by the following principles:

- the role of each link in the supply chain in ensuring workers' health and safety;
- the right of workers to be treated fairly and to 'have the opportunity to contribute to a collective voice';
- involvement in industry initiatives to improve work practices and eliminate incentives to engage in unsafe practices.[8]

The second MOU notes that 'the on demand workforce is part of a new and rapidly evolving workplace environment, based on new technology leading to distinctly different methods of work coordination through digital platforms'. The MOU establishes principles aimed at ensuring that 'on demand workers are not compromised in terms of safety, fairness and engagement', including:

- preventing 'artificial labels' from applying to these workers that 'would limit their access to appropriate payments, leave entitlements, superannuation, safe working conditions and representation';
- promotion of transport as a career rather than 'a one-off "gig"';
- the opportunity of on-demand workers to collectively organise with co-workers.[9]

Assessment

The efforts of Italian and Australian unions to negotiate collective agreements in fissured work contexts demonstrate varying degrees of success in performing Ewing's collective workplace representation function, or Hyman's labour market function. Filcams CGIL Nazionale's 'world-first' collective agreement with Amazon, obtained through industrial action, represents a potent form of worker representation. It resulted in direct improvements in wages and employment conditions, against the resistance of a multinational behemoth notorious for a 'union-busting' model globally. In contrast, the unions covering Amazon workers in Australia do not yet have a foothold for bargaining (although see Karp 2018). In-depth media reporting has highlighted the company's almost total reliance on labour hire casuals (Hatch 2018a; Burin 2019), leading Amazon to create 500 permanent positions (Marin-Guzman 2019).

Unions NSW's agreement with Airtasker is a less effective embodiment of collective workplace representation than the Italian Amazon example. The Airtasker agreement is not legally enforceable, and Unions NSW acknowledges that more is required to effectively regulate gig platforms. Kaine (2017) argues that, in the absence of actually setting minimum pay rates or working conditions, the agreement 'doesn't go far enough'. However, the Unions NSW/Airtasker deal does have *some* value as an exercise in worker representation. As Buchanan observes, '[l]abour standards start from modest bases' and this agreement 'provides a point of reference' in a context 'which has been labour-standards free' (Patty 2017).

The two TWU accords with Coles do not amount to a form of collective worker representation that leads directly to measurable improvements in employment conditions, establishing general principles only. However, the MOUs exhibit other elements of trade union functions which cannot be ignored, going some way towards Ewing's conception of the regulatory role of unions (i.e. rule-making that has the *potential* to extend beyond the union's immediate membership). The commitments given by Coles can shape not only its own practices, but those of other actors in its supply chain. Both MOUs involve recognition of the right of Coles' transport workers to a 'collective voice' (in Freeman and Medoff's terms, the medium for fundamentally transforming the social relations of the workplace). The on-demand work MOU also includes a commitment to avoid sham contracting (a central component of the business model of most platforms).

Union Lobbying to Obtain Improvements in Regulatory Framework

Italy

Food Delivery Platforms

Italy has recently seen considerable activism among self-organised food delivery workers (discussed below). Some of these groups (including the Riders Union Bologna) combined with the established union confederations to negotiate a 'Charter of fundamental digital workers' rights within an urban setting' with the Bologna City Council and a food delivery platform (Zamponi 2018; Liebman and Aloisi 2018). The Charter (signed on 31 May 2018) includes provisions for fixed hourly wage rates as set down in national collective agreements, compensation for overtime work and public holidays, formal notification (with reasons) for excluding workers from a platform, accident/sickness insurance, as well as freedom of association and the right to strike (De Stefano and Aloisi 2018, pp. 20–21; Zamponi 2018; Vandaele 2018, p. 17). Local measures to provide advice and information for food delivery riders, and improved protections for platform workers more broadly, have been adopted in Milan and Lazio, respectively (as well as Bologna).

Dignity Decree

Italian unions have long worked to improve the position of non-standard workers by lobbying for legal reforms and collective bargaining (Johnston and Land-Kazlauskas 2018, pp. 7–8). Although not the direct result of this kind of campaigning, the former League/Five Star Movement Government sponsored enactment of a 'Dignity Decree' which took effect on 14 July 2018. This measure overturned certain elements of the 2015 Jobs Act, reducing the maximum length of fixed-term contracts from 36 to 24 months and limiting the number of renewals of these contracts to four (from five previously) (Merler 2018). De Stefano argues, however, 'that the decree is a limited measure that only deals with categories of temporary workers that are not the most vulnerable' (Merler 2018).

Australia

Rights for Riders

The TWU and the Young Workers Centre (YWC) of the Victorian Trades Hall Council have been pushing hard to highlight the misclassification of food delivery workers engaged by Foodora, Deliveroo and Uber Eats (YWC 2017). YWC is organising food delivery workers through its 'Rights for Riders' campaign,[10] to improve their 'safety, pay, conditions and job security' based on the notion of 'joining with other riders to stand up for your rights'.[11] Information is provided on YWC's website about matters such as where riders stand if they are injured or their bike is damaged, regularity of payment and minimum shift periods. YWC made a submission to a 2017 Senate Inquiry, arguing that the gig economy is simply 'sham contracting rebadged': food delivery riders are engaged as independent contractors although they are really economically dependent on the platforms (YWC 2017, pp. 3, 6). YWC's submission included a comparison of weekly income received by food bike couriers under three different Deliveroo contracts, with the applicable rates under the *Road Transport and Distribution Award* and superannuation legislation. This analysis showed a shortfall ('wages stolen per week') of between A$72.91 and A$158.91 in income and A$32.20 in superannuation (YWC 2017, pp. 6–7; Goods et al. 2019).

In their campaigning on behalf of gig workers, the TWU and YWC have called for higher minimum hourly rates of pay, allowances for working in poor weather conditions and improved rating systems (Bright and Fitzgerald 2018). This activism has led to some reforms and proposals for change at the state level. In mid-2018, the Victorian Government announced that it would extend an existing legal regime protecting the rights of transport industry owner drivers, to digital platform-based food delivery riders. The amending legislation gave these workers access to the dispute resolution mechanism and obligations upon businesses operating under the *Owner Drivers and Forestry Contractors Act 2005* (Vic).[12] The Victorian Government also conducted an independent Inquiry into the On-Demand Workforce, which made extensive recommendations in mid-2020 to counter the spurious presumption of contractor status imposed on gig economy workers (James 2020).

Fair Food Campaign

Since 2015, the United Workers Union (UWU) 'Fair Food Campaign' has highlighted the exploitation of vulnerable workers in Australia's fresh food supply chain (Underhill et al. 2020). The UWU's innovative approach seeks to align the interests of its traditional core membership base in logistics and warehousing with those of workers in the packing sheds on fruit and vegetable farms (Small 2018). A multifaceted strategy is being deployed by the UWU in the agricultural sector: organising workers for collective bargaining; litigation alleging underpayment and other workplace law breaches (Schneiders 2018); and intensive lobbying for legislative reforms to better protect vulnerable migrant workers. The most direct response to those efforts is the enactment of labour hire licensing legislation aimed at eliminating exploitative labour contractors in three states (Queensland, Victoria and South Australia) and the Australian Capital Territory (Forsyth 2019). The public attention to issues highlighted in the UWU's Fair Food Campaign also led to action by the Coalition Government, through the *Fair Work Amendment (Protecting Vulnerable Workers) Act 2017* (Cth).

Assessment

In their initiatives to obtain regulatory changes to improve protections for platform workers and those engaged through complex supply chains, Italian and Australian unions have been reasonably effective in carrying out Ewing's indirect regulatory function and governmental/public administration function. These initiatives also display elements of the societal orientation of trade unions described by Hyman, seeking to challenge central aspects of the social and economic order. The Bologna Charter is a clear example of union intervention leading to increased worker protections at the municipal level. At the national level, the link between union activism and the Italian Government's Dignity Decree is less clear.

In Australia, extensive efforts by the TWU/YWC on behalf of workers engaged by food delivery platforms have resulted in reform proposals in the state of Victoria. More significant legal changes applying across the nation were anticipated if the May 2019 election had resulted in a federal Labor Government (ALP 2018, p. 59), but this did not eventuate. Organising, litigation and campaigning by the UWU on behalf of horticultural workers have delivered tangible results in public policy terms, and Small (2018) hailed the Fair Food Campaign as 'one of the few systematic union organizing drives in Australia today'.

Litigation to Challenge Particular Business Models

Italy

In April 2018, the Employment Tribunal of Turin ruled on a claim brought by six riders engaged by the food delivery platform, Foodora, arguing that they had been misclassified and should be regarded (at law) as employees (De Stefano and Aloisi 2018, p. 12). The workers contended that they had been wrongfully 'dismissed as a form of retaliation against their decision to take part in a collective demonstration against the shift in [Foodora's] payment system from an hourly-based to a piece rate model' (Aloisi 2018). Italian law maintains a 'strict binary divide' between employment and self-employment. The Foodora worker had been engaged via a particular sub-category of self-employment known as 'collaborazione coordinate e continuativa' or 'Co.Co.Co', applicable (under a 1973 law) to 'contractual relations implying a continual performance of work, mainly of a personal character, although not in a position of subordination' (Aloisi 2018).

In the Foodora case, the judge ruled that because the riders were free to decide on matters such as when they would work, and could accept or refuse shifts, they were not subordinate to the employer's power to command and therefore were not employees. However, according to Aloisi's critique (2018):

> ... the judge in Turin decided the case by looking at the rear-view mirror. ... In the search for a legal precedent, the judge applied the same reasoning made thirty years ago for delivery couriers on mopeds, even though technological progress and the regulatory framework have taken significant steps forward.

In January 2019, the Turin Court of Appeal confirmed the Employment Tribunal's finding that the Foodora riders could not be considered employees—but also determined that they were not properly to be viewed as self-employed. Rather, the 'riders belong to a third type of relationship between self-employment and subordinated employment', and must be accorded the same rights as employees working in the same sector (Pedroni 2019). This could also be viewed as a subset of self-employed work to which employment law applies. Then, in January 2020, the Italian Supreme Court finally ruled that although the riders are self-employed, certain employment protections applied to them as they fell into the category of 'etero-organizati' workers (i.e. those effectively organised by the other party) (Sideri 2020; Aloisi 2020, p. 4).

Australia

In three Australian cases, Uber drivers (who were not represented by a union or lawyers) failed to establish that they were employees, a necessary prerequisite for having their unfair dismissal claims determined by the FWC. In each decision,[13] the tribunal applied the common law multi-factor test for distinguishing employees from independent contractors and found that the drivers had control over when to log on and off from the Uber app. Combined with other relevant factors (e.g. the absence of any prohibition on drivers performing work for others), they could not be considered employees of Uber. This reasoning also informed the conclusion of the Fair Work Ombudsman (FWO) that Uber drivers are independent contractors. After a two-year investigation, the enforcement agency decided in June 2019 there was no basis for pursuing compliance action against Uber (i.e. the company's contractor model does not breach the FW Act) (FWO 2019). In April 2020, a Full Bench of the FWC followed similar logic to conclude that a delivery driver for Uber Eats was not an employee (even though the majority members of the bench also found that she was incapable of developing her own independent delivery business using the 'freedom' provided under her contractual arrangements with Uber Eats).[14]

A different result arose from an unfair dismissal claim brought by the TWU on behalf of a Foodora delivery rider, which proceeded despite the company entering into voluntary administration and ceasing operations in Australia in August 2018 (see below). In *Klooger v Foodora Australia Pty Ltd*,[15] the FWC decided that the rider was an employee, the first definitive Australian ruling confirming the employment status of a platform worker. This conclusion was based on the high level of control exercised by Foodora over the rider's work, including the use of a 'batching system' for allocating deliveries based on performance metrics. In the tribunal's view, the rider was not carrying on a trade or business on his own behalf. Rather, he was an employee of Foodora and therefore eligible to pursue an unfair dismissal claim. The FWC rejected Foodora's argument that the rider was sacked for breaching the company's intellectual property rules. Instead, he was unlawfully dismissed for being involved in agitation about the terms and conditions imposed on Foodora riders, and was awarded A$15,559 compensation.

Assessment

The success or otherwise of litigation to establish the employment status of platform workers has depended in part on whether unions were involved in supporting the workers' claims. It is understood that the Turin Foodora riders brought their case as a spontaneous collective group without union support (achieving limited success on appeal). The unsuccessful Australian Uber drivers were not represented, while the TWU intervened in the Uber Eats appeal and backed the only successful platform worker case so far. In these cases, the TWU performed both the service function and the individual representation function of unions as posited by Ewing, but also something akin to his indirect regulatory function: seeking changes to the rules affecting workers' rights, although through favourable precedent rather than legislation. It is interesting that Foodora has been the subject of test cases in each country, with different conclusions reached. In Italy, the company has not only faced litigation testing the legal status of riders, but also considerable self-organised worker activism (see below). In Australia, the TWU stepped in to highlight Foodora's abandonment of its obligations to workers by abruptly leaving the country (Workplace Express 2018c). The FWO and federal/NSW tax authorities were also pursuing the company (Marin-Guzman 2018; Chau 2018), part of a broader regulatory backlash against Foodora's short-lived foray into the Australian market.

Self-Organisation/Spontaneous Worker Protests

Italy

Italian food delivery riders have engaged in protests and strikes, seeking to improve their working conditions, which have attracted significant attention across the country. Zamponi (2018) explains the favourable media coverage and public support for the riders in terms of the image projected by the platforms of the 'the rider as a young adult on a bicycle', reproducing 'an idea of smartness, coolness, and modernity, spiced with techno-enthusiasm and environmental sensitivity'. This image becomes 'a powerful weapon' for the riders, making the platforms 'vulnerable in the public eye' if 'a key element of the value chain' comes under attack.

A public protest by around 50 Foodora riders took place in Turin on 8 October 2016, after they had signed a petition demanding improved conditions (particularly relating to the bike maintenance and Internet costs they have to meet themselves). A bigger concern was Foodora's introduction of a payment by delivery system (rather than an hourly rate). Riders demanded an end to their subordinate legal status, observance of national collective agreement wage levels and conditions, and cessation of 'punitive practices' against perceived 'troublemakers' (Tassinari and Maccarrone 2017a, p. 354). The riders' tactics in the Turin 'proto-strike' were innovative, as explained by Tassinari and Maccarrone (2017a, p. 354):

> … [they] 'unlogged' from the app and encouraged others to do the same, thus impacting the company's capacity to fulfil its orders. They then staged visible protests around the city with their bikes and flags, holding 'flying pickets' that went through restaurants and squares handing out flyers to restaurant owners and members of the public, inviting them to boycott the app. This was coordinated with an online campaign targeting the company's social media pages with critical comments, aimed at negatively affecting its reputation.

The protest was partly effective: Foodora reluctantly met with some of the riders' representatives and agreed to increase the new delivery fee from €2.70 to €3.60; provided limited assistance to riders for bicycle repairs; but refused the key demand to return to the hourly payment structure (Tassinari and Maccarrone 2017a, p. 355). Activists were removed from access to the app, 'thus diluting the unity of the original core of protestors'. However as Tassinari and Maccarrone (2017a, p. 355) observe, a strike involving only 50 workers attracted such widespread attention because: 'this represents the first-known case of worker self-organization in the Italian gig economy' (Tassinari and Maccarrone 2017b). This strike was followed by protests by Deliveroo riders in Milan (in summer 2017), and by cross-platform collectives of riders in Bologna (in autumn 2017) and Rome (November 2018). Self-organised collectives have taken a number of different forms, e.g. Deliveroo Strike Raiders, Riders Union Bologna and Deliverance Milano, pressuring Deliveroo to apply the national collective agreement for transport and pay a minimum wage of €7.50/hour, a minimum of 20 hours per week payment, inclement weather rates and insurance coverage (Zamponi 2018).

In 2018, the Labour and Industry Minister in Italy's new Government proposed a decree that would provide greater protections for workers engaged by food delivery platforms (including paid holidays, sick leave and minimum wages). Further, workers would be paid hourly rather than 'per drop' rates and would obtain the right to disconnect from the app. This legislative proposal followed meetings held by the Minister, Luigi Di Maio, with platform workers' representatives and company managers (De Stefano and Aloisi 2018, p. 13). According to Zamponi (2018), it was a deliberate strategy of Di Maio's Five Star Movement to negotiate directly with self-organised worker collectives rather than the established union confederations, providing 'an unquestionable piece of recognition for the [riders'] movement'. Di Maio stated that the Government wanted 'to ensure minimum protections for this category of the gig economy', describing food delivery workers as the 'symbol of a generation abandoned by the state' (Politi 2018). The CEO of Foodora Italy countered that the Government's 'demonisation of technology is incredible, it's almost medieval' and was intended to drive digital platforms out of Italy (Politi 2018). Ultimately the proposed law was not implemented: the Italian Government instead put forward a more moderate reform statute which was passed in November 2019 (including access to collective bargaining for self-employed riders) (Aloisi 2020, pp. 2–3).

Australia

In addition to the role played by the TWU in representing rideshare drivers, in June 2016 an online workers' forum emerged called 'RideShare Drivers United' (RSDU). RSDU operates in Melbourne, Perth, Sydney and the USA. It offers free membership, and aims 'to help unite [ride-share] drivers anywhere in the world with fellow drivers right next door, to help change our situation right here right now!'[16] Through the RSDU app, drivers are alerted any time a 'collaborative action' is planned for their area or when a 'vote' is required for future collaborative events/actions. RSDU's philosophy bears some hallmarks of traditional trade unionism:

> Download and share the RSDU app among other drivers. *Let's all stand together and ensure* that our rights to a fair days [sic] work are not exploited. It is only through large scale collaborative effort that *we can send a strong message to the ride share companies.* A message they can not [sic] ignore.[17]

RSDU held a driver's strike and protest in Melbourne on 11 April 2017, with 1200–1500 drivers participating (Workplace Express 2017). This was followed by further Uber 'log-offs/strikes' in Australian capital cities on 5 and 22 August 2018 (Thomsen 2018). Key RSDU demands included payment to drivers for the actual time/distance they travel (rather than Uber's 'upfront pricing' model), a 12-hour cap on the working day and compensation for petrol price fluctuations (AAP 2018). Upfront pricing was introduced in 2018, giving passengers the precise cost before their ride, but with the result that drivers 'take home [10%-30%] less pay for doing the same amount of work' (according to 'Max B' who runs RSDU but 'would not reveal his last name for fear of being "deactivated" by Uber') (Hatch 2018b; Stanford 2018). Uber does not engage with RSDU, stating that it has roundtables and focus groups for consultation with its 'driver-partners' (AAP 2018).

Assessment

Self-organisation among gig workers in the food delivery sector has been prominent in Italy, with a moderate level of success in achieving direct improvements in employment conditions at one platform (Foodora, following the Turin protest) and across the sector (the Government's 2019 decree). Various self-organised worker groups were also influential in negotiating the Bologna Charter. These emerging forms of collective representation are seeking to perform functions typically carried out by traditional trade unions: securing economic benefits for those they represent (Hyman's labour market function), providing an expression of collective worker voice to counter managerial power (Freeman and Medoff), and direct/indirect regulatory functions as well as organised political representation (Ewing). The modus operandi of these more spontaneous forms of worker organisation also has elements in common with Hyman's class orientation of unions, with workers engaging in sharp bursts of protest and industrial action aimed at curbing the excesses of capital.

In contrast, the RSDU in Australia has had minimal impact so far. Kaine and Josserand (2017) cite the RSDU as an example of the growing phenomenon of 'alt-unionism': '... a catch-all term that can refer to spontaneous actions by workers that don't conform to the traditional pattern of strike behaviour or other industrial action. ... It's also characterised by the fluid campaigns (often digital) launched outside of regular channels of representation'. However the RSDU appears to have low penetration among rideshare drivers and has obtained no demonstrable improvements in their working conditions. The fact that RSDU's leader feels he needs to remain anonymous speaks volumes about the challenges faced by self-organised groups seeking to collectivise the gig economy.

Conclusions

The evidence and analysis presented in this chapter demonstrate that a new form of solidarity is indeed emerging in response to the adoption of various business models in Australia and Italy—or, that it is proving possible to 'organize the "unorganizable"' (Zamponi 2018). Using the framework provided by literature on the functions performed by trade unions, other forms of worker representation and employee voice, it has been shown that some established unions and emerging forms of collectivism have been quite effective in advancing the interests of workers and challenging the fissuring of work.

The best examples include Filcams CGIL Nazionale's collective agreement with Amazon; union and self-organised rider groups' involvement in obtaining the Bologna Charter; and the UWU's Fair Food Campaign leading to significant regulatory reform. More modest efforts, achieving some improved outcomes for workers and a basis for building stronger collective voice, include Unions NSW's agreement with Airtasker; the TWU's supply chain and on-demand work MOUs with Coles; TWU/YWC's campaigning on behalf of food delivery riders; and the self-organised riders' protests against food delivery platforms in northern Italy. Another self-organised group, Australia's RSDU, represents a weaker form of collective representation. Litigation in both countries to challenge a particular business model (gig work) has resulted in mixed success, the TWU's unfair dismissal claim against Foodora being the best result to date. The strongest examples can be found where unions, like the UWU and TWU, utilise a multi-pronged strategy with the ultimate aim of increasing the collective power of workers: public campaigning, litigation of individual or group claims and grass-roots organising.

The conclusions of this study converge with others which have found that:

- collective representation of workers in the gig economy and other types of fragmented work is most effective when supported by established trade unions (Tassinari and Maccarrone 2017a, p. 356);
- unions need to be willing to experiment with innovative tactics (public/media campaigns; street protests; digital organising) in order to attract workers engaged through new business models (Vandaele 2018, p. 16);
- the most successful unions are looking 'beyond their actual member base' in their efforts to represent the interests of workers in fissured

work contexts (Vandaele 2018, p. 19; see also Benassi and Vlandas 2016, on the concept of 'union inclusiveness').

While the various business models examined here have presented serious challenges to unions, it is clear that new opportunities also arise, offering prospects for the development of different expressions of collectivism. Ultimately, it is up to established unions and emerging worker representatives to intervene and reverse the trend towards fissured work over the last 30 years. Through the implementation of business models like labour hire, franchising, contracting, supply chains and now the gig economy, employers have been able to avoid trade unions. Now though, as De Stefano (2018) has argued: 'Companies can't expect to choose their negotiating partner. They have to negotiate with the collective organisations that the workers have chosen to represent them'. There are significant questions as to whether traditional legal and institutional supports for freedom of association and collective bargaining are sufficient to help achieve that outcome. Further stages of this research will closely examine the supports and barriers to effective exercise of worker power in Australian and Italian law and recommend options for reform.

Acknowledgements Thanks to Valerio De Stefano, Antonio Aloisi, Emanuele Menegatti and Paolo Tomassetti for responding to queries about the Italian scene. Antonio, Emanuele and Kurt Vandaele (ETUI, Brussels) kindly gave helpful feedback on an earlier draft. Thanks also to Kate Minter (formerly of Unions NSW) and Sarah Bright/Carita Kazakoff (formerly of VTHC Young Workers Centre) for providing additional information about Airtasker and Rights for Riders respectively. Any errors are my own.

Notes

1. See, e.g., *R. (on the application of The Independent Workers Union of Great Britain) v Central Arbitration Committee and Roofoods Ltd t/a Deliveroo* [2018] EWHC 3342 (Admin).
2. In contrast to the 'dual channel' of union and works council representation in some continental European countries; see Davies (1994).

3. Peetz (1998, pp. 25–26), noting that union density peaked at 63% of the workforce in 1953, falling to 49% in 1969, returning to as high as 56% in 1975 and 1983, before beginning its steady fall.
4. In addition to the literature discussed here, see Gall and Fiorito (2014).
5. Ewing (2005, pp. 3–5) (the discussion and quotations in this paragraph are drawn mostly from these pages).
6. For examples beyond Amazon, see Curcio (2018).
7. See https://www.airtasker.com/.
8. Coles-TWU MOU, *Principles to Ensure Safety & Fairness for Transport Workers in the Coles Supply Chain* (23 May 2018).
9. Coles-TWU MOU, *Principles to Ensure Safety and Fairness for On Demand Workers* (23 May 2018).
10. See http://www.youngworkers.org.au/rights4riders.
11. See http://www.youngworkers.org.au/rights4ridersfaq.
12. *Owner Drivers and Forestry Contractors Amendment Act 2019* (Vic).
13. *Kaseris v Rasier Pacific V.O.F.* [2017] FWC 6610; *Pallage v Rasier Pacific Pty Ltd* [2018] FWC 2579; *Suliman v Rasier Pacific Pty Ltd* [2019] FWC 4807.
14. *Gupta v Portier Pacific Pty Ltd; Uber Australia Pty Ltd T/A Uber Eats* [2020] FWCFB 1698.
15. [2018] FWC 6836.
16. See http://ridesharedriversunited.com/.
17. See http://ridesharedriversunited.com/mission-statement/ (emphasis added).

References

Ales, Edoardo, and Iacopo Senatori. 2015. "Collective Bargaining and Workers' (Trade Union) Representation: The Company Level in Italy". Paper for the Labour Law Research Network Conference. Amsterdam.

Aloisi, Antonio. 2018. "'With Great Power Comes Virtual Freedom': A Review of the First Italian Case Holding That (Food-Delivery) Platform Workers Are Not Employees." *Comparative Labor Law and Policy Journal*. Dispatch No. 13.

Aloisi, Antonio. 2020. "A Fascinating Chapter in the 'Gig' Saga: How to Deliver Decent Work to Platform Workers in Italy." Mutual Learning Programme. DG Employment, Social Affiars and Inclusion. European Union.

Australian Associated Press (AAP). 2018. "Uber Drivers Log Off in Australia-Wide Protest Against Low Fares". *The Guardian*, August 6.

Australian Bureau of Statistics (ABS). 2010. *Australian Labour Market Statistics*, July 2010. Cat. 6105.0.

Australian Bureau of Statistics (ABS). 2013. *Employee Earnings, Benefits and Trade Union Membership, Australia*. Cat. 6310.0.

Australian Bureau of Statistics (ABS). 2018. *Characteristics of Employment, Australia*. Cat. 6333.0.

Australian Bureau of Statistics (ABS). 2019. *Employee Earnings and Hours, Australia*, May 2018. Cat. 6306.0.

Australian Labor Party (ALP). 2018. *2018 National Platform: Final Draft*.

Benassi, Chiara and Tim Vlandas. 2016. "Union Inclusiveness and Temporary Agency Workers: The Role of Power Resources and Union Ideology." *European Journal of Industrial Relations* 22 (1): 5–22.

Bloodworth, James. 2019. *Hired: Six Months Undercover in Low-Wage Britain*. London: Atlantic Books.

Bogg, Alan, and Tonia Novitz. 2014. "The Purposes and Techniques of Voice: Prospects for Continuity and Change." In *Voices at Work: Continuity and Change in the Common Law World*, edited by Alan Bogg and Tonia Novitz, 3. Oxford: Oxford University Press.

Bright, Sarah, and Amy Fitzgerald. 2018. "Snapshot: On-Demand Food Delivery Riders." Transport Workers Union (TWU), Young Workers Center.

Burin, Margaret. 2019. "What It's Like to Work in an Amazon Australia Warehouse." *ABC News*, February 27.

Carinci, Franco. 2015. "Trade Union Freedom, Organization and Activities." In *Labour Law and Industrial Relations in Italy: Update to the Jobs Act*, edited by Franco Carinci and Emanuele Menegatti, 279–300. Milano: IPSOA, Wolters Kluwer Italia.

Casilli, Antonio. 2017. "Lessons from Amazon's Italian Hub Strike." November 28. http://www.casilli.fr/. Accessed on November 14, 2020.

Cattero, Bruno, and Marta D'Onofrio. 2018. "Organizing and Collective Bargaining in the Digitized 'Tertiary Factories' of Amazon: A Comparison Between Germany and Italy." In *Working in Digital and Smart Organizations: Legal, Economic and Organizational Perspectives on the Digitalization of Labour Relations*, edited by Edoardo Ales, Ylenia Curzi, Tommaso Fabbri,

Olga Rymkevich, Iacopo Senatori, and Giovanni Solinas, 141–164. Cham: Palgrave Macmillan.

Chau, David. 2018. "Foodora Fallout: ATO Comes After Failed Food Delivery Company for Unpaid Taxes." *ABC News*, August 28.

Cooper, Rae, Ellem Bradon, Briggs Chris, and Diane Van Den Broek. 2009. "Anti-Unionism, Employer Strategy, and the Australian State, 1996–2005." *Labor Studies Journal* 34: 339.

Curcio, Anna. 2018. "Italy: The Revolution in Logistics." In *The Class Strikes Back: Self-Organised Workers' Struggles in the Twenty-First Century*, edited by Dario Azzellini and Michael Kraft, 259–275. Chicago: Haymarket Books.

Davies, Paul. 1994. "A Challenge to Single Channel." *Industrial Law Journal* 23 (3): 272–285.

De Stefano, Valerio. 2018. "Amazon, Uber, Deliveroo: Anything but Odd Jobs." *Morning Future*, January 15.

De Stefano, Valerio, and Antonio Aloisi. 2018. "Digital Age: Employment and Working Conditions of Selected Types of Platform Work—National Context Analysis, Italy." Working Paper. European Foundation for the Improvement of Living and Working Conditions.

Ewing, Keith D. 2005. "The Function of Trade Unions." *Industrial Law Journal* 34 (1): 1–22.

Ewing, Keith D. 2014. "The Importance of Trade Union Political Voice: Labour Law Meets Constitutional Law." In *Voices at Work: Continuity and Change in the Common Law World*, edited by Alan Bogg and Tonia Novitz, 277. Oxford: Oxford University Press.

Fair Work Ombudsman (FWO). 2019. "Uber Australia Investigation Finalised." Media Release, 7 June.

Ford, Michael, and Tonia Novitz. 2020. "There Is Power in a Union? Revisiting Trade Union Functions in 2019." In *The Constitution of Social Democracy: Essays in Honour of Keith Ewing*, edited by Alan Bogg, Jacob Rowbottom, and Alison Young, 261–286. Oxford: Hart Publishing.

Forsyth, Anthony. 2017. "The Victorian Inquiry into Labour Hire and Insecure Work: Addressing Worker Exploitation in Complex Business Structures." *E-Journal of International and Comparative Labour Studies* 6 (3).

Forsyth, Anthony. 2019. "Regulating Australia's 'Gangmasters' Through Labour Hire Licensing." *Federal Law Review* 47 (3): 469–493.

Freeman, Richard, and James Medoff. 1984. *What Do Unions Do?* New York: Basic Books.

Gall, Gregor, and Jack Fiorito. 2014. "Union Effectiveness: In Search of the Holy Grail." *Economic and Industrial Democracy* 37 (1): 189–211.

Goods, Caleb, Veen Alex, and Tom Barratt. 2019. "'Is Your Gig Any Good?' Analysing Job Quality in the Australian Platform-Based Food Delivery Sector." *Journal of Industrial Relations* 61 (4): 502–527.

Gregory, Katherine. 2018. "Airtasker: Unions Raise Safety Concerns Over 'Gig Economy' Cowboys." *ABC News*, March 9.

Gumbrell-McCormick, Rebecca, and Richard Hyman. 2013. *Trade Unions in Western Europe: Hard Times, Hard Choices.* Oxford: Oxford University Press.

Hardy, Tess. 2017. "Reconsidering the Notion of the 'Employer' in the Era of the Fissured Workplace: Traversing the Legislative Landscape in Australia." In *The Notion of the Employer in the Era of the Fissured Workplace: Should Labour Law Responsibilities Exceed the Boundary of the Legal Entity?*, edited by Hiroya Nakakubo and Takashi Araki. Alphen aan den Rijn: Kluwer Law International, Wolters Kluwer.

Hardy, Tess. 2019. "Big Brands, Big Responsibilities? An Examination of Franchisor Accountability for Employment Contraventions in the United States, Canada and Australia." *Comparative Labor Law and Policy Journal* 40 (2): 285–324.

Hatch, Patrick. 2018a. "In Amazon's "Hellscape" Workers Face Insecurity and Crushing Targets." *The Sydney Morning Herald*, September 7.

Hatch, Patrick. 2018b. "Uber Drivers Feel "Pay Cut" Pinch as Rivals Grow." *The Age*, July 30.

Hayter, Susan. 2011. "Introduction." In *The Role of Collective Bargaining in the Global Economy: Negotiating for Social Justice*, edited by Susan Hayter, 1. Cheltenham: Edward Elgar Publishing.

Hirschman, Albert O. 1970. *Exit, Voice and Loyalty: Responses to Decline in Firms, Organizations and States.* Cambridge: Harvard University Press.

Hyman, Richard. 2001. *Understanding European Trade Unionism: Between Market, Class and Society.* London: Sage Publications.

Industrial Relations Victoria. 2018. "Inquiry into the Victorian On-Demand Workforce." Background Paper.

James, Natalie. 2020. "Report of the Inquiry into the Victorian On-Demand Workforce." Melbourne: Victorian Government.

Johnston, Hannah, and Chris Land-Kazlauskas. 2018. "Organizing On-Demand: Representation, Voice and Collective Bargaining in the Gig Economy." ILO Conditions of Work and Employment Series No. 94. Geneva: International Labour Office.

Kaine, Sarah. 2017. "All Care and No Responsibility: Why Airtasker Can't Guarantee a Minimum Wage." *The Conversation*, May 2.

Kaine, Sarah, and Emmanuel Josserand. 2017. "Alt-Unionism: Why Businesses May Be Better with the Devil They Know." *The Conversation*, April 3.
Karp, Paul. 2018. "Unions to Step Up Efforts at Amazon Australia After Worker Sacked." *The Guardian*, December 10.
Liebman, Stefano, and Antonio Aloisi. 2018. "The Labor Rights of Riders and Other Gig Workers." July 30. https://www.viasarfatti25.unibocconi.eu/notizia.php?idArt=19849. Accessed on November 14, 2020.
Marin-Guzman, David. 2018. "Foodora Leaked Emails Warn Business Vulnerable over "Sham" Contracts." *Australian Financial Review*, April 29.
Marin-Guzman, David. 2019. "Amazon Promises 500 Permanent Jobs After Casual Flak." *Australian Financial Review*, February 27.
McCrystal, Shae, Creighton Breen, and Anthony Forsyth. 2018. *Collective Bargaining Under the Fair Work Act.* Sydney: Federation Press.
McManus, Sally. 2018. "Speech to John Curtin Research Centre Gala Dinner." *ACTU*, October 5.
Menegatti, Emanuele. 2015. "Mending the Fissured Workplace: The Solutions Provided by Italian Law." *Comparative Labor Law and Policy Journal* 37 (1): 91–120.
Menegatti, Emanuele. 2018. "A Fair Wage for Workers on Demand via App." In *Working in Digital and Smart Organizations: Legal, Economic and Organizational Perspectives on the Digitalization of Labour Relations*, edited by Edoardo Ales, Ylenia Curzi, Tommaso Fabbri, Olga Rymkevich, Iacopo Senatori, and Giovanni Solinas, 67–92. Cham: Palgrave Macmillan.
Merler, Silvia, 2018. "Italy's 'Dignity Decree.'" *Bruegel*, July 23.
Minter, Kate. 2017. "Negotiating Labour Standards in the Gig Economy: Airtasker and Unions New South Wales." *The Economic and Labour Relations Review* 28 (3): 438–454.
OECD (Organization for Economic Co-operation and Development). 2017. *OECD Employment Outlook 2017.* Paris: OECD Publishing.
Pallini, Massimo. 2016. "Italian Industrial Relations: Toward a Strongly Decentralized Collective Bargaining?" *Comparative Labor Law and Policy Journal* 38 (1):1–21.
Patty, Anna. 2017. "Airtasker and Unions Make Landmark Agreement to Improve Pay Rates and Conditions." *The Sydney Morning Herald*, April 30.
Pedroni, Francesco. 2019. "Appeal Court Deems Foodora Riders Self-Employed with Certain Workers' Rights." International Law Office, March 13.
Peetz, David. 1998. *Unions in a Contrary World: The Future of the Australian Trade Union Movement*. Oakleigh: Cambridge University Press.

Pennington, Alison. 2018. "On the Brink: The Erosion of Enterprise Agreement Coverage in Australia's Private Sector." Centre for Future Work: Australia Institute, December.

Politi, James. 2018. "Di Maio Takes Aim at Italy's Gig Economy." *Financial Times*, June 18.

Prassl, Jeremias. 2018. *Humans as a Service: The Promise and Perils of the Gig Economy*. Oxford: Oxford University Press.

Regalia, Ida, and Marino Regini. 2018. "Trade Unions and Employment Relations in Italy During the Economic Crisis." *South European Society and Politics* 23 (1): 63–79.

Rimmer, Malcolm. 2004. "Unions and Arbitration." In *The New Province for Law and Order: 100 Years of Australian Industrial Conciliation and Arbitration*, edited by Joe Isaac and Stuart Macintrye, 275–316. New York: Cambridge University Press.

Rogers, Joel, and Wolfgang Streeck. 1995. *Works Councils: Consultation, Representation and Cooperation in Industrial Relations*. Chicago: University of Chicago Press.

Ronfeldt, Paul, and Ron McCallum. 1995. *Enterprise Bargaining, Trade Unions and the Law*. Leichhardt: Federation Press.

Schneiders, Ben. 2018. "Migrant Farm Workers Launch Landmark $10m Legal Claim." *The Sydney Morning Herald*, July 29.

Sciotto, Antonio. 2018. "Amazon Bows to the Unions: New Shifts and Higher Wages." *Il manifesto, Global Edition*, May 23.

Sideri, Marco. 2020. "Employed or Self-Employed? The Italian Supreme Court Gives New Clarity on Deliver Riders." *Ius Laboris—Global HR Lawyers*, March 4.

Small, Jerome. 2018. "The Melbourne March." *Jacobin*, May 10.

Srnicek, Nick. 2017. *Platform Capitalism*. Cambridge: Polity Press.

Stanford, Jim. 2018. "Subsidising Billionaires: Simulating the Net Incomes of UberX Drivers in Australia." Centre for Future Work: Australia Institute. March 6.

Stewart, Andrew, and Shae McCrystal. 2019. "Labour Regulation and the Great Divide: Does the Gig Economy Require a New Category of Worker?" *Australian Journal of Labour Law* 32 (1): 4–22.

Tassinari, Arianna, and Vincenzo Maccarrone. 2017a. "The Mobilisation of Gig Economy Couriers in Italy: Some lessons for the Trade Union Movement." *Transfer* 23 (3): 353–357.

Tassinari, Arianna, and Vincenzo Maccarone. 2017b. "Striking the Startups." *Jacobin*, January 23.

Taylor, David. 2017. "Airtasker Agrees to Minimum Working Conditions for 'Gig Economy' Contractors'." *ABC News*, May 1.
Thomsen, Simon. 2018. "Uber Drivers Are Holding Another Nationwide Strike in Australia Today." *Business Insider*, August 22.
Underhill, Elsa, Groutsis Dimitria, van den Broek Diane, and Malcolm Rimmer. 2020. "Organising Across Borders: Mobilising Temporary Migrant Labour in Australian Food Production." *Journal of Industrial Relations* 62 (2): 278–303.
UNI Global Union. 2018. "First-Ever Agreement Between Amazon and Unions Halts Inhumane Work Hours in Italy." 23 May.
Unions NSW. 2016. "Innovation or Exploitation? Busting the Airtasker Myth."
Vandaele, Kurt. 2018. "Will Trade Unions Survive in the Platform Economy? Emerging Patterns of Platform Workers' Collective Voice and Representation in Europe." Working Paper 2018.05. Brussels: European Trade Union Institute.
Walker, Michael. 2018. "Tech Innovators Start to See Old-Fashioned Benefits of Collective Bargaining." *The Conversation*, July 19.
Weil, David. 2014. *The Fissured Workplace: Why Work Became So Bad for So Many and What Can Be Done to Improve It*. Cambridge: Harvard University Press.
Workplace Express. 2017. "Uber Drivers Signal Further Strikes After Melbourne 'Log-Off'." *Workplace Express*, April 12.
Workplace Express. 2018a. "Technology Won't Protect Workers from Themselves: Airtasker." *Workplace Express*, May 4.
Workplace Express. 2018b. "'Coles and TWU Sign Accords on Supply Chain, Gig Workers." *Workplace Express*, May 23.
Workplace Express. 2018c. "FWO Drops Foodora Test Case." *Workplace Express*, September 3.
Young Workers Centre (YWC). 2017. *Young Workers Centre Submission: Inquiry into Corporate Avoidance of the Fair Work Act*. January.
Zamponi, Lorenzo. 2018. "Bargaining with the Algorithm." *Jacobin*, June 9.

11

Explaining Failures of Social Dialogue Building in Eastern Europe

Marius Kalanta

Introduction

Social dialogue, undoubtedly, is an essential building block of the EU's normative social and economic order. It is both a fundamental right and a policy priority prominent in the main treaties of the EU. However, despite its political significance social dialogue has not experienced positive developments across the EU since the beginning of the century. While changes in North-Western countries may look more like gradual adaptation to the changing economic conditions, in Central and Eastern Europe (CEE) developments have been either negative or absent at the best. Moreover, the Eastern part of the region, particularly, the Baltic countries represent the Europe's most extreme cases of low bargaining

M. Kalanta (✉)
Institute of International Relations and Political Science, Vilnius University, Vilnius, Lithuania

T. Addabbo et al. (eds.), *The Collective Dimensions of Employment Relations*,
https://doi.org/10.1007/978-3-030-75532-4_11

institutionalization and labour mobilization (Eurofound 2015a; European Commission 2011, 2013, 2015; Kalanta 2015b; Visser 2019; Vitols 2010).

Oddly, the lack of positive changes has taken place in the context of increased political priority for social dialogue, as is evident from recent policy documents such as 'A New Start for Social Dialogue: Statement of the Presidency of the Council of the European Union, the European Commission and the European Social Partners' (Council of the EU 2016), 'Declaration on a new start for a strong Social Dialogue' (European Commission 2016) and 'Europe 2020: A European strategy for smart, sustainable and inclusive growth' (European Commission 2010), and also in speeches by political leaders. For instance, Jean-Claude Juncker in his candidate's for President of European Commission Opening Statement in the European Parliament called social dialogue, however in need for restoring after the crisis, an essential part of the social market economy and wished to become 'a President of social dialogue' (Juncker 2014).

Weak social dialogue in CEE has been mostly associated with a variety of interlinked causes related to demographic, political, historical and economic changes, institutional and organizational deficiencies, and global trends. Low collective bargaining coverage has been attributed to insufficient capacities of social partners organizations, underdeveloped or weakened legal systems of collective agreement extension and enforcement, and a lack of bargaining centralization and coordination (Bernaciak 2015; Eurofound 2015a, 2015c; European Commission 2009, 2013, 2015; Petrylaitė 2017). Furthermore, recent economic changes, particularly, those induced by globalization and further accelerated by the crisis, have increased shares of enterprises and employees, especially in the services sector, reluctant to join associations and unions (Eurofound 2015a; European Commission 2011, 2015; Schnabel 2013). In some cases, for instance in Lithuania, Hungary, Poland and Slovakia, a decline in union density has been linked to outward mobility (Kaminska and Kahancová 2011; Meardi 2012), while in others, for instance in the Visegrad countries, the strengthening of tripartite institutions has been found to reduce social partners incentives for bipartite social dialogue

(Aghion et al. 2008; Bohle and Greskovits 2012; European Commission 2015).

Broadly speaking, European and national measures aimed at strengthening social dialogue in the Central and Eastern periphery have been grounded on two assumptions. First, social dialogue is purely a political problem. Second, it is fully consistent with employers and employees interests; however, they both lack organizational and administrative capacity to engage in social dialogue in a mutually beneficial way. The measures drawn from these assumptions have not proven effective so far. Politically built institutions, such as the dual-channel company-level consultation and information system, and industry and tripartite level collective bargaining, have largely remained formal, suggesting that these institutions have failed in shaping interests, strategies and practices of social partners the way that had been intended to (ESTEP 2016; Eurofound 2017; European Commission 2009, 2013, 2015).

Two limitations can be identified in the existing explanations of weak social dialogue in CEE and measures taken to improve it. First, they all are state- and labour-centred, while employers motivation to engage in social dialogue and power to alter institutional environment according to their interests have been commonly neglected. Second, less attention has been paid to factors that link social dialogue institutions with employers business strategies and institutions in other domains of the political economy, which support or constrain employers in implementing these strategies. Findings in comparative political economy have revealed that, indeed, employers are active actors of institutional design, both by shaping formal rules or changing practices under existing one (Amable and Palombarini 2009; Hall and Soskice 2001; Hall and Thelen 2009; Streeck and Thelen 2005). One of the arguments is that institutions do not perform their function in isolation. They tend to interrelate with each other, both inside an institutional domain or across the domains, and form 'an interlocking ensemble' of institutions that may resist changes in individual elements (Howell 2003).

In this paper, I will aim to contribute to the existing explanations of weak social dialogue in Eastern Europe by suggesting a comparative political economy perspective and applying it to the Baltic countries, which of all CEE countries represent the most extreme cases of low bargaining coverage and labour mobilization, decentralized and uncoordinated wage setting, and weakly institutionalized tripartite and employee representation at the workplace level institutions (Eurofound 2015a; European Commission 2011, 2013, 2015; Visser 2019; Vitols 2010). I will build my argument by integrating three strands of scholarship. First, the literature in comparative political economy that has argued that while the role of unions in establishing social dialogue was crucial in the past, strong evidence indicates that employer interest in social dialogue, and, more broadly, in welfare institutions, is an important force for its contemporary developments (Estevez-Abe et al. 2001; Hall and Soskice 2001; Jackson 2001; Manow 2001; Mares 2001; Swenson 1991). Second, findings in industrial relations have demonstrated that long-run stability or, as in some cases recently, the re-centralization of multi-employer collective bargaining in advanced coordinated market economies of the EU can be linked to its capability to improve the international competitiveness of enterprises (Hancké 2002, 2013). And third, as literature on postcommunist transformation has shown, due to low levels of institutionalization and labour mobilization Eastern European enterprises have relatively superior power to choose institutions and prioritize their interests against those of employees and the government (Bohle and Greskovits 2012).

The aim of this paper is to demonstrate, both theoretically and empirically, that, in CEE, not only 'a sufficient membership base, organisational capacity to negotiate, legal recognition, and the workers' and companies' confidence in these organisations' are required as 'key preconditions for a strong and functioning social dialogue' (Eurofound 2015a, p. 11), but a country's regime of accumulation and the mode of regulation is no less important as they create structural opportunities for certain institutions to be established (Crouch 1993; Traxler 1998). Consequently, I will argue that European recommendations and national measures both aimed at revitalizing social dialogue in CEE are built on assumptions that social partners are motivated to involve in social dialogue, however, they lack capacities in doing so. Instead, I will empirically demonstrate that the primary source of weak social dialogue in the Baltics is not only weak labour or low capacities of social partners but also a lack of motivation and institutional incentives on the employers side. Furthermore, this lack is determined by factors that are external to the industrial relations system and include the prevailing regime of economic growth, institutional characteristics of product markets and macroeconomic conditions.

The paper will focus on bipartite social dialogue in the private sector, and more specifically, on multi-employer bargaining, while public sector social dialogue and tripartite institutions will be given less attention. The rationale behind this choice is that both public sector and tripartite social dialogue are more a political problem and strongly depend on the engagement of the government. In the private sector, in contrast, social dialogue is not only a political, but also, and perhaps even more, an economic problem as well as a problem of collective action, diverging interests, inter-institutional influence and macroeconomic conditions. Therefore, employers business strategies and motivation to involve in social dialogue play a key role.

The paper is structured in four sections. The first section will overview recent political measures aimed at strengthening social dialogue across the CEE region and discuss why these measures have not proved successful so far. The second section discusses the limitations of the labour- and state-centred approaches in explaining the weakness and failures of social dialogue in the Baltic countries and argues that an employer-centred perspective would benefit these explanations. The third section provides a brief theoretical account of the functional benefits of multi-employer bargaining to enterprises, while the fourth section applies this framework empirically for analysing the structural and macroeconomic conditions that emerged in the Baltic countries during and after the economic and financial crisis of 2009 by linking these conditions with enterprises business strategies and motivation to engage in multi-employer bargaining. The last section concludes by interpreting the findings with respect to the current state and prospects for future developments of social dialogue in the Baltics and throughout the Eastern part of the EU.

Strengthening of Social Dialogue in CEE

In this section I analyse recently implemented European and national level political measures aimed at strengthening social dialogue in CEE. I will argue that these measures have been built on incomplete assumptions about social partners' motivation to engage in social dialogue, and the importance of inter-institutional links and mechanisms of institutional change. Therefore, the impact of these measures has been limited. All these measures that have been implemented since the start of their EU accession negotiations aiming at strengthening social dialogue in CEE countries may be grouped in two groups. The first group includes 'hard' measures of institution building and rebuilding via political intervention. The second group consists of 'soft' measures that focus on Europeanization of social dialogue through capacity building of social partner organizations as well as dissemination of European social standards.

Social Dialogue Institution Building via Political Reforms

Measures of the first group have been built on the assumption that social dialogue institutions can be built or changed via the political reform, the best moments for it being critical junctures. The political reform usually depends on the government's exclusive power and takes the form of regulation via legislation. This assumption has received theoretical support in new institutionalist literature (for instance, Amable and Palombarini 2009; Hall and Thelen 2009) and is built on strong empirical evidence demonstrating that political interventions and continuous support by the state can indeed have significant effects on social dialogue. For instance, strong support by the state has been an essential precondition for building worker codetermination institutions that serve to secure statutory participation rights of labour in several European countries; also continuous state sponsorship is still crucial for stability of coordinated collective bargaining institutions in those countries where coverage of these institutions is high (Bosch 2015; Brandl and Traxler 2011).

Social dialogue institutions that were created as a result of the adoption of the social *acquis communautaire* during the EU accession process, a critical juncture, is a good example of political attempts to build new or strengthen existing social dialogue institutions in CEE. For instance, these countries' governments, with the European support, have committed to strengthen institutions of employee representation at the establishment level or build new where these institutions had previously been absent, for instance, in Bulgaria, Latvia, Lithuania and Romania (European Commission 2015). As a result the directives on information and consultation as well as those on working time and equal treatment in the workplace have been transposed into the national legal systems and this transposition has been considered successful (Falkner and Treib 2007).

Unfortunately, these politically built social dialogue institutions do not perform as intended, their incidence or coverage remains low, and their practical application and enforcement has been found problematic, mainly due to an absence of active civic society organizations, shortcomings in the judiciary and ineffective labour inspectorates (Falkner and Treib 2007). The effects of practical application of these politically built institutions have varied significantly between countries and in the impact on the existing industrial relations system. On the one hand, in some countries, namely those that had already had functioning systems of social dialogue, such as Slovakia, Hungary and Romania, the governments and employers have frequently used these EU directives as deregulative instruments for weakening unions and decentralizing collective bargaining (Keune 2008; Meardi 2007; Schulten and Müller 2013). On the other hand, in some other countries, namely those without a previous social dialogue experience, such as the Baltics, the directives have been adopted only formally and literally without intentions to employ them for starting social dialogue (Eamets and Masso 2005; Ost 2000; Woolfson and Sommers 2016).

Although work councils or other official structures of worker representation at the establishment level have become legally possible in all CEE countries, in fact, in some of them, they remain relatively rare. In Latvia, Czech Republic, Hungary, Poland and Bulgaria, the incidence of these structures has not exceeded 30 per cent of establishments with 10 or more employees (Eurofound 2015b).[1] Moreover, in all these countries, except Hungary, and also in Romania and Slovakia, employee representation institutions and employee rights delivered by them, despite some positive developments, notably in Slovakia, have still remained among the weakest in the EU because they include only information and consultation rights but without judicial redress (Visser 2016). Following this lack of positive developments, the European Commission has admitted that its attempts to implement duel-channel company-level consultation and information system had not yet been successful (2013) and has even expressed concerns that practical influence of employee representation institutions had decreased (2011).

Another example of politically built institutions is legal rules and procedures governing extension of collective agreements. Evidence has indicated that a well-functioning system of collective agreement extension is an essential condition of high collective bargaining coverage (Traxler 1998), while its absence or weakening is linked to low or decreasing bargaining coverage in CEE (Eurofound 2015a; European Commission 2009, 2013, 2015). Indeed, as reported by Eurofound (2015a), in all post-accession CEE countries, the extension has become legally possible, however again, its practical application has been limited since it has been used infrequently or never. In some of the countries (Estonia, Czech Republic, Hungary, Latvia and Slovakia) further legal amendments, including simplified rules or lowered thresholds and criteria, have been implemented to make extension of collective agreements even easier, however, these amendments have not affected the extension frequency significantly. For instance, Slovenia has been referred to as a case of the effective political influence on collective agreement extension by the government, oddly, both in positive and negative terms (European Commission 2013; original reference Kahancová 2011). Here, in 2007 the social-democratic government introduced legal mechanism of mandatory horizontal extension, which had an immediate positive effect on bargaining coverage and centralization. However, in 2010 the successive right-wing government revoked this mechanism provoking further fragmentation of bargaining coverage and reducing possibility for the sector-wide extension.

Europeanization Through Capacity Building and Dissemination of Social Standards

After the formal social dialogue institutional structure, including that of worker representation at the establishment level and collective agreement extension, had been built in CEE countries, European and national policy-makers have turned their focus to Europeanization of social standards and industrial relations. Therefore, in the last decade 'hard' recommendations of institutional design have been absent from European Commission's policy documents and Council's of the EU country specific recommendations within the framework of the European Semester. 'Soft' recommendations of social partners involvement and their capacity building have prevailed the current political agenda instead.

In the Declaration on a new start for a strong Social Dialogue, the European Commission (2016) explicitly states that strong social dialogue requires strong, representative, autonomous and capable social partners, and this can be achieved both by improving involvement of social partners in EU policy-making and the European economic governance, and by mutual learning and capacity-building of national social partners. In A New Start for Social Dialogue, a joint statement signed by the Council, the Commission and European social partners, again the main focus is on capacity-building of social partners, so the signatory parties have taken relevant responsibilities to support member organizations, examine possibilities to use the European Social Fund (ESF) by national social partners, organize educational events, exchange good practice and encourage promotion of knowledge-building on social dialogue (Council of the EU 2016). Similarly, in the country specific recommendations for the 2010–2017 period, governments of some CEE countries (Bulgaria, Hungary, Lithuania, Romania and Slovenia) were regularly prompted to involve social partners in consultations, policy design and implementation of reforms, and to build their capacity.

In all these recommendations and measures implemented following them, it has been expected that the Europeanization of social standards and industrial relations, including open method of coordination, engagement of national partners in European-level social dialogue, exchange of information through international networks of trade unions and employers associations, mutual learning, and company-level transfer of social dialogue standards within multinational companies (MNC), will serve as a channel for encouraging convergence of industrial relations in respect to workplace employee representation and coverage of multi-employer bargaining (Eurofound 2015c; European Commission 2013). It has also been expected that the capacity of social partners across CEE will be fostered by their interaction and cooperation with those from old member states, consequently leading to their socialization to new norms (Checkel 2005) and enhancing their position in national settings (Visser and Ramos Martin 2008).

The recommendations and measures aimed at strengthening social dialogue through Europeanization of social standards and industrial relations reveal assumptions they have been built on. Specifically, it is assumed that in CEE countries, social dialogue institutions have become appropriate; therefore, the focus should be shifted towards teaching social partners on how to use these institutions. According to this thinking, political reforms implemented during the critical junctures of the EU accession and the 2009 crisis have created all needed institutional incentives for social partners to engage in social dialogue. As a result, social dialogue is now in social partners hands as they are motivated to involve in it and to make the process work. However, they cannot or they do not know how to do this, as they lack financial, legal, analytical, institutional or political capacity, all for varying reasons, for instance, due to lost membership, poor fee collection or human resources, low organizational and negotiation skills, or insufficient knowledge about benefits of social dialogue (Eurofound 2015c).

Unfortunately, Europeanization through capacity building has not brought any positive changes in CEE yet. Resulting improvements to national level social dialogue have been only minor and mostly 'soft' without altering its major characteristics. This has been acknowledged by the European Commission (2009, 2013, 2015) and illustrated by experiences of individual countries as reported by Eurofound (2017). In a group of countries including Bulgaria, Croatia, the Czech Republic, Latvia and Lithuania, several capacity building programmes supported by the ESF were implemented between 2007 and 2015. At the broad level, the programmes aimed at strengthening social dialogue institutions and improving collective bargaining. Individual goals varied across the countries from improving human resources of social partner organizations and cooperation between them in the Czech Republic and strengthening company-, sector- and region-level social dialogue in Latvia to increasing social dialogue driven labour market flexibility in Bulgaria, and increasing in a number of collective agreements in Lithuania. Despite wide scope and relatively long duration of the programmes, the experts have concluded that the most obvious impact achieved had been only improved qualifications of social partners organizations' staff and access to social dialogue related research and analysis, while sustaining continuation of the achievements had been the biggest difficulty.

The case of Lithuania, which had one of the most ambitious goals of increasing collective bargaining coverage through a higher number of collective agreements, seems to well represent the minor impact of the programmes. The programme 'Strengthening of the Social Dialogue' was co-financed by the state and the ESF and implemented during the period of 2007–2013. According to the final evaluation report (ESTEP 2016), 600 enterprise- and region-level, and 10 industry-level collective agreements were planned to conclude. For this purpose multiple capacity building activities aimed at improving social partner skills were implemented. Nonetheless, only less than half of the total planned number of the agreements, 270 and 12, respectively, were actually signed, with private sector agreements making a smaller fraction, 105 and 5, respectively. Furthermore, the content analysis of the private sector agreements has revealed that the quality of almost all of them was low: the agreements were declarative in nature as informative provisions and provisions from legal acts dominated; several industry-level agreements were copy-pasted from agreements in other industries suggesting that collective bargaining process was simulated; none of the industry-level and only few of the enterprise-level agreements covered wage-setting issues. Consequently, the report has summarized that the main performance criteria of the programme had been reached only formally; however, without commitment to continuous social dialogue, therefore, a breakthrough in social dialogue in Lithuania had not been achieved.

Transfer of social dialogue standards within MNCs as another channel of social dialogue Europeanization has not proven successful too. After the EU enlargement, MNCs were seen as frontrunners to transfer social dialogue practices of their home countries to CEE. It has been expected that MNCs would actively involve in local employer associations and improve their organizational and bargaining capacities, which in turn will push up capacities of unions. In overall, this has not happen. Contrarily, evidence suggests that MNCs tend to adapt to local industrial relations institutions, seek institutional arbitrage and benefit from flexible labour markets and short-term strategies rather than voluntarily 'import' and introduce social dialogue, bargaining or organizational standards (European Commission 2013; Marginson and Meardi 2006). Although, as reported by Eurofound (2009) and also revealed by Meardi (2011), in the majority of CEE countries, company-level social dialogue with respect to bargaining coverage, bargaining agenda, working conditions and wages is better in MNCs if compared with local companies; however, with respect to multi-employer bargaining, MNCs has acted as a major source of pressure for bargaining decentralization by giving greater scope for company-level bargaining. Also, while in some countries (Poland, Bulgaria and Latvia) MNCs helped to establish major employer organizations, more frequently MNCs created their own or joined national but not sectoral organizations thus potentially undermining viability of sector-level bargaining.

Summing up, few conclusions can be drawn from the experiences of social dialogue institution building via political interventions, and the Europeanization through capacity building and dissemination of social standards in CEE. First, the governments are, indeed, capable of setting up the formal institutional structure of social dialogue. This is demonstrated by worker representation at the establishment level and collective agreement extension institutions, which now exist in all CEE countries. However, second, in many cases, the political support for social dialogue institutions has not always been capable of achieving changes in practices of social partners as intended by the formal rules. This is evidenced by the low incidence and weak rights of worker representation official structures across establishments and infrequent use of collective agreement extensions. Actors of industrial relations have not accepted new politically designed institutions and have not adapted their strategies and practices to them despite attempts to improve capacities of social partners in using these institutions.

Third, the political support for social dialogue institutions has frequently worked asymmetrically. On the one hand, dismantling or weakening of collective bargaining institutions through political interventions, as demonstrated by the examples from the crisis period, have been more successful, as legal amendments have been followed by corresponding practices of social partners, especially employers. However, on the other hand, politically modified or newly built institutions that aimed at strengthening social dialogue have been subject to actors' defection or drift. And fourth, although in theory critical junctures, such as the EU accession and the crisis, can represent important turning points in the institutional structure, in reality these junctures have not brought forth significant changes. As admitted by the European Commission (2013, 2015), social dialogue institutions that were built during the critical junctures still remain weak and lack stability; they are viable and capable to shape social partners' practices only while support by the governments last.

The Baltic Extremes

Measures aimed at social dialogue institution building and Europeanization of industrial relations, as described in the previous section, have made only limited impact on social dialogue in CEE countries. Consequently, none of the countries have experienced positive trends in the main social dialogue indicators, such as collective bargaining coverage, union density or the employer organization rate. In all countries, as demonstrated in Table 11.1, these indicators have significantly declined since 2000s. The only positive change has been the increase in the employer organization rate in the Czech Republic. This increase has not reflected in any positive trend in bargaining coverage; however, it might also be assumed that it has been one of the factors responsible for only slight decrease in bargaining coverage in this country.

Table 11.1 Social dialogue characteristics in Central and Eastern Europe

	Bargaining coverage (%)[a]	Bargaining coverage change since 2000s (p. p.)[a]	Union density (%)[b]	Union density change since 2000s (p. p.)[b]	Employer organization rate (%)[c]	Employer org. rate change since 2000s (p. p.)[c]
EE	18.6	−12.9	4.3	−9.7	25.0	−10.0
LV	13.8	−4.2	12.3	−8.7	30.0	–
LT	7.1	−7.9	7.7	−9.1	–	–
BG	22.9	−33.4	13.9	−9.1	43.2	−11.8
CZ	30.4	−4.9	11.7	−15.5	65.1	+30.1
HU	22.8	−15.6	8.5	−15.3	60.0	–
PL	17.2	−7.8	12.3	−7.6	20.0	–
RO	23.0	−77.0	19.2	−15.5	60.0	−20.0
SK	25.0	−26.0	10.7	−21.6	37.5	–
SI	70.9	−29.1	20.4	−23.8	56	−44

Source: ICTWSS, version 6.0., Visser 2019
[a]Adjusted rate; latest available data: 2015 for EE, LT and PL, 2016 for BG, CZ, LV, RO, SK and SI; reference year for change is 2000 for all countries, except 2001 for EE, 2002 for LV, LT and BG
[b]Latest available data for union density: 2016 for BG, HU, LV, LT, PL, RO, SK and SI, 2017 for CZ and EE; reference year for change is 2000 for all countries, except 2001 for LT and HU, 2002 for RO and LV
[c]Latest available data for the employer organizations rate: 2002 for LV, 2004 for HU, 2008 for PL and RO, 2012 for BG, 2013 for SI, 2014 for CZ, 2015 for EE and SK, no data for LT; reference year for change is 2002 for all countries, except 2000 for SI, 2001 for RO, and 2007 for LT, BG and PL

Although the positive impact of the measures aimed at strengthening social dialogue have been limited across CEE countries, different institutional factors and social partners' responses may had been responsible for it. This has already been emphasized by Bohle and Greskovits (2012) who have distinguish between three varieties of political economic institutional structures in CEE, namely, 'liberal' market economies in the Baltic countries, 'embedded liberal' economies in the Visegrád countries and corporatist capitalism in Slovenia. In similar vein, Kahancová (2015) has argued that different levels of bargaining institutionalization implied by different institutional characteristics as well as differences in labour mobilization have led to systemically varying union responses and outcomes. While in the Visegrád countries and Slovenia, union responses are channelled through established negotiation channels, in the Baltic countries, Bulgaria and Romania, unions must rely on the existing level of labour mobilization, which is relatively higher in the latter two countries and the lowest in the former, and the capacity for the action outside the traditional industrial relations structures because they are weakly developed.

The Baltic states also differ from the other countries in the region in two additional respects. First, in contrast to the other CEE countries, in the Baltics, social dialogue is not a phenomenon that has previously existed but declined. In these countries, all-encompassing social dialogue institutions have not been inherited from the past and have not evolved as an outcome of a long-lasting struggle between organized labour and capital in the distributional conflict (Ost 2000). As a result, a long-standing tradition and a culture of social partnership, such as bargaining practices, positive attitudes towards collective action and, more broadly, the priority of social inclusion have been absent (Petrylaitė 2017). Furthermore, normative and causal ideas (Emmerij et al. 2005) about social dialogue, specifically, beliefs about social dialogue's social and economic benefits, and efforts required to establish it, remain shallow (Kalanta 2015b).

Second, if some market economy institutions had already existed in the Visegrád countries before the post-communist transformation, in the Baltics, these institutions were started to build only after their 1990 independence. The reforms taken were aimed at rapid restructuring of the Baltic economies from the centrally planned to market-led economic system, and relied on radical liberalization policies driving on withdrawal of the state from the economy and liberalization of the foreign trade (Bohle and Greskovits 2012). As a result, the governments gave a higher priority to the macroeconomic stabilization leading to an early adoption of the currency board regimes and consequently the euro. Additionally, since the process of privatization of state-owned enterprises resulted in extensive deindustrialization, foreign direct investments (FDI) were seen as a major source of capital inflows and technological modernization (Bohle 2008). Obviously, in these conditions, coupled with the absence of social dialogue institutions and the experience from the past, social and employment policies were not among the priorities to the governments, contrarily, flexible labour markets were seen as the primary adjustment mechanism to economic fluctuations (Kallaste and Woolfson 2013).

Low motivation and capacity of labour and the governments have been common explanations of weak social dialogue as well as of the negligible impact of the measures aimed at improving it in the Baltics. In these countries, labour motivation to mobilize has been effectively mitigated by a lack of experience in interest representation in a market economy, negative public attitudes towards unions and wide exit opportunities. Unions have lost their organizational capacities built during the Soviet regime, while political and structural conditions to develop new capacities have been unfavourable. Although the governments' capacity to impose national and European formal rules, as demonstrated in the previous section by the examples of practical application of the European directives, has been limited, governments motivation has always been more of a problem. The Baltic governments have never been motivated in social dialogue, again, for a variety of reasons including a higher priority given to market building economic reforms and attraction of FDIs than to social inclusion, a lack of relevant policy ideas and comfort of unilateral decision-making.

More importantly, one actor has been commonly missing from the explanations of weak social dialogue in the Baltics. It is employers or, more specifically, enterprises. Although it has become evident that MNCs' motivation to disseminate social standards of their countries of origin has been low despite potentially high capacity to do so, motivation and the capacity of local enterprises have been paid less attention in the literature implicitly assuming them as low and therefore, peripheral to the explanations. While it is certainly true with respect to the capacity as demonstrated by the low employer organization rates in Table 11.1, below it is argued that motivation is a more complex and significant phenomenon requiring a special attention.

There are three reasons suggesting that focusing on employers motivation might be of special relevance for explaining failures of social dialogue in the Baltic countries. First, in the market economy, enterprises should not be treated as passive but, instead, active actors of institution building and welfare provisions. This has been demonstrated by studies in comparative political economy finding that motivation of enterprises to engage in social dialogue is a phenomenon shaped endogenously by a complex interplay between institutions, actors' strategies and power configuration in the political economy (Amable and Palombarini 2009). Labour or the state can force enterprises to adapt their business strategies to the institutions they face; however, if an institutional domain is weakly institutionalized or institutions within it are weakly enforced, enterprises can complement their strategies by changing institutions or even creating new one (Hall and Thelen 2009). It has also been revealed that, on the one hand, interests of enterprises can be compatible with constructing and maintaining collective industrial relations and welfare state institutions; therefore, enterprises can actively involve in building these institutions, as they permit 'decentralized cooperation' (Culpepper 2001, 279) with regard to skill provision, labour market risks, productivity gains and competitiveness improvements, and, therefore, are supportive of certain production or growth strategies (for instance, Iversen and Soskice 2010; Mares 2001). On the other hand, the state and labour are seldom capable of building these institutions without support from capital.

The second reason is region-specific. In the Baltic countries, the main political economic institutions are relatively young, established only after the 1990 independence. Some institutions remain weak. This is indicated not only by traditional industrial relations indicators such as weak unions and employers organizations, low bargaining coverage, weak employment, income and unemployment protection as well as weak institutionalization and enforcement of tripartite bargaining, employment protection legislation and employee representation at the workplace level (Eurofound 2015a; European Commission 2011, 2013, 2015; Kalanta 2015a, 2015b; Visser 2019; Vitols 2010). Some other political-economic institutions are still absent. As a result, the Baltic economies are characterized by significant shares of shadow economy, undeveloped capital markets, low incidence of contemporary corporate governance structures and practices, and missing links between skill provision and the labour market (Baltic institute of corporate governance 2011, 2012; Cedefop 2013; Lane 2007; Norkus 2012). All this suggests that, on the one hand, the Baltic governments frequently experience difficulties in enforcing and enacting in practice formal institutions, and on the other hand, enterprises have wider possibilities to develop their business strategies in isolation from the existing institutions or build new institutions to complement to these strategies.

The third reason concerns possible paths of social dialogue development in countries where it has initially been weak. While in the West, the role of unions in establishing social dialogue was crucial in the past, recent literature has revealed that employers—but not employees—have become the force driving contemporary developments. Three arguments support this claim. First, unions have been losing membership and power since the 1990s, and views on possibilities of their revitalization across the EU are strongly pessimistic (Avdagic and Baccaro 2014; Hyman 2016; Ibsen and Tapia 2017). Second, bargaining coverage strongly correlates with the employer organization rate but not with union density suggesting that where a high rate of bargaining coverage still exists, it mostly depends on employers mobilization (Traxler 1998). Third, the importance of social dialogue, particularly, multi-employer wage setting, for enterprises has increased over time for reasons brought by trade globalization (Hancké 2002, 2013).

These arguments suggest that in the Baltics, if there is a possibility for social dialogue to progress, this possibility might be strongly linked to employers motivation to engage in the development of social dialogue institutions. This points out to the importance of studying employer motivation to engage in social dialogue; therefore, the question is why employers should be motivated in doing this? The next section addresses the question.

Why Should Employers Be Motivated in Social Dialogue?

In this section I will focus on employers motivation to engage in multi-employer bargaining, a form of social dialogue that has one of the highest potentials to improve the overall situation in a country. Indeed, substantial evidence supports that multi-employer bargaining can be highly beneficial for enterprises. Accounts of these benefits, however, differ between the industrial relations literature, which traditionally has been labour-centric, and the comparative political economy literature, which commonly is firm-centric. These benefits, however, are scarcer in the former and more salient in the latter.

Traxler (1998) provides a good generalization of the industrial relations perspective. He lists three reasons why employers might be interested in multi-employer bargaining as a form of social dialogue. First, it may perform a 'cartelizing' function and take wages out of competition, reducing wage fluctuations and inflationary over-heating of the labour market (se also Calmfors and Driffill 1988). Second, multi-employer bargaining may neutralize the workplace from trade union activities as it shifts major decisions from the enterprise- to sector- or industry-level. Third, multi-employer bargaining may perform a coordinating function by reducing the transaction costs of regulating employment relations, for instance, through applying uniform standards to the workforce or containing industrial conflicts.

In Traxler's view, the relevance of these benefits to employers has changed over time. On the one hand, the cartelizing and neutralizing functions have lost their importance. It has become difficult to perform the cartelizing function since the heterogeneity of interests of enterprises, especially those in exposed high-value added sectors, has increased. The neutralizing function has been shifted to the enterprise level, where it has become easier to implement due to the increased availability of decentralized and deregulated forms of employment relations. On the other hand, the role of the coordinating function has tended to increase. This happens because higher industry- or sector-wide stability and the need for industrial peace has gained new importance as enterprises had become more functionally interdependent in intra- and inter-enterprise networks and global value chains.

Scholarship in comparative political economy has taken a different approach that allowed for a different conclusion. This scholarship focuses on explanations for how distinct institutional configurations enable certain economic actions, capacities and outcomes (Jackson and Deeg 2006; Nölke 2016), so it views the benefits of multi-employer bargaining to enterprises through complementary inter-institutional links. The possibility of revealing these links, notably links between industrial relations institutions, on the one hand, and skill formation and product market institutions and monetary and fiscal regimes, on the other hand, opens when the industrial relations system is studied within the broad national and international context of political economic institutions. Studies within this analytical tradition have demonstrated that the importance of multi-employer bargaining (and more specifically coordinated wage-setting) for enterprises has not diminished but instead increased in internationalized economies. The remainder of this section reviews this argument in more detail.

It has already become conventional wisdom that multi-employer bargaining can reduce the scope of competition between enterprises both on labour costs and for labour, eventually leading to higher employment stability and lower employee turnover (Manow 2001). It can also perform a wage protection function that enables employees to estimate their lifelong earnings (Estevez-Abe et al. 2001). Through inter-institutional links, these two effects have in turn been found capable of securing employees and employers investments in company- and industry-specific skills, making high-quality high-value-added production strategies possible (Estevez-Abe et al. 2001; Hall and Soskice 2001; Thelen 2001).

More complex mechanisms, however, are set in motion when a dimension of the international competitiveness is added. There are three ways how enterprises can ensure that their products remain competitive on international markets: they can hold down labour costs, produce high value-added goods or substitute capital for labour to improve quality and productivity (Hall 2012). The evidence suggests that multi-employer bargaining can have positive, but not always direct effects on all of them. These effects involve the capacity of multi-employer bargaining to align nominal wages with productivity and thus to restrain labour costs in both tradable and sheltered sectors of the economy. This occurs via two channels.

First, the moderation of labour costs has a direct impact on cost competitiveness of exports (Baccaro and Pontusson 2016; Hall 2018; Hancké 2002; Iversen and Soskice 2013). Although wage restraint is in the direct interest of both employers and the government (if it chooses to support an export-led growth model), it can be achieved only if employers are organized and engage in multi-employer bargaining with centralized unions. Unions can agree with wage restraints if they see the potential of increasing demand for exports as providing the prospect of higher employment stability. Higher demand for exports also increases demand for labour in the tradable sector, which in turn helps unions to absorb new workers while containing shop-floor pressure against wage restraints (Iversen and Soskice 2010). If unions are fragmented and push for higher wages without externalizing the impact on employment and competitiveness, the central bank by adopting a non-accommodating monetary policy can provide additional incentives for unions to exercise restraint as the trade-off between wages and employment becomes steeper (Iversen and Soskice 2013). Wage moderation in the tradable sector, however, cannot be implemented if wages in sheltered domestically oriented sectors are not also moderated. Horizontal bargaining coordination, which can take the forms of state (or central bank as above) sponsored or inter-associational coordination, or pattern bargaining, helps to overcome this obstacle (Traxler 2003; Traxler et al. 2008).

The second effect links labour cost moderation with improvement in productivity and higher value-added production. Two mechanisms have been found in place here. First, coordinated wage restraint tied to productivity may provide strong incentives for unions, work councils or individual employees to cooperate with management in improving establishment-level productivity, quality or innovation in return for local wage and benefit improvements and expectations for a wage increase in the next bargaining round (Hancké 2002). Second, as emphasized previously and since the tradable sector is usually the most advanced in the economy, coordinated wage restraint increases demand for high-skilled labour. More specifically, higher capacity to absorb skilled labour induced by wage restraints is one of the main features of a contemporary high-value-added production regime that Sorge and Streeck (2018) have described as Diversified Quality Production Mark II and of which Germany is the most characteristic example.

The link between multi-employer bargaining and the export-oriented product market strategy is striking. Coordinated wage-setting can strongly support international competitiveness and is essential to the export-led growth regime. Macro-level evidence shows that economies with coordinated wage-setting are the most successful and competitive in exports; as a result, their share of exports is higher (Iversen and Soskice 2010, 2015). These economies include all the advanced coordinated market economies of the North-Western core of the EU (Hope and Soskice 2016). In these economies, at the micro-level, coordinated wage-setting institutions are primarily and highly beneficial for enterprises because they align wages with productivity and contribute to productivity, innovation, quality and the competitiveness. Since these institutions serve the interests of enterprises, they have been found to contain an intrinsic resilience to decentralization and deregulation (Hancké 2002). This can explain why a decline in union density that occurred in recent decades was not followed by a corresponding decrease in bargaining coverage in most of the North-Western countries (Iversen et al. 2016). It also suggests that countries at the macro-level and enterprises at the micro-level, both aiming to pursue export-led growth and production strategies, would benefit from adopting coordinated wage-setting.

The latter recommendation might be especially relevant if the single currency Euro and the monetary regime of the Eurozone are taken into consideration. Scholarship dedicated to the causes and outcomes of the recent Eurozone crisis has revealed that the Economic and Monetary Union (EMU) has been designed in a way that supports coordinated wage-setting institutions and the competitiveness of exports and disadvantages less-coordinated institutional arrangements and demand-led growth regimes. For this reason, the EMU is more favourable to the economies of the North-Western core than to the economies of the Southern and Central-Eastern periphery; as a result, the former can always out-compete the latter (Nölke 2016). Two interlinked mechanisms through which this occurs have been identified. First, after joining the Eurozone South European economies were deprived of the possibility of periodic devaluations of their domestic currencies, which they had been using to restore international competitiveness that had deteriorated due to higher inflation. In this situation, the Euro added to the competitiveness of North-Western economies as it reduced demand fluctuations in their export markets (Hall 2012; Iversen et al. 2016) and thus helped to advance the North-Western export-led growth model as these countries' exports and competitiveness soared (Johnston and Regan 2016).

Second, the European Central Bank's 'one-size-fits-all' monetary policies, which are non-accommodating and inflation averse, produce diverging outcomes with respect to the competitiveness in political economies with different institutional settings and production regimes. These policies again are favourable to the North-Western export-led economies and unfavourable to the Southern demand-led economies because the former support fiscal austerity and are capable to contain inflation through disinflationary wages, while the latter prefer counter-cyclical policies and lack the institutional capacity to contain inflation through wage coordination (Hall 2018). As a result, under the same monetary policy, the North-Western economies have improved their competitiveness, while the Southern economies have lost theirs (Hancké 2013).

Multi-employer Bargaining and the Competitiveness of Baltic Exports

This section aims at providing an empirical account for whether the capability of multi-employer bargaining to strengthen enterprises' international competitiveness through wage moderation and productivity improvement may be relevant for the Baltic political economies. This account will help to link the lack of any favourable social dialogue developments in these countries with a lack of motivation on the enterprises side.

Baltic Exports

Estonia, Latvia and Lithuania are strongly export-driven economies. In these countries, the ratios of exports of goods and services to GDP are among the highest in the EU, amounting to the ratios in major exporting EU economies, for instance, Germany and Belgium (Table 11.2, second column).[2] Furthermore, all three countries export more than domestic

Table 11.2 Export performance

	Exports of goods and services to GDP ratio (%, 2013–17 average)[a]	Share of intra-EU exports (%, 2017)[a]	Share of exports of goods in total exports (%, 2013–17 average)[a]	Share of high and medium-high technology value added manufacturing (%, 2016)[b]	Wage-setting coordination level (2017)[c]
EE	80.4	71.7	67.3	24.4	1
LV	60.4	66.7	70.5	19.7	1
LT	79.4	58.2	78.5	20.5	1
BE	82.6	72	71.3	47.9	5
CZ	79.8	83.7	84.8	49.8	1
DE	46.3	58.5	82.9	61.6	4
IT	29.8	55.6	81.9	39.3	3
PL	49.9	79.7	80.6	28.5	1
SE	44.8	59.2	69.2	40.8	4
UK	28.8	47.6	56.3	43.1	1

[a]Source: Eurostat
[b]In total manufacturing. Source: Eurostat
[c]1—Fragmented wage bargaining confined largely to individual firms or plants; 2—Mixed industry and firm-level bargaining, weak government coordination through MW setting or wage indexation; 3—Negotiation guidelines based on centralized bargaining; 4—Wage norms based on centralized bargaining by peak associations with or without government involvement; 5—Maximum or minimum wage rates/increases based on centralized bargaining. Source: ICTWSS, version 6.0., Visser 2019

demand-led economies such as Italy and the UK—the difference in the ratios is more than twofold.

A strong focus on exports has been a characteristic feature of the Baltic economies since their independence in 1990. This focus has recently increased, with the growth rates of exports being among the highest in the EU. Latvian and Lithuanian exports of goods and services to GDP ratios were approximately 60 per cent higher in 2017 than in 2007, a pre-crisis year in which these economies grew fastest. In Estonia, the share grew in more moderate terms, 20 per cent, indicating that it had initially been high. During the same period, the Baltic countries increased their market shares of world exports of goods by 25 per cent in the cases of Latvia and Lithuania and by 8 per cent in the case of Estonia.[3] Again, these increases were among the largest in the EU.

The EU is the biggest market for all Baltic countries accounting for approximately two-thirds of total Estonian and Latvian exports (Table 11.2, third column). In Lithuania, the share increases from 58.2 to 78.8 per cent if oil, tobacco and fertilizers are deducted from total exports. This indicates these countries' strong reliance on the single market, even stronger than that of Germany, Sweden, Italy and the UK.

In the Baltics, like in the advanced exporting economies of the EU, exports of goods constitute a major share of total exports (Table 11.2, fourth column); however, the composition of those goods varies widely. The Baltic manufacturing industry, serving as a good proxy for exports composition, focuses on low and medium-low technology goods suggesting that these types of goods also dominate exports. In strong contrast to the advanced exporting economies of Germany, Belgium and Sweden, a share of high and medium-high technology manufacturing value-added is only approximately 24 per cent in Estonia and 20 per cent in Latvia and Lithuania (Table 11.2, fifth column). These shares also contrast with those of the other CEE countries, which have traditionally been considered lower value-added producers, for instance, the Czech Republic, Hungary (not in the table) and Poland. Only Greece and Portugal (both not in the table) have lower shares in the EU.

Summing up these descriptive findings, Estonia, Latvia and Lithuania are economies with a strong and continuously increasing focus on exports. With regard to the exports-to-GDP ratio and the importance of the intra-EU market, these economies are similar to other exporting economies of the EU. In this respect, the Baltic countries, as members of the Eurozone, are among those capable of benefitting from the EU's monetary and fiscal policies favouring exports. However, the Baltic economies differ from advanced exporting economies in one important respect. In the former, low and medium-low technology goods account for a major part of exports positioning these countries among the few countries with the lowest technology intensity in exports within the EU. This implies lower R&D intensity and thus, as has been demonstrated by Carlin et al. (1999), higher cost sensitivity of exports.

Competitiveness of Baltic Exports

The previous section has demonstrated the existence of a strong link between the export competitiveness of the economy and the capacity for the non-market coordination of wages. The examples of Belgium, Germany and Sweden clearly represent this link. These three countries are export-oriented and have well developed social dialogue characterized by strong multi-employer bargaining covering more than half of employees and making their wage-setting systems highly coordinated (Table 11.2, sixth column). The Baltic countries, however, appear to be an exception from this rule. Although they are also export-oriented economies, in all of them, bargaining coverage is low and wages are mostly set on an individual contract basis. This raises two questions. First, expanding shares of exports suggest that Baltic enterprises are indeed competitive in international markets. How do they achieve this competitiveness? Second, since there are no coordinated wage-setting institutions in place, are there any structural reasons for this absence or alternative institutional mechanisms at work upon which these countries' competitiveness relies?

Real unit labour costs (RULC) is an indicator commonly considered a good proxy for international competitiveness. Figure 11.1 demonstrates RULC dynamics in the manufacturing sector in the Baltics, several other CEE countries and in the EU15 at the aggregate level. It compares how the cost competitiveness of CEE countries has changed since their accession to the EU's single market, even though, as discussed previously, these countries' exports with regard to technological intensity do not always compete directly. Not all major CEE economies have succeeded in preserving and improving the competitiveness of their manufacturing industries in terms of RULC. Developments in Poland, Czech Republic, Slovenia and Hungary have followed the EU15 trend. Currently, these countries are in a better competitive position than they were before the crisis or even in 2004. Slovakia, Latvia and Estonia experienced the biggest deterioration in competitiveness during the pre-crisis years, and while all three countries succeeded in restoring their competitiveness during the crisis and in the years that followed, they all seem to return to the same negative trend. Lithuania presents a rather different picture.

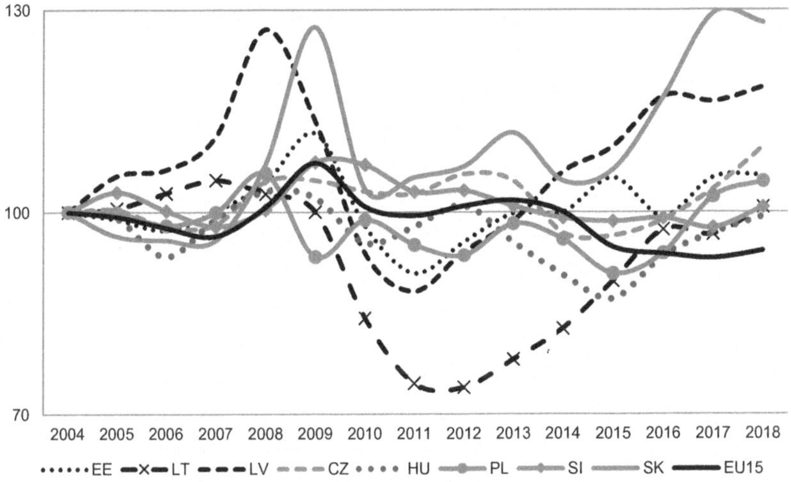

Fig. 11.1 Real unit labour costs in manufacturing, index 2004 = 100. *Source* AMECO

Although it did not experience significant competitiveness problems before the crisis, it achieved the biggest and longest-lasting competitiveness improvements during and after the crisis. Nevertheless, these gains were not stable and currently show a diminishing trend.

The capacity of the Baltic countries for significant competitiveness improvements during the crisis and afterwards constitutes a puzzle with potentially strong implications with respect to multi-employer bargaining. To solve the puzzle, attention should be paid to individual components of RULC—labour compensation and labour productivity—and their dynamics throughout the boom, bust and recovery. The scholarship dedicated to experiences of the crisis in the Baltics (Blanchard et al. 2013; Feldmann 2013, 2017; Kuokštis 2011, 2015; Raudla and Kattel 2011) has most agreed that these countries represent successful though unconventional cases of macroeconomic adjustment. All three countries were hit similarly harshly by the crisis: in 2009 real GDP contracted by almost fifteen per cent—the largest contraction in the EU, and unemployment at its peak ranged from 16.7 per cent in Estonia to 29.5 per cent in Latvia.[4] Instead of an option of external devaluation and unpegging exchange rates of their domestic currencies, the governments chose measures aimed at internal devaluation. These measures included wage cuts and reductions in employment in the public sector; cuts in social protection spending on sick leave, pensions, maternity and unemployment benefits; reductions in personal income tax allowances; and increases in VAT, pollution fees and excises.

Outcomes of this internal devaluation have not exactly been what one might have expected. Indeed, public-sector wages were cut sharply, up to 30 per cent (Blanchard et al. 2013; European Commission 2013; Kattel and Raudla 2013; Nakrošis et al. 2015). However, as argued in Blanchard et al. (2013), the effect on private-sector wages was limited. The effect on wages in the manufacturing sector was also limited, as demonstrated in Fig. 11.2. During the peak of the crisis, a decrease in nominal compensation per employee in manufacturing was slight—approximately 10 per cent in Latvia and Lithuania and less than 3 per cent in Estonia—and importantly, it was temporary, lasting no longer than a year in Estonia and Lithuania and up to three years in Latvia. After this slight decrease, nominal wages rocketed by 45–55 per cent by 2016 and the trend seems to continue.

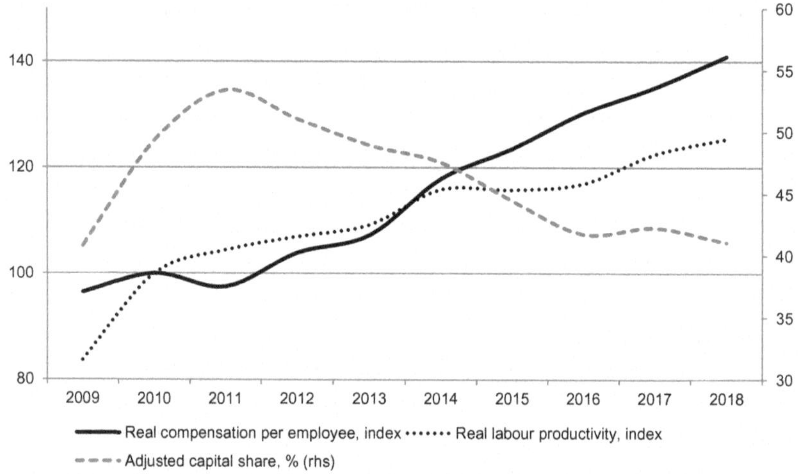

Fig. 11.2 Compensation per employee, labour productivity and capital share in manufacturing in the Baltics Unweighted averages 2010 = 100 for compensation per emploee and labour productivity. *Source* AMECO

The high rates of wage growth in manufacturing before and after the crisis and only the slight adjustment during the crisis pose a question of whether there was any need for wage coordination between sectors or coordinated alignment between manufacturing wages and productivity in the Baltics. Three facts point out that this was not a necessity. First, the prevalence of decentralized highly flexible wage-setting systems (Dabušinskas and Rõõm 2011; Fadejava and Krasnopjorovs 2015) suggests that possibilities of achieving larger wage cuts at the peak of the crisis were real; however, these possibilities were not implemented. Second, wage-setting issues in the private sector were not among the objectives of the 2009 social pacts concluded in all three countries. These pacts were primarily targeted at fiscal consolidation, public-sector wage cuts and securing both electoral support and social peace, but not at improving the cost competitiveness of the tradable sector (Gruževskis and Blažiene 2013; Meardi 2011). Third, none of the industry-level and only few of the enterprise-level collective agreements signed during the 2007–2013 period covered wage-setting issues (ESTEP 2016; Eurofound 2017).

Summing up these facts, Baltic enterprises *did not* need large wage adjustments. Obviously, wage cuts were not the primary source that led to significant improvements in these countries' international competitiveness. One should turn to labour productivity, another component of RULC, instead. Here, gains have been more pronounced. The dynamics of labour productivity expressed as gross value added per person employed demonstrate that, in manufacturing, obviously, major competitiveness improvements occurred through a steep increase in labour productivity, not through wage cuts (Fig. 11.2). In all three countries, during the pre-crisis boom period labour productivity grew aligned with labour compensation, but it soared much faster from its recovery in 2009 onwards. Over the next 5 years, labour productivity increased by around 30 per cent on average in all three countries.

Answering the question about the causes of this recent labour productivity surge and its future prospects, obviously, is key to understanding the potential role of multi-employer bargaining in the competitiveness of Baltic exports. The literature on this issue suggests that in these countries, the sudden labour productivity increase after the crisis was a result of a combination of several favourable factors. First, the 2004 EU accession and its earlier prospects have had large positive effects on industry upgrading and restructuring, and changes in trade geography. The period between 2006 and 2008 was marked by the highest levels of investments in gross fixed capital formation—the levels that several times exceeded the previous levels and have never been repeated later. Political frictions with Russia, the largest trade partner since the fall of the Soviet Union, and the accession to the EU single market have worked favourably for exports diversification. Although Russia has remained an important exports market, the EU market has accumulated the largest shares of exports growth. The easier access to the EU market has also created better possibilities for integration into global value chains for Baltic manufacturers. If Russia has mainly been a market for exports of final product, intermediate industrial inputs have become main goods exported to global value chains.

The second group of factors points to the place of the Baltic countries in the global economy. As Blanchard et al. (2013) and Notten (2012) have argued on Latvia and Lithuania, respectively, the Baltic countries are small, with small market shares in world exports. These countries' products can be easily substituted, and thus demand for their exports mainly depends on their capacity to supply. Thus, Baltic exporters are price takers that are highly responsive to price incentives. Their export prices mainly depend on export partners' import prices. From this perspective, the after-crisis productivity increase in the Baltics might be linked to favourable price-related developments in exports markets. It might be hypothesized that if these prices were to increase, Baltic exporters could sell their goods at higher prices that aggregated into larger value-added without a need for efficiency improvements. Empirical evidence supports this explanation. The IMF database of world prices demonstrates that prices of food and intermediate industrial goods that both account for the biggest share in manufacturing exports in all three countries have indeed increased significantly, 66 and 28 per cent in 2011 compared to 2007, respectively.

The policies and factors that produced the gap between labour productivity and labour compensation in the Baltics during the after-crisis period were capable to improve these countries' international competitiveness leading to faster economic recovery through stronger reliance on exports. These policies and factors were more favourable to employers than to labour because they resulted in both higher shares of profits and large wage restraint. Figure 11.2 demonstrates this. Year 2011 with the biggest gap between labour compensation and labour productivity also saw the manufacturing capital share at historically high 53 per cent as a result of strong increase from 41 per cent in 2009. At the country level capital share varied from 43 per cent in Estonia to 63 per cent in Lithuania in 2011 in contrast to 29 and 50 per cent in 2009, respectively.

The increased capital share did not signify a new structural equilibria, however. This is seen both from sectoral characteristics of manufacturing output, and recent trends in labour productivity and labour compensation. In the period between 2008 and 2016, in all three Baltic countries, the share of high- and medium-high technology sectors in total manufacturing value added remained stable on average, while at the individual country level it decreased by 1.0 and 2.7 percentage points in Estonia and Lithuania, respectively, and increased by 2.9 percentage points in Latvia, where it had always lagged behind the former two (see Table 11.2 for recent data). This suggests that the countries continue to rely on resource-driven growth, in which more efficient utilization of resources and the capacity of aligning labour compensation and labour productivity growth rates or keeping the former below the latter should play an important role.

Nevertheless, labour compensation and labour productivity dynamics have recently demonstrated a reversed trend. In all three countries, the impact of wage restraint achieved through the internal devaluation quickly became exhausted. As demonstrated in Fig. 11.2, from 2012 labour compensation started picking up and grew at the average rate of 4.7–7.0 per cent per year. The period of strong productivity growth was short too and its growth rate fell sharply afterwards. After 2010 labour productivity grew in more moderate terms ranging from 2.4 per cent on average per year in Latvia to 2.8 per cent in Estonia and 3.4 per cent in Lithuania.

This recent trend also suggests, that policies and factors responsible for the post-crisis competitiveness improvements were short-lasting. This by no way meant deterioration of the countries' competitiveness. Enterprises were able to absorb increasing labour costs through the profits bumper. This is seen from wage share dynamics in Fig. 11.2. By 2018 in all three countries, wage shares returned to their pre-crisis levels and almost reached the EU average. Therefore, it might be hypothesized that if the trend continues resource-driven growth and the international competitiveness based on it may start to deteriorate. To avoid this the countries will have to find new policies or employ new factors capable of both restoring labour productivity growth and realigning it with labour compensation.

Conclusion

The paper has searched for answers why in CEE countries, social dialogue lacks positive developments despite European and national policy measures aimed at strengthening it. These measures that have been implemented since the start of these countries' EU accession negotiations have mainly focused on social dialogue institution building via political interventions, and the Europeanization of social dialogue through capacity building and dissemination of social standards. However, as the paper has argued, these measures have overestimated the power of European and national political actors to establish strong and functioning social dialogue institutions and underestimated the role of social partners motivation to engage in it. National governments have indeed been capable to set up the formal institutional structure of social dialogue, while the critical junctures of the EU accession and the Global financial crisis constituted favourable moments for this. Nevertheless, industrial relations actors have not accepted these new politically designed institutions and have not adapted their strategies and practices to them.

While in the industrial relations literature, failures to strengthen social dialogue in CEE have commonly been attributed to a lack of social partners capacity to engage in it, and this lack has been attempted to address with the capacity building programmes in practice, the paper has argued that insufficient motivation and relative power to not accept the newly built institutions on the side of enterprises have also played a major role. This argument has been grounded on findings in comparative political economy and applied to the case of the Baltic countries, and started with two assumptions. The first assumption locates social dialogue in a broader institutional context suggesting that motivation of enterprises to engage in social dialogue is a phenomenon determined by factors external to the industrial relations system, such as the prevailing regime of economic growth, institutional characteristics of product markets and surrounding macroeconomic conditions. The second assumption characterizes a specific institutional context in the Baltic countries, in which the enforcement of formal industrial relations institutions or the enactment of them in practice is frequently imperfect due to the limited capacity of the governments and labour; therefore, enterprises have wider possibilities to develop business strategies in isolation from the existing institutions or complement to these strategies by establishing new institutions.

The paper has empirically studied motivation of Baltic enterprises in the tradable sector to engage in multi-employer bargaining, a form of social dialogue. The literature on the stability and strength of social dialogue institutions in advanced export-driven European economies has argued that multi-employer bargaining can be compatible with the interests of tradable sector enterprises to improve their international competitiveness. Specifically, in these export-driven European economies, multi-employer bargaining widely serves as an instrument for coordinated alignment between labour costs and labour productivity growth rates and also has positive effects on productivity. In this respect, multi-employer bargaining constitutes an essential component in the competitiveness of these economies' tradable sectors. Hence, the paper has assumed that a deeper look into factors that enabled Baltic tradable sector enterprises to build up and sustain high export competitiveness during the last decade would shed light on why these enterprises have lacked motivation in coordinated wage-setting institutions, and in social dialogue in general.

The findings have revealed that although the Baltic economies are strongly and increasingly export-driven, multi-employer bargaining, as an institutional toolkit for labour cost coordination and productivity improvement, is not a component of the business strategies of tradable sector enterprises. Instead, enterprises rely on 'price taker' strategies that coupled with low-skill and low value-added production, and cheap labour take advantage of favourable market opportunities but not of competitiveness improvements via cooperation and coordination at the intra- or inter-sectorial level. Therefore, these strategies are not complementary with social dialogue institutions and suggest a convincing explanation of why Baltic enterprises do not demonstrate any interest in multi-employer bargaining and why measures aimed at strengthening social dialogue do not return positive outcomes.

It is obvious that in the Baltic political economies, prospects for strengthening social dialogue, especially at the above-establishment level, cannot come from labour, as it has been continuously weakly mobilized and politically supported. Instead, these prospects would strongly depend on employers interests and mobilization. During the last decade business strategies of Baltic enterprises relied on labour cost moderation via internal devaluation, and productivity improvements via higher efficiency and favourable price-related conditions in export markets. While the competitiveness sustaining effects of these internal and external factors last, it does not seem likely that the enterprises or the governments would attempt for investing in social dialogue institutions.

Recent trends are not so favourable though. In all three Baltic countries, labour compensation growth rate overtook that of labour productivity signalling, on the one hand, that if the trend continues resource driven growth and the international competitiveness based on it may start to deteriorate. On the other hand, it also suggests that a new critical juncture is about to accumulate. If no positive external shocks supporting the current business strategies emerge (it is yet to be seen if the COVID-19 pandemics will provoke this kind of shock), it may open new opportunities for social dialogue in the Baltics via incentivizing attempts to increase sustainability of these countries' export-driven growth regimes and establishing new institutions capable of both restoring labour productivity growth and realigning it with labour compensation.

Notes

1. The data on the incidence of employee representation in Lithuania is ambiguous. While the 2009 wave of the European Company Survey reported that only approximately 20 per cent of establishments had an official structure of worker representation (Eurofound 2010), this share, due to changes in the methodology, which now includes informal representatives, increased to more than 50 per cent in the 2013 wave (Eurofound 2015b).
2. Here and further in the section, countries for comparison are chosen to represent certain political economic types, namely, export-led coordinated market economies are represented by Germany, Belgium and Sweden, demand-driven liberal market economies are represented by the UK, demand-driven mixed market economies are represented by Italy and coordinated post-communist economies are represented by Central European countries.
3. Source: AMECO.
4. Source: Eurostat.

References

Aghion, Philippe, Yann Algan, and Pierre Cahuc. 2008. *Can Policy Influence Culture? Minimum Wage and the Quality of Labor Relations.*

Amable, Bruno, and Stefano Palombarini. 2009. "A Neorealist Approach to Institutional Change and the Diversity of Capitalism." *Socio-Economic Review* 7 (1): 123–143.

Avdagic, Sabina, and Lucio Baccaro. 2014. "The Future of Employment Relations in Advanced Capitalism: Inexorable Decline?" In *The Oxford Handbook of Employment Relations: Comparative Employment Systems*, edited by Adrian Wilkinson, Geoffrey Wood, and Richard Deeg. Oxford University Press.

Baccaro, Lucio, and Jonas Pontusson. 2016. "Rethinking Comparative Political Economy." *Politics & Society* 44 (2): 175–207.

Baltic institute of corporate governance. 2011. *Corporate Governance Guidance and Principles for Unlisted Companies in the Baltics*. Vilnius.

Baltic institute of corporate governance. 2012. *Governance of State-Owned Enterprises in the Baltic States*. Vilnius.
Bernaciak, Magdalena. 2015. "All Roads Lead to Decentralization? Collective Bargaining Trends and Prospects in Central and Eastern Europe." *Transfer: European Review of Labour and Research* 21 (3): 373–381.
Blanchard, Olivier J., Mark Griffiths, and Bertrand Gruss. 2013. "Boom, Bust, Recovery: Forensics of the Latvia Crisis." *Brookings Papers on Economic Activity* 2013 (2): 325–388.
Bohle, Dorothee. 2008. "Race to the Bottom? Transnational Companies and Reinforced Competition in the Enlarged European Union." In *Contradictions and Limits of Neoliberal European Governance: From Lisbon to Lisbon*, edited by Bastiaan Van Apeldoom, Jan Drahokoupil, and Laura Hom, 163–186. Palgrave Macmillan.
Bohle, Dorothee, and Béla Greskovits. 2012. *Capitalist Diversity on Europe's Periphery*. Ithaca, NY: Cornell University Press.
Bosch, Gerhard. 2015. "Shrinking Collective Bargaining Coverage, Increasing Income Inequality: A Comparison of Five EU Countries." *International Labour Review* 154 (1).
Brandl, Bernd, and Franz Traxler. 2011. "Labour Relations, Economic Governance and the Crisis: Turning the Tide Again?" *Labor History* 52 (1): 1–22.
Calmfors, Lars, and John Driffill. 1988. "Bargaining Structure, Corporatism and Macroeconomic Performance." *Economic Policy* (April 1988).
Carlin, Wendy, Andrew Glyn, and John Van Reenen. 1999. *Export Market Performance of OECD Countries: An Empirical Examination of the Role of Cost Competitiveness.*
Cedefop. 2013. *Vocational Education and Training in Lithuania*. Luxembourg.
Checkel, Jeffrey T. 2005. "International Institutions and Socialization in Europe: Introduction and Framework." *International Organization* 59: 801–826.
Council of the EU. 2016. "A New Start for Social Dialogue: Statement of the Presidency of the Council of the European Union, the European Commission and the European Social Partners.".
Crouch, Colin. 1993. *Industrial Relations and European State Traditions*. 1st ed. Oxford University Press.
Culpepper, Pepper D. 2001. "Employers, Public Policy, and the Politics of Decentralized Cooperation in Germany and France." In *Varieties of Capitalism: The Institutional Foundations of Comparative Advantage*, edited by Peter A. Hall and David Soskice, 275–304. Oxford University Press.

Dabušinskas, Aurelijus, and Tairi Rõõm. 2011. *Survey Evidence on Wage and Price Setting in Estonia*. Tallinn.

Eamets, Raul, and Jaan Masso. 2005. "The Paradox of the Baltic States: Labour Market Flexibility but Protected Workers?" *European Journal of Industrial Relations* 11 (1): 71–90.

Emmerij, Louis, Richard Jolly, and Thomas G Weiss. 2005. "Economic and Social Thinking at the UN in Historical Perspective." *Development and Change* 36 (2): 211–235.

ESTEP. 2016. *Evaluation of Results, Efficiency and Impact of the 2007–2013 Measure to Facilitate Social Dialogue in Lithuania: Summary of the Final Report*. Vilnius.

Estevez-Abe, Margarita, Torben Iversen, and David Soskice. 2001. "Social Protection and the Formation of Skills: A Reinterpretation of the Welfare State." In *Varieties of Capitalism: The Institutional Foundations of Comparative Advantage*, edited by Peter A. Hall and David Soskice. Oxford: Oxford University Press.

Eurofound. 2009. *Multinational Companies and Collective Bargaining*. Dublin.

Eurofound. 2010. *European Company Survey 2009: Overview*. Luxembourg.

Eurofound. 2015a. *Collective Bargaining in Europe in the 21st Century*. Luxembourg.

Eurofound. 2015b. *Third European Company Survey—Overview Report: Workplace Practices—Patterns, Performance and Well-Being*. Luxembourg.

Eurofound. 2015c. "Towards a New Start for Social Dialogue? Collective Employment Relations—Q1 2015.".

Eurofound. 2017. *National Capacity-Building Initiatives for Social Partners: Experiences in Five EU Member States*. Luxembourg.

European Commission. 2009. *Industrial Relations in Europe 2008*. Luxembourg.

European Commission. 2010. *Europe 2020: A European Strategy for Smart, Sustainable and Inclusive Growth*. Luxembourg.

European Commission. 2011. *Industrial Relations in Europe 2010*. Luxembourg: Publications Office of the European Union.

European Commission. 2013. *Industrial Relations in Europe 2012*. Luxembourg.

European Commission. 2015. *Industrial Relations in Europe 2014*. Luxembourg: Publications Office of the European Union.

European Commission. 2016. "Declaration on a New Start for a Strong Social Dialogue".

Fadejava, Ludmila, and Olegs Krasnopjorovs. 2015. *Labour Market Adjustments during 2008–2013 in Latvia: Firm Level Evidence*. Riga.

Falkner, Gerda, and Oliver Treib. 2007. *Three Worlds of Compliance or Four?* Vienna.

Feldmann, Magnus. 2013. "Varieties of Capitalism and the Estonian Economy: Institutions, Growth and Crisis in a Liberal Market Economy." *Communist and Post-Communist Studies* 46 (4): 493–501.

Feldmann, Magnus. 2017. "Crisis and Opportunity: Varieties of Capitalism and Varieties of Crisis Responses in Estonia and Slovenia." *European Journal of Industrial Relations* 23 (1): 33–46.

Gruževskis, Boguslavas, and Inga Blažiene. 2013. *The Social and Employment Situation in Lithuania*. Brussels: European Parliament Directorate-General for Internal Policies.

Hall, Peter A. 2018. "Varieties of Capitalism in Light of the Euro Crisis." *Journal of European Public Policy* 25 (1): 7–30.

Hall, Peter A., and David Soskice. 2001. "An Introduction to Varieties of Capitalism." In *Varieties of Capitalism: The Institutional Foundations of Comparative Advantage*, edited by Peter A. Hall and David Soskice, 1–68. Oxford University Press.

Hall, Peter A. 2012. "The Economics and Politics of the Euro Crisis." *German Politics* 21 (4): 355–71.

Hall, Peter A, and Kathleen Thelen. 2009. "Institutional Change in Varieties of Capitalism." *Socio-Economic Review Economic Review* 7 (1): 7–34.

Hancké, Bob. 2002. "The Political Economy of Wage-Setting in the Eurozone." In *Wage Policy in the Eurozone*, edited by Philippe Pochet, 131–148. Brussels: Peter Lang Publishing.

Hancké, Bob. 2013. "The Missing Link. Labour Unions, Central Banks and Monetary Integration in Europe." *Transfer: European Review of Labour and Research* 19 (1): 89–101.

Hope, David, and David Soskice. 2016. "Growth Models, Varieties of Capitalism, and Macroeconomics." *Politics & Society* 44 (2): 209–226.

Howell, Chris. 2003. "Varieties of Capitalism: And Then There Was One?" *Comparative Politics* 36 (1): 103–124.

Hyman, Richard. 2016. "The Very Idea of Democracy at Work." *Transfer* 22 (1): 11–24.

Ibsen, Christian Lyhne, and Maite Tapia. 2017. "Trade Union Revitalisation: Where Are We Now? Where to Next?" *Journal of Industrial Relations* 59 (2): 170–191.

Iversen, Torben, and David Soskice. 2010. "Real Exchange Rates and Competitiveness: The Political Economy of Skill Formation, Wage Compression, and Electoral Systems." *American Political Science Review* 104 (3): 601–623.

Iversen, Torben, and David Soskice. 2013. *An Structural-Institutional Explanation of the Eurozone Crisis.*

Iversen, Torben, and David Soskice. 2015. "Politics for Markets." *Journal of European Social Policy* 25 (1): 76–93.

Iversen, Torben, David Soskice, and David Hope. 2016. "The Eurozone and Political Economic Institutions." *Annual Review of Political Science* 19 (1): 163–185.

Jackson, Gregory. 2001. "The Origins of Nonliberal Corporate Governance in Germany and Japan." In *The Origins of Nonliberal Capitalism: Germany and Japan in Comparison*, edited by Wolfgang Streeck and Kozo Yamamura. Cornell University Press.

Jackson, Gregory, and Richard Deeg. 2006. 06/2 MPIfG Discussion Paper *How Many Varieties of Capitalism? Comparing the Comparative Institutional Analyses of Capitalist Diversity.*

Johnston, Alison, and Aidan Regan. 2016. "European Monetary Integration and the Incompatibility of National Varieties of Capitalism." *Journal of Common Market Studies* 54 (2): 318–336.

Juncker, Jean-Claude. 2014. *A New Start for Europe: My Agenda for Jobs, Growth, Fairness and Democratic Change. Political Guidelines for the Next European Commission Opening. Opening Statement in the European Parliament Plenary Session.* Strasbourg, 15 July 2014.

Kahancova, M. 2015. "Central and Eastern European Trade Unions after the EU Enlargement: Successes and Failures for Capacity Building." *Transfer: European Review of Labour and Research* 21 (3): 343–357.

Kahancová, Marta. 2011. "Slovakia: From Extension to Dilution. Experiences with the Extension of Higher-Level Collective Agreements." In *WSI Expert Workshop on the Practice of Extension Mechanisms across the EU*, Düsseldorf.

Kalanta, Marius. 2015a. "Kapitalizmo Lietuvoje tipologinė analizė institucinės kaitos diskurso aspektu." Daktaro disertacija, Vytauto Didžiojo universitetas. Kaunas.

Kalanta, Marius. 2015b. "Typological Analysis of Capitalism in Lithuania in Terms of a Discourse on Institutional Change. Summary of Doctoral Dissertation." Vytautas Magnus University. Kaunas.

Kallaste, E, and C Woolfson. 2013. "Negotiated Responses to the Crisis in the Baltic Countries." *Transfer* 19 (2): 253–266.

Kaminska, Monika Ewa, and Marta Kahancová. 2011. "Emigration and Labour Shortages: An Opportunity for Trade Unions in the New Member States?" *European Journal of Industrial Relations* 17 (2): 189–203.
Kattel, Rainer, and Ringa Raudla. 2013. "The Baltic Republics and the Crisis of 2008–2011." *Europe—Asia Studies* 65 (3): 426–449.
Keune, Maarten. 2008. *EU Enlargement and Social Standards: Exporting the European Social Model?* Brussels.
Kuokštis, Vytautas. 2011. "What Type of Capitalism Do the Baltic Countries Belong To?" *Emecon* 1.
Kuokštis, Vytautas. 2015. "Jingle Bells and Struggling GIPS: Comparing the Baltic and the Southern Euro Zone's Crisis Experience Using the Varieties of Capitalism Framework." *Acta Oeconomica* 65 (1): 39–64.
Lane, David. 2007. "Post-State Socialism: A Diversity of Capitalisms?" In *Varieties of Capitalism in Post-Comunist Countries*, edited by David Lane and Martin Myant. Palgrave Macmillan.
Manow, Philip. 2001. "Welfare State Building and Coordinated Capitalism in Japan and Germany." In *The Origins of Nonliberal Capitalism: Germany and Japan in Comparison*, edited by Wolfgang Streeck and Kozo Yamamura, 94–120. Ithaca and London: Cormell University Press.
Mares, Isabela. 2001. "Firms and the Welfare State: Whe, Why, and How Does Social Policy Matters to Employers?" In *Varieties of Capitalism: The Institutional Foundations of Comparative Advantage*, edited by Peter A. Hall and David Soskice, 184–212. Oxford University Press.
Marginson, Paul, and Guglielmo Meardi. 2006. "European Union Enlargement and the Foreign Direct Investment Channel of Industrial Relations Transfer." *Industrial Relations Journal* 37 (2): 92–110.
Meardi, Guglielmo. 2007. "More Voice after More Exit? Unstable Industrial Relations in Central and Eastern Europe." *Industrial Relations Journal* 38 (6): 503–23.
Meardi, Guglielmo. 2011. "Social Pacts: A Western Receipe for Central and Eastern Europe?" *Warsaw Forum of Economic Sociology* 2 (1): 73–87.
Meardi, Guglielmo. 2012. *Social Failures of the EU Enlargement. The Case of Workers Voting with Their Feet*. Abingdon and New York: Routledge.
Nakrošis, Vitalis, Ramūnas Vilpišauskas, and Vytautas Kuokštis. 2015. "Fiscal Consolidation and Structural Reforms in Lithuania in the Period 2008–2012: From Grand Ambitions to Hectic Firefighting." *International Review of Administrative Sciences* 81 (3): 522–540.

Nölke, Andreas. 2016. "Economic Causes of the Eurozone Crisis: The Analytical Contribution of Comparative Capitalism." *Socio-Economic Review* 14 (1): 141–161.

Norkus, Zenonas. 2012. *On Baltic Slovenia and Adriatic Lithuania: A Qualitative Comparative Analysis of Patterns in Post-Communist Transformation.* Vilnius: Apostrofa.

Notten, Thomas E. H. 2012. "The Role of Supply and Demand Factors for Lithuanian Exports: An ARDL Bounds Testing Approach." *Monetary Studies* 2.

Ost, David. 2000. "Illusory Corporatism in Eastern Europe: Neoliberal Tripartism and Post Communist Class Identities." *Politics and Society* 28 (4): 503–530.

Petrylaitė, Daiva. 2017. "Post-Crisis Social Dialogue in Lithuania: The Contentious Path of Social Policy Reform." In *Talking Through the Crisis: Social Dialogue and Industrial Relations Trends in Selected EU Countries*, edited by Igor Guardiancich and Oscar Molina, 171–87. ILO.

Raudla, Ringa, and Rainer Kattel. 2011. "Why Did Estonia Choose Fiscal Retrenchment after the 2008 Crisis?" *Journal of Public Policy* 31 (2): 163–186.

Schnabel, Claus. 2013. "Union Membership and Density: Some (Not so) Stylized Facts and Challenges." *European Journal of Industrial Relations* 19 (3): 255–272.

Schulten, Thorsten, and Torsten Müller. 2013. "A New European Interventionism? The Impact of the New European Economic Governance on Wages and Collective Bargaining." In *Social Developments in the European Union 2012*, edited by David Natali and Bart Vanhercke, 181–213. The European Trade Union Institute and the European Social Observatory.

Sorge, Arndt, and Wolfgang Streeck. 2018. "Diversified Quality Production Revisited: Its Contribution to German Socio-Economic Performance over Time." *Socio-Economic Review* 16 (3): 587–612.

Streeck, Wolfgang, and Kathleen Thelen. 2005. "Introduction: Institutional Change in Advanced Political Economies." In *Beyond Continuity: Institutional Change in Advanced Political Economies*, edited by Wolfgang Streeck and Kathleen Thelen. Oxford University Press.

Swenson, Peter. 1991. "Bringing Capital Back In, or Social Democracy Reconsidered: Employer Power, Cross-Class Alliances, and Centralization of Industrial Relations in Denmark and Sweden." *World Politics* 43 (4): 513–544.

Thelen, Kathleen. 2001. "Varieties of Labor Politics in the Developed Democracies." In *Varieties of Capitalism: The Institutional Foundations of Comparative Advantage*, edited by Peter A. Hall and David Soskice. Oxford University Press.

Traxler, Franz. 1998. "Collective Bargaining in the OECD: Developments, Preconditions and Effects." *European Journal of Industrial Relations* 4 (2): 207–226.

Traxler, Franz. 2003. "Coordinated Bargaining: A Stocktaking of Its Preconditions, Practices and Performance." *Industrial Relations Journal* 34 (3): 194–209.

Traxler, Franz, Bernd Brandl, and Vera Glassner. 2008. "Pattern Bargaining: An Investigation into Its Agency, Context and Evidence." *British Journal of Industrial Relations* 46 (1): 33–58.

Visser, Jelle. 2016. "What Happened to Collective Bargaining during the Great Recession?" *IZA Journal of Labor Policy* 5 (1): 1–35.

Visser, Jelle. 2019. *ICTWSS Data Base. Version 6.0*. Amsterdam.

Visser, Jelle, and Nuria Ramos Martin. 2008. *Expert Report on the Implementation of the Social Partner's Framework Agreement on Telework*. Amsterdam.

Vitols, Sigurt. 2010. *The European Participation Index (EPI): A Tool for Cross-National Quantitative Comparison.*

Woolfson, Charles, and Jeffrey Sommers. 2016. "Austerity and the Demise of Social Europe: The Baltic Model Versus the European Social Model." *Globalizations* 13 (1): 78–93.

12

New Challenges for the Collective Representation of Platform Workers in Russia and China

Olga Rymkevich and Ronald C. Brown

Introduction

The paper compares the situation of platform workers engaged in ride-hailing and food delivery services in Russia and China. These countries share communist experience, similar trajectory of trade unionism development and have witnessed rapid growth of platform work in the last two decades. The lack of labor rights and benefits for gig workers is

The present paper is a result of joint work of the authors. However, sections are authored as follows: all paragraphs regarding Russia, introduction and conclusion by Olga Rymkevich. All paragraphs regarding China—by Ronald Brown.

O. Rymkevich (✉)
Marco Biagi Foundation, University of Modena and Reggio Emilia, Modena, MO, Italy
e-mail: rymkevich@unimore.it

R. C. Brown
University of Hawaii Law School, Honolulu, HI, USA
e-mail: ronaldc@hawaii.edu

T. Addabbo et al. (eds.), *The Collective Dimensions of Employment Relations*, https://doi.org/10.1007/978-3-030-75532-4_12

a global issue. It is complicated by the diversity of gig workers who generally vary from self-employed, independent contractors, part-timers, irregular workers, etc. However, the facts are becoming clear that platform entrepreneurialism is a business model designed to cut costs by shifting labor costs to the workers. It is particularly true for workers who work for one employer upon whom they are dependent on for their livelihood. Some countries have protected this group of "dependent employees." Stirrings in China and Russia are beginning to call for that recognition. The problem of granting them the status of "employee" thus entitling these workers to an employment contract and eligibility for labor rights and benefits and the right to become members of unions has gained increasing attention both in China and in Russia albeit to a different extent and with different success. In the meantime, the frustrations of these workers sometimes result in public protests. The paper focuses on the experience of Russia and China in relation to ride-hailing and food delivery services. After an overview of the general trends of the development of gig work in these countries, the paper briefly analyzes the approaches toward the problem of the legal classification of these workers and trade unions' responses.

Shared Economy: Gig Drivers and Couriers

Russia

Recent pandemic became a trigger for the more rapid development of platform work in the Russian labor market which during 2020 increased by 76%[1] mainly due to the possibility to use flexible time arrangements and work from outside the company premises. By the volume of the freelance market in 2020 Russia entered the top ten countries with around 14 million of such workers. At present around one-quarter of employers plan to substitute at least 30% of their workforce by freelancers.[2]

During the pandemic the demand for ride-hailing and food delivery services has significantly grown, especially for the latter. According to the statistics in spring 2020, there was a 120% increase of the food delivery market[3] with the domination of two leaders Delivery Club and Yandex food which pushed Uber from the Russian market. Their income has been doubled, and this tendency is expected also after the end of the pandemic due to the persisting risks of coronavirus and positive customer experience of the use of online services.[4] On the taxi market, two leaders Citimobil and Yandex taxi actually dominate, controlling more than 50% of the Russian ride-hailing market followed by smaller companies such as Gett, Rutaxi, Maxim-taxi, etc.

Growing unemployment[5] stimulated the demand among the Russian population, especially for such professions as couriers, which before the pandemic were traditionally occupied by the immigrants from Central Asia. This position became required not only among the low-skilled, young, and immigrant workers, but also among highly skilled professionals who, for some reasons, lost their jobs. The increasing popularity of this job may be explained by the high demand, higher respect for the average national income,[6] relatively easy procedure of hiring[7] and flexible working schedule. There are no reliable statistics regarding the number of couriers engaged with the platforms. According to the data of publishing agency, the Bell, only in Moscow, the number of couriers working for Yandex Food and Delivery Club in the first months of the pandemic was at least 3000 couriers in each platform.[8] According to the other sources, these numbers are much higher, but because of the constantly changing situation, and high turnover in this market segment statistical data are very approximate.

China

The shared economy in China has grown just as it has in the rest of the world (Ma and Zhang 2019, pp. 467–484). It is estimated some "110 million freelance writers, cab drivers, pet sitters, live-streamers, house cleaners, couriers, and others have become part of China's gig economy, accounting for about 15 percent of the entire labor force—compared to about 10 percent in the United States."[9]

According to the Annual Report on the Development of China's Sharing Economy (2018) released by the China E-Business Research Center, the market scale of China's sharing economy has reached RMB

4,920.5 billion, with 70 million service providers and 7.16 million workers in the gig economy.[10]

In China, Didi Chuxing—the immense ride-hailing service pushed Uber out of the Chinese market. Its workforce primarily used migrant labor, so they lacked proper authorization to work in the cities (Beijing had 90% migrants and Shanghai had 97%) and had to leave, causing customer dissatisfaction due to delays.[11]

According to a recent report by the Chinese Academy of Social Sciences, "in 2016, the emergent gig economy indirectly led to an 8.1% increase in GDP. For China's workforce, it has been billed as a viable alternative both for millennials who prefer a more flexible schedule, and, on the other end of the spectrum, for a growing number of retirees seeking supplementary income". The rapid expansion intended to reboot China's slowing economic growth and propel the transition from a manufacturing to a service-based economy. In 2015, Premier Li Keqiang unveiled the Internet Plus strategy to encourage "hundreds of thousands of people's passion for innovation to build the new engine for economic development."[12]

However, it was soon reported that in China and elsewhere these workers often have no access to benefits such as retirement programs, compensation for workplace injuries, vacation time, and health care that attach to a formal labor contract.[13]

Legal Status of Platform Workers

Russia

The Russian Labour Code (2001) does not recognize the intermediate contractual form between subordinate work and self-employment. As for the self-employed, according to the Russian laws, a person may be registered with the status of the individual entrepreneur or be self-employed without the official registration.[14] As a rule, couriers are qualified as self-employed either because of their personal choice or (more frequently) under the employer's (platform) pressure. In Russia, self-employed workers are insured and are obliged to pay on their own respective social contributions to the pension fund and for health insurance. In order to avoid paying these taxes, many workers opt to be self-employed without registration or work in the informal sector.[15] (Chesalina 2018, p. 24).

Currently many couriers remain in the grey zone from the point of view of their employment status. Often these workers do not have with the platform, neither an employment contract nor a contract to provide services. In these cases they are classified by the tribunals as false self-employed and are excluded from the contributory social security system (Davletgildeev and Klimovskaya 2019).

Self-employed, without the status of individual entrepreneurs have to pay 5% as a pension insurance (3%) and health insurance (2%). Normally, couriers are employed or as individual entrepreneurs or as false self-employed and have a reduced level of social security protection respect to subordinate worker. (Chesalina 2018, p. 24).

Differently from many European countries and the USA, in Russia the problem regarding the regulation of the legal status of platform worker is not a matter of heated debates. Until now only a few claims to recognize the relationship between the driver and the platform were forwarded against Yandex taxi. In all the cases the courts rejected the claims to recognize employment relationship with the platform and adopted a formal approach considering the existing civil law contract between the parties without due consideration of the factual evidence. The court, in particular, considered the declared tax-payer status of the claimant, the fact of the stipulation of civil law contract, the fact the driver could refuse the order, and that he rented the vehicle from the third party and not from the platform which role was defined as intermediary[16] (Lyutov and Voytkovskaya 2020).

Actually, Russian labor and civil law does not provide necessary instruments for self-employed and platform workers to defend their rights.

China

The Chinese approach is not to have a legal category for an independent contractor classification, rather designating a non-employee worker as allowing individual business contracts, perhaps similar to Western notions of "self-employed" and some countries' adoption of the dependent employee doctrine, such as Canada.[17]

Under Chinese law, workers classified as "workers with a labor contract" (not those with "contracts for labor") are entitled to the rights and benefits of the labor laws. (Brown 2010, pp. 36–43). However, questions arise which worker should be issued a labor contract. For example, a driver raised the issue, asking "[if] I do the work arranged on the platform, [and] I get a salary every month, how am I not the platform's employee? If it's not a labor relationship, what is it?"[18]

"Ridesharing drivers that litigate their rights often claim to be employees entitled to a labor contract, but the trend in the Chinese courts is to find them outside that classification." Chinese specialists have noted,

> [I]t certainly appears that China is loosening the employer employee strings and its courts are no longer treating all situations where employee-like individuals had independence and flexibility as traditional employees. Do note that the courts did not use the concept 'independent contractor' as we commonly see in the U.S.[19]

Chinese scholars argue for a new category of "independent worker" between "employee" and "independent contractor."[20] The rights accorded to this category of worker should include social security, joining a trade union and collectively bargaining, having fair and equitable conditions of work, and anti-discrimination guarantees (Quanxing and Qian 2018, pp. 7–14).

Academia has reached a consensus that the existing "all-or-nothing" dual framework of labor laws in China can no longer protect a large number of workers in the gig economy and other new employment modes and it is thus necessary to break through the existing legal framework and find a new way out. One of the suggested and practiced solutions is the creation of the third kind of workers outside labor relations and service relations. Many countries in the world have started the systematic practice of the third kind of workers[21] (Zhu 2018; Zengyi 2018; Tianyu 2018; Silu 2019).

"In a series of cases concerning ride-hailing service drivers, China's courts have held that the drivers were not employees. In each case, the driver and the company entered into an e-ride-hailing driver cooperation agreement."[22] Often there is a "business cooperation agreement" wherein the driver says he is not in an employment relationship. Criteria used by a Beijing Intermediate Court that held the plaintiff driver failed to prove an employment relationship existed reaching that considered:

> (1) "whether the employer and the employee qualified as employer and employee for purposes of the Chinese labor and employment laws; (2) whether the employee was subject to the employer's rules and regulations and the labor management of the employer and undertook work arrangements from the employer for remuneration; and (3) the employee's services constituted a part of employer's business." Id. Often there is a "business cooperation agreement" wherein the driver says he is not in an employment relationship.[23]

A 2019 study analyzes the labor processes and labor supply of drivers on a Chinese mobile-travel platform and examines them in deciding whether the drivers on the platform are employees.[24] They conclude as follows.

> Although workers enjoy a certain degree of work autonomy, platforms hold stronger and more-covert control over workers' online working process. Through motivational payment systems and task designs, workers are unknowingly integrated into the game and finish or even exceed their task targets. At the same time, the star rating system allows platforms to utilize consumers' supervision to obtain de facto control over the time, form, and environment of workers' work, as well as to use practices resembling an employer's sanction. With the design of these motivation mechanisms, rating system, supervising system, and so on, platforms obtain de facto control over the labor process, generating more approval than grievances and more cooperation than resistance among workers, and thereby reproducing capital.[25]

Trade Unions and Gig Workers

Russia

Considering the legal vacuum in which these workers are forced to operate, their weak bargaining power vis-a-vis the employer and the scarce probability to be recognized as employees in the courts, one of the possible alternatives to defend their rights remains the collective defense through the established trade unions. However, as it will be demonstrated further, also this option is actually limited by the current political, economic, and legal environment.

There is no statistical data regarding the unionization rate of the couriers. Notwithstanding their large number, they are rarely members of trade unions. The reasons are multiple and common not only for Russia. First of all, the workers themselves are not interested to become union members for various reasons including mistrust, fear of management retaliation measures, unwillingness to pay membership fees, or little knowledge about such possibilities considering that many of the couriers are immigrants who do not know well Russian language. Also their attitude toward trade unions is often opportunistic and related to the short-term needs regarding individual problems (normally the delays in payments or legal assistance).

On the other hand, also trade unions encounter different problems to unionize these workers because of different obstacles mainly of legal and economic nature which will be explained below.

According to Russian scholars, from the 90's, trade union movement has been split and has been characterized by the lack of trade union solidarity (Bizyukov 2001, p. 1). After the collapse of the USSR, trade unions have been conditionally divided between the traditional ones (belonging to the Federation of Independent Trade Unions (FNPR) which became an official successor of the main Soviet Trade union, the All-Union Central Council of Trade Unions (VTsSPS). FNPR inherited not only substantial economic resources but also the ideology and working methods of its predecessor. Considering deeply changed economic, legal, and political context it would be erroneous to continue to define them as "transmission belt" between the government and the workers (Olimpieva 2012, p. 277). However, arguably traditional Russian trade unions neither possess the characteristics of traditional western unions whose main goal consists in the promotion of the class fight and defending the workers by means of collective bargaining, conclusion of collective agreements, and organization of the strikes and other forms of protest. Even if under the new Labor Code and extensive legislation on social partnership trade unions carry out collective bargaining and conclude agreements,[26] however, their main mission often remains limited to the mitigation of the escalation of conflicts and ensure industrial peace (Kulaev 2020). They rarely organize strikes and go to open conflicts with the management limiting themselves to distributing various monetary and non-monetary benefits to their members and providing legal assistance, mainly regarding individual labor relations. Traditional unions from the very beginning demonstrated scarce interest toward outsiders (atypical workers, immigrants, and later, gig workers) considering precarious work a threat to the economic stability. It was especially evident in the case of temporary agency workers whose status for many years had remained unregulated mainly because of the trade union hostility, until its complete prohibition in 2016.[27]

Quite different is a position of the alternative trade unions which in the Russian scientific literature are conventionally referred to as those which do not belong to the traditional ones. These unions are more similar to the trade unions in traditional understanding and more often resort to the open confrontation with the management and promote strikes and other "aggressive" methods of fighting. However, they are structurally weak, often lack financial resources, are mistreated by the management, and normally need to form coalitions with other stakeholders (as a rule with the left-wing political parties) to survive. Moreover, they are usually fragmented and see other traditional and alternative trade unions mainly as rivals and not as possible allies which do not strengthen their position as bargaining agents.[28]

The government has traditionally supported the "representational monopoly" of the FNPR. Existing trade union legislation and other laws are aimed to reinforce its position and restrict the room for maneuvering by the other unions not belonging to it.

Such restrictions are laid down in the Labor Code (2001) which applies the principle of proportional representation for the commissions for collective bargaining and dispute resolution. In this way minor trade unions became excluded from these processes; the level of protection to trade union activists was diminished; the possibility to organize strikes or protest actions was significantly restricted due to very burdensome procedural requirements.[29] (Olimpieva 2012, p. 275). In addition, a federal law limiting possibilities to organize meetings and other forms of protests (2004) should be mentioned.[30] It imposes restrictive procedures on the organization of protests. [31]These measures resulted in a very low number of official strikes which is in sharp contrast with the overall number of registered protests.[32]

Among other pieces of the restrictive legislation also the law on "Foreign Agents" (2012)[33] should be mentioned. This law requires the organizations and natural persons participating in any way in political life of the country and receiving money from abroad to register themselves at the Ministry of Justice as foreign agents. The non-observance of this requirement may have extremely negative consequences including penal responsibility. These requirements may concern also trade unions as it happens with the MPRA (Inter-regional Trade unions workers association) of the automobile sector which risked its liquidation as it was recognized as a foreign agent for having received financial aid from Industrial All and, most recently, with the Alliance of Doctors which was included in the register of foreign agents on 3 March 2021.[34]

Clearly such restrictive legislation significantly undermines not only the possibilities to organize strikes but also creates obstacles to the inter-union solidarity at the international level as well as limits the options to receive economic help from abroad which is especially relevant in case of smaller unions which in this way not only lose economic possibilities but also the chances to learn from their international counterparts.

Considering general reluctance of traditional trade unions to organize gig workers and objective difficulties for these workers to organize themselves, they have more chances to find support among the alternative trade unions which took this opportunity and organized a few protest actions of couriers which notwithstanding a modest scale[35] attracted mass media attention and customer support.

Couriers' and Gig Drivers' Protests

Couriers protests are among the main protest events of the year together with the protest of the workers employed in the medical sector.[36] Recent actions among the couriers of Delivery Club were organized by the alternative trade union *Courier*. It was created in 2020 by the former courier. A major part of its members are immigrants, but since the pandemic brought to the sharp reduction of immigrant labor force, the number of Russian members has been increasing which is a positive sign as they are more prepared to defend their labor rights. The trade union operates mainly in Moscow and St. Petersburg, but it is expanding its activities in other Russian cities where also protest actions against Delivery Club were organized. It does not receive membership fees and maintains itself due to the mutual help among the members and support from some left-wing organizations such as "Social alternative", "Sozfrem Alternativa", "Left Block" and "Marxist Tendency". On 5 June, 9 July, and 30 October 2020[37] it organized some local actions of protest against blatant violations of labor rights by the platform. In fact, couriers working for Delivery Club were initially attracted by the perspectives of above the average income, relative working time flexibility, and easy hiring procedure. However, after the initial period needed to occupy the market niche, the company, strengthened the belts and downgraded working conditions.[38]

The major workers' claims concerned several months' salary delay as well as generally poor working conditions including disproportionately high and non-transparent fines, disappearance of the accomplished orders, too long distances (especially for on-foot couriers),[39] requirements to work in bad weather conditions, lack of support in case of the broken transportation means and customers' aggressive behavior, etc. The trade union required the managers of Delivery Club the payment of the delayed salaries, the stipulation of the employment contracts, abolishing of fines system (which is illegal under the Russian labor legislation), and restatement of the couriers who were discriminately blocked by the system. In addition, a claim to the labor inspectorate regarding bogus employment contracts and labor rights violation was forward.[40] Due to the resonance of these strikes, the company partially satisfied the claims mainly regarding the payment of the salaries and promised to reconsider the motivation system and distances. However, the possibility of permanent employment contracts stipulation was not taken into consideration.

Ride-hailing drivers demonstrated more active protest activity throughout 2019–2021. They organized a number of unsanctioned and spontaneous protests all over Russia against platforms claiming worsened employment conditions, increased interest rate required by platform, and low income. No data emerged regarding the claims to employment contract with the platform. Generally, the success and the effects of these strikes were very limited due to the number of participants (around 30–50 in average) and lack of solidarity among the drivers. Most parts of them continued working during the organized protest actions being even pleased to have more orders. On the other hand, the "striking" drivers used aggressive methods to induce the others to take part in the action like sending fake orders, damaging cars, sending offensive messages in chat, etc. However, the limited number of participants resulted in non-interruption of the service and in most of the cases management simply ignored the fact of the strike preventing the drivers from obtaining any serious improvement of their working conditions. The lack of success of these protests can be explained by the lack of coordination mainly due to the absence of trade union and lack of solidarity among the drivers who were mainly worried about their personal income. The trade unions belonging to the traditional taxi sector demonstrated very scarce support for these actions and in most cases even condemned the illegal actions of the drivers.

China

The Trade Union Law of the People's Republic of China is the country's key piece of legislation on trade union organization. Notably absent from the Trade Union Law is the right of union members to strike—a cornerstone of trade unions in the West[41]; and it is argued the ACFTU operates "not to uphold workers' rights. Rather, the modus operandi of the AFCTU is to ensure that the country's labor force runs smoothly and in line with CCP targets."[42]

Industrial action in China was once primarily confined to the manufacturing and construction sectors, the traditional mainstay of China's growth, but labor unrest has moved into the retail and service sectors, with strike action doubling in the former and growing by a fifth in the latter. "When combined with the transport sector – which continued its upwards surge in incidents by registering a 25 percent increase – labor strikes in these three sectors outweighed those in manufacturing for the first time. As in previous years, 2016's strikes were organized by the workers themselves and not through the All-China Federation of Trade Unions (ACFTU). The ACFTU is the country's sole legally mandated trade union, with which all enterprise-level trade unions must be affiliated."[43]

In China, the issue of independent gig-platform drivers forming a union appears not to have arisen, nor has China's solitary union, the All China Federation of Trade Unions ("ACFTU"), expressed interest in organizing them. It is reported there are some informal worker's networks, often based around secondary affiliations such as hometown or faith,[44] but none that purports to be a trade union, which would be illegal. There is no meaningful collective bargaining, in the Western sense, (Brown 2010) though a Guangdong Provincial collective bargaining statute was put in place, without much-reported success (Brown 2015). However, the gig-platform drivers, like other gig workers, do not appear uniformly content with their current economic relationship with the platform controllers.

However, so far there has not been labor union involvement on assisting these drivers, most likely due to their legal status of not being workers with labor contracts.

> The growing pervasiveness of the gig economy has raised serious and pressing concerns within China, as in other countries, about workers' access to social insurance, compensation, pensions, and health care—all of which are generally based on formal labor contracts. Victimized by predatory corporate cyber-giants that play a powerful role in the state as well as in the rapidly changing and expanding domain of the gig economy,

> the worker, once the top star on the Chinese flag and the proud hero marching at the vanguard of the revolution, is now struggling against exploitative employment practices.[45]

Stories appear showing protests by China's ride-hailing drivers. For example, in June 2018, hundreds of Didi drivers went on strike to protest an employer policy change that made it more difficult for them to claim their bonus payments. A few days later, in Hangzhou, Zhejiang nearly one hundred Didi drivers gathered in front of the company office protesting its new guarantee plan that claimed to provide drivers with a stable income but required them to work at least ten hours a day. Didi drivers in China protest pay cuts and restrictive work practices.[46]

Overall, the number of protests by gig-economy workers has risen: in 2019 there were a reported 142 protests by food-delivery, logistics, and transport workers.[47] In 2018, it was reported that China's transport and logistics sector accounted for 20% of all the strikes and protests recorded on China labor Bulletin's strike map.[48] Truck-hailing conglomerate Manbang, a logistics company that runs an app connecting businesses with drivers has had ongoing driver protests over the low prices charged by Manbang.[49]

Conclusion

Undoubtedly the pandemic was a trigger for the rapid development of platform labor all over the world. Increasing unemployment forced people to search for new sources of income and platform labor presents in this regard numerous opportunities due to its high degree of adaptability to the crisis situations.

Both Russia and China share similar trajectory of the development of trade unionism due to their communist experience (Clarke 2005). In both countries the share of platform work and in particular ride-hailing and food delivery services has exploded after the pandemic and currently neither Russian nor Chinese labor legislation possesses sufficient legal mechanisms to ensure legal and social security guarantees for these workers. At the current stage, this problem is taken into serious consideration, neither by the legislators nor by the main trade unions. As a result, in practice platform workers remain outside both from the labor law protective scope and from the possibilities of collective defense. In the meantime, their number is growing, feeding a kind of new digital precariat and promoting in-work poverty.

While the law in China and in Russia does not currently grant gig platform workers in the transportation industry any labor rights or benefits, the society is taking notice and the protests by these workers will likely continue. However, to trigger a considerable change the protests need to reach a certain threshold level making thus impossible for the society to ignore them (Crowley and Olimpieva 2017, p. 8). Nevertheless, apparently both Russian and Chinese leadership have enough legal and non-legal tools to prevent the protests from reaching such a dangerous scale. The potential for labor protests in Russia and in China is seriously limited by the trade unions not having sufficient power and willingness to be engaged in the class actions. On the other hand, restrictive framework impeding unions activity and strikes organization as well as workers' lack of structural power, which is especially evident in the situation of the economic downturn, deprives the workers from legal institutional channels to defend their rights. This most likely will bring in future to the increase of spontaneous uncontrolled forms of protests. It may also encourage the appearance of new unions or new workers' coalitions in the future. In the meantime, considering the current state of art, the only feasible way to ensure the recognition of the rights of platform workers is the legislative route which, however, also seems hardly possible without the active involvement of leading trade unions able to perform a regulatory function in pushing for necessary reforms in the sector.

Notes

1. *Illusion of freedom: in Russia the number of freelancers is increasing*, Gazeta, 24.12.2020, https://www.gazeta.ru/business/2020/12/24/13413338.shtml (accessed on 15 January 2021).

2. Research on the freelance market. Gig economy 2021, February 2021 https://www.pwc.ru/ru/publications/issledovaniye-rynka-freelance-uslug.html (accessed on 10 January 2021).
3. Experts: what expects Russian food delivery market after the pandemic, 2.21.2021, https://secretmag.ru/news/eksperty-rasskazali-chto-zhdyot-rossiiskii-rynok-dostavki-edy-posle-pandemii.htm.
4. Ibid.
5. According to the latest statistics Russia was placed at 18 position in Europe on the level of unemployment: unemployment for October–December 2020 was 6,1%: https://www.km.ru/economics/2021/02/24/rynok-truda-i-bezrabotitsa-v-rossii/885850-rossiya-zanyala-18-e-mesto-v-evrope and https://www.km.ru/economics/2021/02/24/rynok-truda-i-bezrabotitsa-v-rossii/885850-rossiya-zanyala-18-e-mesto-v-evrope.
6. According to website Zarplata.ru, couriers of Yandex in Moscow may earn between 30.000–70.000 rubles per months (around 330–800 euro) (average for Moscow on February 2021 was 55.530 rubles (around 660 euro); in St. Petersburg- 25.000–55.000 rubles (against average of 44.723 rubles): https://moskva.trud.com/salary/693.html), in other cities 20.000–50.000 rubles. Official minimum wage for Russia for 2021 is 12 792 rubles per month (around 142 euro).
7. The citizenship is not required and often the candidates must undergo only a short instruction course.
8. Russia: the boom in online delivery has spawned a new sector of cheap and poorly protected workforce, Eurasianet, 6.01.2021 https://russian.eurasianet.org/%D1%80%D0%BE%D1%81%D1%81%D0%B8%D1%8F-%D0%B1%D1%83%D0%BC-%D0%BE%D0%BD%D0%BB%D0%B0%D0%B9%D0%BD-%D0%B4%D0%BE%D1%81%D1%82%D0%B0%D0%B2%D0%BA%D0%B8-%D0%BF%D0%BE%D1%80%D0%BE%D0%B4%D0%B8%D0%BB-%D0%BD%D0%BE%D0%B2%D1%8B%D0%B9-%D1%81%D0%B5%D0%BA%D1%82%D0%BE%D1%80-%D0%B4%D0%B5%D1%88%D0%B5%D0%B2%D0%BE%D0%B9-%D0%B8-%D0%BF%D0%BB%D0%BE%D1%85%D0%BE-%D0%B7%D0%B0%D1%89%D0%B8%D1%89%D0%B5%D0%BD%D0%BD%D0%BE%D0%B9-%D1%80%D0%B0%D0%B1%D0%BE%D1%87%D0%B5%D0%B9-%D1%81%D0%B8%D0%BB%D1%8B (accessed on 22 January 2021).
9. Rothschild, Viola. *China's Gig Economy is Driving Close to the Edge*, https://foreignpolicy.com/2018/09/07/chinas-gig-economy-is-driving-close-to-the-edge/. Another source from 2015 showed a higher figure.

China's State Information Center has estimated that the value of China's sharing economy in 2015 reached nearly RMB 1.956 trillion (about $300 billion), with just 500 million users, cited in Mimi Zou, supra note 9 (citing State Information Centre, Report on the Development of the Chinese Sharing Economy 1, February 2016); see also Borak, Masha. *Before Uber, Didi Drivers Had Their Own Strikes, ABACUS* (May 10, 2019), https://www.abacusnews.com/big-guns/uber-didi-drivers-had-their-own-strikes/article/3009646; Report on China's Collaborative Economy Development, CHINESE ST. INFO. CTR. & CHINA INTERNET.

10. Lu, Haina and Chen Yiheng The Protection of the "Third Kind of Workers" in Gig Economy from the Perspective of Social Rights, http://www.chinahumanrights.org/html/2020/MAGAZINES_0727/15397.html.
11. Rothschild, Viola, op. cit.
12. Ibid.
13. Yang Ming, As China's Gig Economy Booms, Concerns Grow Over Worker Protections, https://www.voanews.com/east-asia-pacific/voa-news-china/chinas-gig-economy-booms-concerns-grow-over-worker-protections.
14. This option became available after the amendment of the Civil Code in 2017 (art 23) which allowed people to work as individual entrepreneurs without state registration.
15. Art 430, 431 of the Tax Code.
16. Judgment of Tushinsky Court of Moscow from 26 June 2019, case no. № 2–2238/19, Scherbinin vs. Yandex Taxi; Judgment of Zamoskvoretsky Court from 14 May 2019, case № 2–2792/2019 Golovanov vs. Yandex taxi on https://www.mos-gorsud.ru, cited in Nikita L. Lyutov, Ilona V. Voytkovskaya, "Taxi Drivers Performing Work through Online Platforms: What Are the Legal Consequences of Labor "Uberization"?", *Aktualne problemy rossiyskogo prava* 2020 15 (6): 149–159.
17. Eickelberg, Henry, *Gig Workers in Canada Found to be Employees and Allowed to Unionize*, https://www.hrpolicy.org/news/story/gig-workers-in-canada-found-to-be-employees-and-allowed-to-unionize-18078.
18. "Network Appointments" Are Not Easy to be True "Dongjia" is Not Easy to Find", *Guangzhou Daily* (March 5, 2019), http://www.xinhuanet.com/info/2019-05/03/c_138030757.htm.
19. *Id.*; *see also How to Solve the Biggest Problems with Independent Contractors in China?*, HRONE (September 13, 2017), https://www.hrone.com/solve-biggest-problems-independent-contractors-china/; Eunice.

Ku & Adam Livermore, *Independent Contractors in China and Available Alternative Options*, CHINA BRIEFING (July 18, 2013), https://www.china-briefing.com/news/independent-contractors-in-china-andavailable-alternative-options/ (regarding possible use of dispatch workers, not necessarily in the ridesharing industry).

20. "After a comparative analysis on various theories and national practices, this paper argues that the term "independent worker" put forward by American scholars is closer to the rights-based approach in terms of concept and theoretical framework. Besides having the legal basis of international laws, it conforms to the legislative purpose of balancing the protection of the workers and the sustainable development of the gig economy and is also operable; therefore, it has the most referential significance to China." Lu, Haina and Chen Yiheng, The Protection of the "Third Kind of Workers" in Gig Economy from the Perspective of Social Rights, at 2, http://www.chinahumanrights.org/html/2020/MAGAZINES_0727/15397.html.
21. Lu, Haina and Chen Yiheng, *The Protection of the "Third Kind of Workers" in Gig Economy from the Perspective of Social Rights*, at 2, http://www.chinahumanrights.org/html/2020/MAGAZINES_0727/15397.html.
22. Yang, Grace, *China Employees and Independent Contractors: The O2O Business Carve-Out*, CHINA L. BLOG: CHINA L. FOR BUS. (September 25, 2016), https://www.chinalawblog.com/2016/09/china-employees-and-independent-contractors-the-o2o-businesscarve-out.html.
23. Ibid.
24. Wu, Qingjun and Zhen Li, *Labor Control and Task Autonomy under the Sharing Economy: A Mixed-Method Study of Drivers' Work*, https://journalofchinesesociology.springeropen.com/articles/10.1186/s40711-019-0098-9.
25. Ibid.
26. However, these agreements often not add much more respect to the existing labor legislation.
27. Federal law from 05.05.2014 N 116-FZ.
28. Of course, the division between traditional and alternative unions is conventional and also alternative union may become "mediator" of management interests as well as traditional one may become militant and pro-labor oriented.
29. Art 37 of the RF Constitution and art. 398, 409–415 LC RF.
30. On meetings, rallies, demonstrations, processions and picketing " from 19.06.2004 No 54-FZ.

31. *The law on rallies has been tightened again,* Kommersant, 17.11.2020 https://www.kommersant.ru/doc/4575418; the sanctions for the organization of illegal actions are laid down in the art 20.2 Code of Administrative Infringements and may vary from the administrative fines up to the imprisonment.
32. See more on the statistics on legal and illegal strikes and unsanctioned protests at http://trudprava.ru/news/protestnews.
33. On Amendments to Legislative Acts of the Russian Federation regarding the Regulation of the Activities of Non-profit Organizations Performing the Functions of a Foreign Agent", is a law in Russia that requires non-profit organizations that receive foreign donations and engage in "political activity" to register and declare themselves as foreign agents.
34. *Trade union withdrawn from the list of foreign agents*, Kommersant, 24.05.2018 https://www.kommersant.ru/doc/3637406; *The Alliance of Doctors is recognized as a foreign agent*, Lenta, 3.03.2021, https://lenta.ru/news/2021/03/03/alians_agent/.
35. Only few hundred of participants between workers and mass media representatives and activists took part in the actions,

    'Not even apologised': How the Delivery Club couriers rally in Moscow took place and who convened the trade union Courier, 9.07.2020: https://vc.ru/food/140863-dazhe-ne-izvinilis-kak-proshel-miting-kurerov-delivery-club-v-moskve-i-kto-sobral-profsoyuz-kurer.
36. *Medics go to the picket*, Kommersant, N. 168, 16.09.2020, https://www.kommersant.ru/doc/4493029.
37. *Mining method of couriers*, Novaya Gazeta, 1.11.2020, https://novayagazeta.ru/articles/2020/11/12/87939-kuriernyy-metod-dobychi.
38. From 2019 the distance was progressively increased from initial 5 to 6, 7 and then 15–20 km which increased relative expenses for the couriers as well as sanctions for the delays or refusals to accept the order; there was introduced system of payment for order delivery and not for the order waiting time; the sanctions included dismissals in case of claims to the administration or request of holidays.
39. According to the report of the couriers it happens that after the whole 12 day and 30 km on foot they remain in debts with the company or in case of the refusal of an order because of the distance and even if it was taken by another courier the fine is two times higher than the order cost; if the courier switches off the GPS on his phone for more than half an hour, he will be fined by day wage.
40. Still pending at the time of writing of this paper.

41. On the other hand, strikes are not explicitly prohibited and do occur, often spontaneously without the urging or support of the ACFTU.
42. Wrest, Samuel, *Evaluating Trade Union Law and Collective Bargaining in China: Key Considerations for Foreign Firms*, https://www.china-briefing.com/news/chinas-trade-union-law/.
43. Ibid.
44. Viola Rothschild, op. cit.
45. Viola Rothschild, op. cit.
46. *Didi drivers in China protest pay cuts and restrictive work practices*, https://clb.org.hk/content/didi-drivers-china-protest-pay-cuts-and-restrictive-work-practices.
47. *Precariat unite! The gig economy challenges China's state-run labor unions*, https://www.economist.com/china/2021/01/27/the-gig-economy-challenges-chinas-state-run-labour-unions.
48. Viola Rothschild, op. cit.
49. Ibid.

References

Bizyukov, Petr. 2001. "Alternative Trade Unions on the Way to the Development of Social Space." *Socialogical Studies*: 5.

Brown, Ronald C. 2010. *Understanding Labor and Employment Law in China.*

Brown, Ronald C. 2015. "Collective Bargaining in China: Guangdong Regulation a Harbinger of National Model?" *China-EU Law Journal* 4: 135.

Chesalina, Olga. 2018. "Access to Social Security for Digital Platform Workers in Germany and in Russia: A Comparative Study." *Spanish Labour Law and Employment Relations Journal*. EISSN 2255–2081. 19. 7 (1–2): 17–28.

Clarke, Simon. 2005. "Post-Socialist Trade Unions: China and Russia." *Industrial Relations Journal* 36 (1): 2–18.

Crowley, Stephen, and Irina Olimpieva. 2017. "Labor Protests and their Consequences in Putin's Russia, problems of Post-Communism." *Problems of Post-Communism* 65 (5): 1–15.

Davletgildeev, Rustem, and Lenara Klimovskaya. 2019. "Legal Status of Platform Workers in Russia: Right on Unemployment and Social Assistance." *Humanities & Social Sciences Reviews* 7 (6): 639–643.

Kulaev, Maxim. 2020. "Russian Trade Unions and the De-Escalation of Protests in Russian Regions." *International Journal of Politics, Culture, and Society*.

Lyutov, Nikita, and Ilona Voytkovskaya. 2020. "Taxi Drivers Performing Work through Online Platforms: What are the Legal Consequences of Labor "Uberization"?" *Aktualnye Problemy Rossiyskogo Prava* 15 (6): 149–159.

Ma, Yide, and Haoran Zhang. 2019. "Development of the Sharing Economy in China: Challenges and Lessons." In *Innovation, Economic Development, and Intellectual Property in India and China*, edited by Kung-Chung Liu and Uday Racherla, 467–84.

Olimpieva, Irina. 2012. "Labor Unions in Contemporary Russia: An Assessment of Contrasting Forms of Organization and Representation." *The Journal of Labor and Society* 15: 267–283.

Quanxing, Wang, and Wang Qian. 2018. "Identification of Labor Relations and Protection of Rights and Interests for Chinese 'Online Gig Workers.'" *Law Science* 4: 7–14.

Silu, Tian. 2019. "Subordinate Labor Theory in the Era of Industry 4.0." *China Law Review*, 1.

Tianyu, Wang. 2018. "Is Online Labor Service a Challenge to Labor Laws." *China Law Review* 6 (2018).

Zengyi, Xie. 2018. "Identification of Labor Relations in the Employment of Internet Platforms." *Peking University Law Journal* 6 (2018).

Zhu, Xiao. 2018. "Theoretical Reflection and Alternative Path of the Third Kind of Workers." *Global Law Review* 6 (2018).

13

Evidence from Monitoring on Tax Incentives on the Performance Related Pay in Italy

Massimo Resce and Enrico Sestili

Introduction

One of the crucial aspects that has characterized Western economies since the 1990s is the low dynamic of labour productivity. This trend is particularly critical for Italy, which in the last twenty years has recorded productivity performance well below the countries in the eurozone. The

The present chapter is the result of the joint work of the authors. However, sections were authored as follows: "Introduction", "Measures for Labour Productivity in Decentralized Bargaining" and related sub-sections ("Evolution of productivity measures in decentralized bargaining" and "The integration by company size, industry and region") and the sub-section "New features in the installation of concession measures: the incremental nature and verifiability of target values" by Massimo Resce; "Conclusions" and the sub-sections "Objectives and criteria for measuring performance bonuses" and "Performance indicators", by Enrico Sestili.

M. Resce (✉) · E. Sestili
INAPP - National Institute for the Analysis of Public Policies, Rome, Italy
e-mail: m.resce@inapp.org

E. Sestili
e-mail: e.sestili@inapp.org

T. Addabbo et al. (eds.), *The Collective Dimensions of Employment Relations*,
https://doi.org/10.1007/978-3-030-75532-4_13

limited growth in productivity is due to various factors (Schlitzer 2015). Economists and policy makers find it difficult to compose what is now defined as a "paradox" and none has yet proved convincing enough to propose shared and effective solutions.

The causes do not exclude the effects of the institutions that regulate the labour market and in particular the mechanism for negotiating wages introduced by the Protocol of 1993,[1] currently in force, which envisages two specialized negotiation levels that are not comparable between different institutions and are non-repetitive (Resce 2018). At the first level, the national collective bargaining agreement (CCNL) operates and regulates the issue of remuneration coherently with the planned inflation adopted as a common objective.[2] At the second level, in which both the corporate and the local-level agreement operate, the resulting salary is contracted linked to increases in productivity,[3] quality and other elements of competitiveness.

Some authors have criticized the functioning of this second level of bargaining, which is unable to affect wage conditions and labour productivity levels due to its scarce diffusion[4] (Tronti 2009, 2010, 2013). According to the European Institutions[5] this circumstance represents a real obstacle to the mechanisms for adjusting wages to local conditions and to productivity growth.[6]

In order to guarantee a greater prevalence of decentralized negotiations, in recent years the government has adopted, also according to European recommendations, a preferential tax regime on productivity bonuses in the 2016 Stability Law (Article 1 para. 182–190 of Law 208/2015) and subsequently in the Budget Law for 2017 (Law 232/2016). Monitoring[7] activity was also envisaged for the measures, through a repository initiated by the Ministry of Labour and Social Policy (MLPS).

The proposed analysis focuses on the emerging evidence of the monitoring activity. In particular, the first paragraph describes the main characteristics of the measures adopted for the growth of productivity in decentralized bargaining and their integration at a local level and by company size and industry. The second paragraph, instead, deals with the problems of measurability of performance increases and the choices made by the companies in terms of objectives and growth indicators. Finally, the conclusions try to give a summary of the main emerging evidence also through company profiling with respect to the choices in adopting the tax incentive.

Measures for Labour Productivity in Decentralized Bargaining

Evolution of Productivity Measures in Decentralized Bargaining

The policy of supporting labour productivity in Italy launched in recent years forms part of system of negotiation with well-defined characteristics, intervening on the second level of bargaining, i.e. in corporate and local-level bargaining.

The various interventions that have taken place since 1997 (see Table 13.1) have been experimental and, even when seeking to make the system more organic and systematic (with Law 92/2012, known as the "Fornero reform"), the lack of allocation of resources made the measures precarious (Morocco 2018). From the initial incentive of a contributory nature we have moved to a tax incentive, introducing a substitute tax on the income tax of individuals and regional and municipal surcharges. In some cases, the regional authorities have also been given the opportunity to intervene independently, and arrange for the deduction of taxable income from regional tax on productive activity (IRAP) (Law 183/2011).

In this twenty-year evolution, it is possible to recognize two main historical phases lasting ten years each: a first one that goes from 1997 to 2007 characterized by the contribution incentive (Legislative Decree No. 67 of 25th March 1997—Article 2), and a second one from 2008 to today characterized by the tax incentive (Law No. 247 of 24 December 2007—Article 1 paragraph 67).

Focusing on this last decade, the incentive initially had an a-selective nature that concerned not only productivity-related compensation, but also overtime and services performed after the reduced hours agreed in the context of part-time work contracts (Legislative Decree 93/2008). The link with the collective agreement was short-lived and concerned

Table 13.1 Evolution in the last 20 years of variable-wage incentives in the context of decentralized bargaining

Regulation	Period	Incentive characteristics
Legislative Decree No. 67 of 25 March 1997 and conversion law No. 135 of 23 May 1997—Article 2	1997 2007	Exclusion from the taxable earnings and pensionable earnings within 3% of the perceived contractual remuneration (to be reached progressively: 1% for 1997 and 2% for 1998 and subsequent increases established by interministerial decree)
Law No. 247 of 24 December 2007 Article 1, para. 67	2008 2010	Repeal Article 2 of Legislative Decree 67/1997 and Institution Fund for the financing of tax relief to encourage second-level bargaining. Launch of three-year testing 2008-2010 with contribution relief relating to the amount of taxable salary up to a maximum limit of 5% of the contractual salary received and relief within 25% on social security contributions due by employers
Legislative Decree No. 93 of 27 May 2008 and Conversion Law No. 126 of 24 July 2008—Article 2	2008 2010	Substitutive tax on income tax levied on individuals and regional and municipal additional tax of 10%, up to a total amount of €3,000 for: overtime; additional work; productivity gains, innovation and organizational efficiency and other elements of competitiveness and profitability

(continued)

different elements of remuneration, united by the uncertain nature of their payment. Only since 2011 has the incentive been reserved for "productivity agreements" implemented according to the provisions of agreements or local-level or corporate collective agreements (Legislative Decree 78/2010). The extent of the delegation to collective bargaining

Table 13.1 (continued)

Regulation	Period	Incentive characteristics
Legislative Decree No. 78 of 31 May 2010 and Conversion Law 220 of 30 July 2010—Article 53	2011	Productivity contracts with substitute tax on the income of individuals and regional and municipal surcharges within the total limit of €6,000 and for bearers of income from employment not exceeding €40,000, for increases in productivity, quality, profitability, innovation, organizational efficiency
Law No. 220 of 13 December 2010 Article 1, para. 47	2011	Extension of relief Article 53 para. 2 Legislative Decree 78/2010
Legislative Decree No. 98 of 06 July 2011 and conversion law No. 111 of 15 July 2011—Article 26	2012	Tax reductions on workers' income and tax abatements for the employee and the employer
Law No. 183 of 12 November 2011 Articles 22, para. 7 and 33, para. 12	2012	Possibility for the regional authorities to order the deduction of IRAP from the taxable income and extension of the incentives referred to in Article 2 para. 1 letter C of Legislative Decree 93/2008 (Council of Ministers Presidential Decree 23 May 2012)

(continued)

in the identification of parameters has determined the need for ex-post monitoring (Law 183/2011). Subsequently, in 2013 an attempt was made to regulate a greater definition of the asset awarded with the introduction of "productivity compensation" (Council of Ministers Presidential Decree 22nd January 2013) by imposing, for monitoring purposes, the customary obligation to file decentralized agreements with the competent ministerial offices.

In the last decade, in addition to the rates, the methods of disbursement of the incentive have also changed, no longer granted automatically but behind a specific request of the company and within the availability

Table 13.1 (continued)

Regulation	Period	Incentive characteristics
Law No. 92 of 28 June 2012 ("Fornero Reform")—Article 4—para. 62	2012 2014	Delegation to the Government to encourage forms of employee involvement in the company, activated through the stipulation of a corporate collective agreement, in order to allow for organic and systematic rules on information and consultation for workers, as well as employee participation in profits and capital (Council of Ministers Presidential Decree of 22 January 2013 and Council of Ministers Presidential Decree of 19 February 2014)
***	2015	Suspension
Law No. 208 of 28 December 2015 Article 1 paras. 182, 189, 190	2016	Substitute tax: 10% Total amount limit: €3,000.00. Employee income limit: €80,000.00. Type of increases: productivity, profitability, quality, efficiency and innovation. Monitoring of corporate and regional contracts. (Ministerial Decree 25 March 2016)
Law No. 232 of 11 December 2016—Article 1 para. 160	2017	Substitute tax: 10% Total amount limit: €3,000.00 –€4,000.00 (involvement of workers). Employee income limit: €80,000.00. Type of increases: productivity, profitability, quality, efficiency and innovation. Monitoring of corporate and regional contracts

(*Source* Resce 2018)

of a dedicated fund. The incentive has been designed from time to time with variable geometry in the various annuities especially in the definition of thresholds. A clear tendency, however, was that of widening the limit of income from employment to access the concessions, which grew progressively from 30,000 euros (2007–2008) to 80,000 (2017), extending the range of beneficiaries also to employees with medium-high incomes, thus not only workers but also a part of management (Leonardi 2017).

The most important changes introduced in recent years, starting in 2016, have also concerned the introduction of reward mechanisms for worker participation and company welfare[8] and greater definition with criteria for measuring the expected increase in productivity.

The following is an analysis of the main evidence taken from the agreement filing form, which we will call for simplicity "application" (attached to the Ministerial Decree of 25 March 2016).[9]

The Integration by Company, Size, Industry and Region

For the preferential taxation regime on the productivity bonuses provided for by the 2016 Stability Law (Article 1 paras. 182–190 of Law 208/2015), subsequently strengthened by the Budget Law for 2017 (Law 232/2016), action was taken to monitor the applications based on the repository rolled out by the Ministry of Labour and Social Policies (MLPS), as a tool for collecting summary data on agreements.[10] These data, as with all data from administrative sources, underwent a process of verification and integration with other sources to increase the quality of the information[11] (Centra 2018).[12]

The first characteristic that can be seen by comparing the applications filed in the repository is that most (83.1%) concern corporate agreements, while 16.9% refer to local-level agreements (see Table 13.2).

This gap between the two types of decentralized bargaining is even more marked if we consider the beneficiaries involved,[13] which in the first case represent around 94.5%, while in the second case, only 5.5%. The reason for this further gap could be structural since local-level

Table 13.2 Types of contract: corporate and local level

Type of contract	Applications		Beneficiaries		
	No.	%	No.	%	Average values
Corporate	28,150	83.11	7,278,300	94.46	259
Local	5,719	16.89	427,019	5.54	75
Total	33,869	100.00	7,705,319	100.00	*228*

(*Source* Our processing on MLPS repository "Repository for corporate and local-level contracts and preferential taxation of performance bonuses")

bargaining should cover micro and small companies, where union representatives are few or completely absent, and which are not able to initiate corporate-type bargaining processes (See Fig. 13.1). The trend is clearly outlined despite the presence of missing data (n/a) and would be further accentuated if we consider the hypothesis that the missing data refer to large companies (in fact the average beneficiaries involved per company for the n/a amount to 276, which makes one assume that it is indeed a large company).

The dimensional aspect is therefore one of the first factors that affects the activation of decentralized bargaining (see Fig. 13.2). It is clear in all the reference literature that the use of decentralized bargaining increases as the size of the company increases. In fact, this statement in the experience of incentives on the performance bonus is backed by some particular evidence. After deducting missing data which has a considerable bearing (15%), the number of applications presented is distributed almost uniformly between the different classifications of company size. When considering the beneficiaries involved, it is clear that a large company with over 250 employees has a greater capacity for involvement, covering 66% of the total beneficiaries of the measure. If we consider that the missing data refers, as already mentioned, to companies with an average of over 250 employees, an additional 18% of beneficiaries should be added, so the ability to involve employees of all the other types of companies is around 16%. In particular, micro and small businesses (respectively up to 10 employees and 11 to 50 employees)[14] cover only 3% of beneficiaries; medium-sized companies (from 51 to 250 employees) cover 13% of the beneficiaries. Therefore, it can be concluded

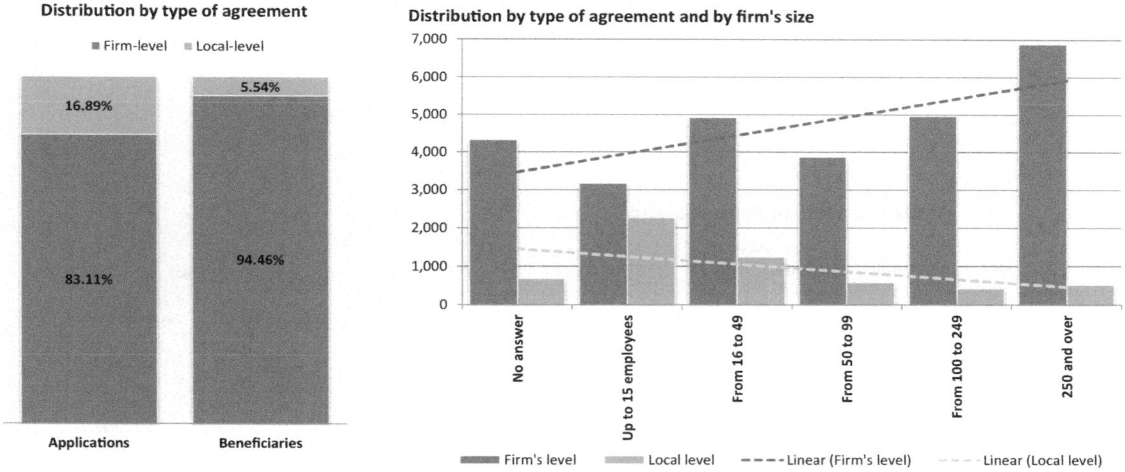

Fig. 13.1 Distribution by type of contract and by company size (*Source* Our processing on MLPS repository "Repository for corporate and local-level contracts and preferential taxation of performance bonuses")

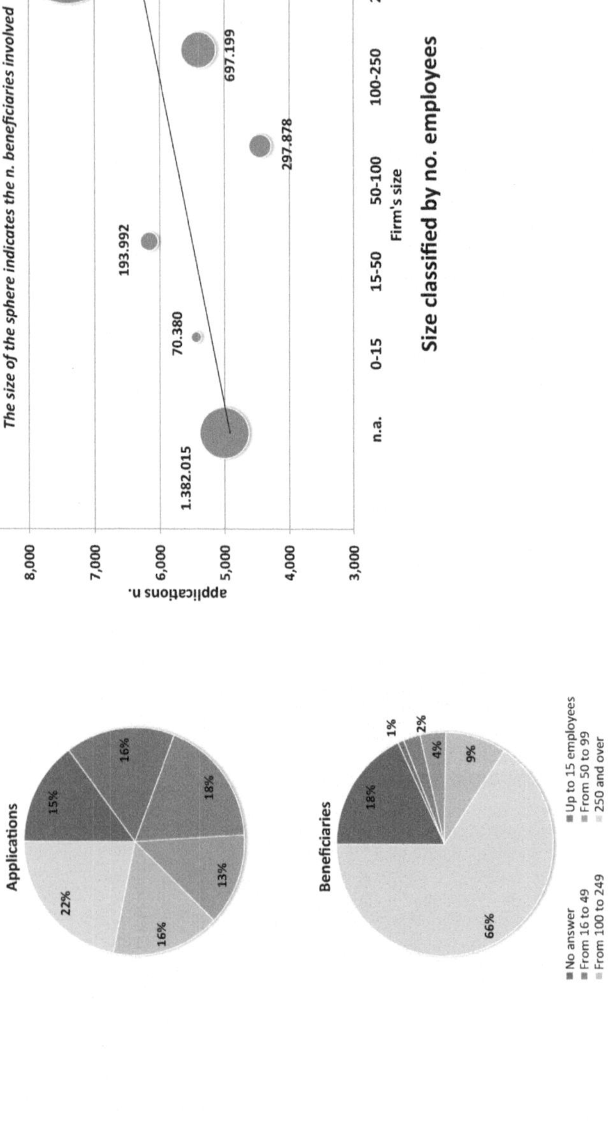

Fig. 13.2 Distribution of applications and beneficiaries by company size (*Source* Our processing on MLPS repository "Repository for corporate and local-level contracts and preferential taxation of performance bonuses")

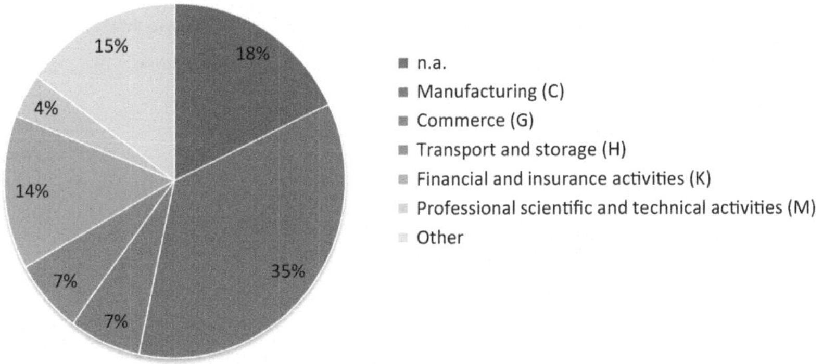

Fig. 13.3 Distribution of beneficiaries by economic sector (*Source* Our processing on MLPS repository "Repository for corporate and local-level contracts and preferential taxation of performance bonuses")

that the measure remains mainly reserved for employees of medium and large companies.

The industry that most integrated the measure (see Fig. 13.3), after deduction of the missing data, was manufacturing with 35.3% coverage,[15] followed by financial and insurance activities with 14.1%, then by trade—6.8%, and logistics (transportation and storage) 6.8%, and finally from professional scientific and technical activities, at around 4%. All the other industries, which represent the remaining 15%, taken individually, do not even reach the minimum 4% threshold.

In reality, the greater and lesser uptake was also affected by a different sectoral propensity to activate decentralized bargaining, for which it was considered appropriate to measure the propensity to integrate the measures with a summary indicator given by the difference between the amount of beneficiaries integrated by the industry and the amount employed in the industry (see Fig. 13.4). In this way, it is possible to highlight the greater dynamism of some industries compared to others. It emerges that the industries that have shown themselves to be most likely to integrate the measure are manufacturing and financial and insurance activities (with a difference between the portion of beneficiaries and the portion employed of approximately 13.4 and 10.6% respectively). Other industries are practically consistent: "B—mining of quarries and mines",

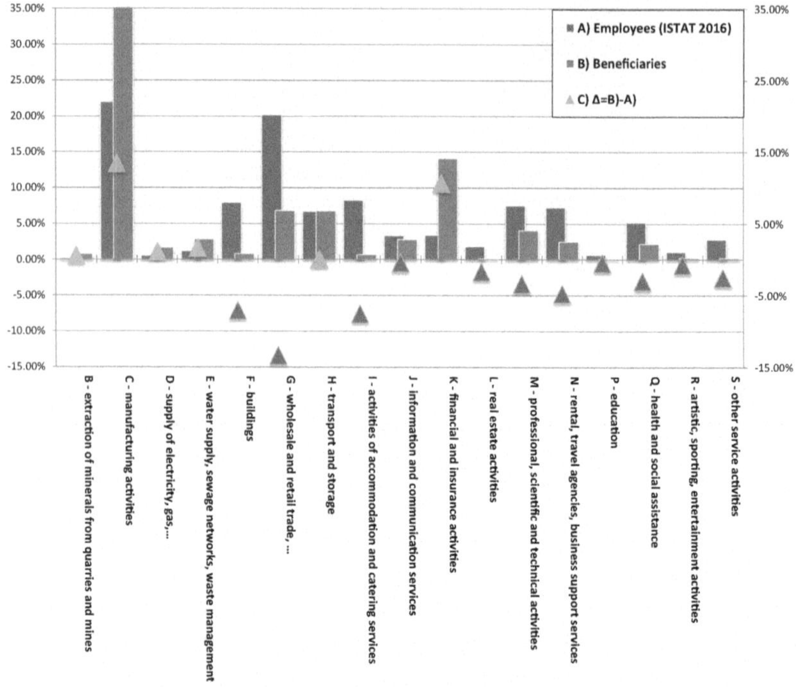

Fig. 13.4 Sectoral inclination to the activation of the measure (*Source* Our processing on MLPS repository "Repository for corporate and local-level contracts and preferential taxation of performance bonuses")

"D—supply of electricity, gas, steam and air conditioning", "E—supply of water to sewage networks, waste management activities and redevelopment", "H—transportation and storage". On the other hand, all the other industries show a negative gap and therefore a low propensity to integrate the measure. In particular, the industries that, with regard to the size of their workforce, have integrated the measure less, were trade (−13.4%), construction (7.1%), accommodation and food service activities (−7.6%).

In addition to polarizations by type of contract, by company size and by sector, there are also strong regional polarizations[16] of the adoption of the measure.

In fact, there were only five regions to have made use, in a more massive manner, of the tax concessions over productivity bonuses (Fig. 13.5). These are: Lombardy (with 2,224,147 beneficiaries accumulated over the years), Lazio (1,185,656); Piedmont (1,020,437); Emilia Romagna (891,131) and Veneto (733,363). Then there is another group of regions whose companies have indicated a total of beneficiaries above 100,000 units: Abruzzo; Sicily; Campania; Liguria; Friuli VG; Tuscany. The remaining regions are all below this threshold.

Beyond the data that is not available for the various years, which have a strong bearing (about 39%), it can be said that the adoption of the

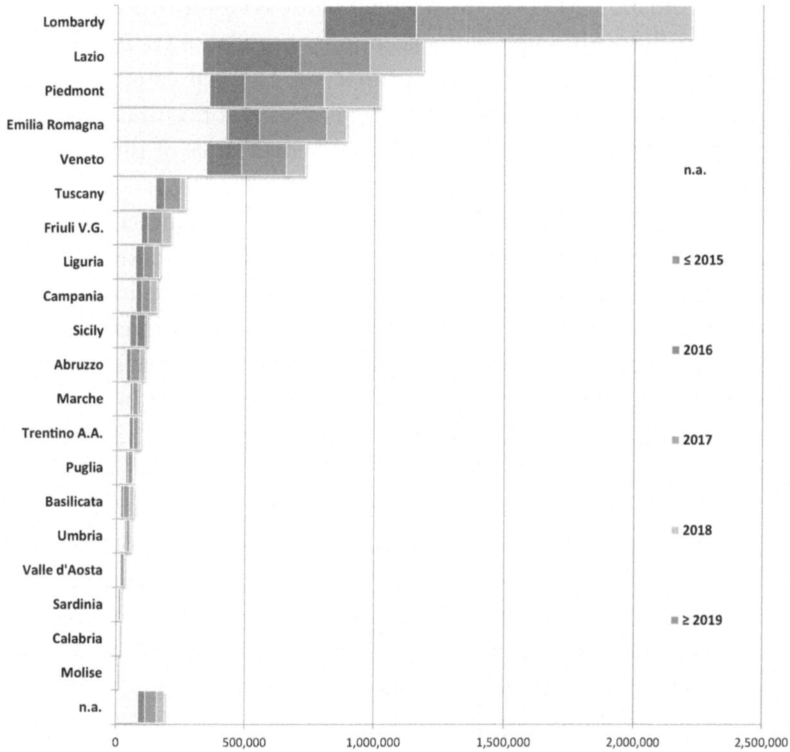

Fig. 13.5 Distribution of beneficiaries by region and by year of activation of the bonus (*Source* Our processing on MLPS repository "Repository for corporate and local-level contracts and preferential taxation of performance bonuses")

performance bonuses is concentrated mainly in the three years 2016, 2017 and 2018.[17]

To better understand the regional differences in the activation of productivity measures, the regional incidence was calculated[18] to highlight the adoption of incentives with respect to the size of local labour markets.

Under this point of analysis, a discrepancy emerges between the northern regions with the central regions (with the exception of Lazio) and an even sharper divergence with the regions of Southern Italy (with the exception of Basilicata and Abruzzo).

Going down to the provincial level or rather, the level of territorial directorate of labour (DTL), the regional figure is confirmed but another trend is also clear. Although with exceptions, a model of territorial adoption emerges characterized by the primacy of regional capitals. In fact, in these units the greatest number of employees is concentrated but also a more than the proportionate number of beneficiaries of incentives for productivity (Fig. 13.6).

From the joint reading of Figs. 13.6 and 13.7,[19] it emerges that after the Aosta Valley, where the limited size of the local market gives the region the primacy by regional incidence (33.4%), the region with the highest incidence is Piedmont (29.4%). At the infra-regional level, the highest incidence of DTL is Turin, which is also in first place nationally (39.7%). The Lazio region (25.7%) then follows, with Rome holding the second place nationally (30.3%), Emilia Romagna (22.0%) with Bologna in third place (29.7%) and Lombardy (21.3%) with Milan in fourth place (27.5%). From these figures, it seems clear that the regions are driven by large centres characterized by wider and more dynamic labour markets. This results in marked variability in distribution within these regions. For example, the regions with the greatest variability of incidences in the different DTLs,[20] or greater asymmetry, are precisely those driven by the regional capitals, in decreasing order of variability: Lazio; Piedmont; Emilia Romagna; Lombardy.

Those with the most uniformly distributed local incidence are precisely the regions of the South where there is no influence from the capitals. In fact, in Sicily the DTL with the highest incidence is Ragusa (12.0%) and not Palermo (5.0%); in Campania it is Caserta (8.0%)

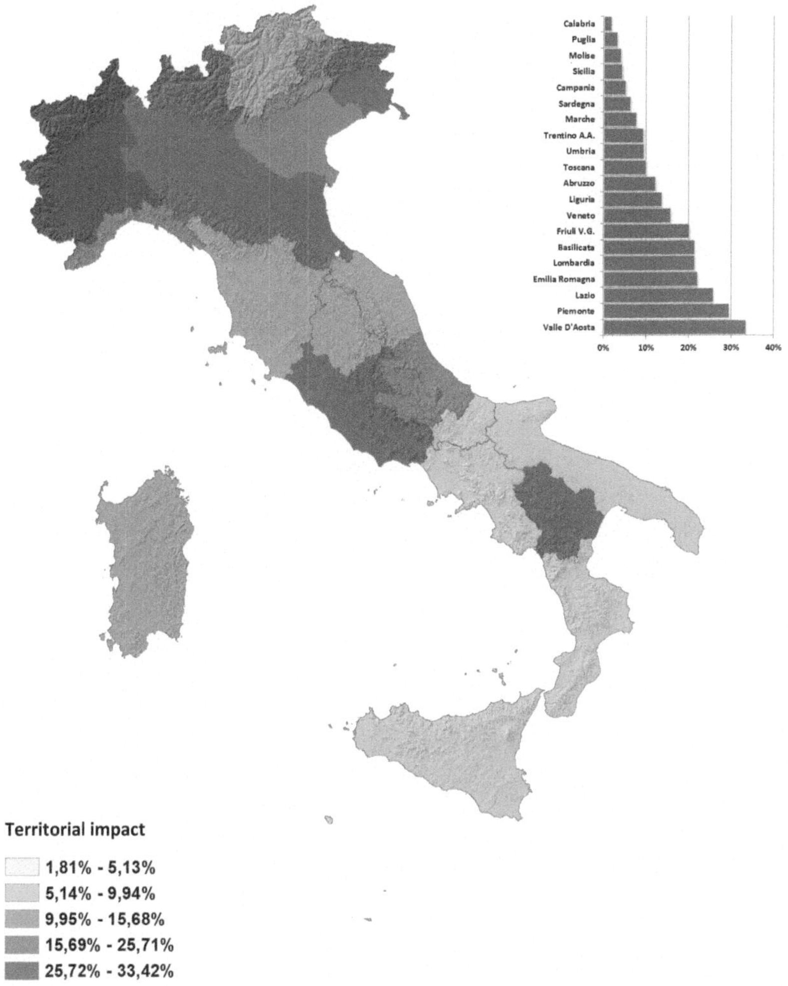

Fig. 13.6 Local impact by region of the beneficiaries of the productivity bonus (*Source* Our processing on MLPS repository "Repository for corporate and local-level contracts and preferential taxation of performance bonuses")

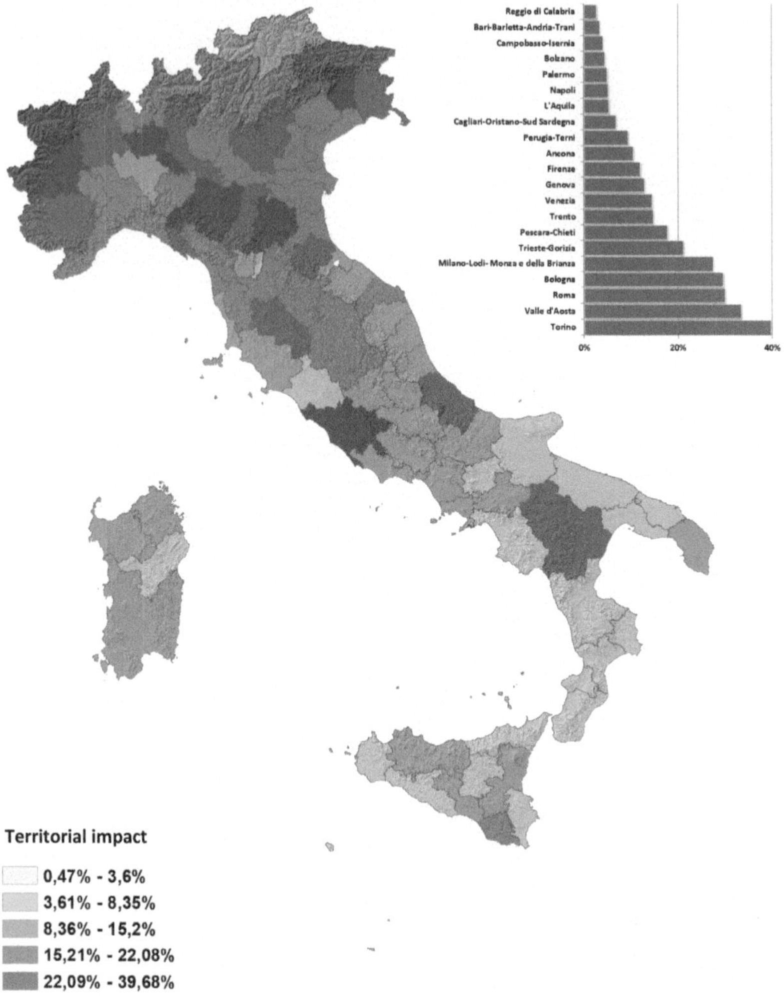

Fig. 13.7 Territorial impact by DTL of the beneficiaries of the productivity bonus (*Source* Our processing on MLPS repository "Repository for corporate and local-level contracts and preferential taxation of performance bonuses")

instead of Naples (5.2%); in Puglia it is Foggia (3.6%) instead of Bari (3.35%).

From this evidence, which demonstrates different rates of integration of incentives by company size, by economic sector and by local area, a first assessment emerges.

Where these measures[21] might lead to actual increases in productivity, the way in which the uptake by companies is formed could trigger off phenomena of polarization in terms of local area or by type of company (size and industry). In this way, the polarization of productivity (Resce 2016) of labour and the imbalances within a labour market that is still not solid and characterized by divergence processes would increase.

Problems of Measurability of *Performance* Increases and Choices Made by Companies

New Features in the Installation of Concession Measures: The Incremental Nature and Verifiability of Target Values

The tax relief regime on productivity bonuses provided for by the 2016 Stability Law, differs from the previous tax incentives to support business productivity, due to the fact that it restricts access to the tax benefit upon reaching a verifiable increase in productivity. The new incentive is based on two requisites: the "objectives incrementality" of the target values and the "verifiability" of the increases.[22]

First of all, it should be pointed out that even if we generally refer to productivity bonuses, in reality the spectrum of performance bonuses is much broader and is based on a more overall *performance* of which productivity is only one of the components. In fact, by reconstructing in detail, the performance bonuses paid to workers are awarded by increases in[23]:

1. productivity;
2. profitability;
3. quality;

4. efficiency;
5. innovation.

These are the decentralized, corporate and local-level collective agreements, which must include the criteria for measuring and verifying these increases in various ways[24]:

a. increased production;
b. savings on production factors;
c. improving the quality of products and processes.

This last modality can be pursued also through the reorganization of the normal working hours or the use of agile work as a flexible way of executing the employment relationship.

To ensure the *target* values are verified, contracts must also define an "appropriate" period in which to reach the declared increases and this achievement must be ascertained in an objective manner through the identification of numerical or other specifically identified indicators. The duration of the period in which the increase is to be reached is referred to second-level bargaining and "can be annual, interim or over one year, indifferently, since what is relevant is that the result achieved by the company in this period can be measured and is better than the result before the start of the same period".[25]

The tendency to increase of a target value is therefore not sufficient alone, but must take place over a given period. Therefore, the dynamic nature of the measurements is clear, comparing *pre-* with *post-* values.

In order to facilitate collective bargaining in identifying the parameters with which to measure *performance*, 19 indicators are listed in the annex to the Ministerial Decree of 25 March 2016, namely, by way of example but not exhaustive: (1) production volume/number of employees; (2) turnover or value added (VA) of the budget/number of employees; (3) earnings before interest, taxes, depreciation, and amortization (MOL)/value added (VA); (4) customer satisfaction indicators; (5) decrease in the number of repairs, reworking; (6) reduction of processing waste; (7) % of compliance with delivery times; (8) compliance with work progress forecasts; (9) changes in work organization; (10) agile work (*smart working*); (11) changes to the schedule regimes; (12) actual costs/expected costs ratio; (13) reduction of absenteeism; (14) number of patents filed; (15) reduction of new product development times; (16) reduction of energy consumption, (17) reduction in number of accidents; (18) reduction of internal processing throughput times; (19) reduction of delivery times.

From the first reading of this list it is clear that there is a will to consider not only the orthodox indicators of the business economy, such as the budget ratios, but also other parameters that seem to be organizational levers rather than indicators, to reach performance gains, i.e. productivity, profitability, quality, efficiency and innovation.

It is still too early to evaluate the effectiveness of this policy, above all in terms of productivity increases,[26] but it is possible, thanks to the processing of data contained in the repository of the Ministry of Labour, to identify and analyze bargaining choices in determining objectives and indicators.

Objectives and Criteria for Measuring Performance Bonuses

As already mentioned, the stricter approach of lawmakers in 2015 in defining the asset that was fiscally awarded implied the imposition on the part of collective actors of the obligation to include in the second-level agreement "criteria for measuring and verifying increases in productivity, profitability, quality, efficiency and innovation (...), compared to an appropriate period defined in the agreement, the achievement of which can be verified in an objective manner through the identification of numerical indicators (...) specifically identified" (article 2, 2nd para. of 25 March 2016). The payment of the performance bonuses is linked to the verified increase in the indicators. In essence, the collective parts are required to agree and declare in advance the expected business result and that this result is measurable, i.e. it is possible to verify at the end of the time period (also declared *ex ante*) a better result than the result before beginning of the period considered.

This obligation was reflected in sections no. 5 and 6 of the "declaration of compliance with the agreement"—the monitoring sheet—where the companies that intend to benefit from the tax discount must specify, respectively, "objectives" and "indicators". The following pages will analyze the information provided in these two sections, which have never been analyzed so far, thus providing a first picture of the contents of the collective agreements filed for access to the tax allowance.

Starting with the analysis of the objectives, the available data show that the collective agreements decided, in most cases, to reward the increase in productivity and profitability with variable pay (see Table 13.3). Productivity in particular is considered in just under 4/5 of the agreements, while profitability in 59.8%.

In less than half of the agreements submitted, on the other hand, the objectives of increasing efficiency (47.1%) and quality (45.5%) were declared. The figure for innovation is still lower (9.1% of agreements), reflecting perhaps how much some systemic backwardness is discounted on this objective, even in sectors where R&D takes on a central role for the growth of business and commercial activities.

Productivity growth was a decidedly high objective and across the board, with respect to the production industries. In the construction industry in particular, productivity is essentially the "guiding" objective (84.3%, Table 13.4).

The influence of the sector characteristics on the trends is more evident when passing from the macro divisions to some categories of detail of the ATECO code, especially for the heavier sector in terms of participation, such as "manufacturing" in the strict sense. In particular,

Table 13.3 Objectives of decentralized bargaining (% val.)

Objectives	Yes	No	Total
Productivity	79.6	20.4	100.0
Profitability	59.8	40.2	100.0
Quality	45.5	54.5	100.0
Efficiency	47.1	52.9	100.0
Innovation	9.1	90.9	100.0

(*Source* Our processing on MLPS repository "Repository for corporate and local-level contracts and preferential taxation of performance bonuses")

Table 13.4 Objectives of decentralized bargaining based on macro-economic sectors (% val.)

Industries	Productivity	Profitability	Quality	Efficiency	Innovation
Industry	79.0	61.8	53.5	50.1	7.1
Construction	84.3	41.8	25.5	27.6	6.1
Services	79.9	62.4	33.7	42.5	10.4
Total	***79.6***	***59.8***	***45.5***	***47.1***	***9.1***

(*Source* Our processing on MLPS repository "Repository for corporate and local-level contracts and preferential taxation of performance bonuses")

in Table 13.5 it is shown that, in addition to construction, productivity adopts a decidedly prevalent function also in the companies of mining industries (90.9%), in transportation (87.1%) and in services related to energy, gas, water and the environment (85.7%).

On the profitability front, an overall homogeneous figure emerges (with the exception of construction, 41.8%), with a high incidence in decentralized bargaining in companies in the sectors of financial and insurance activities (83.2%), of services related to energy, gas, water and environment (76.4%), accommodation and catering (76.3%).

In industry, on average the number of bargaining targets appears on average much more complex, essentially due to the presence of a greater number of submitted contracts aimed at increasing quality (53.5%) and efficiency (50.1%). Quality in particular assumes a high importance in the bargaining of the food, beverages and tobacco (67.9%), chemical, pharmaceutical and oil (59.2%), metallurgy (56.0%) and machinery, equipment and vehicles sectors (55.9%).

Still in industry, the indication of the objective of innovation (7.1%) is instead limited, which is linked to performance bonuses, and would appear to be a critical issue.

For the service industries, it should be emphasized that only 33.7% of the contracts submitted provided for the objective of quality, while innovation seems to have a greater importance (10.4%) at least compared to the average for companies, especially in areas such as education (14.7%), information and communication (13.4%) and services related to energy, gas, water and the environment (13.0%).

Table 13.5 Objectives of decentralized bargaining based on macro-economic sectors (% val.)

Industries		Productivity	Profitability	Quality	Efficiency	Innovation
B MINING AND MINERALS FROM QUARRIES AND MINES	Mining	90.9	39.9	14	30.8	0
C MANUFACTURING	Food, drink and tobacco		59.3	67.9	45.5	5.9
	Clothing textiles; footwear	65.3	58.5	23.5	29.5	1.3
	Wood and paper	82.7	50.9	53.1	54.7	5.5
	Chemicals, pharmaceutics, oil	82.6	68.4	59.2	53.9	10
	Manufacturing of basic metals and fabricate metals	80.8	46.3	56	47,6	4.1
	Medical electronic optical electronics	76.4	68.1	51.5	48.9	8
	Machinery, equipment, vehicles	76.9	64.7	55.9	53.2	6.2
	Other manufacturing industries	78.2	51.7	45.9	49.2	6.7
D - E SUPPLIES	Public utilities (energy, gas, water, environment)	85.7	76.4	53.4	60.4	13
F CONSTRUCTION	Construction	84.3	41.8	25.5	27.6	6.1
G TRADE	Trade	82	61.2	33.8	42.5	8.8
H TRANSPORTATION AND STORAGE	Transportation	87.1	47.5	41.7	47.4	6.7

Industries		Productivity	Profitability	Quality	Efficiency	Innovation
I ACCOMMODATION AND CATERING ACTIVITIES	Accommodation and catering	76.3	76.3	33.3	28.4	4.9
J INFORMATION AND COMMUNICATION	Information and communication	72.8	62.3	39	46.3	13.4
K FINANCIAL AND INSURANCE ACTIVITIES	Financial and insurance activities	73.3	83.2	23.6	32.2	12.8
M PROFESSIONAL, SCIENTIFIC AND TECHNICAL ACTIVITIES	Professional, scientific and technical activities	78.5	64.1	41.3	51.1	11.4
P EDUCATION	Education	77.6	60.6	31.8	43.5	14.7
Q HEALTHCARE AND SOCIAL WORK	Healthcare	77.7	62.2	27.1	41.2	13.5
S OTHER SERVICE ACTIVITIES	Other service activities	83.2	56.1	30.8	41.8	10
Total		***79.6***	***59.8***	***45.5***	***47.1***	***9.1***

(*Source* Our processing on MLPS repository "Repository for corporate and local-level contracts and preferential taxation of performance bonuses")

Table 13.6 Objectives of decentralized bargaining based on the class of company employees (val. %)

Company Size	Productivity	Profitability	Quality	Efficiency	Innovation
Up to 15	78.2	53.0	30.5	34.7	8.1
From 15 to 50	77.2	60.3	37.5	42.2	7.8
50 to 100	80.6	59.4	42.6	43.8	6.9
From 100 to 250	80.2	64.2	49 3	50.0	8.1
250 and over	81.4	67.5	55.9	56.1	10.6
Total	***79.6***	***59.8***	***45.5***	***47.1***	***9.1***

(*Source* Our processing on MLPS repository "Repository for corporate and local-level contracts and preferential taxation of performance bonuses")

The monitoring of objectives also confirms that the contents and the dynamics of decentralized bargaining are strongly influenced by the size of the company. Basically, as the size increases, there is a greater propensity to foresee a greater number of objectives (see Table 13.6). This relationship appears first of all very evident not only considering the percentages related to the contracts submitted by companies with 250 employees and more, but above all by observing the variation of the data due to the number of employees. This trend clearly emerges considering the percentages relating to quality and efficiency objectives (direct growth with the increase in the number of employees) and to a certain extent, albeit less linearly, the data on productivity and profitability.

The innovation objective deserves a separate mention, which assumes a relatively greater importance on the one hand for the very small companies with less than 15 employees (8.1%), and on the other for companies with 100 to 250 employees (8.1%) and for those with 250 or more employees (10.6%). Without prejudice to the correlation between objectives and the size of the company, this data would seem to confirm the role of small businesses—the so-called "innovative SMEs" facilitated by a particular support discipline[27]—as an engine of innovation.

The analysis of the objectives by geographical area shows a substantial homogeneity, without high deviations from the average figure (see Fig. 13.7). Nevertheless, it should be noted that in the south and the islands, the percentage of decentralized agreements submitted that provide for performance bonuses related to productivity (85.7%), quality (52.4%), efficiency (56.3%) and innovation (12.9%) is relatively higher when compared to the average figures. Bearing in mind that the decentralized agreements by the companies of the south and the islands constitute only 8% of the total of agreements submitted the results analyzed here lead to a series of hypotheses and in-depth investigations needing to be carried out, in order to verify the reasons for such percentage values in the south (Table 13.7).

In detail, for the individual regions (See Table 13.8), these brief and initial reflections on the local level find some confirmation. In particular, although on the one hand the number of decentralized agreements submitted by companies in the south is very small, in terms of percentages these latter agreements most frequently propose specific objectives. As an example, we note that in terms of productivity, the highest percentages are found in all southern regions and in particular in Molise (92.5%), Campania (87.7%), Calabria (87.1%) and Sardinia (87.1%).

In other areas, the data on the objective of productivity is high in Umbria (89.4%) and in Lazio (88.1%).

Overall, the indication of the profitability objective is confirmed as a substantially structural element. Analyzing Table 13.8 in detail, no significant deviations and differentiations are reported on a regional basis, with

Table 13.7 Objectives of decentralized bargaining based on geographical area (% val.)

Division	Productivity	Profitability	Quality	Efficiency	Innovation
North West	79.1	60.5	49.8	50.4	10.4
North East	77.8	58.2	41.6	42.2	6.9
Centre	82.0	62.5	40.3	45,3	8.8
South & Islands	85.7	57.5	52.4	56.3	12.9
Total	*79.6*	*59.8*	*45.5*	*47.1*	*9.1*

(*Source* Our processing on MLPS repository "Repository for corporate and local-level contracts and preferential taxation of performance bonuses")

Table 13.8 Objectives of decentralized bargaining based on region (% val.)

Regions	Productivity	Profitability	Quality	Efficiency	Innovation
Piedmont	79.0	59.5	59.0	56.1	8.0
Aosta Valley	82.4	72.1	47.1	30.9	4.4
Lombardy	78,7	60.3	47.5	49.1	11.6
Trentino-Alto Adige	66.7	69.0	29.5	39.9	9.5
Veneto	80.2	52.9	42.8	47.5	7.8
Friuli Venezia Giulia	84.4	58.2	50.2	55.8	9.1
Liguria	83.3	66.3	42.1	46.4	5, 6
Emilia Romagna	76.3	60.8	41	35.6	5.2
Tuscany	75.7	59.5	30.4	37.3	4.4
Umbria	89.4	53.5	48.9	61.2	10.8
Marche	77.8	66.5	40.1	48.1	7.9
Lazio	88.1	66.3	49.1	50.0	13.2
Abruzzo	82.1	60.1	50.1	57.8	13.7
Molise	92.5	58.2	56,7	70.1	14.9
Campania	87.7	51.3	60.5	62.7	13.2
Apulia	85.8	63.8	44.2	45.4	9.5
Basilicata	85.5	54.7	54.1	44.2	7.0
Calabria	87.1	59.2	40,8	59.9	19.0
Sicily	83.3	59.1	57.4	66.3	17.2
Sardinia	87.1	57.2	45.0	42.1	10.1
Total	*79.6*	*59.8*	*45.5*	*47.1*	*9.1*

(*Source* Our processing on MLPS repository "Repository for corporate and local-level contracts and preferential taxation of performance bonuses")

the exception of the Aosta Valley (72.1%), Trentino-Alto Adige (69.0%), Marche (66.5%), and Liguria (66, 3%) and Lazio (66.3%).

The overall figure relating to quality is more complex, which in essence confirms what has been said previously. As for productivity, in several regions of the south and the islands, there are high percentages of submitted agreements in which quality is an incremental objective to which the performance bonuses are attached: Campania (60.5%), Sicily (57.4%), Molise (56.7%). Added to this is the figure for Piedmont (59.0%).

Very similar considerations can be made with respect to the objective of efficiency and taking into consideration in detail the percentages relating to the regions of Molise (70.1%), Sicily (66.3%), Campania

(62.7%), Calabria (59.9%), Abruzzo (57.8%). As for the other areas of the country, significant percentages of decentralized agreements with the objective of efficiency can be found in Umbria (61.2%), Piedmont (56.1%) and Friuli Venezia Giulia (55.8%).

Therefore, if a substantial homogeneity is found between the objectives of quality and efficiency, with regard to innovation, some evidence emerges. In particular, compared to the average figure, this objective occurs more frequently in agreements submitted in regions such as Calabria (19.0%), Sicily (17.2%) and Molise (14.9%).

Finally, it seems appropriate to carry out a verification of the relationship between the objectives of the contract and the type of collective agreement(corporate-local level). Table 13.9 shows that productivity, profitability and innovation are largely present in a similar measure both in business and in local-level agreements: with the partial exception of profitability, in this respect the percentage differences either between the two types of agreement, or respect of the average figure for all companies do not appear to be particularly marked.

Likewise, it is equally significant that the quality and efficiency objectives are largely present in corporate agreements, with significantly lower percentages in local-level bargaining (respectively 21.0 and 26.3%).

Summarizing in the comparison, it would seem that a sectorial vocation appears in the choice of objectives, determined by the very characteristics of the sector. In fact, construction seems to prefer productivity objectives relatively more, while industry is relatively more oriented to quality and efficiency. In the services, on the other hand, profitability is decisive (see Fig. 13.8).

Table 13.9 Objectives of decentralized bargaining based on the type of collective agreement (% val.)

Type	Productivity	Profitability	Quality	Efficiency	Innovation
Corporate	79.1	61.1	50.6	51.4	9.5
Regional	82.0	53.6	21.0	26.3	7,2
Total	*79.6*	*59.8*	*45.5*	*47.1*	*9.1*

(*Source* Our processing on MLPS repository "Repository for corporate and local-level contracts and preferential taxation of performance bonuses")

Fig. 13.8 Hierarchy choice of objectives by sector (*Source* Our processing on MLPS repository "Repository for corporate and local-level contracts and preferential taxation of performance bonuses")

It is worth noting the low propensity of all sectors to set goals in terms of innovation. Some reflections should be made on the capacity of the measure to stimulate processes that increase innovation. A first reflection derives from the very nature of the measure that rewards the accessory salary. The salary is notoriously the price of labour, so this low propensity could be explained by the fact that the measure is mainly adapted to labour-intensive production processes rather than those with a high capital/technology intensity. Another hypothesis that could be made is the displacement of the choices of entrepreneurs due to other measures that reward technological innovation such as those proposed by the simultaneous plan for Industry 4.0.[28]

Despite the general lack of propensity to set innovation objectives, it is clear that this objective plays a part in the strategic choices of competition, especially for small businesses and those in the south.

Some qualitative surveys show that decentralized bargaining is rarely used as a lever to introduce and accelerate innovation processes, but for those companies that focus on staff organization and cognitive capital, as the first element of competitiveness, it assumes an essential strategic role (Marocco and Resce 2020).

Performance Indicators

As stated, at least one indicator for measuring the productivity gains to which to link the variable part of the salary should be declared in Sect. 6 of the filing sheet. A list of these indicators was provided in the same sheet, only for illustrative and not exhaustive purposes (see the following Table 13.10).

Table 13.10 Indicators of decentralized bargaining (val. %)

Indicators provided for in the contract	Yes	No	Total
Production volume/no. employees	27.9	72.1	100.0
Budgetary revenue or VA/no. employees	26.0	74	100.0
Budgetary MOL/VA	27.2	72.8	100.0
Customer satisfaction indexes	18.4	81.6	100.0
Decrease no. repairs, rework	10.6	89.4	100.0
Waste reduction	16.6	83.4	100.0
% respect of delivery times	9.2	90.8	100.0
Compliance with work progress forecasts	5.3	94.7	100.0
changes to the organization of work	9.0	91.0	100.0
Agile work (smart working)	1,2	98.8	100.0
Changes to the working schedule	6.9	93.1	100.0
Report actual costs/expected costs	9.6	90.4	100.0
Reduction in absenteeism	35.8	64.2	100.0
Patents applied for.	0.2	99.8	100.0
Reduction of new product development times	1.4	98.6	100.0
Reduction of energy consumption	4.4	95.6	100.0
Reduction in number of accidents	12.2	87,8	100.0
Reduction internal processing throughput times	3.2	96.8	100.0
Job time reduction	4.6	95.4	100.0
Rebates	0.1	99.9	100.0
Other	19.3	80.7	100.0

(*Source* Our processing on MLPS repository "Repository for corporate and local-level contracts and preferential taxation of performance bonuses")

First, it is extremely significant to note that the reduction in absenteeism represents the indicator used in well over 1/3 of the contracts deposited (35.8%). In over 1/4 of the contracts there are indicators such as the ratio between the volume of production by number of employees (27.9%), the ratio between gross operating margin (MOL) and value added (VA) of the budget (27.2%) and the ratio between revenue or VA of the budget by number of employees (26.0%). Definitely low—and far off in terms of recurrence—is therefore agile working (1.2%), to say that the performances of the workers, to whom the remuneration premium is linked, are still measured on the basis of the criterion presence/absence in the workplace (Table 13.11).

The result does not change considering the product sector to which it belongs: generally speaking, the reduction in absenteeism constitutes a very significant content in the decentralized bargaining of companies in the industry (42.2%). Indicators such as the ratio between the volume of production by number of employees (42.2%) and the ratio between revenue or budget VA by the number of employees (40.3%) are instead used more frequently in construction, while in services they do not emerge significant deviations from the average figure.

Even at a greater level of detail (See Table 13.12), the reduction in absenteeism is the indicator present in the majority of agreements submitted by companies in the textile, clothing and footwear (60.7%),

Table 13.11 Indicators of decentralized bargaining based on macroeconomic sectors (% val.)

Industries	Reduction in absenteeism	Production volume/no. employees	Budgetary MOL/VA	Budgetary revenue or VA/no. employees
Industry	42.2	28.8	30.7	22.9
Construction	14.9	42.2	19.5	40.3
Services	28.3	25.1	25.6	29.3
Total	***35.8***	***27.9***	***27.2***	***26.0***

(*Source* Our processing on MLPS repository "Repository for corporate and local-level contracts and preferential taxation of performance bonuses")

Table 13.12 Indicators of decentralized bargaining based on economic sectors (% val.)

Industries	Reduction in absenteeism	Production volume/no. employees	Budgetary MOL/VA	Budgetary revenue or VA/no. employees
Mining	35.7	37.8	18.2	11.9
Food, drink and tobacco	31.6	39.9	20.7	18.2
Clothing textiles; footwear	60.7	16.6	48.1	12.6
Wood and paper	55.8	37.7	23.6	16.7
Chemicals, pharmaceutics, oil	53.8	38.2	32.7	25.4
manufacturing of basic metals and fabricate metals	41.2	33.9	18.8	22.5
Medical electronic optical electronics	37.9	19.7	28.2	33.7
Machinery, equipment, vehicles	36.6	24.7	28.1	33.5
Other manufacturing industries	36.9	34.1	26.5	27.0
Public utilities (energy, gas, water, environment)	34.3	12.9	49.2	9.6
Construction	14.9	42.2	19.5	40.3
Trade	36.3	22.0	23.5	41
Transportation	43.2	36.7	16.7	13.2
Accommodation and catering	18.3	21.5	17.5	23.7
Information and communication	19.9	18.7	28.1	36.5
Financial and insurance activities	5.2	24.0	22.7	21.8

(continued)

Table 13.12 (continued)

Industries	Reduction in absenteeism	Production volume/no. employees	Budgetary MOL/VA	Budgetary revenue or VA/no. employees
Professional, scientific and technical activities	27.8	26.5	29.8	33.1
Education	25.3	30.0	34.7	42.9
Healthcare	21.7	25.2	36.9	30.6
Other service activities	34.6	21.1	26.8	26.8
Total	***35.8***	***27.9***	***27.2***	***26.0***

(*Source* Our processing on MLPS repository "Repository for corporate and local-level contracts and preferential taxation of performance bonuses")

wood and paper (55.8%), of the chemical, pharmaceutical and oil industries (53.8%), with equally significant peaks in the transport companies (43.2%) and in metallurgy and metal products (41.2%).

Still with regard to the sector, the data on the ratio between production volume by number of employees (with the exception of construction, as mentioned above) is more homogeneous, with a greater presence in the contracts submitted by companies in the food, beverage and tobacco sectors (39.9%), chemical, pharmaceutical and oil (38.2%), mining industry (37.8%), wood and paper (37.7%) and transportation (36.7%).

The gross operating surplus (MOL)/value added (VA) budget ratio is widely applied in slightly fewer companies operating in the energy, gas, water and environment services (49.2%) and textile, clothing and footwear (48.1%), as well as in a high percentage of healthcare sector companies (36.9%).

In addition to construction, the ratio between revenue or budget VA by number of employees is a relatively more present indicator in decentralized bargaining in the education (42.9%), commerce (41.0%) and information and communication sectors (36.5%).

The data shows a tendential correlation between indicators used in decentralized bargaining and the size of the company. In Table 13.13, in particular and with extreme clarity, it is shown that the reduction

Table 13.13 Indicators of decentralized bargaining based on the class of company employees (% val.)

Company size	Reduction in absenteeism	Production volume/no. employees	Budgetary MOL/VA	Budgetary revenue or VA/no. employees
Up to 15	26.8	28.4	24.2	32.6
From 15 to 50	31.0	25.7	26.9	29.5
50 to 100	36.7	28.4	27.1	27.4
From 100 to 250	40.1	29.2	29.7	24.6
250 and over	40.6	27.2	31.4	19.5
Total	***35.8***	***27.9***	***27.2***	***26.0***

(*Source* Our processing on MLPS repository "Repository for corporate and local-level contracts and preferential taxation of performance bonuses")

in absenteeism and the MOL/VA budget ratio grow as the number of employees increases. The opposite is true for the indicator of the ratio between revenue or budget VA by number of employees, which decreases in percentage terms with the increase in the number of employees. On the other hand, these correlations do not seem to exist for the production volume ratio by number of employees. Therefore, the company size clearly determines the indicator selection strategies, reflecting the different organizational needs, in particular with the increasing size, the problem of absenteeism grows, as the company needs to measure itself with budget ratios avoiding measuring budget increases with the number of employees.

The following Table 13.14 shows that the reduction in absenteeism is the indicator present in just under half of the contracts submitted by companies in the south (47.8%). Still in percentage terms, in this area of the country there is a high incidence of the indicator of the production volume ratio by number of employees (36.6%), while the budget MOL/VA ratio occurs relatively more in the agreements submitted by companies in the centre (31.0%).

Considering the individual regions (See Table 13.15), the reduction in absenteeism is a recurring indicator in more than half of the agreements submitted by companies in Basilicata (59.9%), Campania (59.5%) and Umbria (51.8%).

Table 13.14 Objectives of decentralized bargaining based on geographical area (val. %)

Division	Reduction in absenteeism	Production volume/no. employees	Budgetary MOL/VA	Budgetary revenue or VA/no. employees
North West	37.6	27.8	26.1	25.9
North East	29.7	27.0	27.9	27.9
Centre	38.6	26.2	31.0	23.4
South & Islands	47.8	36.6	21.7	23.9
Total	***35.8***	***27.9***	***27.2***	***26.0***

(*Source* Our processing on MLPS repository "Repository for corporate and local-level contracts and preferential taxation of performance bonuses")

Still on the subject of reducing absenteeism, equally substantial percentages are present in the agreements submitted in Piedmont (48.4%), Abruzzo (47.8%), Sicily (46.7%) and Molise (44.8%).

The ratio between production volume and number of employees is included in a large number of contracts submitted in the Molise Regions (55.2%), Apulia (39.2%), Basilicata (37.8%), Abruzzo (37.6%) and Campania (37.4%).

Again, among the most significant data, it should be noted that the budget ratio between MOL and VA is present in 41.6% of the contracts submitted by companies in Tuscany, while the ratio between revenue or budget VA for the number of employees is included in 33.9% of contracts submitted by companies in Emilia Romagna and 32.9% by those relating to Apulia.

Finally, the indicators considered so far do not vary significantly due to the type of bargaining (see Table 13.16): only with regard to the reduction in absenteeism is it possible to observe a lower incidence in percentage terms in local-level bargaining (28.5%).

Conclusions

In Italy the Cross-Sectoral Agreement (Protocollo 1993), signed 23 July 1993, promoted new forms of decentralized bargaining. One of the

Table 13.15 Indicators of decentralized bargaining based on the Region (% val.)

Regions	Reduction in absenteeism	Production volume/no. employees	Budgetary MOL/VA	Budgetary revenue or VA/no. employees
Piedmont	48.4	27.7	30.1	20.2
Aosta Valley	26.5	25.0	29.4	14.7
Lombardy	34.2	28.4	24.4	28.0
Trentino-Alto Adige	38.2	14.9	15.9	10.1
Veneto	40.7	26.9	28.8	25.8
Friuli Venezia Giulia	35.2	25.7	19.1	22.4
Liguria	39.0	20.4	31.2	22.8
Emilia Romagna	17.7	29.4	30.9	33.9
Tuscany	40.4	22.0	41.6	18.2
Umbria	51.8	30.2	31.2	25.2
Marche	43.8	24.9	25.3	26.4
Lazio	32.9	30.0	21.5	27.5
Abruzzo	47.8	37.6	27.4	29.2
Molise	44.8	55.2	29.9	25.4
Campania	59.5	37.4	19.6	17.8
Apulia	39,7	39.2	19.6	32.9
Basilicata	59.9	37.8	17.4	14.5
Calabria	29.9	24.5	15.6	20.4
Sicily	46.7	35.4	25.2	26.2
Sardinia	35.3	32.0	20.1	20.5
Total	***35.8***	***27.9***	***27.2***	***26.0***

(*Source* Our processing on MLPS repository "Repository for corporate and local-level contracts and preferential taxation of performance bonuses")

Table 13.16 Indicators of decentralized bargaining based on the type of contract (val. %)

Type of Agreement	Reduction in absenteeism	Production volume/no. employees	Budget MOL/VA	Budgetary revenue or VA/no. employees
Corporate	37.3	27.7	27.2	25.3
Local	28.5	29.2	27.3	29.4
Total	***35.8***	***27.9***	***27.2***	***26.0***

(*Source* Our processing on MLPS repository "Repository for corporate and local-level contracts and preferential taxation of performance bonuses")

aims was to stimulate the productivity growth in the second level of bargaining, by linking wages dynamics to productivity. Recently, the Italian government has encouraged the second-level bargaining through the provision of tax incentives related to performance bonuses and corporate welfare programmes set forth in the company/territorial collective bargaining agreement. Monitoring measures were also envisaged through a special instrument for collecting summary data and the Italian Ministry of Labour and Social Policy activated a Repository for this purpose. The paper proposes some analyses of the Italian second-level bargaining, using data collected by this the Repository. In particular, it focuses on the choices made by companies to improve labour productivity, proposing an analysis by sector and by territory.

It is not yet possible to establish whether this policy has actually contributed to a growth in labour productivity, it would require counterfactual analyzes which are difficult to carry out since the determinants of productivity to be taken into consideration are innumerable.

It has certainly contributed to a greater diffusion of decentralized bargaining and to lower labour costs.

This circumstance can raise doubts about the quality of the bargaining activated, which may have been tainted by a "race to the incentives", widely criticized aspect (Paliotta and Resce 2019).

Faced with very different realities, which would imply different solutions to increase productivity, we are witnessing local agreements that reproduce homologated approaches, confirming an exclusive attention on tax relief (Fazio and Tiraboschi 2011).

In fact, a practice of negotiations characterized by a purely formal and insubstantial link between accessory salary and performances, which some authors define as "cosmetic agreements" (Antonioli and Pini 2013), has spread.

Other authors have highlighted the risk at local level of an improper use of the measure (Tomassetti 2016b) with the preparation of photocopy agreements (Tomassetti 2016a) aimed at guaranteeing access to the tax bonus for workers of companies without union representation.

Finally the Council of the European Union was also critical[29]: "Tax rebates on productivity-related wage increases have not proved effective in significantly extending the use of second-level bargaining", although it recently revised its judgment, recognizing the difficulty of evaluating this policy.

It is difficult to assess the policy as a whole, but some indications can be drawn from the monitoring evidence on this first experience of tax relief measures.

First of all, it is possible to outline a company profile for those more inclined to use these measures. We could say, in very broad terms, that this is a medium-large company, which chooses the type of company bargaining, which operates in the manufacturing and financial services and insurance sectors, which is based in a regional capital in north-central Italy, and whose main objectives are growth in productivity and profitability.

Instead on the overall experience of the activation of the measures envisaged in the 2016 Stability Law (Article 1 para. 182–190 of Law 208/2015) and subsequently in the Budget Law for 2017 (Law 232/2016), we could enucleate some pros and cons.

Among the "pros" we can make the following points:

- in comparison with the past, the new tax discounts on wage increases linked to productivity are more rigorous, also due to a mandatory planning process of the company areas for improving performance and monitoring required by law;
- certainly, the new incentives, even if they are not fully effective in the growth of labour productivity, certainly generate a reduction in the tax wedge;
- among the primary objectives selected by the applicants the "productivity" and the "profitability" are the most pursued;
- the variability of the choices of the objectives and of the indicators on which to measure performance reveals a capacity for collective bargaining to adapt to the complexity of the organizational and productive needs of companies.
- Among the "cons" we can list:
- second-level bargaining is not yet widely used and therefore the potential advantages of its application are not currently evenly distributed in the productive fabric;

- the measure has pro-cyclical characteristics so that, if it were to really work, it could generate a phenomenon of polarization of productivity between territories and between types of companies (by size and sector);
- absenteeism seems to be—still—one of the main concerns of companies;
- innovation is the least taken into consideration performance objective in second-level bargaining.

Notes

1. Interconfederal protocol of 23 July 1993 on income and employment policy, contractual aspects, labour policies and support for the production system.
2. The 2009 inter-confederal agreement between Confindustria, CISL and UIL is significant, having introduced the forecast of the trend of the Harmonized Consumer Price Index. The agreement, although not signed by the CGIL, influenced the negotiations in the following CCNLs. See D'Amuri and Nizzi (2018, p. 12).
3. Some studies show substantial gains from moving from sectoral-to firm-level wage setting of at least 3.5 percentage points lower unemployment (or higher employment) rate and a notable improvement in Italy's competitiveness over the medium term (Kangur, 2018).
4. The lack of widespread adoption is confirmed by the various sample surveys, not least that reported in the "First report on second level bargaining" by the FDV—CGIL which speaks of a diffusion of around 20%.
5. See for example "Council Recommendation on Italy's National Reform Programme 2017—COM (2017) 511 final" and "Council Recommendation on Italy's National Reform Programme 2018—COM (2018) 411 final".
6. This is an approach that aims to resolve the conditions of productivity growth from a micro point of view at the corporate level (Boeri, 2014, 2015). According to this vision, capping wages in phases of economic crisis, the CLUP (labour cost per unit of product) would be controlled, guaranteeing the company's own competitiveness and therefore adequate productivity. In reality, this approach finds wide criticism, especially among

non-mainstream economists, who highlight that at the macroeconomic level, wage growth is in fact also important in times of crisis in the economic cycle which, by supporting domestic demand, can guarantee the conditions for productivity growth (Resce 2018).

7. Before the introduction of this law some authors argued that "the effectiveness of tax breaks encouraging a closer link between wage and productivity at the firm level has been undermined by poor monitoring and frequent changes to the eligibility criteria" (D'Amuri and Giorgiantonio, 2015).
8. Corporate welfare with the stability law for 2017 (Law No. 232/2016) is awarded regardless of the level, neutralizing in part the advantage in second-level bargaining. In addition to tax relief there are also contribution reliefs, the prerequisite of wich is to have provided for welfare programmes in contracts at firm level (Armaroli and Massagli, 2017; Massagli, 2018).
9. Decree of the Minister of Labour and Social Policies in agreement with the Minister of Economy and Finance. The guidelines for completing the application were then made explicit in guideline note no. of 22 July 2016 ref. no. 33-4274 "Form for filing corporate and local-level contracts and preferential taxation of performance bonuses (Article 1, paragraph 188, law 28 December 2015, No. 208)".
10. Data made available by the MLPS for the preparation of the Labour Market and Collective Bargaining Report, prepared by the National Council for Economics and Labour (CNEL), the National Agency for Active Labour Market Policies (ANPAL) and INAPP.
11. First of all, the data of the Repository were integrated with information on the sectors of economic activity and on the company size obtained from the Statistical Archive of Active Companies (ASIA), published by the National Institute of Statistics (ISTAT), and by the Information System on mandatory online communications, of the MLPS (SISCO).
12. The data used refers to the update of therepository issued by the MLPS in June 2018 systematized by Marco Centra on the occasion of the "Report on the Labour Market and Collective Bargaining 2017–2018" prepared by CNEL-ANPAL-INAPP.
13. i.e. foremployees for whom the performance bonus is envisaged.
14. For the definition of company size, see the classification in the "Recommendation of the Commission of 06 May 2003, relating to the definition of micro-companies, small and medium-sized companies [noted with number C (2003) 1422] (Text relates to the purposes of the SEE) (2003/361/CE)".
15. Number of beneficiaries integrated over the total number of beneficiaries.

16. For more information on territorial differentials, see also Casadio (2010).
17. The contract filing form, being free in the indication of the annuities, allowed the inclusion of values before 2015 and post 2019, which even if in fact do not give the right to the tax incentive have been reported for completeness as a testimony of the planning intentions of applicants.
18. The indicator was constructed as a ratio by territory (region and DTL—Regional Labor Directorate) among the average of the beneficiaries in the three years 2016–2017–2018 (integrated with the missing data na) on the number of total employees minus employees apprentices in 2016.
19. The authors wish to thank Francesco Manente for the cartographic processing shown in the figures.
20. A variance index of the DTL incidences on a single region was calculated.
21. Government intervention through tax breaks and financial incentives are not necessarily efficient (Lucifora, 2015).
22. Previous facilitation measures, in force from 2008 to 2014, fiscally rewarded specific remuneration items regardless of the increase in productivity.
23. Article 2, para. 1, of 25 March 2016.
24. Article 2, para. 2, of 25 March 2016.
25. As specified in the aforementioned Opinion of the Revenue Agency of 19 October 2018.
26. On this point, it is possible to refer to Resce (2018).
27. See the Report on the state of implementation of the legislation supporting start-ups and innovative SMEs—2017, https://bit.ly/2EonVpq.
28. It is possible to refer to Iadevaia et al. (2018).
29. Ref. "Council Recommendation on Italy's National Reform Program 2017—COM (2017) 511 final" and "Council Recommendation on Italy's National Reform Program 2018—COM (2018) 411 final".

References

Antonioli, Davide, and Paolo Pini. 2013. "Retribuzioni e contrattazione decentrata. L'accordo sbagliato tra le parti sociali." *Argomenti* 37: 45–70.

Armaroli, Ilaria, and Emmanuele Massagli. 2017. "Nuovi sgravi per le misure di conciliazione e welfare aziendale: doppio vantaggio?" *Bollettino ADAPT*.

Boeri, Tito. 2014. "Two-Tier Bargaining." *IZA Discussion Paper* No. 8358.

Boeri, Tito. 2015. "Perverse Effects of Two-Tier Wage Bargaining Structures." *IZA World of Labor*.

Casadio, Piero. 2010. "Contrattazione aziendale integrativa e differenziali salariali territoriali: informazioni dall'indagine sulle imprese della Banca d'Italia." *Politica Economica* XXVI (2): 241–291.

Centra, Marco. 2018. "La detassazione del salario di risultato: le evidenze ricavate dal repository centrale del Ministero del lavoro." In *XX Rapporto. Mercato del lavoro e contrattazione collettiva 2017–2018*, edited by CNEL, 291–318.

D'Amuri, Francesco, and Cristina Giorgiantonio. 2015. "The Institutional and Economic Limits to Bargaining Decentralization in Italy." *IZA Policy Paper* no. 98.

D'Amuri, Francesco, and Raffaella Nizzi. 2018. "Recent Developments of Italy's Industrial Relations System." *E-Journal of International and Comparative Labour Studies* 7 (2): 19–47.

Fazio, Francesca and Michele Tiraboschi. 2011. "Una occasione mancata per la crescita. Brevi considerazioni a proposito della misura di detassazione del salario di produttività." *Bollettino ADAPT*.

Iadevaia, Valeria, Massimo Resce, and Claudio Tagliaferro. 2018. "Tendenze evolutive del mercato del lavoro ed ecosistemi 4.0." *Professionalità e studi* n. 5/2018: 5–38.

Kangur, Alvar. 2018. "Competitiveness and Wage Bargaining Reform in Italy." IMF Working Paper No. 18/61.

Leonardi, Marco. 2017. "Le nuove norme sui premi di produttività e il welfare aziendale." In *Salari, produttività, disuguaglianze—Verso un nuovo modello contrattuale?*, edited by Carlo Dell'Aringa, Claudio Lucifora, and Tiziano Treu. Roma: il Mulino—Arel.

Lucifora, Claudio. 2015. "Performance-Related Pay and Labor Productivity". *IZA World of Labor*.

Marocco, Manuel. 2018. "Gli incentivi economici al salario variabile." *Diritto delle relazioni industriali* 28 (2): 668–686.

Marocco, Manuel and Massimo Resce. 2020. "L'obiettivo innovazione nella contrattazione di secondo livello—Studio di casi di imprese beneficiarie degli incentivi al premio di risultato." *INAPP Report* No. 15.

Massagli, Emmanuele. 2018."Le novità (e le mancanze) della Circolare 5/E sul welfare aziendale." *Bollettino ADAPT*.

Paliotta, Achille P., and Massimo Resce. 2019. "Decentralized Bargaining and Measures for Productivity and Occupational Welfare Growth in Italy.

Empirical Evidence from Administrative Data." *E-Journal of International and Comparative—Labour Studies* 8 (3): 114–152.
Protocollo. 1993. interconfederale tra Governo e parti sociali del 23 luglio sulla politica dei redditi e dell'occupazione, sugli aspetti contrattuali, sulle politiche del lavoro e sul sostegno al sistema produttivo.
Resce, Massimo. 2016. "Le incursioni della Bce sul mercato del lavoro italiano." *Economia e Politica* 12 sem. 2.
Resce, Massimo. 2018. "Produttività del lavoro in Italia e misure di sostegno nella contrattazione aziendale." *Economia & Lavoro* 3: 153–178.
Schlitzer, Giuseppe. 2015. "L'economia italiana e il paradosso della produttività." *LIUC Papers in Economics—Serie Economia e Impresa 77* No. 285.
Tomassetti, Paolo. 2016a. "Detassazione 2016: il ritorno degli accordi "fotocopia" di livello territoriale." *Bollettino ADAPT*.
Tomassetti, Paolo. 2016b. "Luci e ombre della nuova detassazione." *Bollettino ADAPT*.
Tronti, Leonello. 2009. "La crisi di produttività dell'economia italiana: scambio politico ed estensione del mercato." *Economia & Lavoro* 2: 139–157.
Tronti, Leonello. 2010. "La crisi di produttività dell'economia italiana: modello contrattuale e incentivi ai fattori." *Economia & Lavoro* 2: 47–70.
Tronti, Leonello. 2013. "Riforma della contrattazione, produttività e crescita: un dialogo tra economisti." *Economia & Lavoro* 3: 7–9.

Index

T. Addabbo et al. (eds.), *The Collective Dimensions of Employment Relations*, https://doi.org/10.1007/978-3-030-75532-4

L

M

N

O

P

The manufacturer's authorised representative in the EU is Springer Nature Customer Service Centre GmbH, Europaplatz 3, 69115 Heidelberg, Germany. If you have any concerns regarding our products, please contact ProductSafety@springernature.com

Printed and bound by CPI Group (UK) Ltd, Croydon, CR0 4YY
30/09/2026
02225701-0016